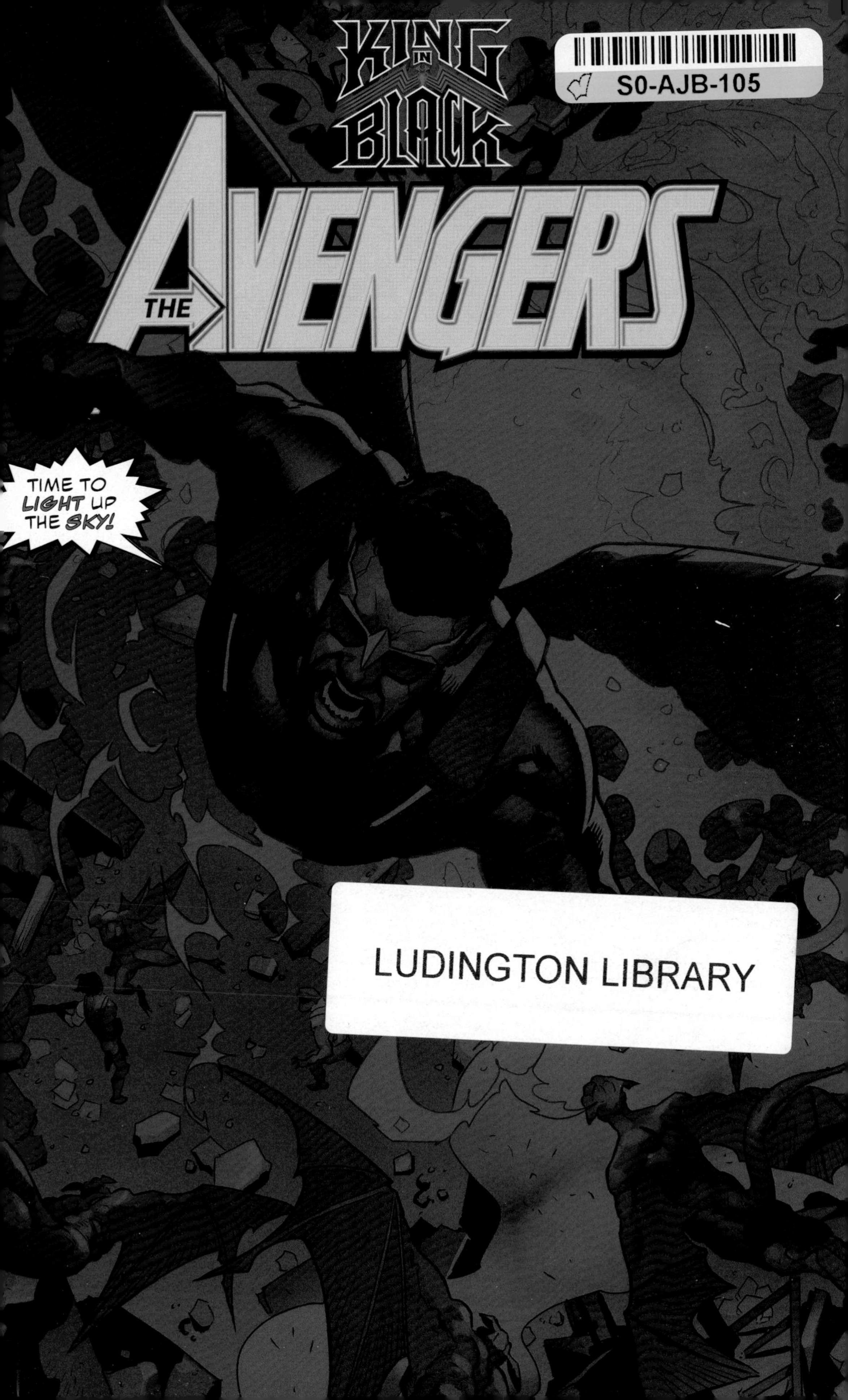
KING IN BLACK
THE AVENGERS
TIME TO LIGHT UP THE SKY!

KING IN BLACK

THE AVENGERS

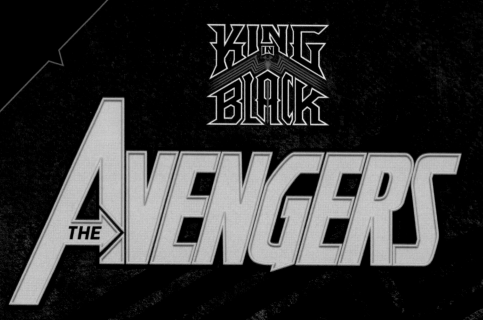

KING IN BLACK: BLACK PANTHER

GEOFFREY THORNE WRITER
GERMÁN PERALTA ARTIST
JESUS ABURTOV COLOR ARTIST

VC'S JOE SABINO LETTERER
LEINIL FRANCIS YU & SUNNY GHO COVER ART
SARAH BRUNSTAD ASSOCIATE EDITOR
WIL MOSS EDITOR

KING IN BLACK: CAPTAIN AMERICA

DANNY LORE WRITER
MIRKO COLAK, STEFANO LANDINI, ROGÊ ANTÔNIO & NICO LEON ARTISTS
ERICK ARCINIEGA COLOR ARTIST

VC'S JOE CARAMAGNA LETTERER
SALVADOR LARROCA & GURU-eFX COVER ART
MARTIN BIRO ASSISTANT EDITOR
ALANNA SMITH EDITOR
TOM BREVOORT EXECUTIVE EDITOR

KING IN BLACK: GHOST RIDER

ED BRISSON WRITER
JUAN FRIGERI ARTIST
JASON KEITH COLOR ARTIST

VC'S JOE CARAMAGNA LETTERER
WILL SLINEY & CHRIS SOTOMAYOR COVER ART
SHANNON ANDREWS BALLESTEROS ASSISTANT EDITOR
JAKE THOMAS EDITOR

KING IN BLACK: AVENGERS. Contains material originally published in magazine form as KING IN BLACK: BLACK PANTHER (2021) #1, KING IN BLACK: CAPTAIN AMERICA (2021) #1, KING IN BLACK: GHOST RIDER (2021) #1, KING IN BLACK: IMMORTAL HULK (2021) #1, KING IN BLACK: IRON MAN/DOOM (2021) #1 and KING IN BLACK: WICCAN AND HULKLING (2021) #1. First printing 2021. ISBN 978-1-302-93034-9. Published by MARVEL WORLDWIDE, INC., a subsidiary of MARVEL ENTERTAINMENT, LLC. OFFICE OF PUBLICATION: 1290 Avenue of the Americas, New York, NY 10104. © 2021 MARVEL No similarity between any of the names, characters, persons, and/or institutions in this magazine with those of any living or dead person or institution is intended, and any such similarity which may exist is purely coincidental. **Printed in Canada.** KEVIN FEIGE, Chief Creative Officer; DAN BUCKLEY, President, Marvel Entertainment; JOE QUESADA, EVP & Creative Director; DAVID BOGART, Associate Publisher & SVP of Talent Affairs; TOM BREVOORT, VP, Executive Editor; NICK LOWE, Executive Editor, VP of Content, Digital Publishing; DAVID GABRIEL, VP of Print & Digital Publishing; JEFF YOUNGQUIST, VP of Production & Special Projects; ALEX MORALES, Director of Publishing Operations; DAN EDINGTON, Managing Editor; RICKEY PURDIN, Director of Talent Relations; JENNIFER GRÜNWALD, Senior Editor, Special Projects; SUSAN CRESPI, Production Manager; STAN LEE, Chairman Emeritus. For information regarding advertising in Marvel Comics or on Marvel.com, please contact Vit DeBellis, Custom Solutions & Integrated Advertising Manager, at vdebellis@marvel.com. For Marvel subscription inquiries, please call 888-511-5480. **Manufactured between 5/28/2021 and 6/29/2021 by SOLISCO PRINTERS, SCOTT, QC, CANADA.**

10 9 8 7 6 5 4 3 2 1

KNULL, THE CREATOR AND GOD OF THE ALIEN SYMBIOTES, HAS BEEN FREED FROM HIS PRISON AT THE EDGE OF THE GALAXY. HE LED A HORDE OF SYMBIOTE DRAGONS ACROSS THE COSMOS, AND NOW THEY HAVE ARRIVED ON EARTH — THE GALAXY'S FINAL LINE OF DEFENSE AGAINST THE KING IN BLACK.

KING IN BLACK: IMMORTAL HULK

AL EWING WRITER

AARON KUDER ARTIST

FRANK MARTIN & **ERICK ARCINIEGA** COLOR ARTISTS

VC'S COREY PETIT LETTERER
AARON KUDER & **FRANK MARTIN** COVER ART
SARAH BRUNSTAD ASSOCIATE EDITOR
WIL MOSS EDITOR

KING IN BLACK: IRON MAN/DOCTOR DOOM

CHRISTOPHER CANTWELL WRITER

SALVADOR LARROCA ARTIST

GURU-eFX COLOR ARTIST

VC'S TRAVIS LANHAM LETTERER
SALVADOR LARROCA & **GURU-eFX** COVER ART

MARTIN BIRO ASSISTANT EDITOR
ALANNA SMITH ASSOCIATE EDITOR
TOM BREVOORT EDITOR

KING IN BLACK: WICCAN AND HULKLING

TINI HOWARD WRITER

LUCIANO VECCHIO ARTIST

ESPEN GRUNDETJERN COLOR ARTIST

VC'S ARIANA MAHER LETTERER
JIM CHEUNG & **ALEJANDRO SÁNCHEZ RODRÍGUEZ** COVER ART
WIL MOSS & **SARAH BRUNSTAD** EDITORS

AVENGERS CREATED BY STAN LEE & JACK KIRBY

JENNIFER GRÜNWALD COLLECTION EDITOR
DANIEL KIRCHHOFFER ASSISTANT EDITOR
MAIA LOY ASSISTANT MANAGING EDITOR
LISA MONTALBANO ASSISTANT MANAGING EDITOR
JEFF YOUNGQUIST VP PRODUCTION & SPECIAL PROJECTS
SARAH SPADACCINI WITH **ANTHONY GAMBINO**
& **JAY BOWEN** BOOK DESIGNER

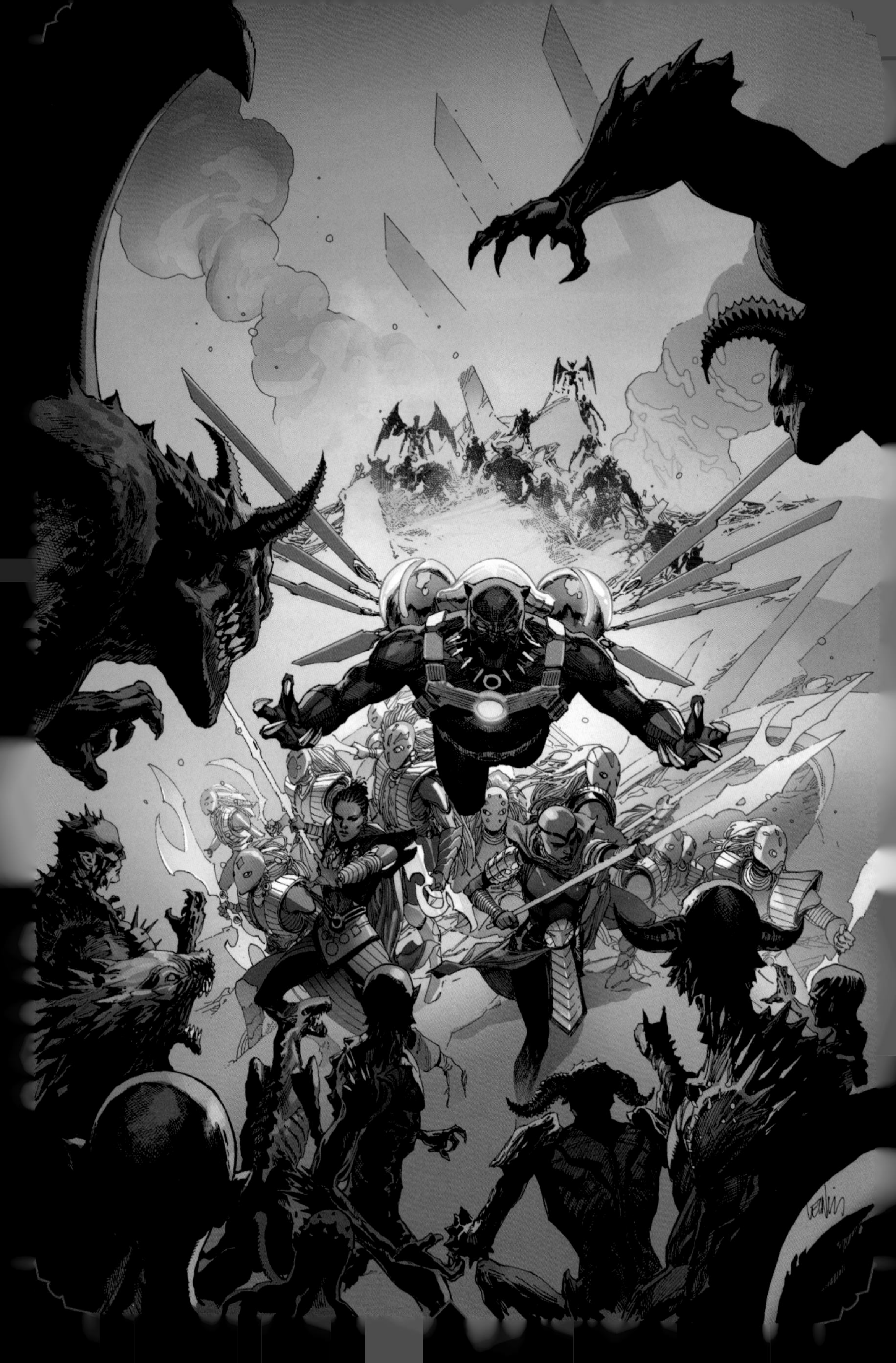

BLACK PANTHER

CATHEXIS

All of EARTH'S MIGHTIEST HEROES have assembled
to stop KNULL — but some of them have now fallen
prey to the symbiotes' dark influence, and Knull's
army only continues to spread across the globe.

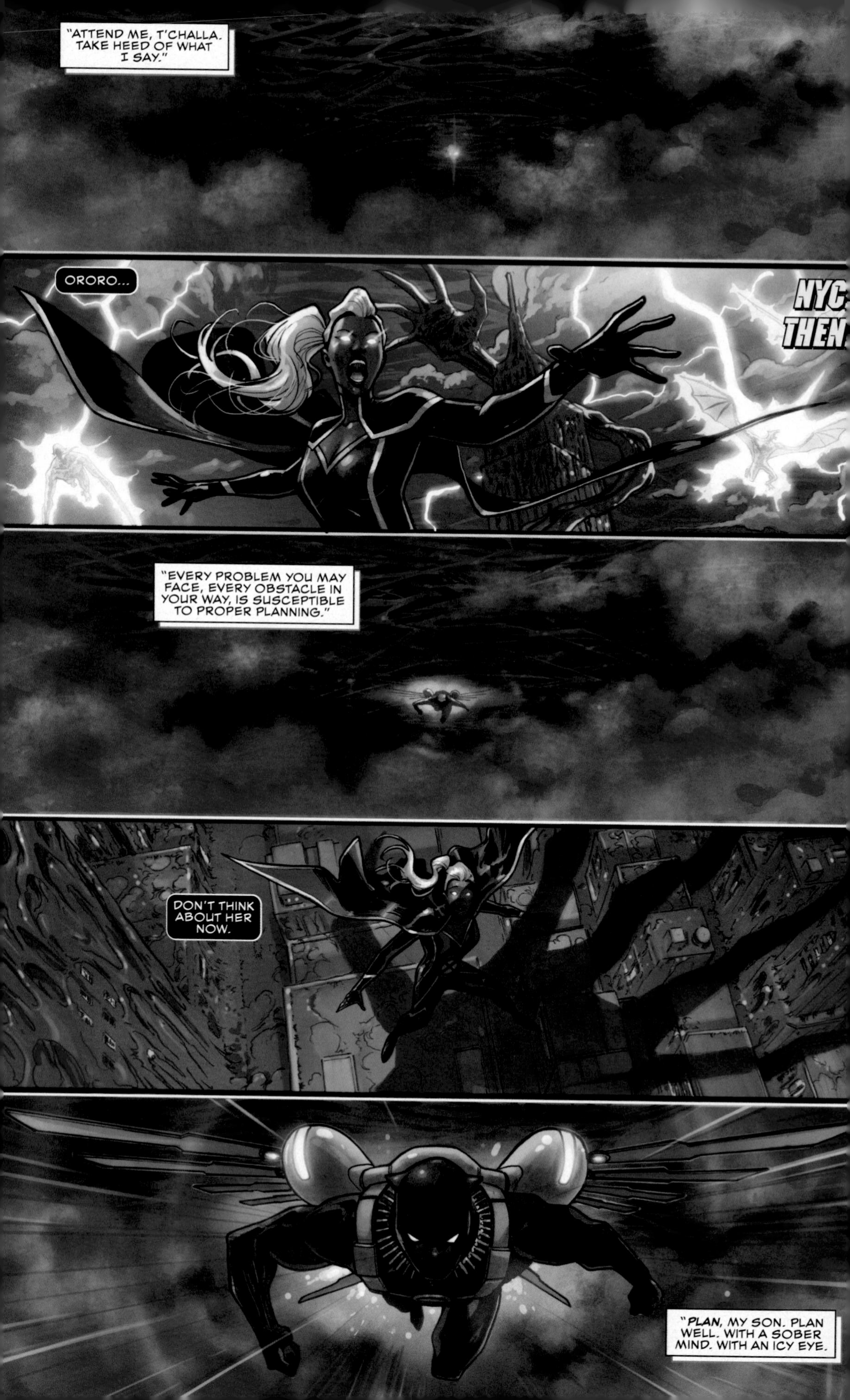
"ATTEND ME, T'CHALLA. TAKE HEED OF WHAT I SAY."
ORORO...
NYC THEN
"EVERY PROBLEM YOU MAY FACE, EVERY OBSTACLE IN YOUR WAY, IS SUSCEPTIBLE TO PROPER PLANNING."
DON'T THINK ABOUT HER NOW.
"PLAN, MY SON. PLAN WELL. WITH A SOBER MIND. WITH AN ICY EYE.

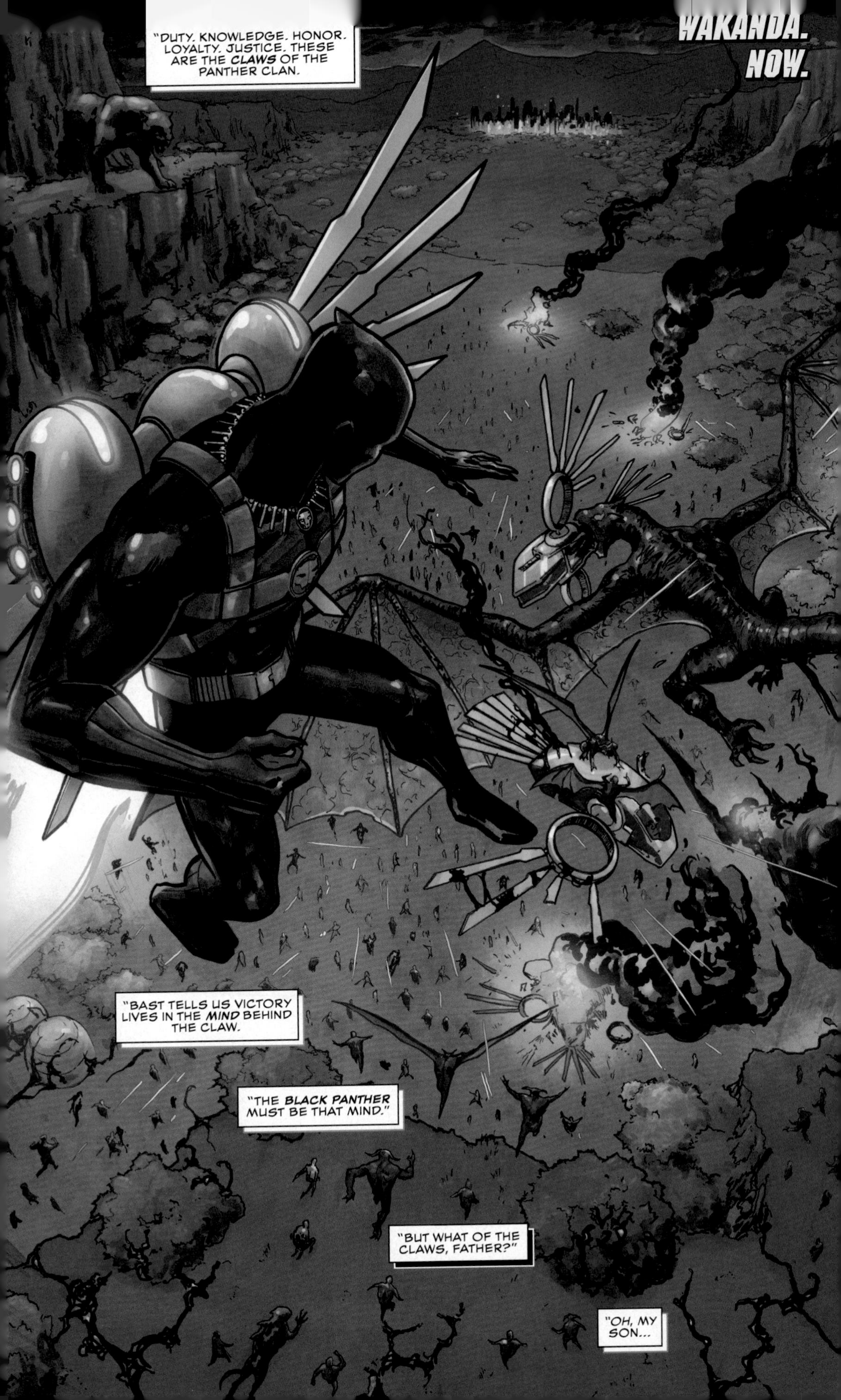

WAKANDA. NOW.
"DUTY. KNOWLEDGE. HONOR. LOYALTY. JUSTICE. THESE ARE THE *CLAWS* OF THE PANTHER CLAN.
"BAST TELLS US VICTORY LIVES IN THE *MIND* BEHIND THE CLAW.
"THE *BLACK PANTHER* MUST BE THAT MIND."
"BUT WHAT OF THE CLAWS, FATHER?"
"OH, MY SON...

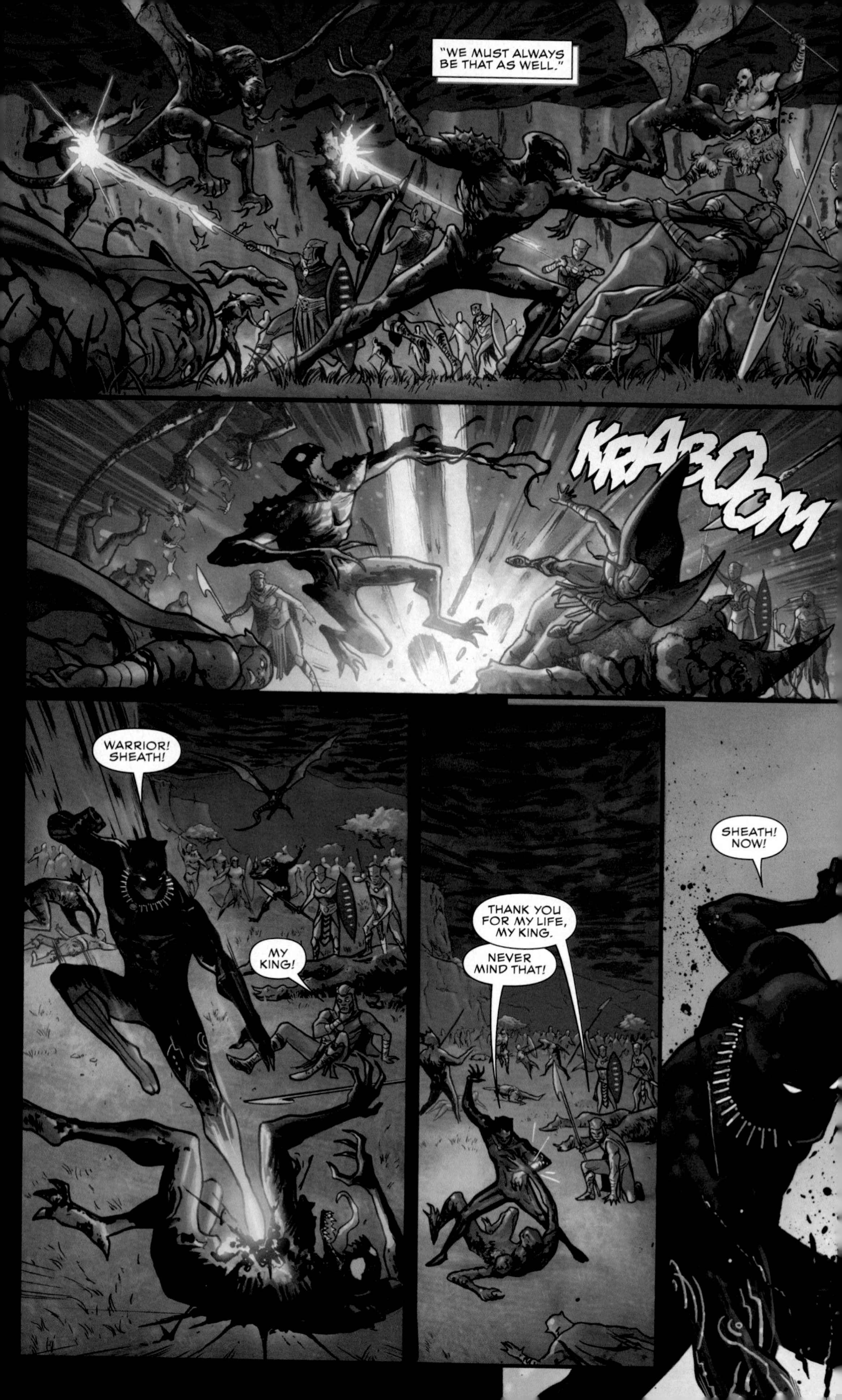
"WE MUST ALWAYS BE THAT AS WELL."
KRABOOM
WARRIOR! SHEATH!
MY KING!
THANK YOU FOR MY LIFE, MY KING.
NEVER MIND THAT!
SHEATH! NOW!

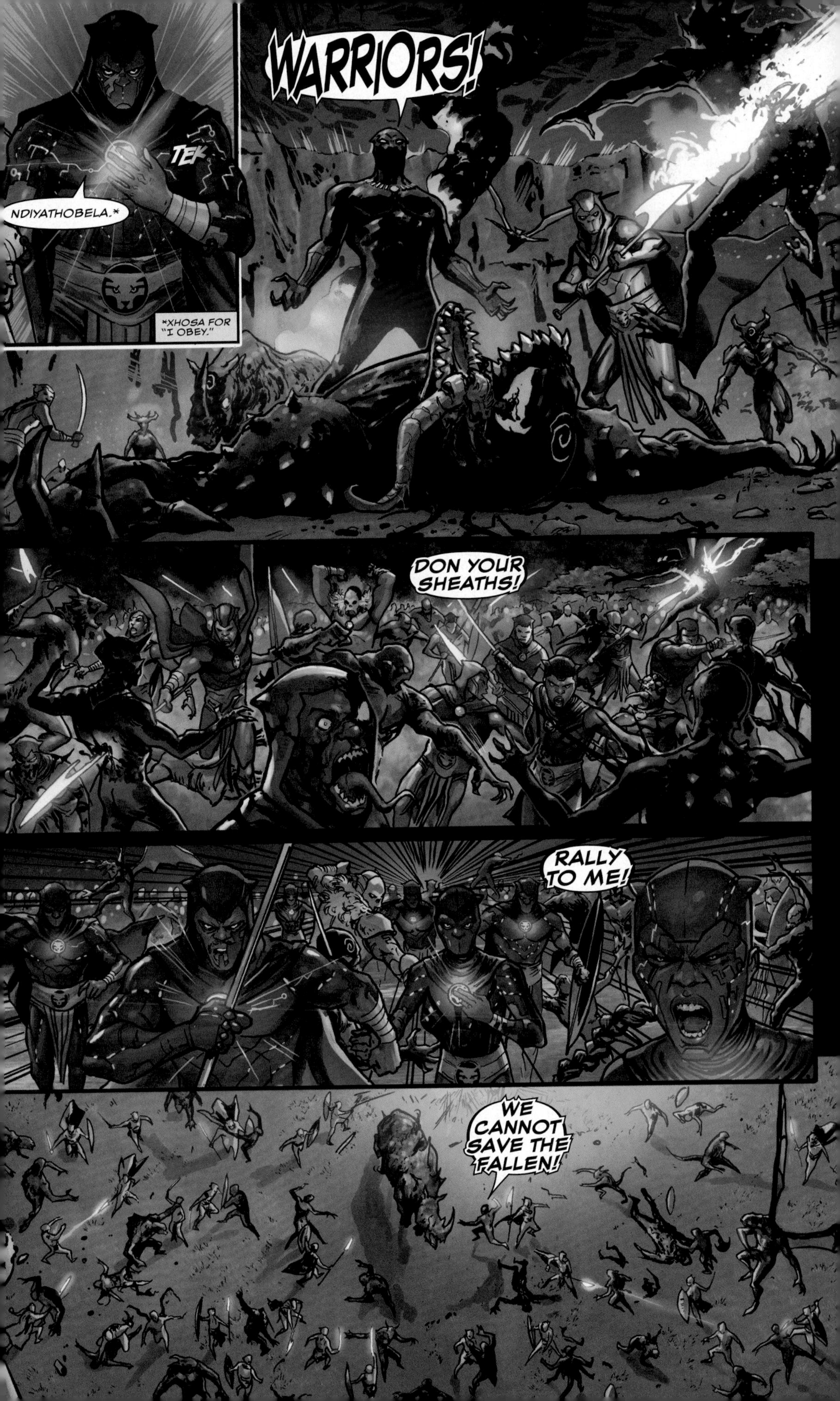
NDIYATHOBELA.*
*XHOSA FOR "I OBEY."
WARRIORS!
DON YOUR SHEATHS!
RALLY TO ME!
WE CANNOT SAVE THE FALLEN!

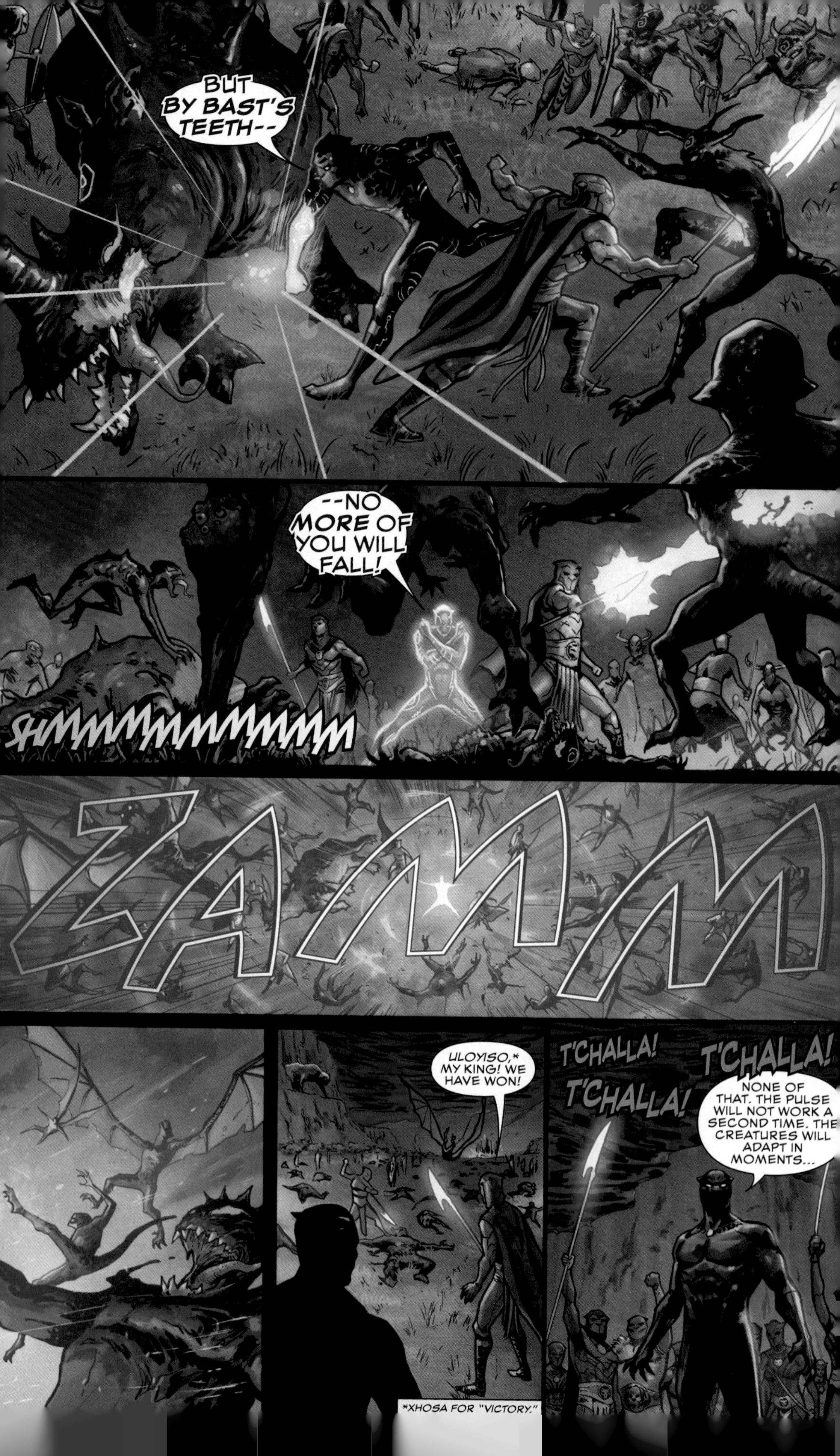
BUT BY BAST'S TEETH--
--NO MORE OF YOU WILL FALL!
SHMMMMMMMMMMM
ZAMM
ULOYISO,* MY KING! WE HAVE WON!
T'CHALLA! T'CHALLA! T'CHALLA!
NONE OF THAT. THE PULSE WILL NOT WORK A SECOND TIME. THE CREATURES WILL ADAPT IN MOMENTS...
*XHOSA FOR "VICTORY."

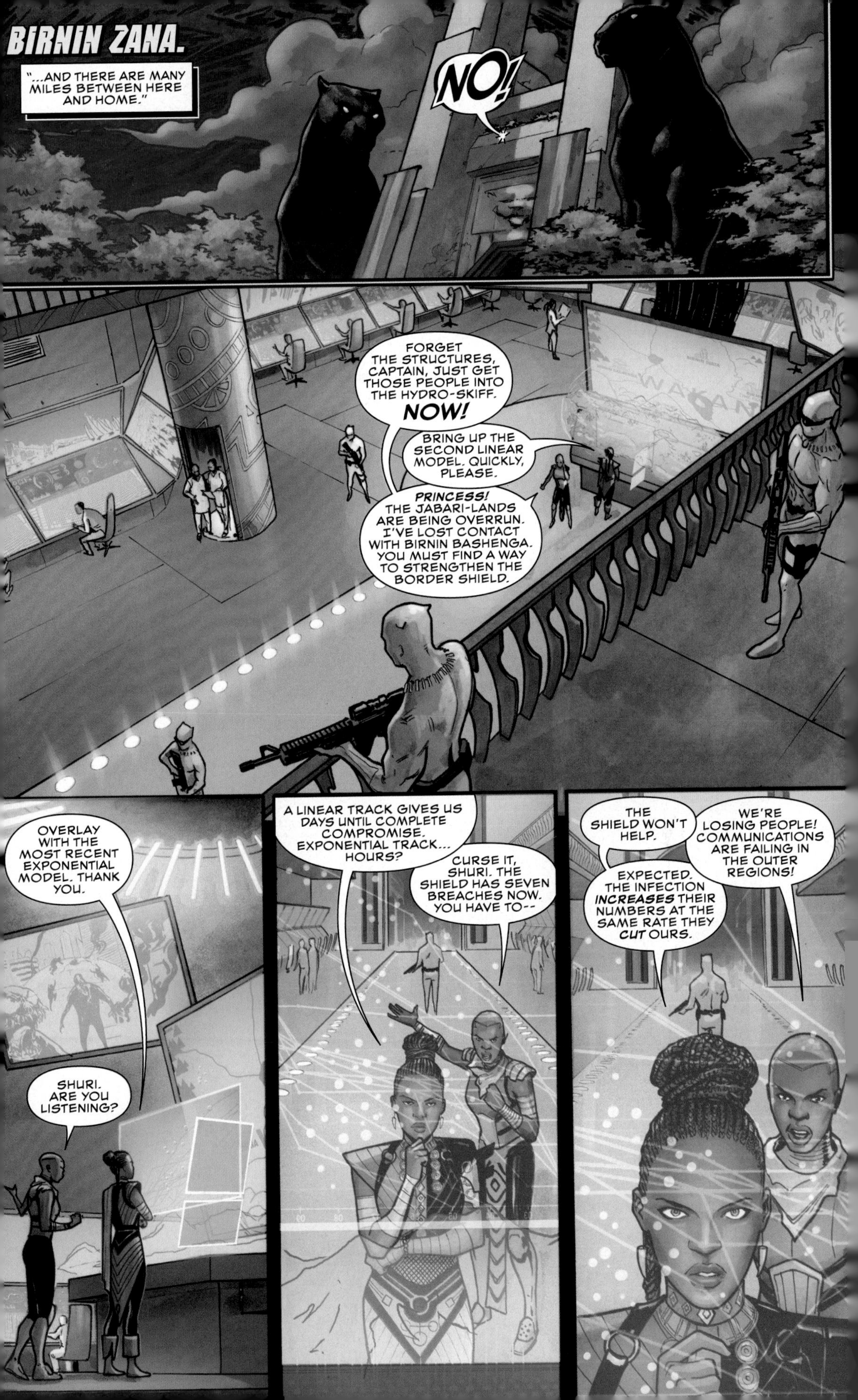
BIRNIN ZANA.
"...AND THERE ARE MANY MILES BETWEEN HERE AND HOME."
NO!
FORGET THE STRUCTURES, CAPTAIN, JUST GET THOSE PEOPLE INTO THE HYDRO-SKIFF. NOW!
BRING UP THE SECOND LINEAR MODEL. QUICKLY, PLEASE.
PRINCESS! THE JABARI-LANDS ARE BEING OVERRUN. I'VE LOST CONTACT WITH BIRNIN BASHENGA. YOU MUST FIND A WAY TO STRENGTHEN THE BORDER SHIELD.
OVERLAY WITH THE MOST RECENT EXPONENTIAL MODEL. THANK YOU.
SHURI. ARE YOU LISTENING?
A LINEAR TRACK GIVES US DAYS UNTIL COMPLETE COMPROMISE. EXPONENTIAL TRACK... HOURS?
CURSE IT, SHURI. THE SHIELD HAS SEVEN BREACHES NOW. YOU HAVE TO--
THE SHIELD WON'T HELP.
WE'RE LOSING PEOPLE! COMMUNICATIONS ARE FAILING IN THE OUTER REGIONS!
EXPECTED. THE INFECTION INCREASES THEIR NUMBERS AT THE SAME RATE THEY CUT OURS.

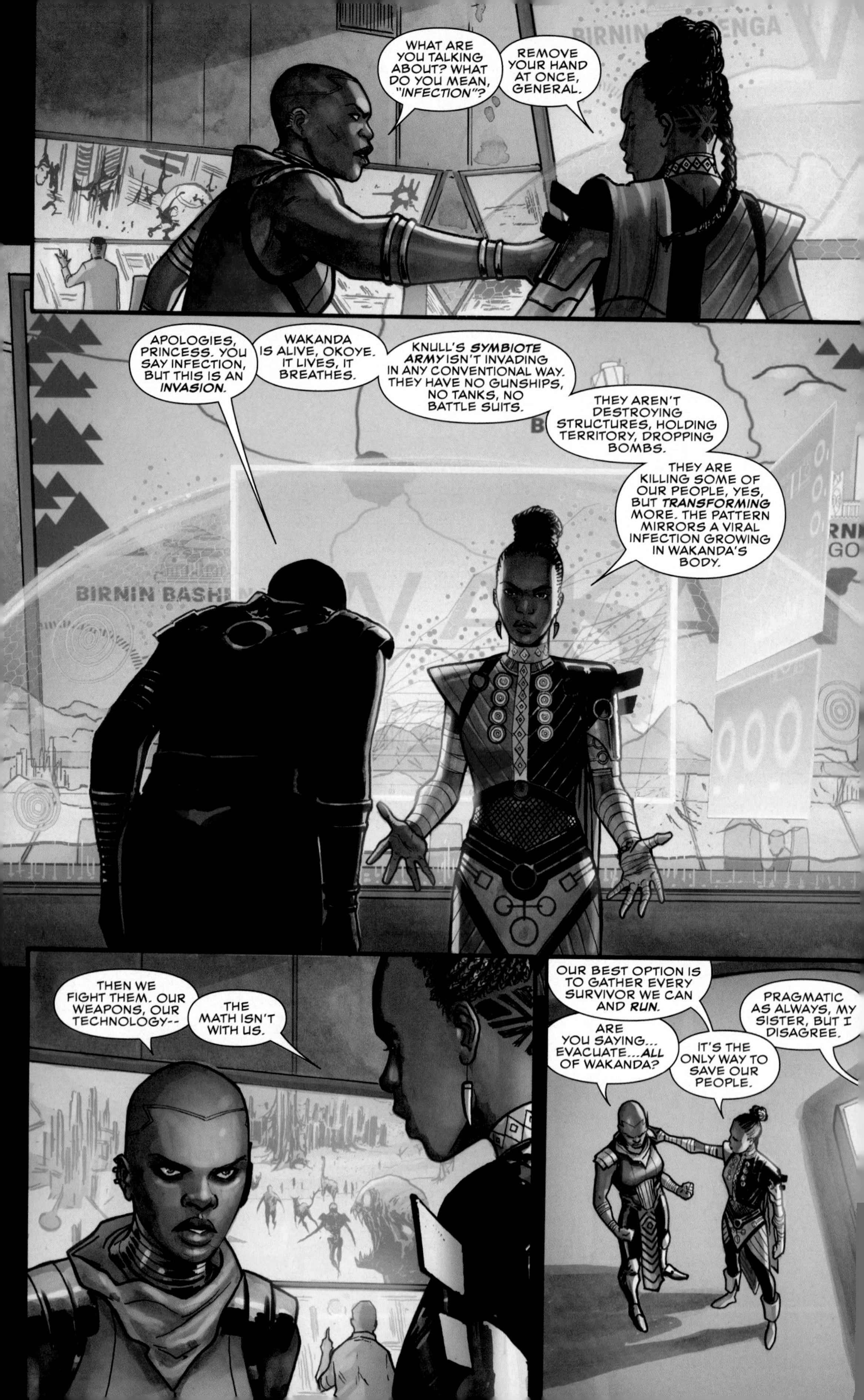
WHAT ARE YOU TALKING ABOUT? WHAT DO YOU MEAN, "INFECTION"?
REMOVE YOUR HAND AT ONCE, GENERAL.
APOLOGIES, PRINCESS. YOU SAY INFECTION, BUT THIS IS AN INVASION.
WAKANDA IS ALIVE, OKOYE. IT LIVES, IT BREATHES.
KNULL'S SYMBIOTE ARMY ISN'T INVADING IN ANY CONVENTIONAL WAY. THEY HAVE NO GUNSHIPS, NO TANKS, NO BATTLE SUITS.
THEY AREN'T DESTROYING STRUCTURES, HOLDING TERRITORY, DROPPING BOMBS.
THEY ARE KILLING SOME OF OUR PEOPLE, YES, BUT TRANSFORMING MORE. THE PATTERN MIRRORS A VIRAL INFECTION GROWING IN WAKANDA'S BODY.
BIRNIN BASHE
THEN WE FIGHT THEM. OUR WEAPONS, OUR TECHNOLOGY--
THE MATH ISN'T WITH US.
OUR BEST OPTION IS TO GATHER EVERY SURVIVOR WE CAN AND RUN.
ARE YOU SAYING... EVACUATE...ALL OF WAKANDA?
IT'S THE ONLY WAY TO SAVE OUR PEOPLE.
PRAGMATIC AS ALWAYS, MY SISTER, BUT I DISAGREE.

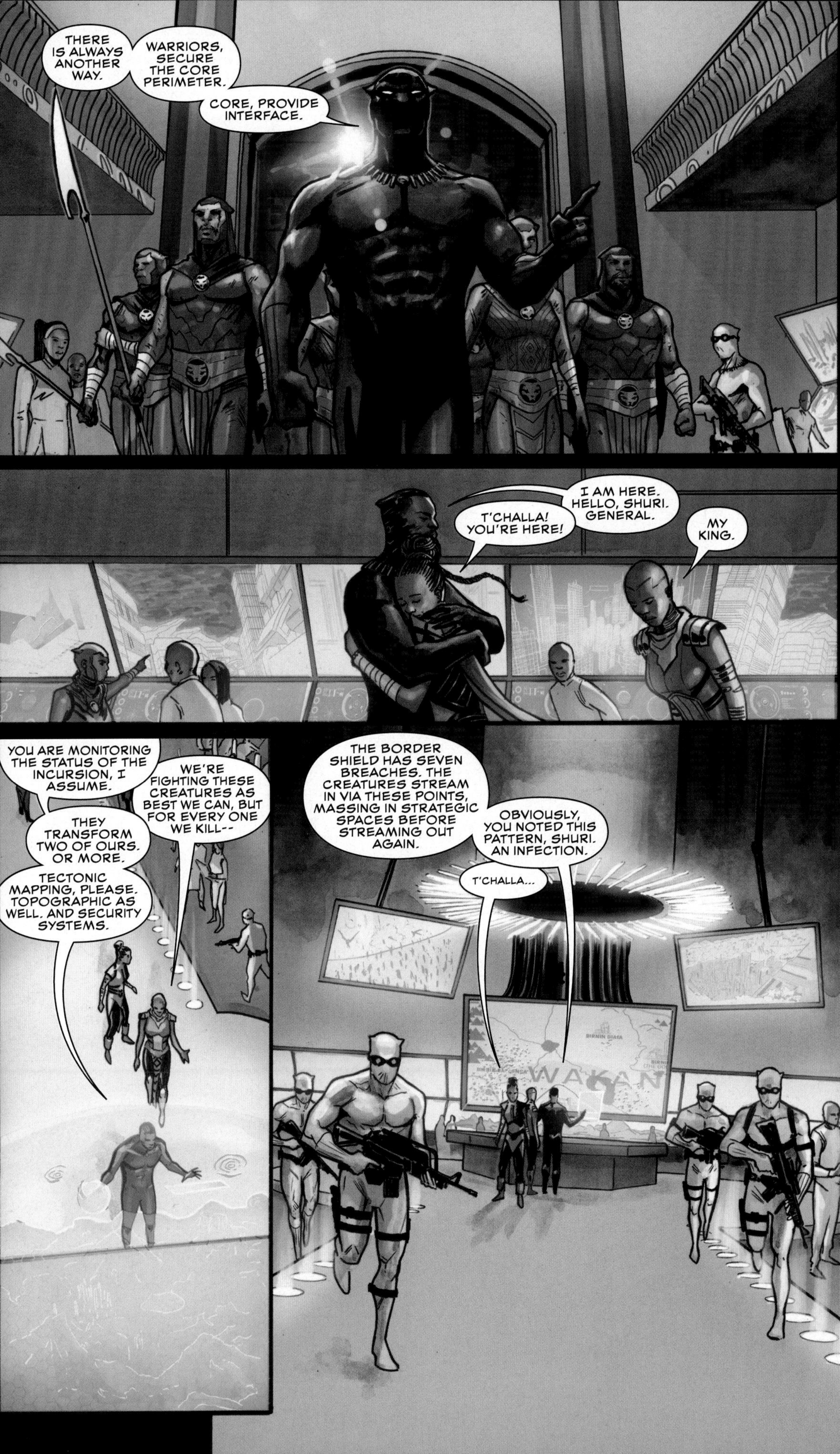
THERE IS ALWAYS ANOTHER WAY.
WARRIORS, SECURE THE CORE PERIMETER.
CORE, PROVIDE INTERFACE.
I AM HERE. HELLO, SHURI. GENERAL.
T'CHALLA! YOU'RE HERE!
MY KING.
YOU ARE MONITORING THE STATUS OF THE INCURSION, I ASSUME.
WE'RE FIGHTING THESE CREATURES AS BEST WE CAN, BUT FOR EVERY ONE WE KILL--
THEY TRANSFORM TWO OF OURS. OR MORE.
TECTONIC MAPPING, PLEASE. TOPOGRAPHIC AS WELL. AND SECURITY SYSTEMS.
THE BORDER SHIELD HAS SEVEN BREACHES. THE CREATURES STREAM IN VIA THESE POINTS, MASSING IN STRATEGIC SPACES BEFORE STREAMING OUT AGAIN.
OBVIOUSLY, YOU NOTED THIS PATTERN, SHURI. AN INFECTION.
T'CHALLA...

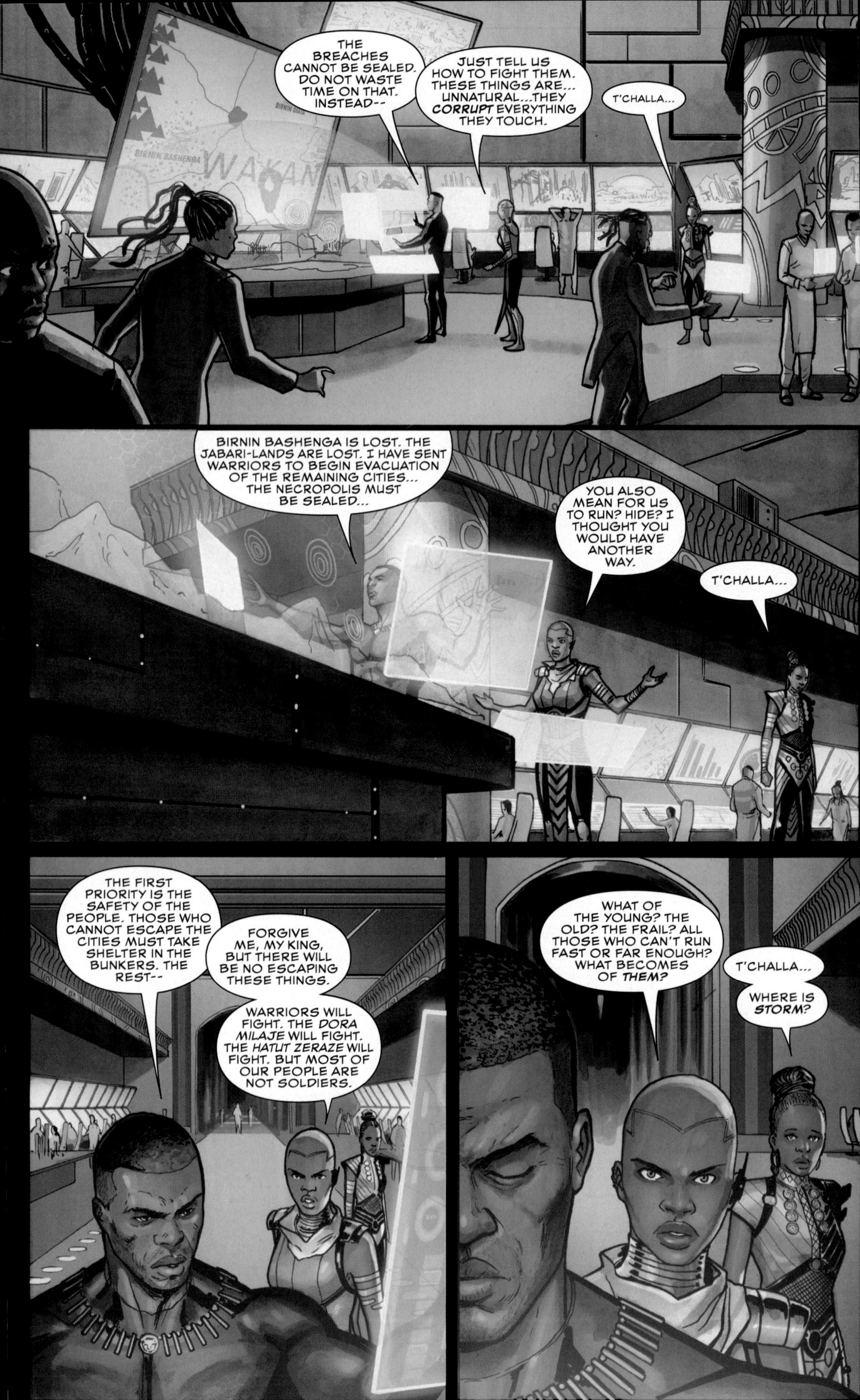
THE BREACHES CANNOT BE SEALED. DO NOT WASTE TIME ON THAT. INSTEAD--
JUST TELL US HOW TO FIGHT THEM. THESE THINGS ARE... UNNATURAL...THEY CORRUPT EVERYTHING THEY TOUCH.
T'CHALLA...
BIRNIN BASHENGA
WAKAN
BIRNIN BASHENGA IS LOST. THE JABARI-LANDS ARE LOST. I HAVE SENT WARRIORS TO BEGIN EVACUATION OF THE REMAINING CITIES... THE NECROPOLIS MUST BE SEALED...
YOU ALSO MEAN FOR US TO RUN? HIDE? I THOUGHT YOU WOULD HAVE ANOTHER WAY.
T'CHALLA...
THE FIRST PRIORITY IS THE SAFETY OF THE PEOPLE. THOSE WHO CANNOT ESCAPE THE CITIES MUST TAKE SHELTER IN THE BUNKERS. THE REST--
FORGIVE ME, MY KING, BUT THERE WILL BE NO ESCAPING THESE THINGS.
WARRIORS WILL FIGHT. THE DORA MILAJE WILL FIGHT. THE HATUT ZERAZE WILL FIGHT. BUT MOST OF OUR PEOPLE ARE NOT SOLDIERS.
WHAT OF THE YOUNG? THE OLD? THE FRAIL? ALL THOSE WHO CAN'T RUN FAST OR FAR ENOUGH? WHAT BECOMES OF THEM?
T'CHALLA...
WHERE IS STORM?

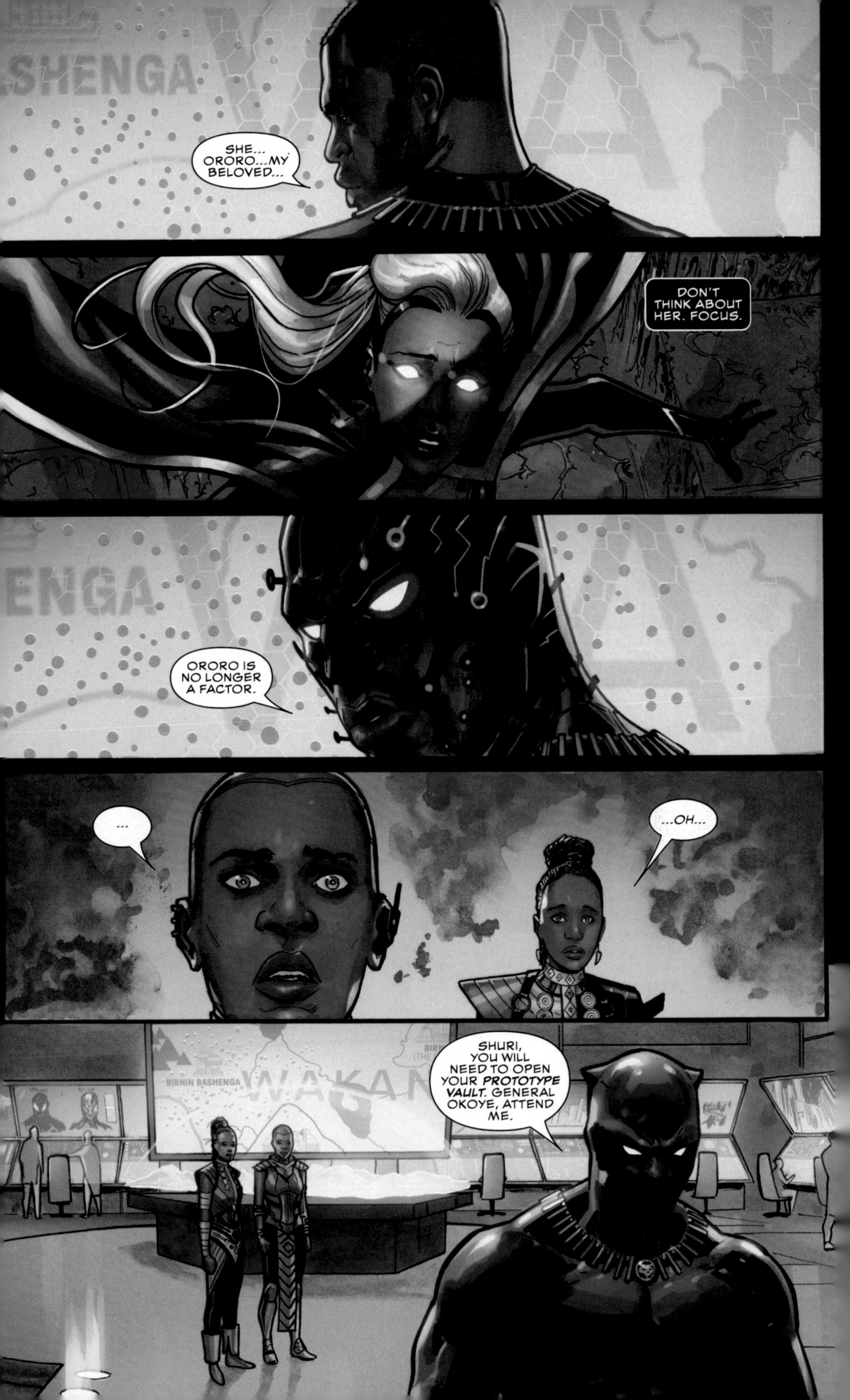
SHE... ORORO...MY BELOVED...
DON'T THINK ABOUT HER. FOCUS.
ORORO IS NO LONGER A FACTOR.
...
...OH...
BIRNIN BASHENGA
WAKAN
SHURI, YOU WILL NEED TO OPEN YOUR *PROTOTYPE VAULT.* GENERAL OKOYE, ATTEND ME.

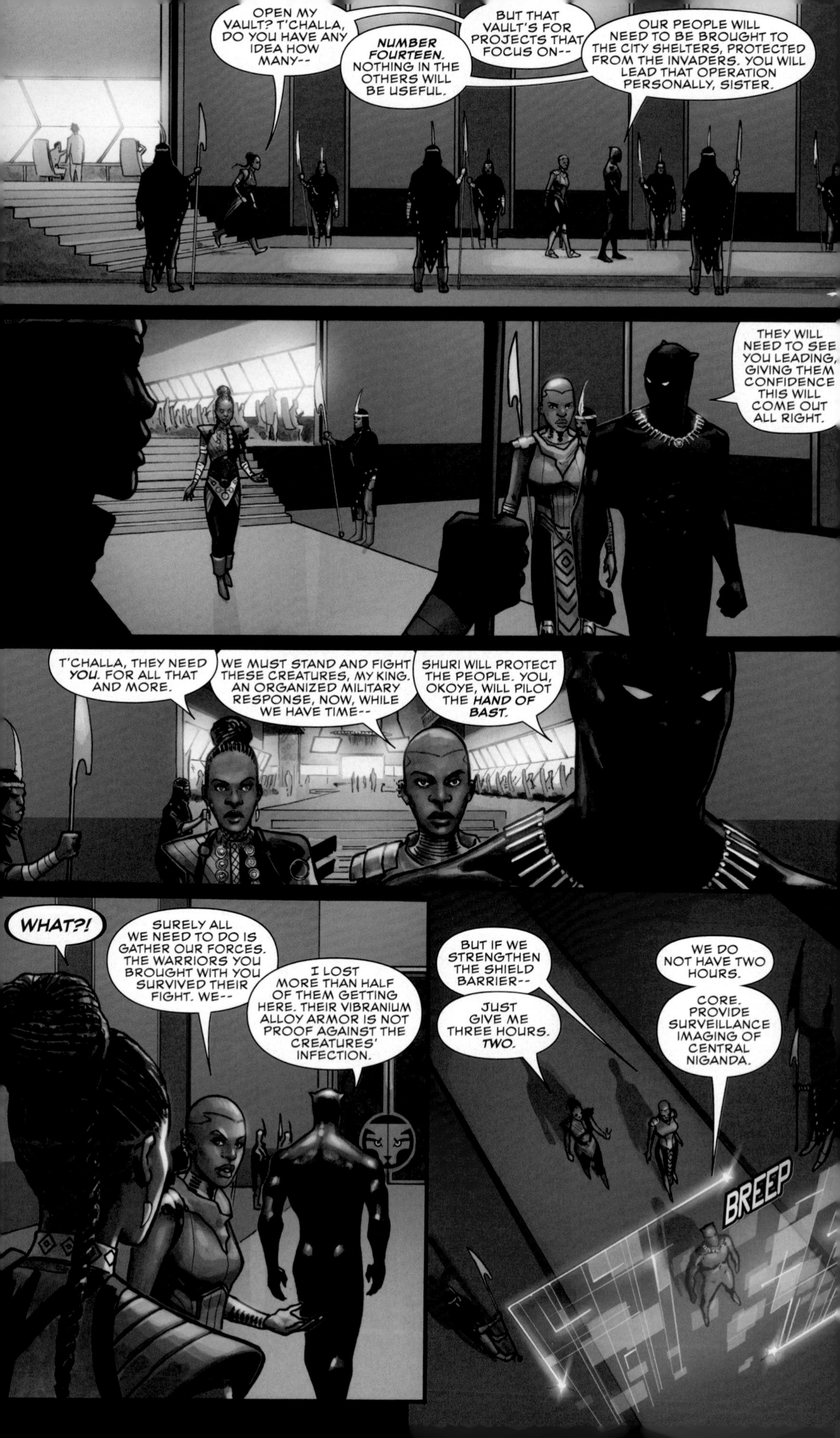
OPEN MY VAULT? T'CHALLA, DO YOU HAVE ANY IDEA HOW MANY--
NUMBER FOURTEEN. NOTHING IN THE OTHERS WILL BE USEFUL.
BUT THAT VAULT'S FOR PROJECTS THAT FOCUS ON--
OUR PEOPLE WILL NEED TO BE BROUGHT TO THE CITY SHELTERS, PROTECTED FROM THE INVADERS. YOU WILL LEAD THAT OPERATION PERSONALLY, SISTER.
THEY WILL NEED TO SEE YOU LEADING, GIVING THEM CONFIDENCE THIS WILL COME OUT ALL RIGHT.
T'CHALLA, THEY NEED YOU. FOR ALL THAT AND MORE.
WE MUST STAND AND FIGHT THESE CREATURES, MY KING. AN ORGANIZED MILITARY RESPONSE, NOW, WHILE WE HAVE TIME--
SHURI WILL PROTECT THE PEOPLE. YOU, OKOYE, WILL PILOT THE HAND OF BAST.
WHAT?!
SURELY ALL WE NEED TO DO IS GATHER OUR FORCES. THE WARRIORS YOU BROUGHT WITH YOU SURVIVED THEIR FIGHT. WE--
I LOST MORE THAN HALF OF THEM GETTING HERE. THEIR VIBRANIUM ALLOY ARMOR IS NOT PROOF AGAINST THE CREATURES' INFECTION.
BUT IF WE STRENGTHEN THE SHIELD BARRIER--
JUST GIVE ME THREE HOURS. TWO.
WE DO NOT HAVE TWO HOURS.
CORE. PROVIDE SURVEILLANCE IMAGING OF CENTRAL NIGANDA.
BREEP

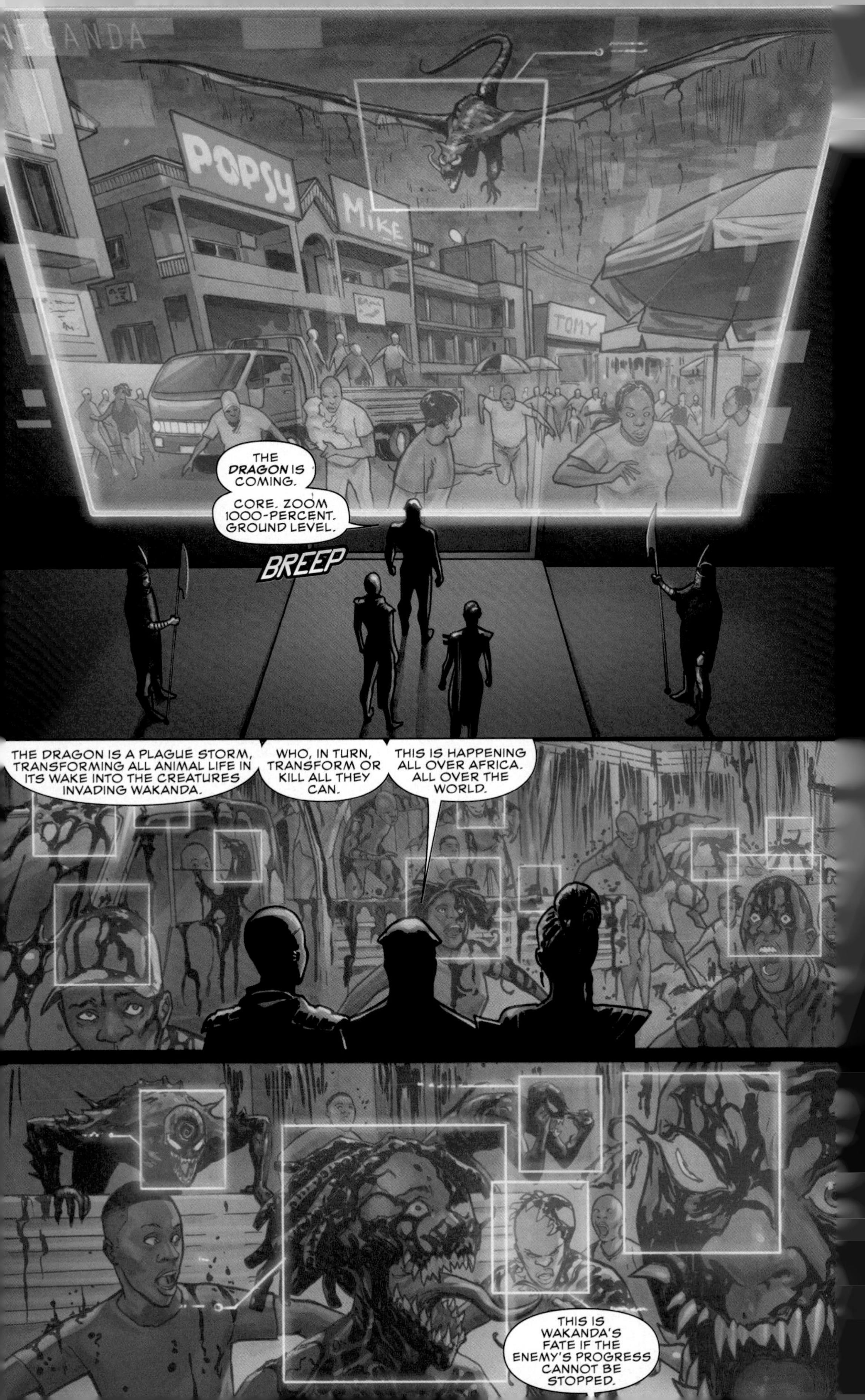
NIGANDA
POPSY
MIKE
TOMY
THE DRAGON IS COMING.
CORE. ZOOM 1000-PERCENT. GROUND LEVEL.
BREEP
THE DRAGON IS A PLAGUE STORM, TRANSFORMING ALL ANIMAL LIFE IN ITS WAKE INTO THE CREATURES INVADING WAKANDA.
WHO, IN TURN, TRANSFORM OR KILL ALL THEY CAN.
THIS IS HAPPENING ALL OVER AFRICA. ALL OVER THE WORLD.
THIS IS WAKANDA'S FATE IF THE ENEMY'S PROGRESS CANNOT BE STOPPED.

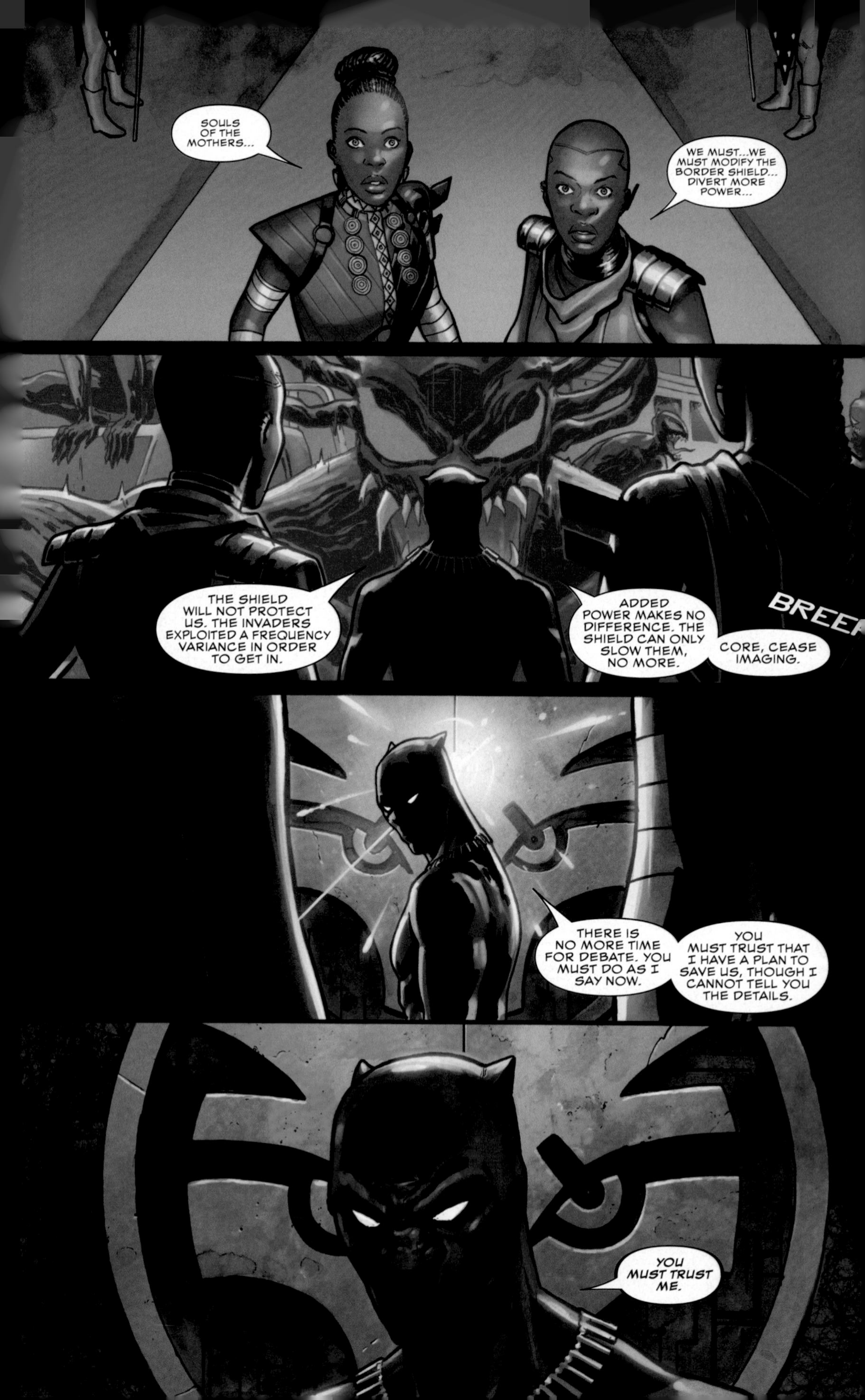
SOULS OF THE MOTHERS...
WE MUST...WE MUST MODIFY THE BORDER SHIELD... DIVERT MORE POWER...
THE SHIELD WILL NOT PROTECT US. THE INVADERS EXPLOITED A FREQUENCY VARIANCE IN ORDER TO GET IN.
ADDED POWER MAKES NO DIFFERENCE. THE SHIELD CAN ONLY SLOW THEM, NO MORE.
CORE, CEASE IMAGING.
THERE IS NO MORE TIME FOR DEBATE. YOU MUST DO AS I SAY NOW.
YOU MUST TRUST THAT I HAVE A PLAN TO SAVE US, THOUGH I CANNOT TELL YOU THE DETAILS.
YOU MUST TRUST ME.

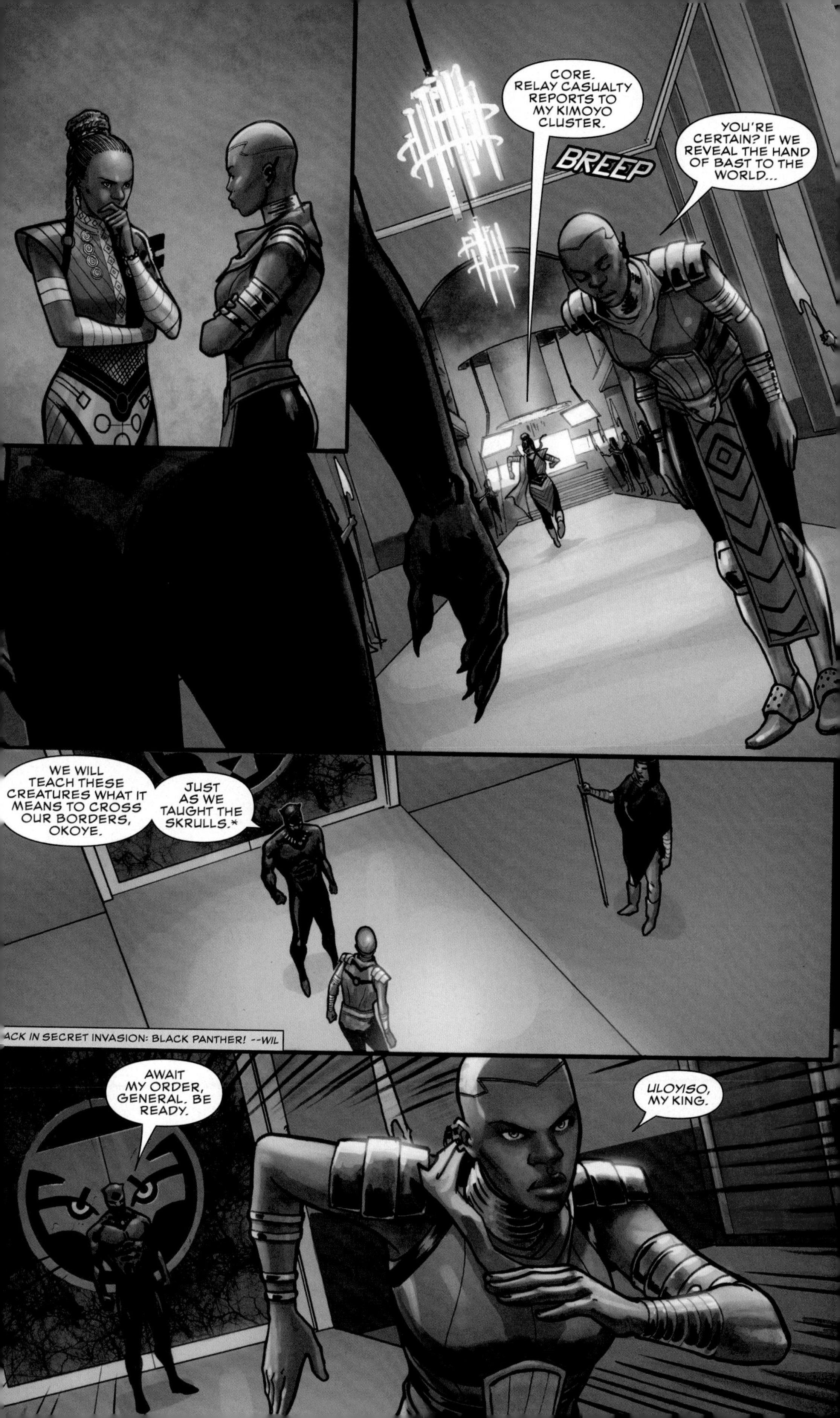
CORE. RELAY CASUALTY REPORTS TO MY KIMOYO CLUSTER.
BREEP
YOU'RE CERTAIN? IF WE REVEAL THE HAND OF BAST TO THE WORLD...
WE WILL TEACH THESE CREATURES WHAT IT MEANS TO CROSS OUR BORDERS, OKOYE.
JUST AS WE TAUGHT THE SKRULLS.*
ACK IN SECRET INVASION: BLACK PANTHER! --WIL
AWAIT MY ORDER, GENERAL. BE READY.
ULOYISO, MY KING.

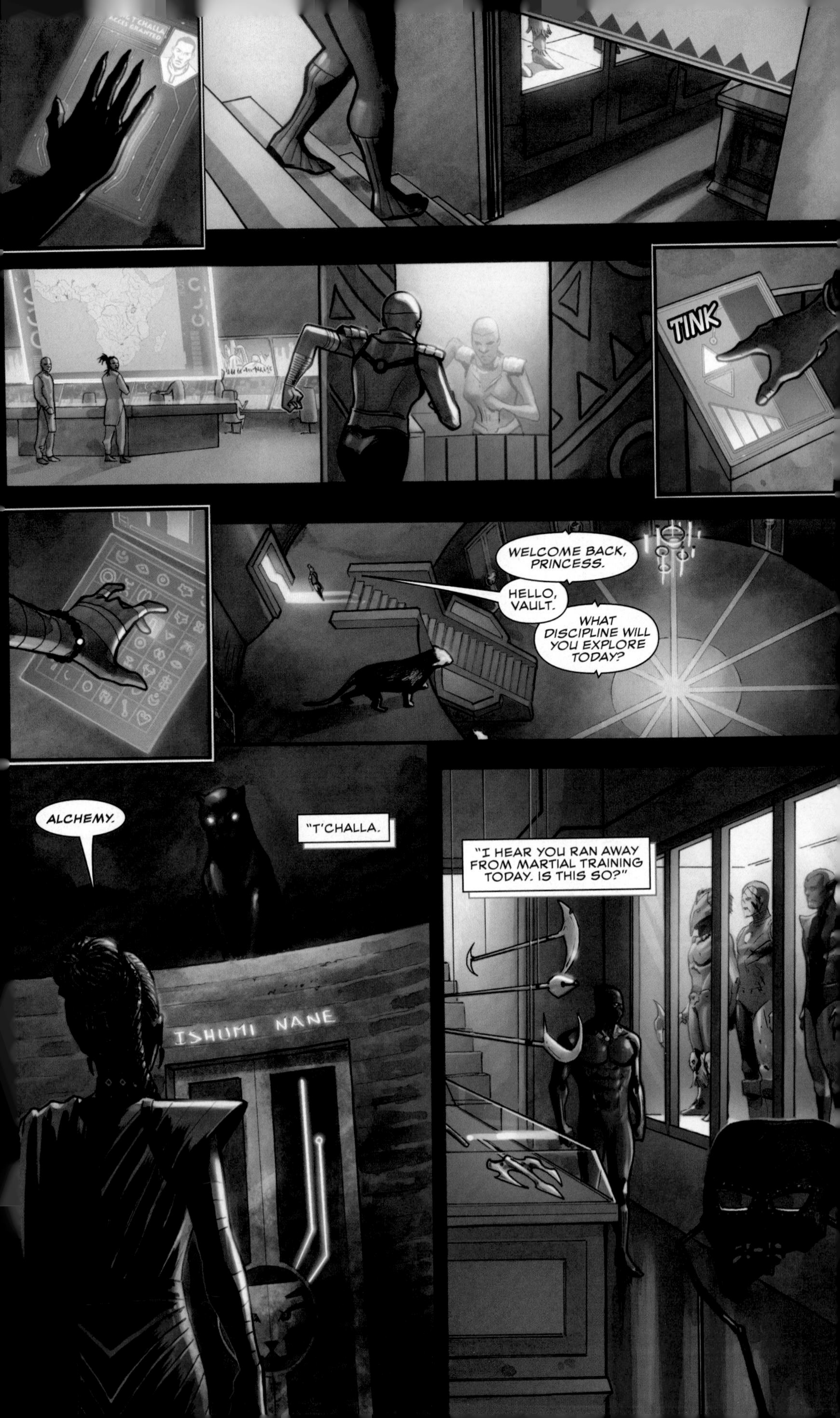
TINK
WELCOME BACK, PRINCESS.
HELLO, VAULT.
WHAT DISCIPLINE WILL YOU EXPLORE TODAY?
ALCHEMY.
"T'CHALLA.
"I HEAR YOU RAN AWAY FROM MARTIAL TRAINING TODAY. IS THIS SO?"
ISHUMI NANE

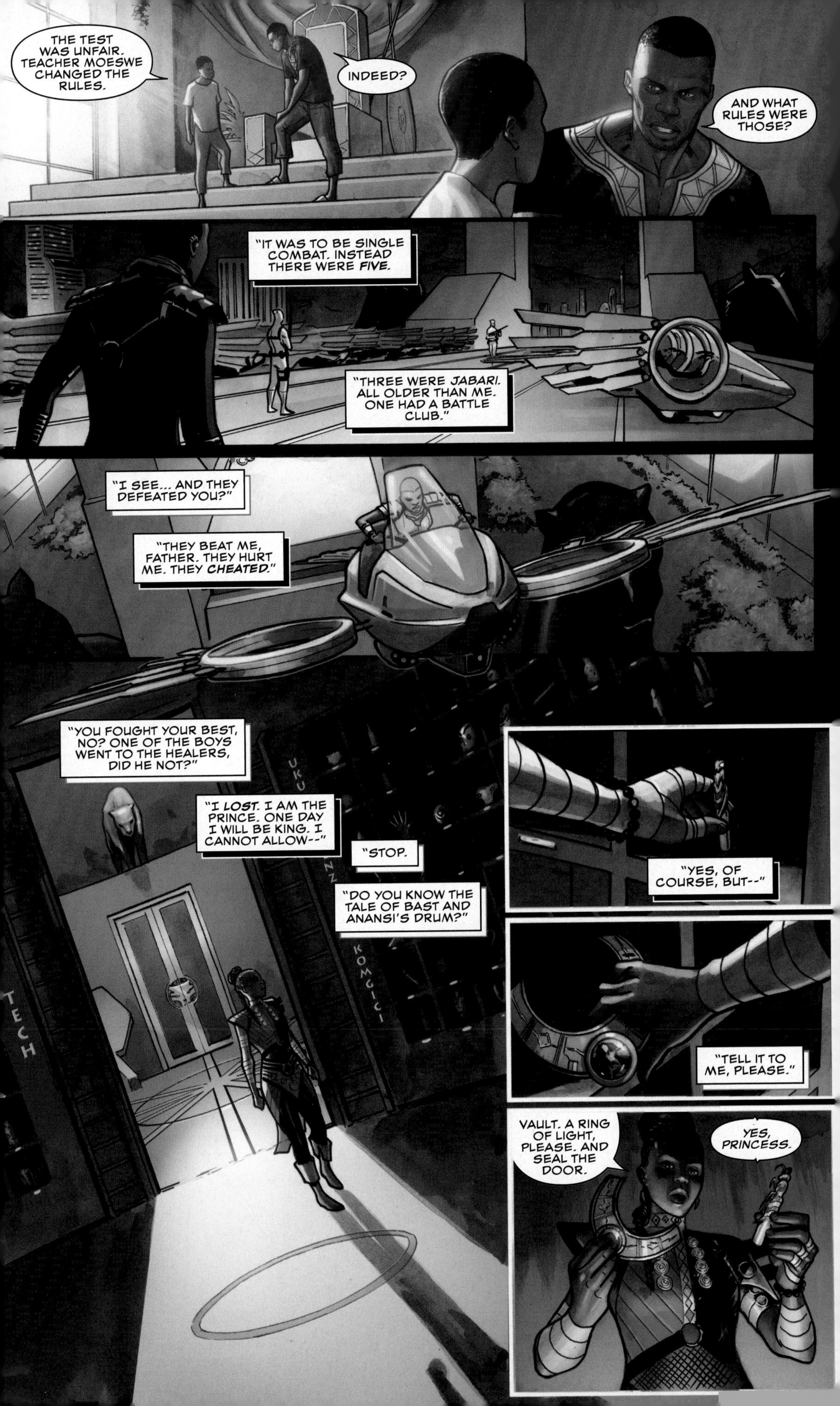
THE TEST WAS UNFAIR. TEACHER MOESWE CHANGED THE RULES.
INDEED?
AND WHAT RULES WERE THOSE?
"IT WAS TO BE SINGLE COMBAT. INSTEAD THERE WERE FIVE.
"THREE WERE JABARI. ALL OLDER THAN ME. ONE HAD A BATTLE CLUB."
"I SEE... AND THEY DEFEATED YOU?"
"THEY BEAT ME, FATHER. THEY HURT ME. THEY CHEATED."
"YOU FOUGHT YOUR BEST, NO? ONE OF THE BOYS WENT TO THE HEALERS, DID HE NOT?"
"I LOST. I AM THE PRINCE. ONE DAY I WILL BE KING. I CANNOT ALLOW--"
"STOP.
"DO YOU KNOW THE TALE OF BAST AND ANANSI'S DRUM?"
TECH
KOMGICI
"YES, OF COURSE, BUT--"
"TELL IT TO ME, PLEASE."
VAULT. A RING OF LIGHT, PLEASE. AND SEAL THE DOOR.
YES, PRINCESS.

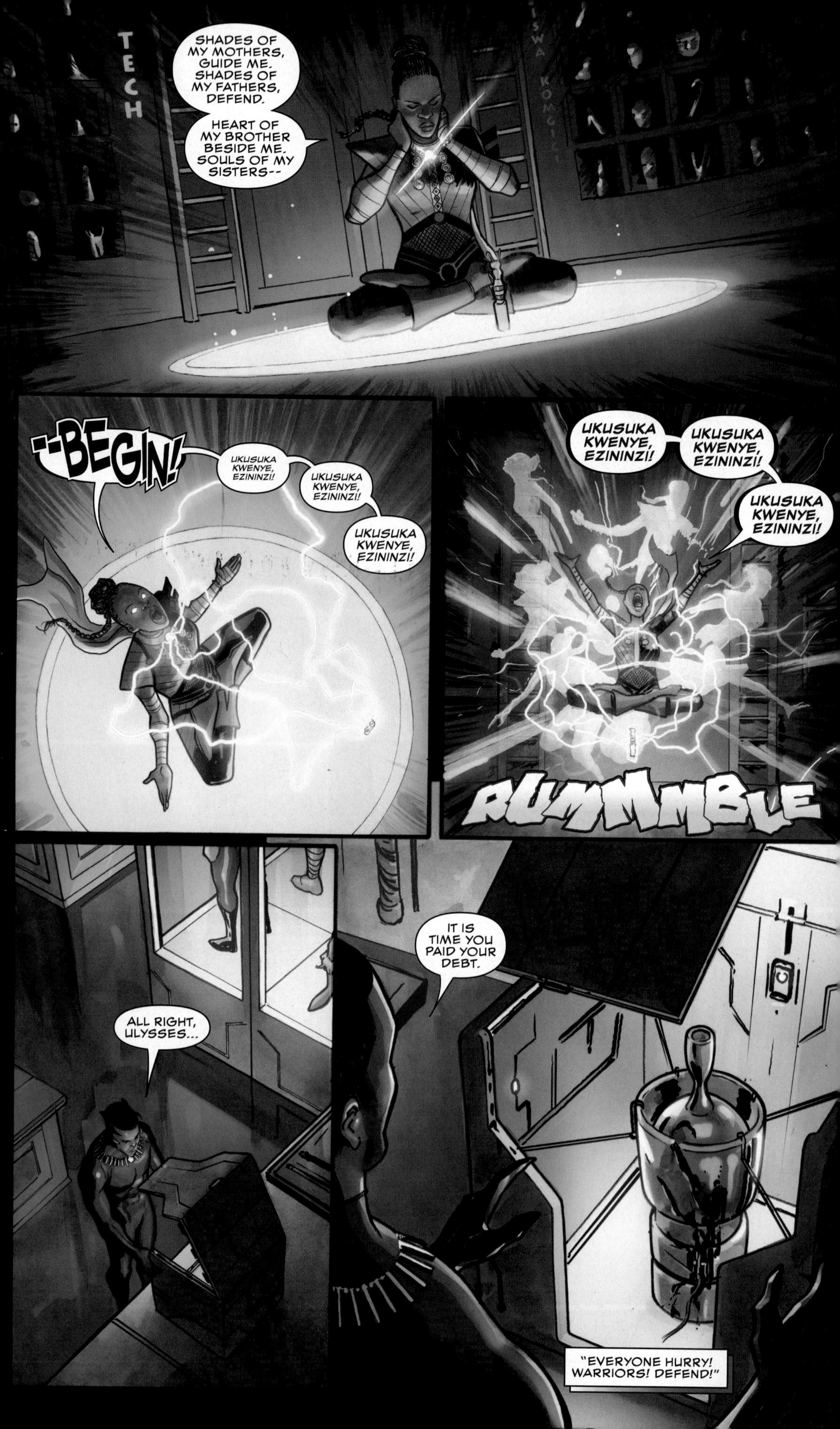
TECH
SHADES OF MY MOTHERS, GUIDE ME. SHADES OF MY FATHERS, DEFEND.
HEART OF MY BROTHER BESIDE ME. SOULS OF MY SISTERS--
--BEGIN!
UKUSUKA KWENYE, EZININZI!
UKUSUKA KWENYE, EZININZI!
UKUSUKA KWENYE, EZININZI!
UKUSUKA KWENYE, EZININZI!
UKUSUKA KWENYE, EZININZI!
UKUSUKA KWENYE, EZININZI!
RUMMMBLE
ALL RIGHT, ULYSSES...
IT IS TIME YOU PAID YOUR DEBT.
"EVERYONE HURRY! WARRIORS! DEFEND!"

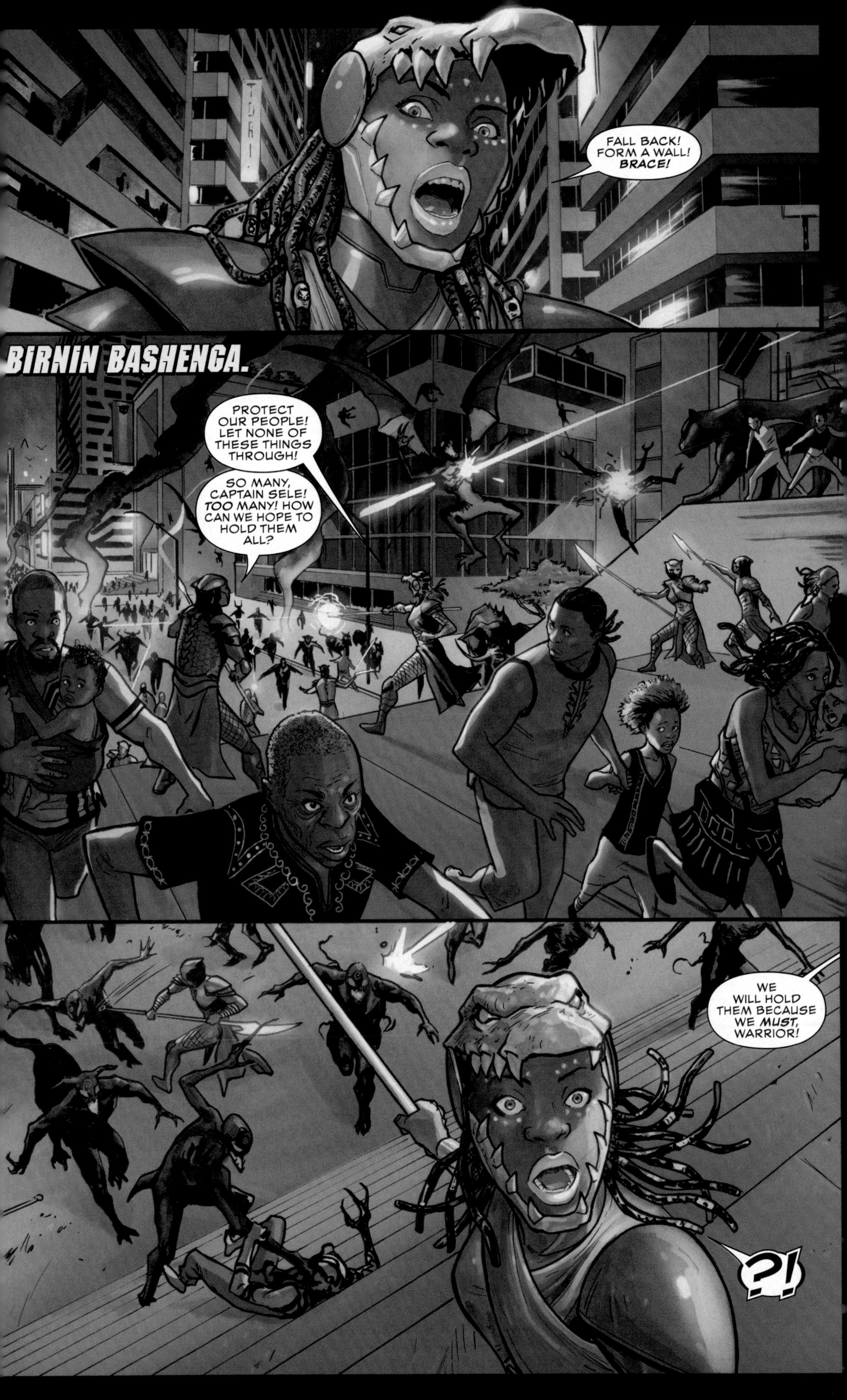
FALL BACK! FORM A WALL! BRACE!
BIRNIN BASHENGA.
PROTECT OUR PEOPLE! LET NONE OF THESE THINGS THROUGH!
SO MANY, CAPTAIN SELE! TOO MANY! HOW CAN WE HOPE TO HOLD THEM ALL?
WE WILL HOLD THEM BECAUSE WE MUST, WARRIOR!
?!

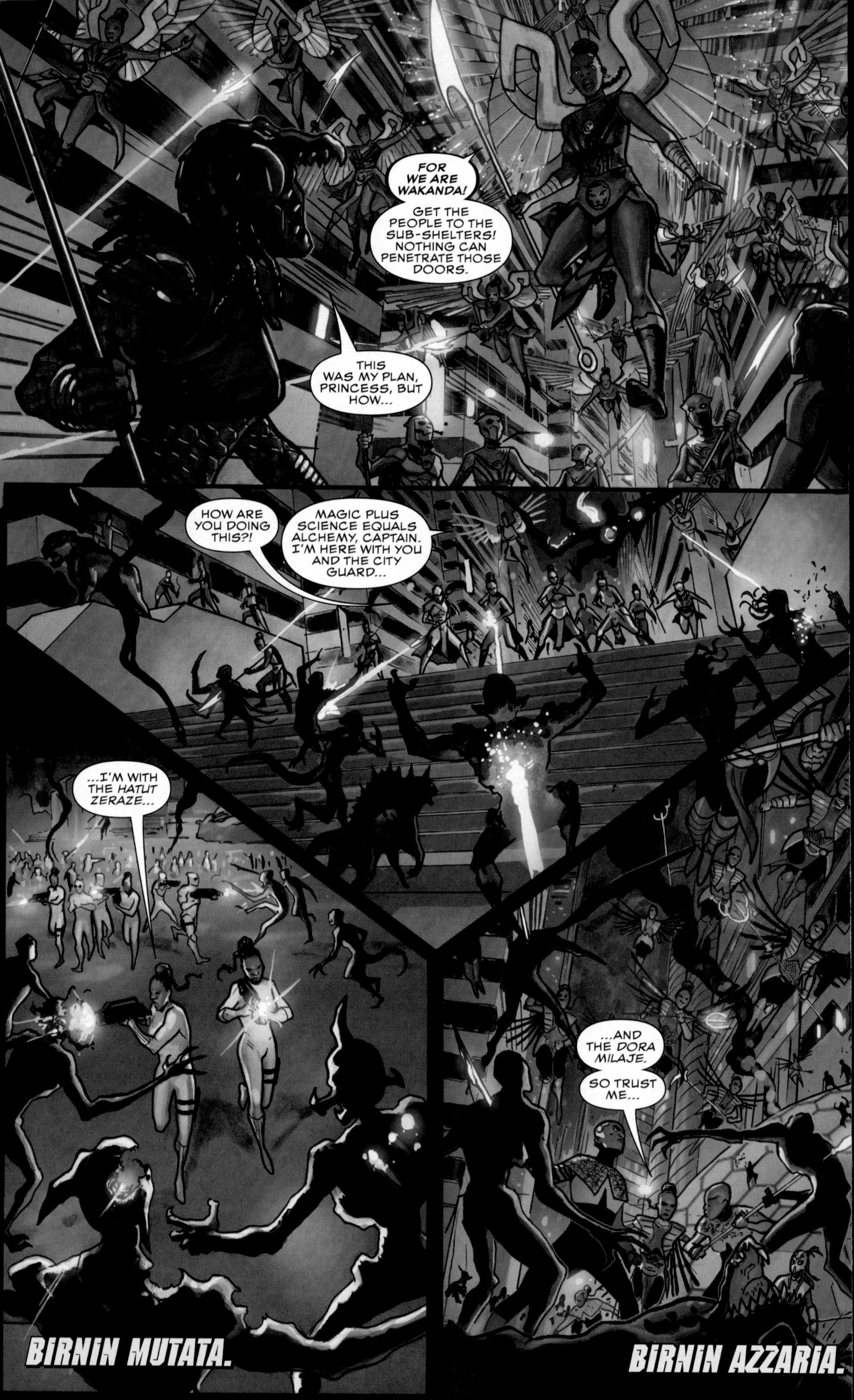

FOR WE ARE WAKANDA!
GET THE PEOPLE TO THE SUB-SHELTERS! NOTHING CAN PENETRATE THOSE DOORS.
THIS WAS MY PLAN, PRINCESS, BUT HOW...
HOW ARE YOU DOING THIS?!
MAGIC PLUS SCIENCE EQUALS ALCHEMY, CAPTAIN. I'M HERE WITH YOU AND THE CITY GUARD...
...I'M WITH THE HATUT ZERAZE...
...AND THE DORA MILAJE.
SO TRUST ME...
BIRNIN MUTATA.
BIRNIN AZZARIA.

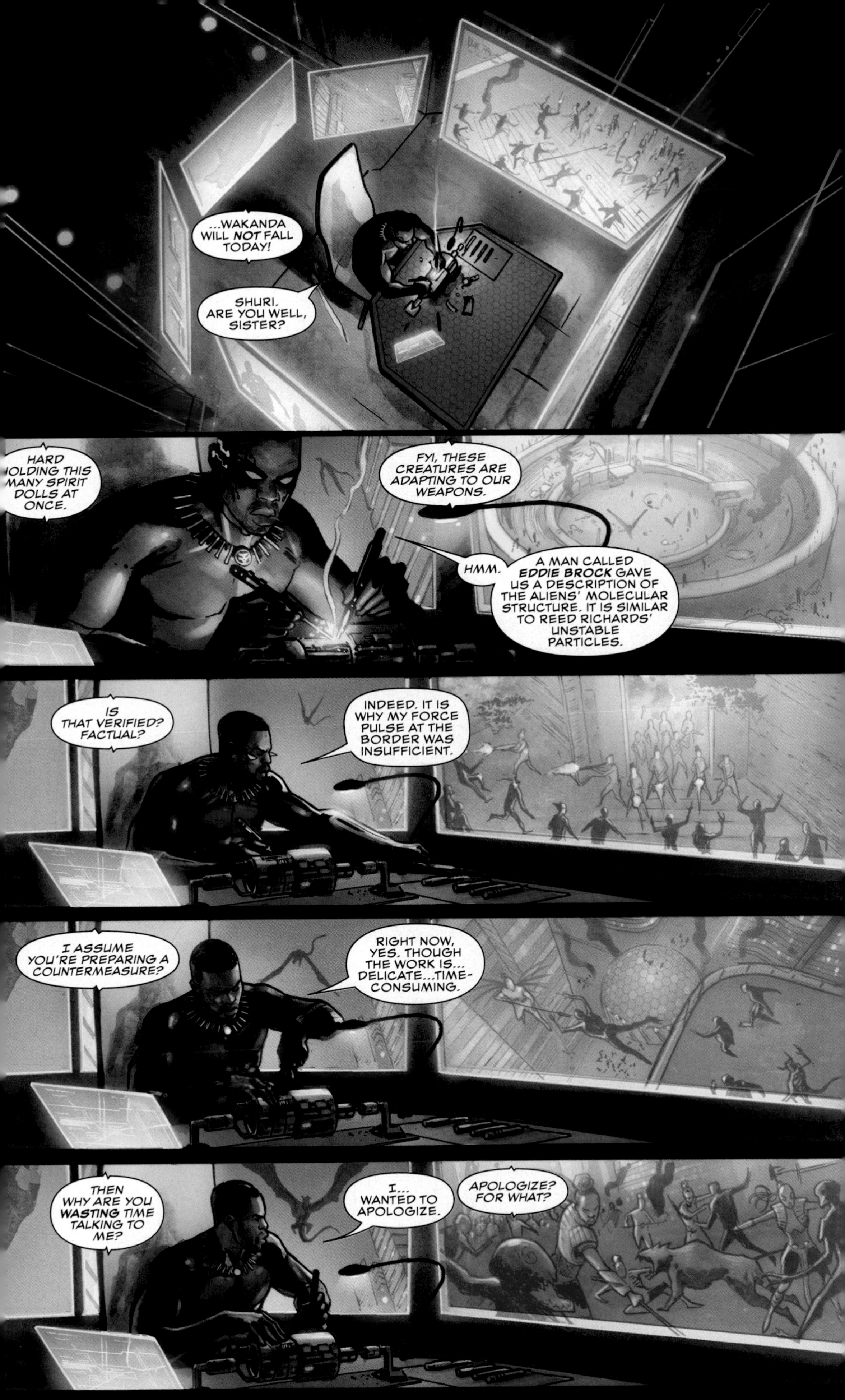
...WAKANDA WILL NOT FALL TODAY!
SHURI. ARE YOU WELL, SISTER?
HARD HOLDING THIS MANY SPIRIT DOLLS AT ONCE.
FYI, THESE CREATURES ARE ADAPTING TO OUR WEAPONS.
HMM.
A MAN CALLED EDDIE BROCK GAVE US A DESCRIPTION OF THE ALIENS' MOLECULAR STRUCTURE. IT IS SIMILAR TO REED RICHARDS' UNSTABLE PARTICLES.
IS THAT VERIFIED? FACTUAL?
INDEED. IT IS WHY MY FORCE PULSE AT THE BORDER WAS INSUFFICIENT.
I ASSUME YOU'RE PREPARING A COUNTERMEASURE?
RIGHT NOW, YES. THOUGH THE WORK IS... DELICATE...TIME-CONSUMING.
THEN WHY ARE YOU WASTING TIME TALKING TO ME?
I... WANTED TO APOLOGIZE.
APOLOGIZE? FOR WHAT?

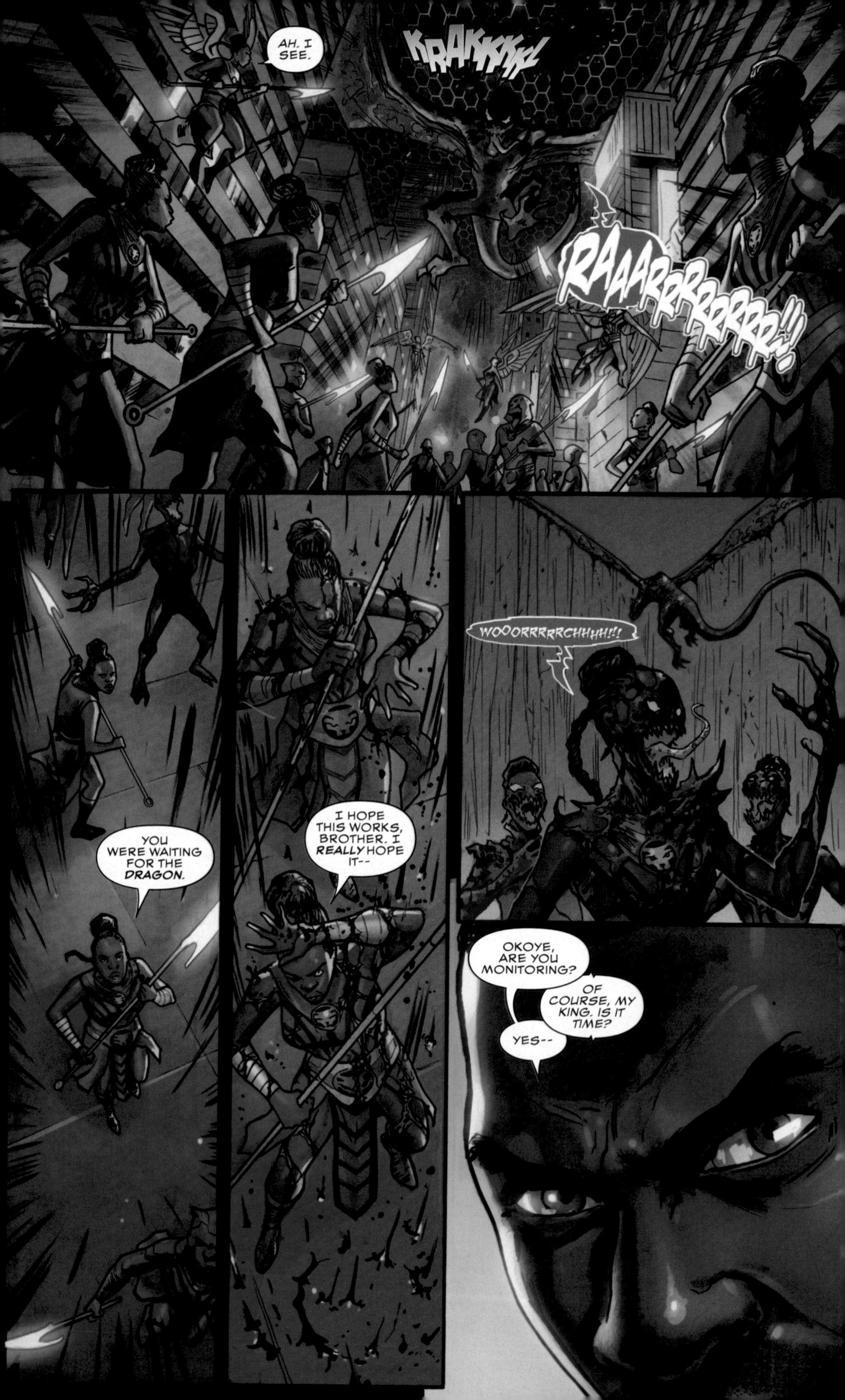
AH. I SEE.
KRAKKKK!
RAAARRRRRRRR!!!
YOU WERE WAITING FOR THE DRAGON.
I HOPE THIS WORKS, BROTHER. I REALLY HOPE IT--
WOOORRRRRCHHHH!!!
OKOYE, ARE YOU MONITORING?
OF COURSE, MY KING. IS IT TIME?
YES--

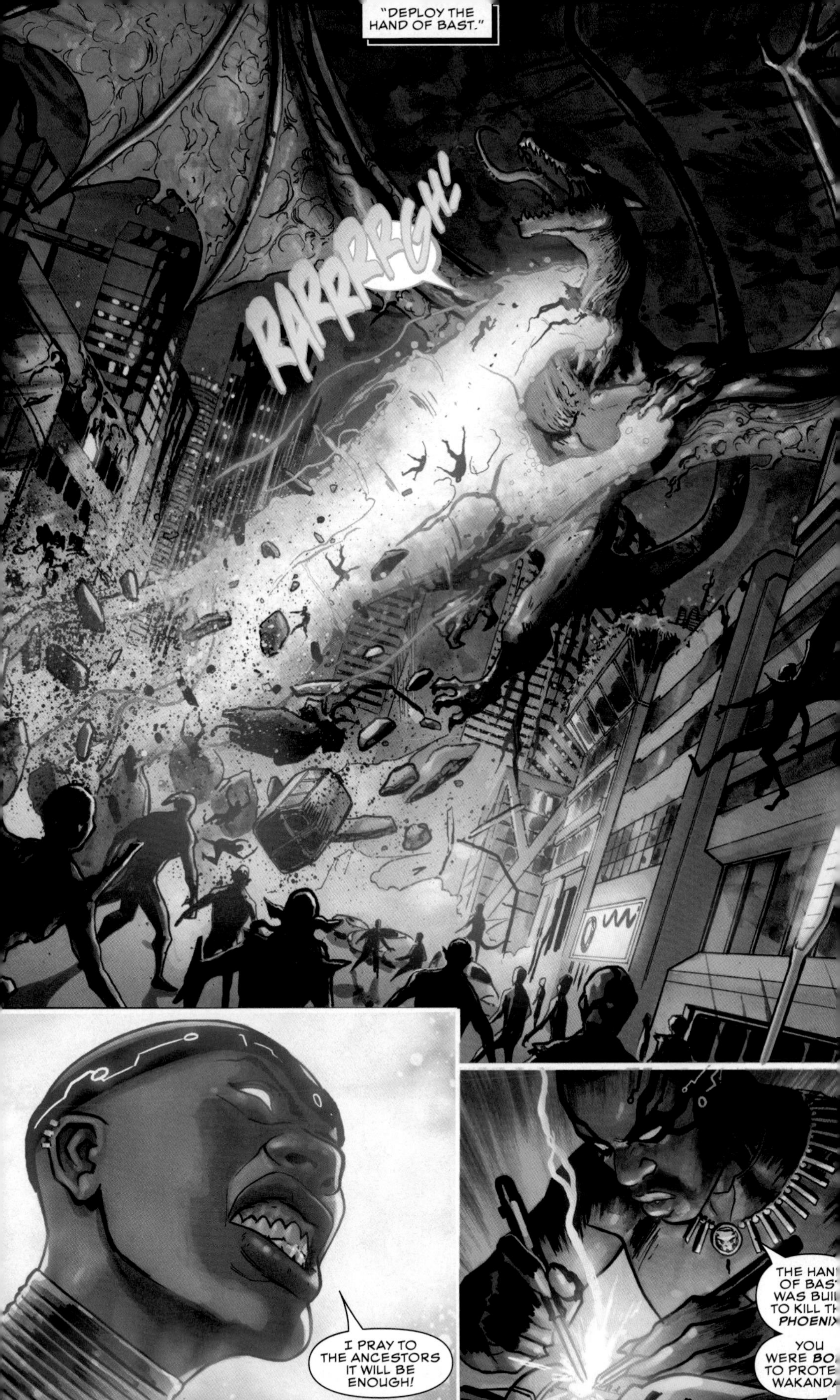
"DEPLOY THE HAND OF BAST."
RARRRGH!
I PRAY TO THE ANCESTORS IT WILL BE ENOUGH!
THE HAN OF BAS WAS BUI TO KILL TH PHOENIX
YOU WERE BO TO PROTE WAKANDA

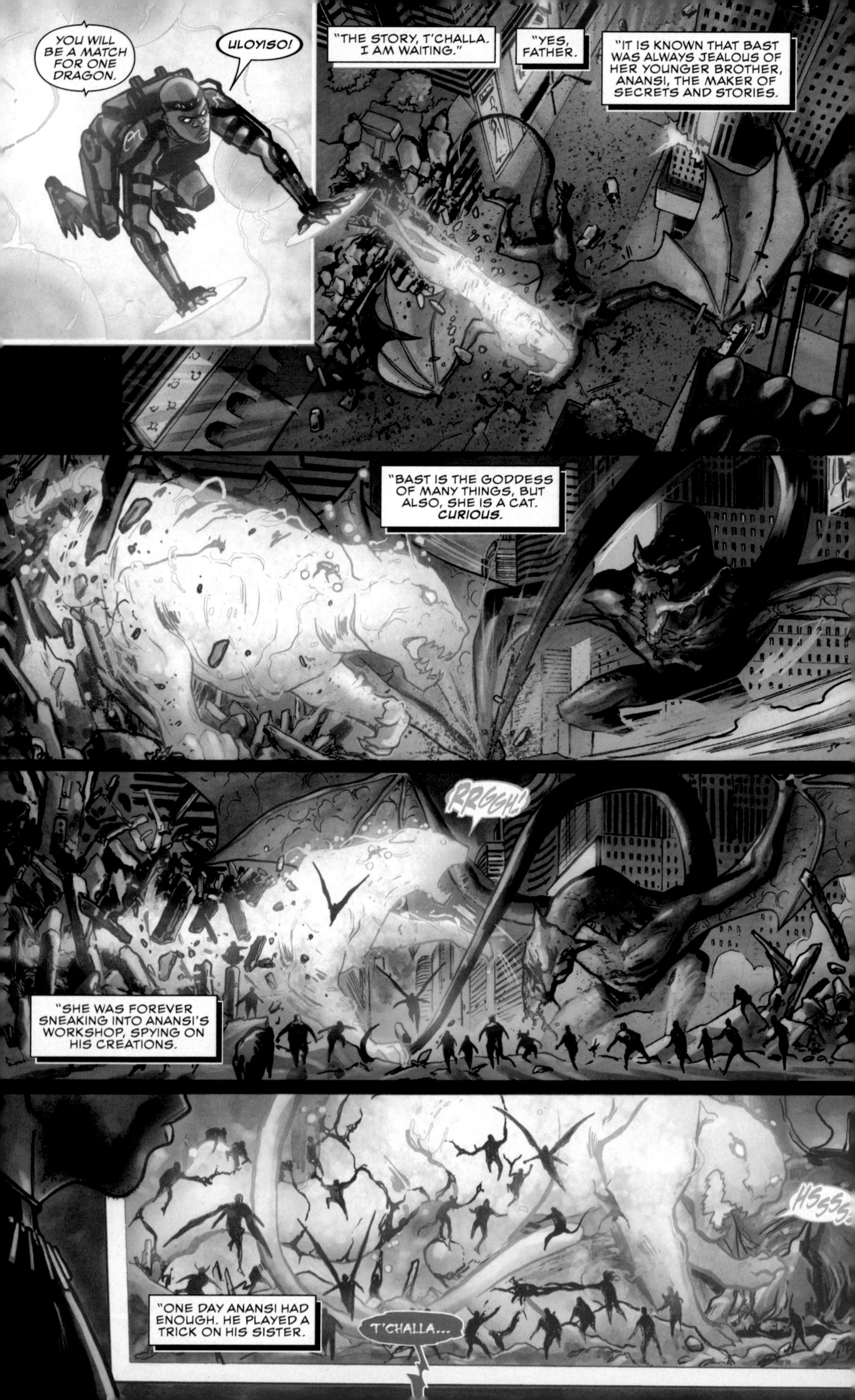
YOU WILL BE A MATCH FOR ONE DRAGON.
ULOYISO!
"THE STORY, T'CHALLA. I AM WAITING."
"YES, FATHER.
"IT IS KNOWN THAT BAST WAS ALWAYS JEALOUS OF HER YOUNGER BROTHER, ANANSI, THE MAKER OF SECRETS AND STORIES.
"BAST IS THE GODDESS OF MANY THINGS, BUT ALSO, SHE IS A CAT. CURIOUS.
RRGGH!
"SHE WAS FOREVER SNEAKING INTO ANANSI'S WORKSHOP, SPYING ON HIS CREATIONS.
HSSSS.
"ONE DAY ANANSI HAD ENOUGH. HE PLAYED A TRICK ON HIS SISTER.
T'CHALLA...

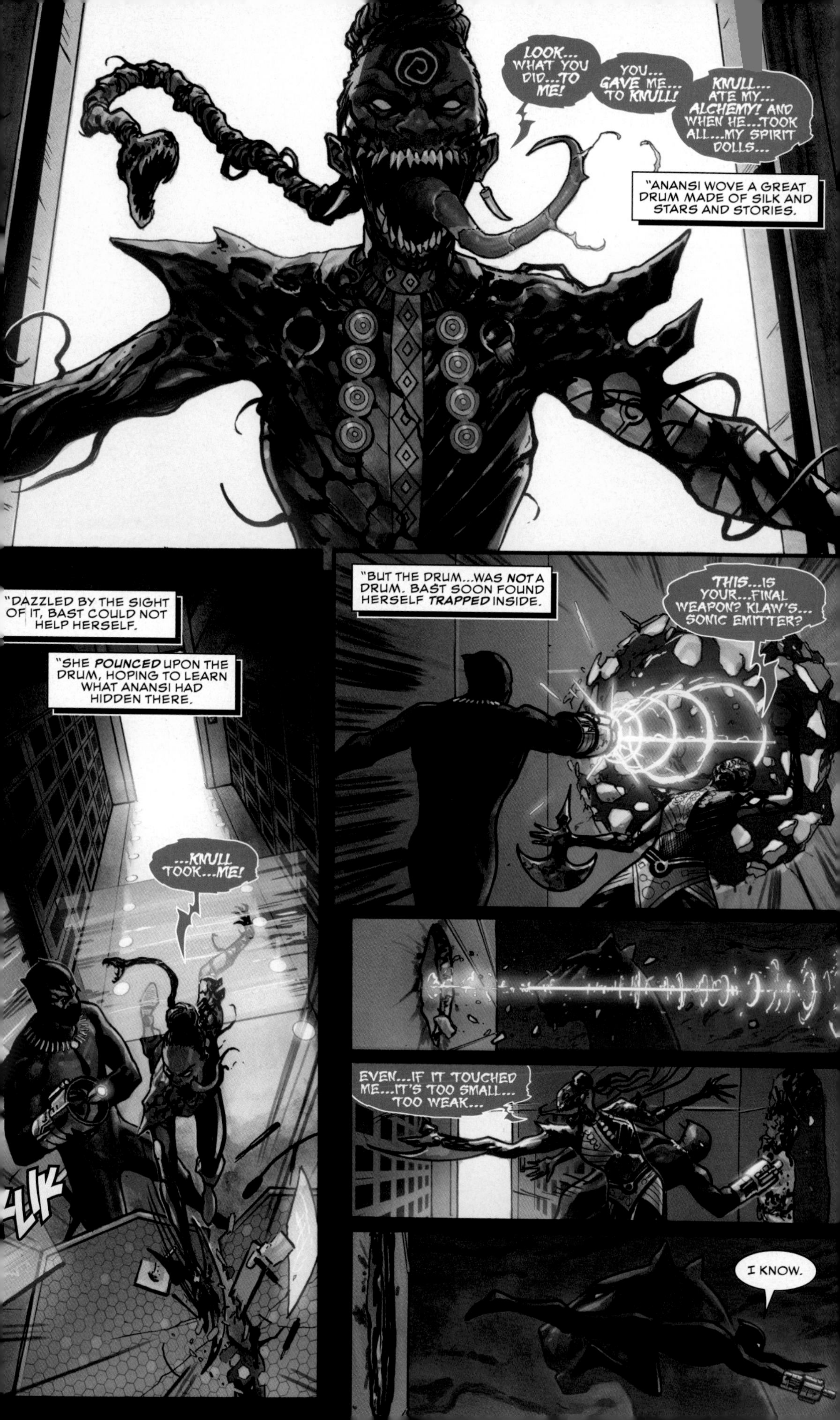
LOOK... WHAT YOU DID...TO ME!
YOU... GAVE ME... TO KNULL!
KNULL... ATE MY... ALCHEMY! AND WHEN HE...TOOK ALL...MY SPIRIT DOLLS...
"ANANSI WOVE A GREAT DRUM MADE OF SILK AND STARS AND STORIES.
"DAZZLED BY THE SIGHT OF IT, BAST COULD NOT HELP HERSELF.
"SHE POUNCED UPON THE DRUM, HOPING TO LEARN WHAT ANANSI HAD HIDDEN THERE.
...KNULL TOOK...ME!
"BUT THE DRUM...WAS NOT A DRUM. BAST SOON FOUND HERSELF TRAPPED INSIDE.
THIS...IS YOUR...FINAL WEAPON? KLAW'S... SONIC EMITTER?
EVEN...IF IT TOUCHED ME...IT'S TOO SMALL... TOO WEAK...
I KNOW.

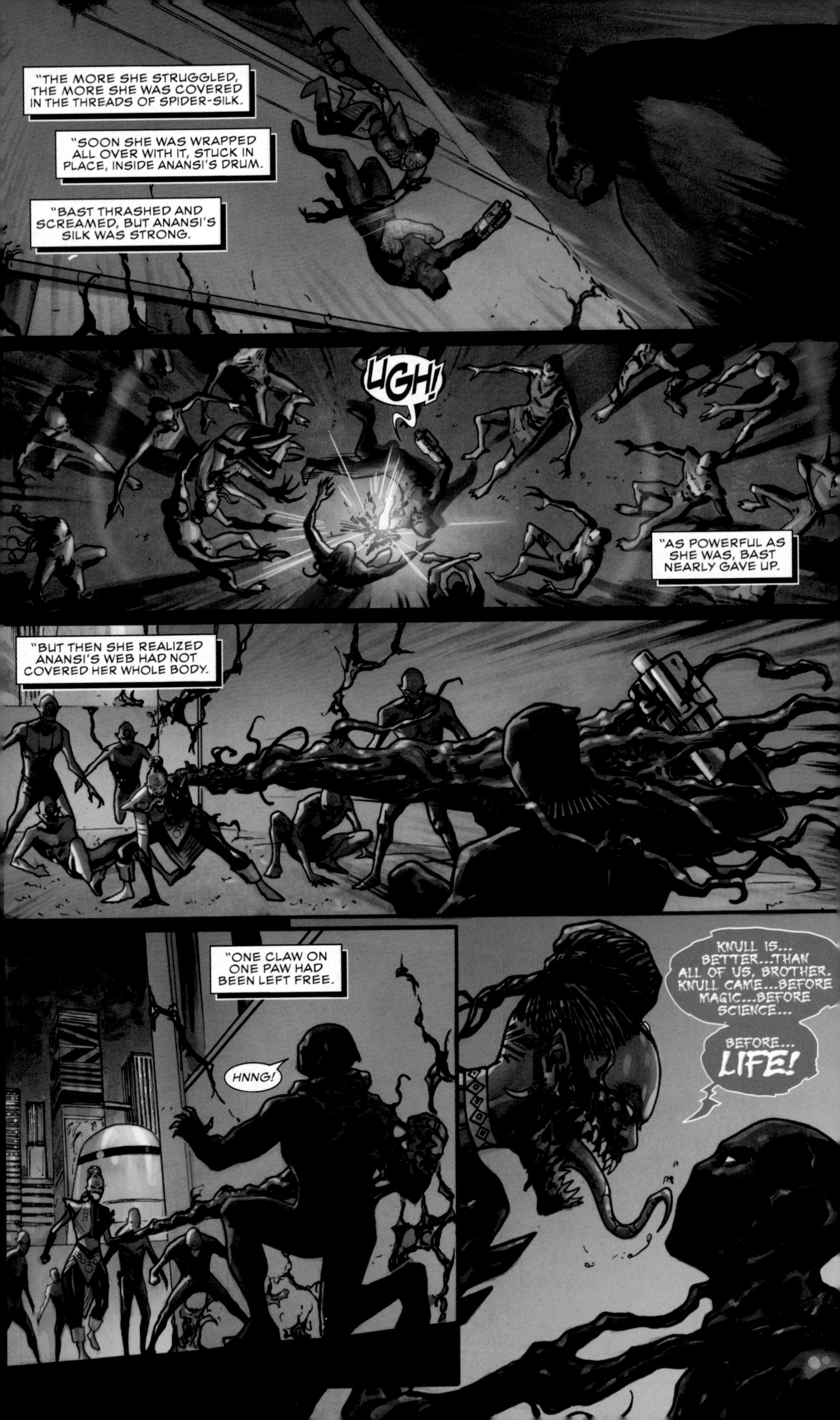
"THE MORE SHE STRUGGLED, THE MORE SHE WAS COVERED IN THE THREADS OF SPIDER-SILK.
"SOON SHE WAS WRAPPED ALL OVER WITH IT, STUCK IN PLACE, INSIDE ANANSI'S DRUM.
"BAST THRASHED AND SCREAMED, BUT ANANSI'S SILK WAS STRONG.
UGH!
"AS POWERFUL AS SHE WAS, BAST NEARLY GAVE UP.
"BUT THEN SHE REALIZED ANANSI'S WEB HAD NOT COVERED HER WHOLE BODY.
"ONE CLAW ON ONE PAW HAD BEEN LEFT FREE.
HNNG!
KNULL IS... BETTER...THAN ALL OF US, BROTHER. KNULL CAME...BEFORE MAGIC...BEFORE SCIENCE...
BEFORE... LIFE!

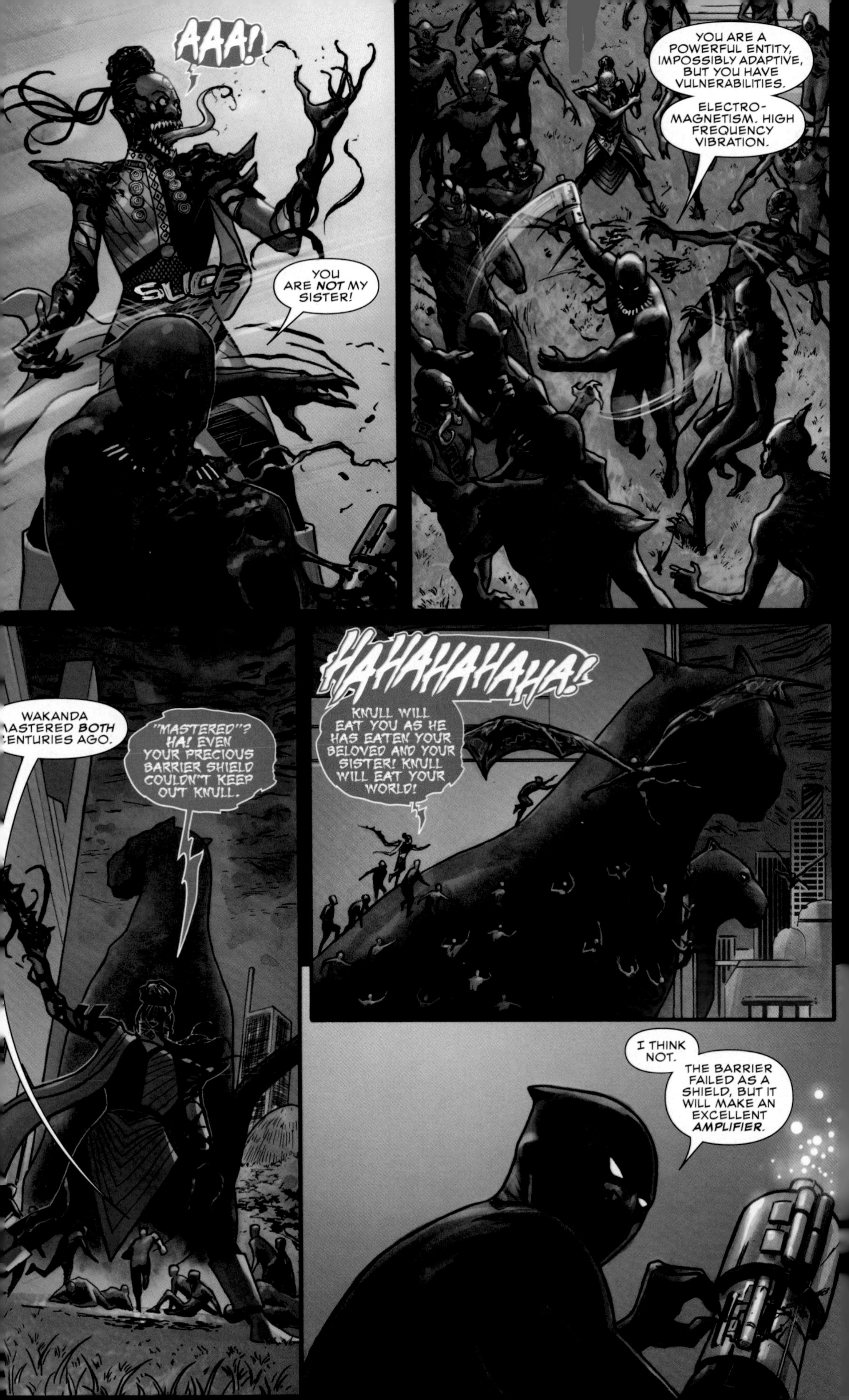
AAA!
SLICE
YOU ARE NOT MY SISTER!
YOU ARE A POWERFUL ENTITY, IMPOSSIBLY ADAPTIVE, BUT YOU HAVE VULNERABILITIES.
ELECTRO-MAGNETISM. HIGH FREQUENCY VIBRATION.
WAKANDA MASTERED BOTH CENTURIES AGO.
"MASTERED"? HA! EVEN YOUR PRECIOUS BARRIER SHIELD COULDN'T KEEP OUT KNULL.
HAHAHAHAHAHA!
KNULL WILL EAT YOU AS HE HAS EATEN YOUR BELOVED AND YOUR SISTER! KNULL WILL EAT YOUR WORLD!
I THINK NOT.
THE BARRIER FAILED AS A SHIELD, BUT IT WILL MAKE AN EXCELLENT AMPLIFIER.

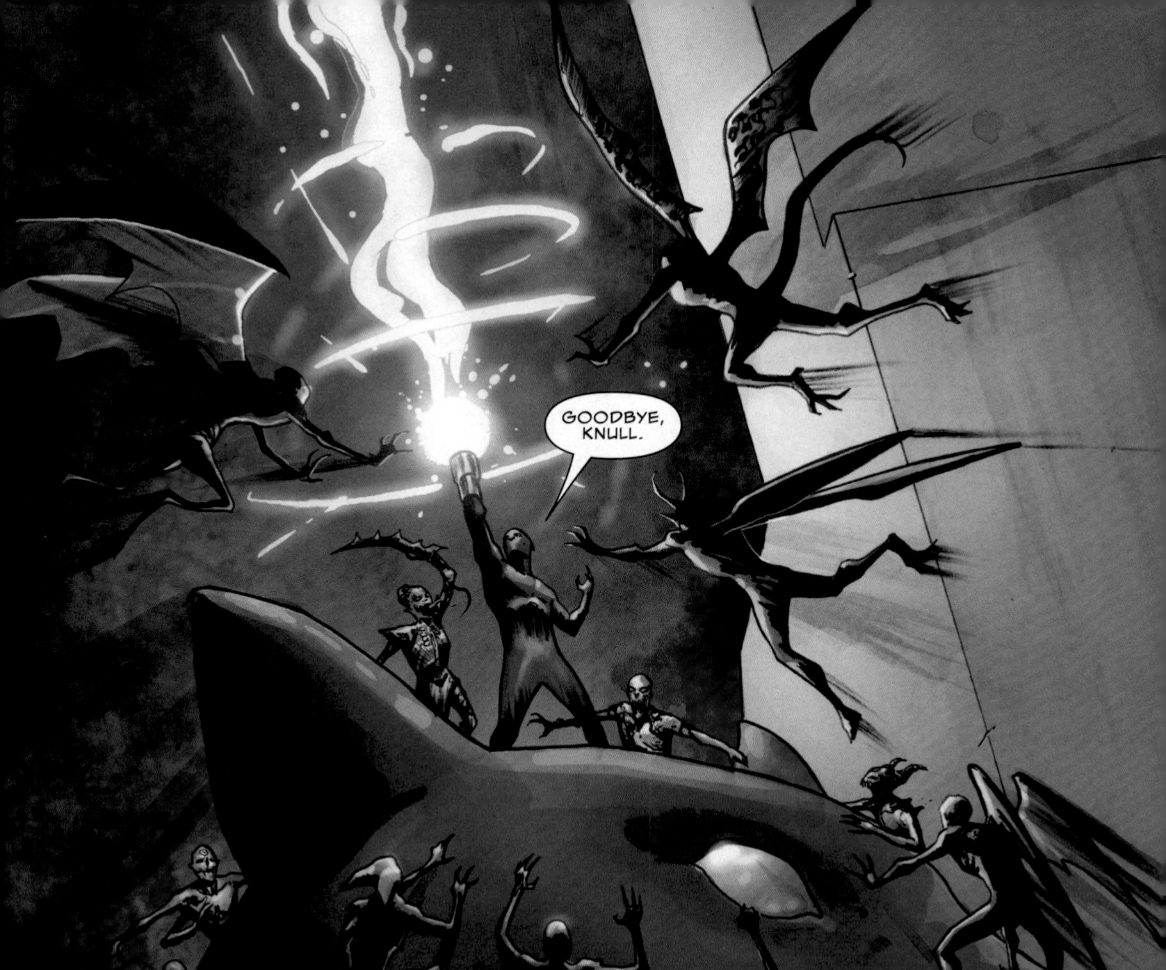
GOODBYE, KNULL.

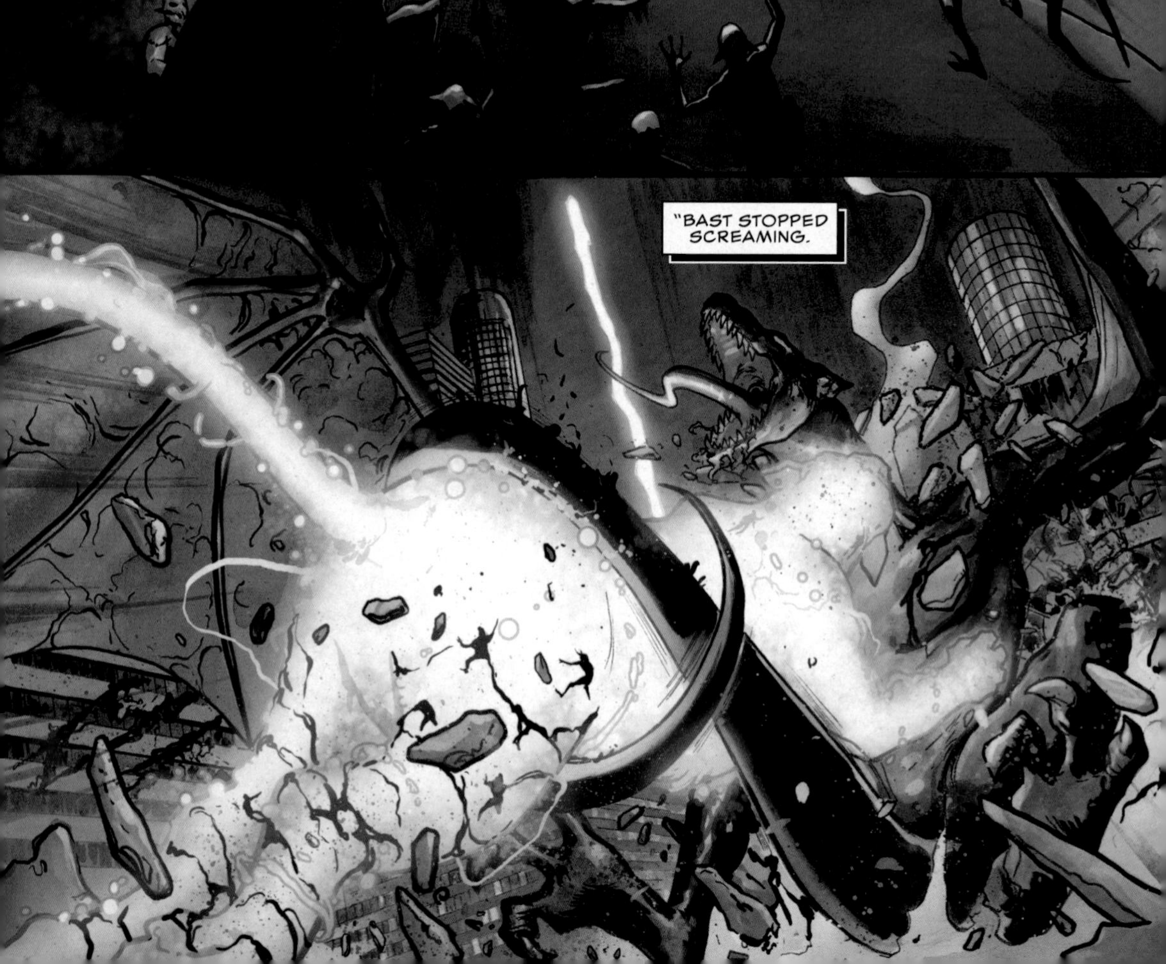
"BAST STOPPED SCREAMING.

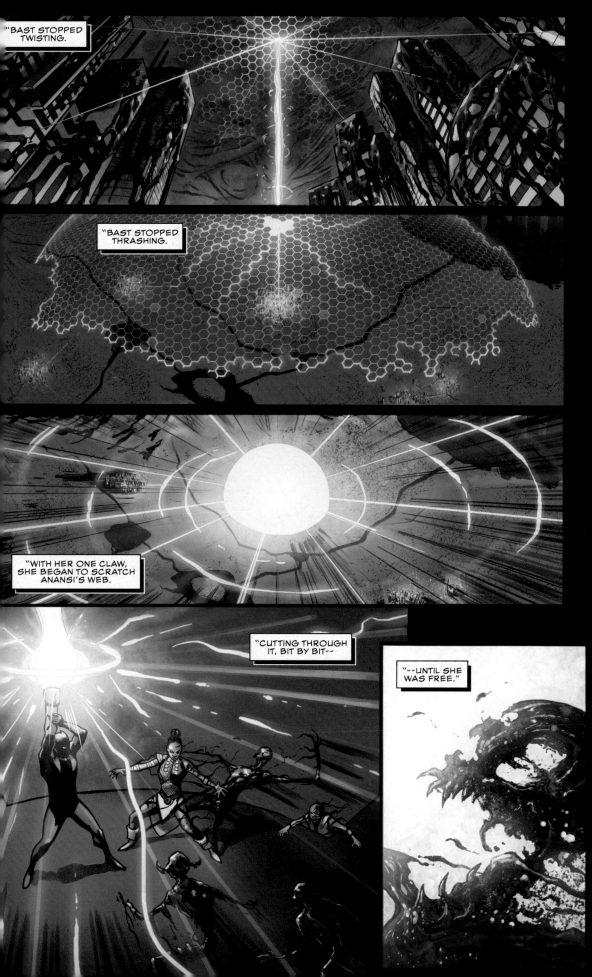

"BAST STOPPED TWISTING.

"BAST STOPPED THRASHING.

"WITH HER ONE CLAW, SHE BEGAN TO SCRATCH ANANSI'S WEB.

"CUTTING THROUGH IT, BIT BY BIT--

"--UNTIL SHE WAS FREE."

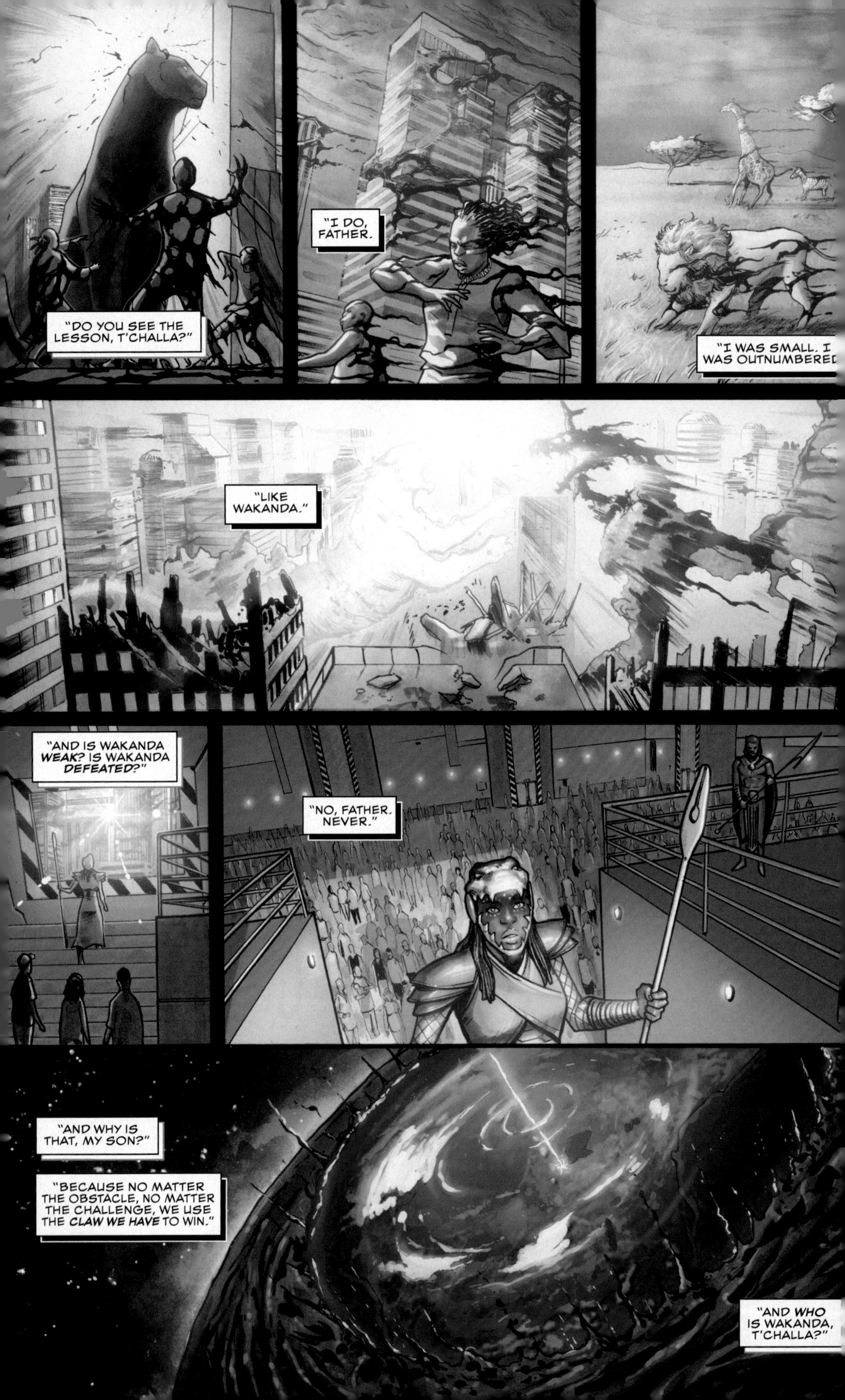
"DO YOU SEE THE LESSON, T'CHALLA?"
"I DO, FATHER.
"I WAS SMALL. I WAS OUTNUMBERED
"LIKE WAKANDA."
"AND IS WAKANDA *WEAK?* IS WAKANDA *DEFEATED?*"
"NO, FATHER. NEVER."
"AND WHY IS THAT, MY SON?"
"BECAUSE NO MATTER THE OBSTACLE, NO MATTER THE CHALLENGE, WE USE THE *CLAW WE HAVE* TO WIN."
"AND *WHO* IS WAKANDA, T'CHALLA?"

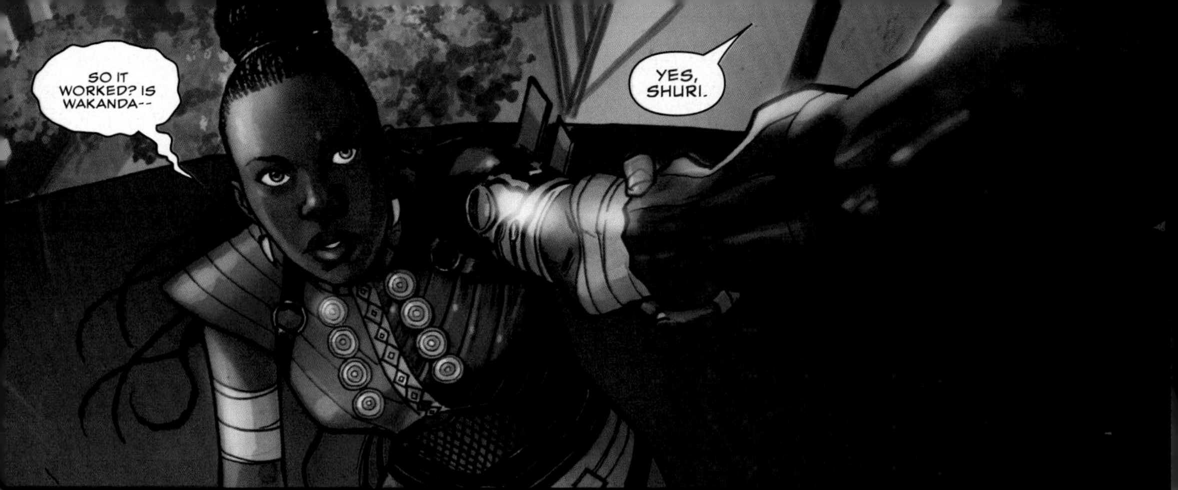
SO IT WORKED? IS WAKANDA--
YES, SHURI.

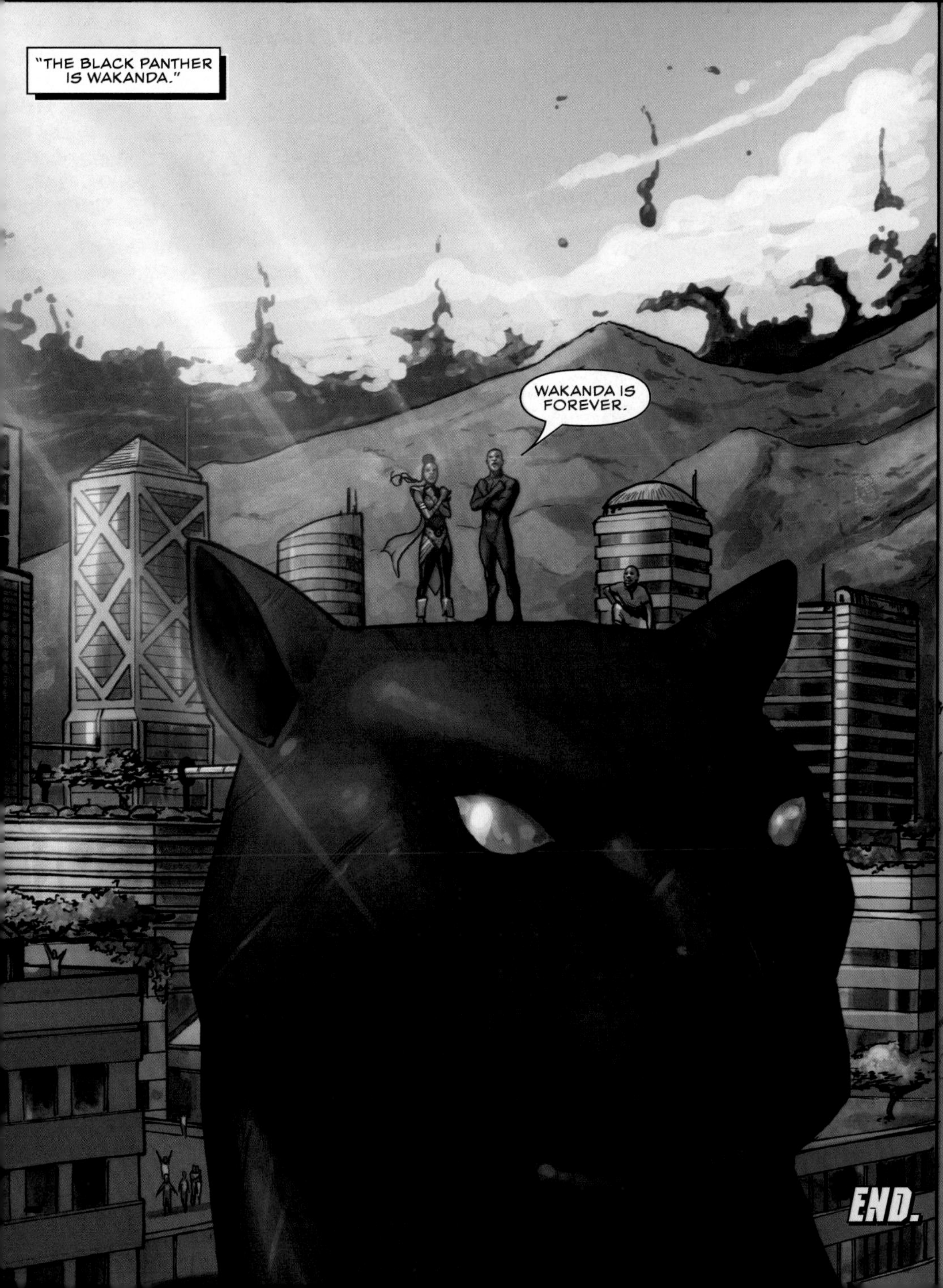
"THE BLACK PANTHER IS WAKANDA."
WAKANDA IS FOREVER.
END.

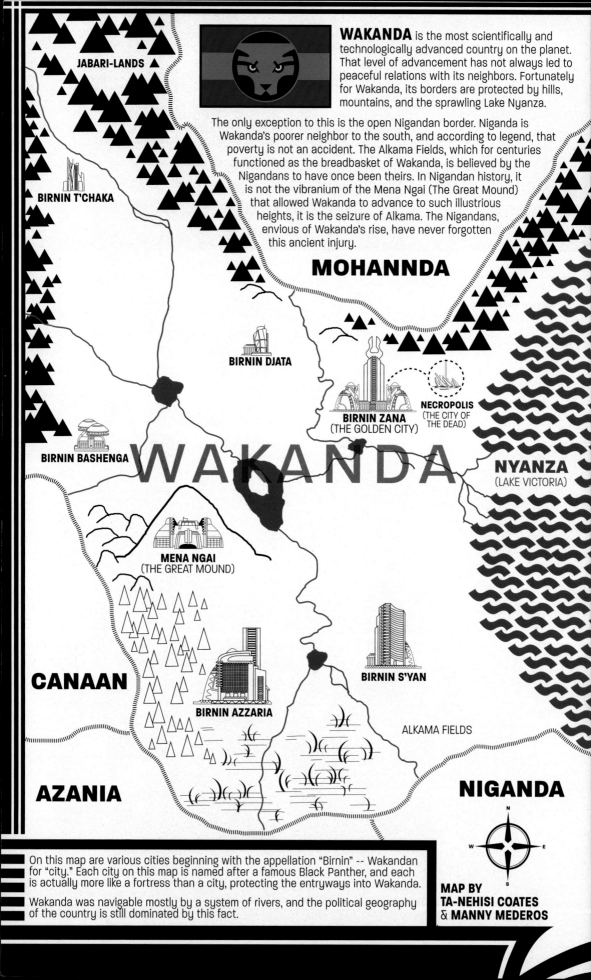

WAKANDA is the most scientifically and technologically advanced country on the planet. That level of advancement has not always led to peaceful relations with its neighbors. Fortunately for Wakanda, its borders are protected by hills, mountains, and the sprawling Lake Nyanza.

The only exception to this is the open Nigandan border. Niganda is Wakanda's poorer neighbor to the south, and according to legend, that poverty is not an accident. The Alkama Fields, which for centuries functioned as the breadbasket of Wakanda, is believed by the Nigandans to have once been theirs. In Nigandan history, it is not the vibranium of the Mena Ngai (The Great Mound) that allowed Wakanda to advance to such illustrious heights, it is the seizure of Alkama. The Nigandans, envious of Wakanda's rise, have never forgotten this ancient injury.

JABARI-LANDS

BIRNIN T'CHAKA

MOHANNDA

BIRNIN DJATA

BIRNIN ZANA
(THE GOLDEN CITY)

NECROPOLIS
(THE CITY OF
THE DEAD)

BIRNIN BASHENGA

W A K A N D A

NYANZA
(LAKE VICTORIA)

MENA NGAI
(THE GREAT MOUND)

BIRNIN S'YAN

CANAAN

BIRNIN AZZARIA

ALKAMA FIELDS

AZANIA

NIGANDA

On this map are various cities beginning with the appellation "Birnin" -- Wakandan for "city." Each city on this map is named after a famous Black Panther, and each is actually more like a fortress than a city, protecting the entryways into Wakanda.

Wakanda was navigable mostly by a system of rivers, and the political geography of the country is still dominated by this fact.

**MAP BY
TA-NEHISI COATES
& MANNY MEDEROS**

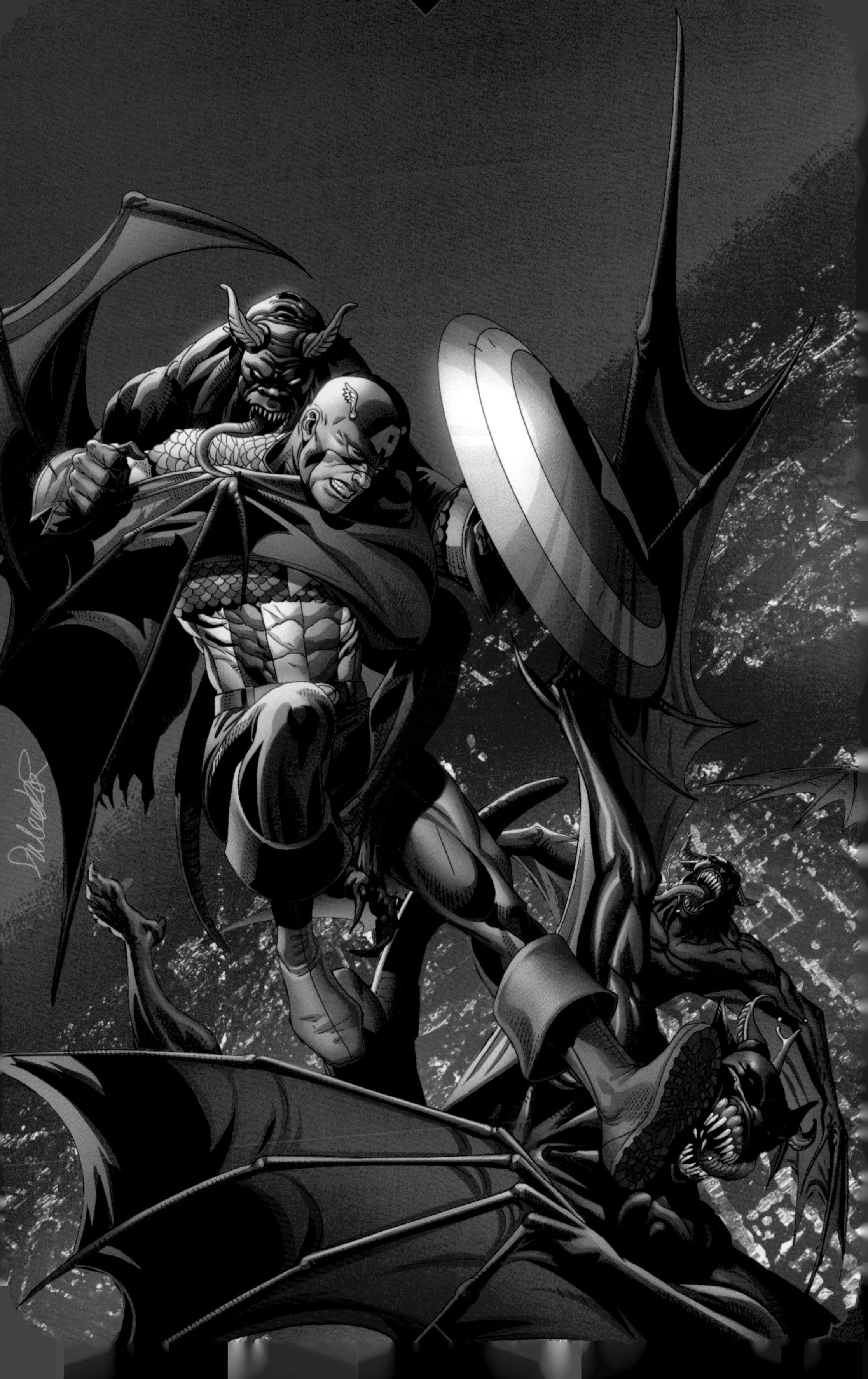

CAPTAIN AMERICA

BLACKENED BLUE

Early in the battle, CAPTAIN AMERICA and several
other heroes were subsumed by KNULL and
transformed into monstrous versions of themselves.
Venom's son Dylan was able to free Steve, but
the scars of his possession remain, AND THE WAR
AGAINST THE SYMBIOTES RAGES ON...

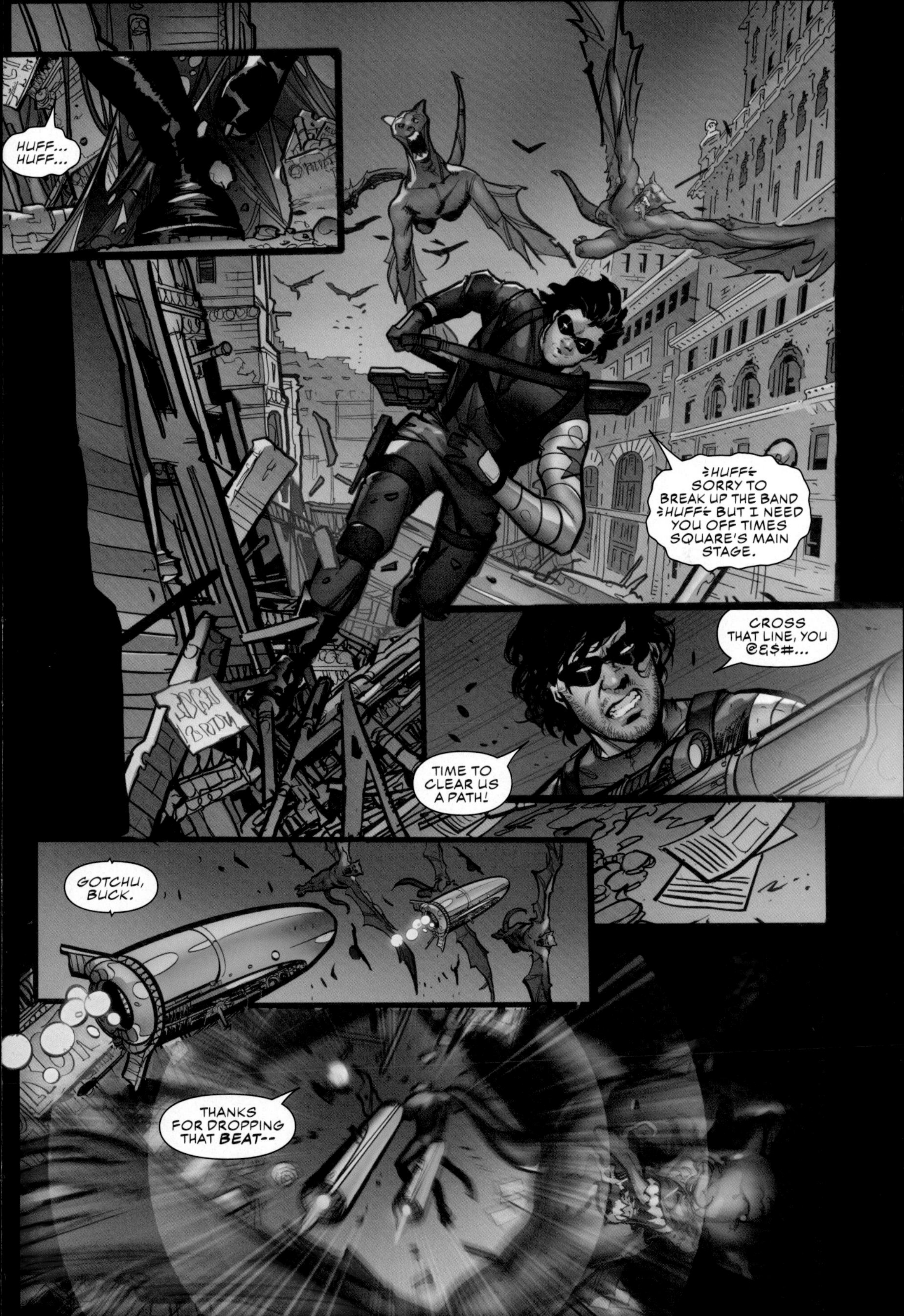
HUFF... HUFF...
≑HUFF≑ SORRY TO BREAK UP THE BAND ≑HUFF≑ BUT I NEED YOU OFF TIMES SQUARE'S MAIN STAGE.
CROSS THAT LINE, YOU @&$#...
TIME TO CLEAR US A PATH!
GOTCHU, BUCK.
THANKS FOR DROPPING THAT BEAT--

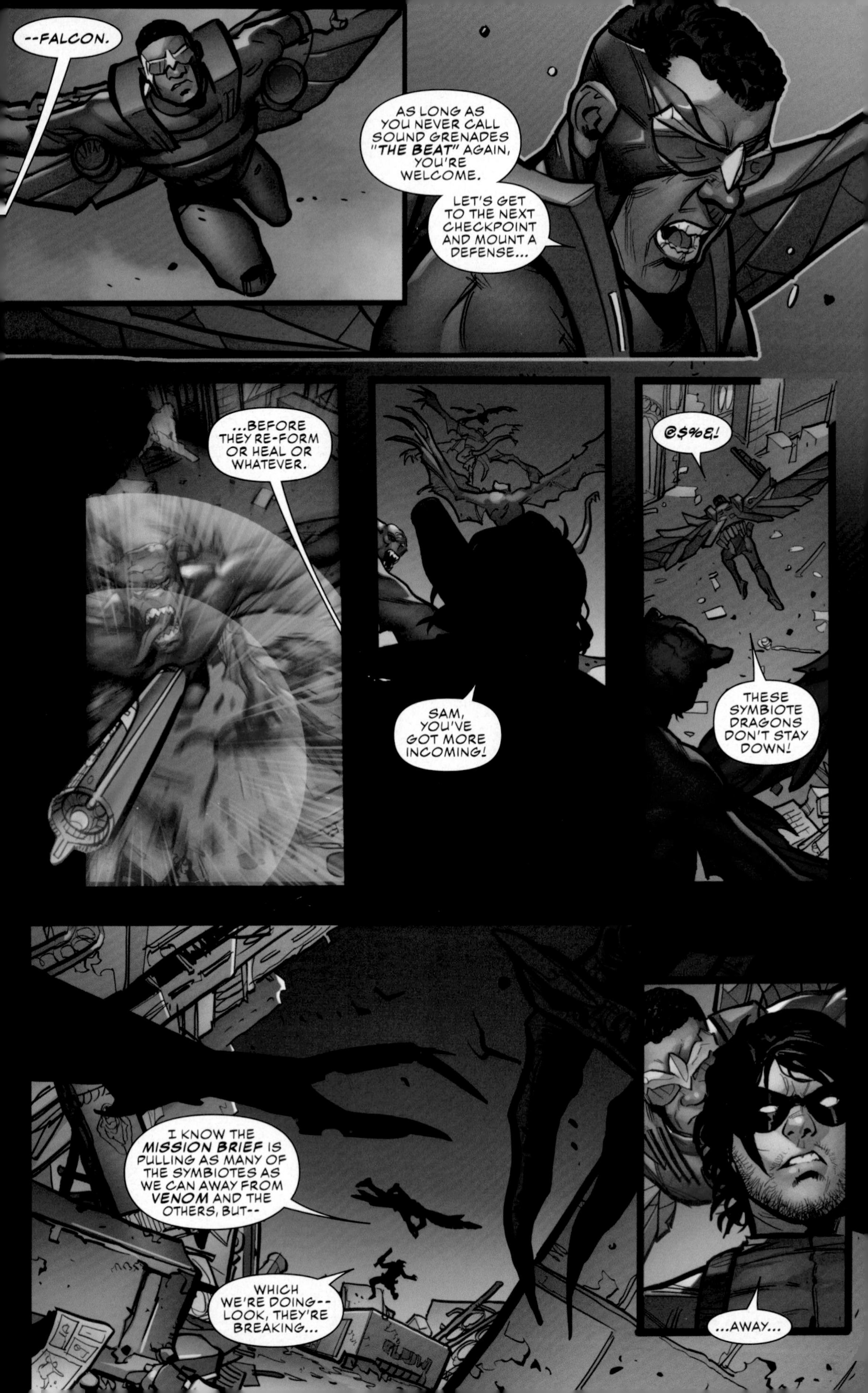
--FALCON.
AS LONG AS YOU NEVER CALL SOUND GRENADES "THE BEAT" AGAIN, YOU'RE WELCOME.
LET'S GET TO THE NEXT CHECKPOINT AND MOUNT A DEFENSE...
...BEFORE THEY RE-FORM OR HEAL OR WHATEVER.
SAM, YOU'VE GOT MORE INCOMING!
@$%&!
THESE SYMBIOTE DRAGONS DON'T STAY DOWN!
I KNOW THE MISSION BRIEF IS PULLING AS MANY OF THE SYMBIOTES AS WE CAN AWAY FROM VENOM AND THE OTHERS, BUT--
WHICH WE'RE DOING-- LOOK, THEY'RE BREAKING...
...AWAY...

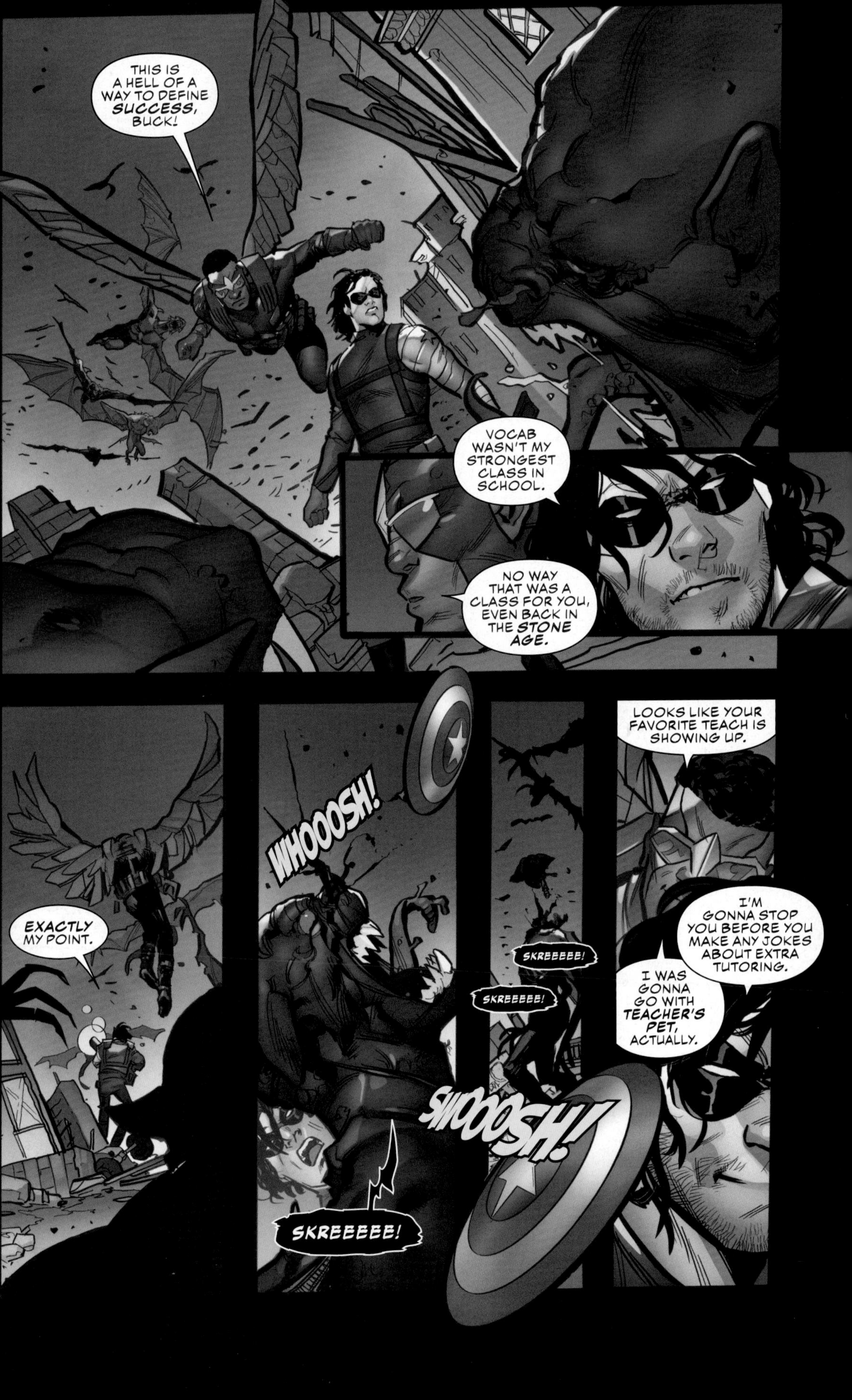

THIS IS A HELL OF A WAY TO DEFINE *SUCCESS*, BUCK!
VOCAB WASN'T MY STRONGEST CLASS IN SCHOOL.
NO WAY THAT WAS A CLASS FOR YOU, EVEN BACK IN THE *STONE AGE*.
EXACTLY MY POINT.
WHOOOSH!
SKREEEEE!
SKREEEEE!
SKREEEEE!
LOOKS LIKE YOUR FAVORITE TEACH IS SHOWING UP.
I'M GONNA STOP YOU BEFORE YOU MAKE ANY JOKES ABOUT EXTRA TUTORING.
I WAS GONNA GO WITH *TEACHER'S PET*, ACTUALLY.
SWOOOSH!

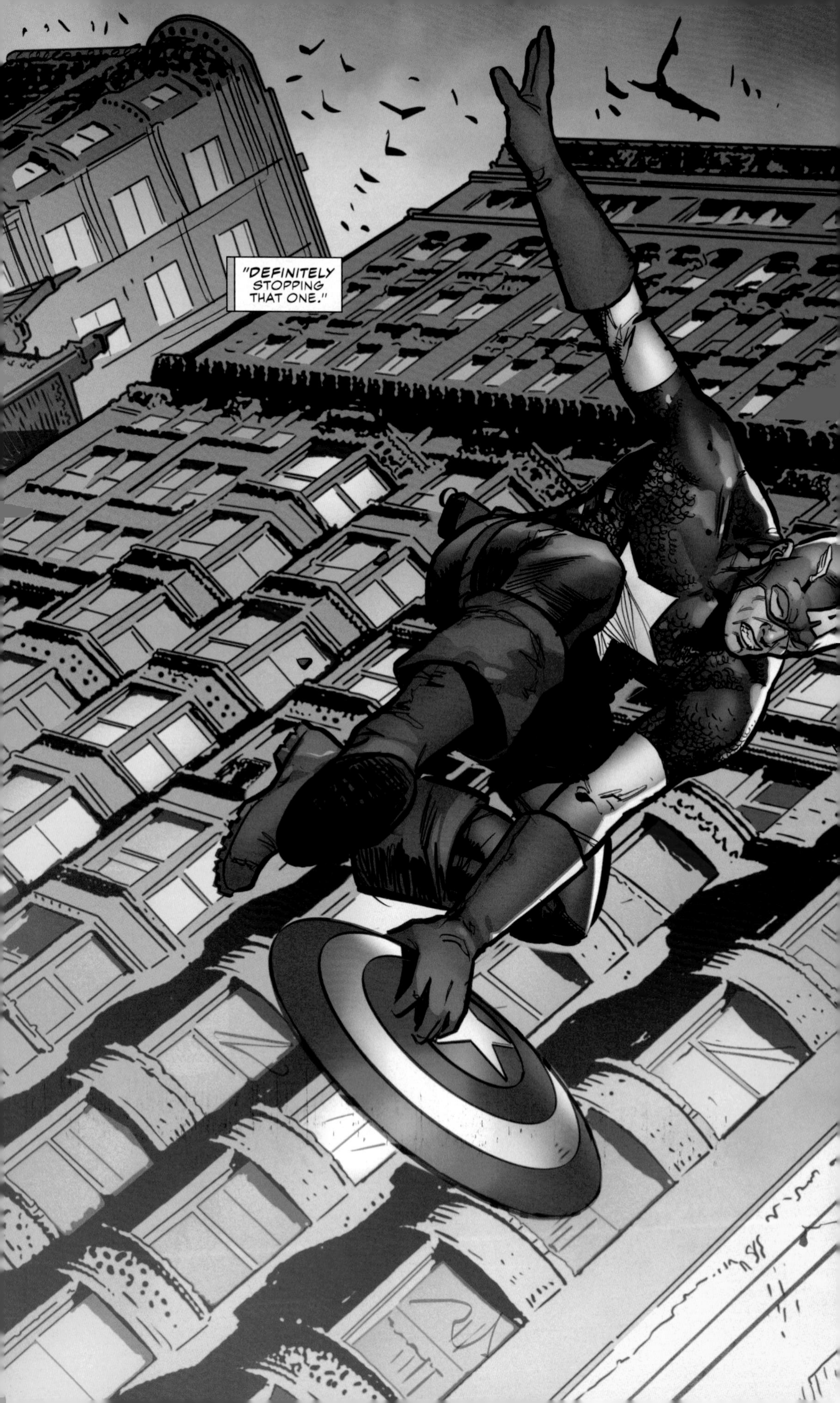
"DEFINITELY STOPPING THAT ONE."

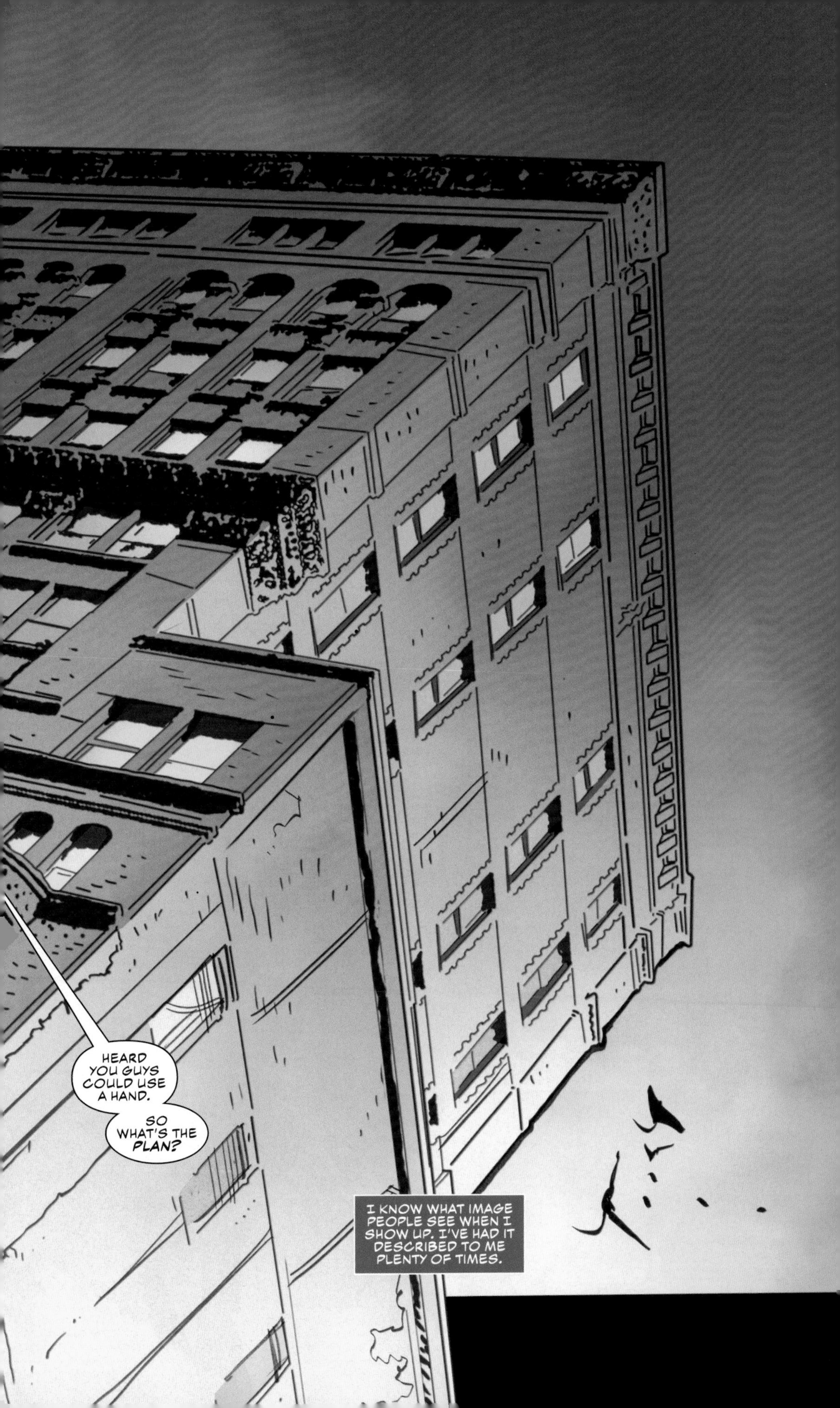

HEARD YOU GUYS COULD USE A HAND.
SO WHAT'S THE *PLAN?*
I KNOW WHAT IMAGE PEOPLE SEE WHEN I SHOW UP. I'VE HAD IT DESCRIBED TO ME PLENTY OF TIMES.

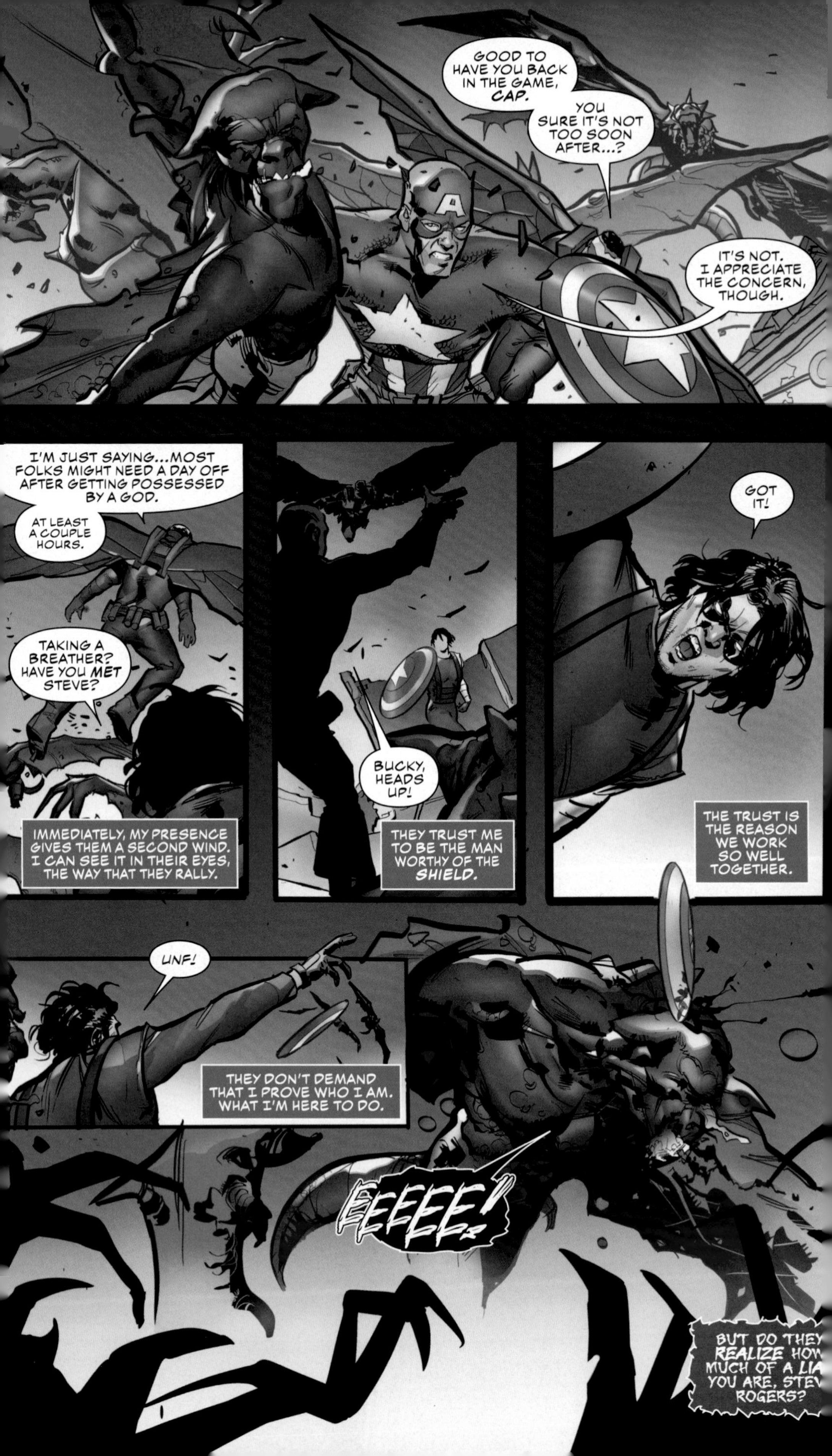
GOOD TO HAVE YOU BACK IN THE GAME, CAP.
YOU SURE IT'S NOT TOO SOON AFTER...?
IT'S NOT. I APPRECIATE THE CONCERN, THOUGH.
I'M JUST SAYING...MOST FOLKS MIGHT NEED A DAY OFF AFTER GETTING POSSESSED BY A GOD.
AT LEAST A COUPLE HOURS.
TAKING A BREATHER? HAVE YOU MET STEVE?
IMMEDIATELY, MY PRESENCE GIVES THEM A SECOND WIND. I CAN SEE IT IN THEIR EYES, THE WAY THAT THEY RALLY.
BUCKY, HEADS UP!
THEY TRUST ME TO BE THE MAN WORTHY OF THE SHIELD.
GOT IT!
THE TRUST IS THE REASON WE WORK SO WELL TOGETHER.
UNF!
THEY DON'T DEMAND THAT I PROVE WHO I AM. WHAT I'M HERE TO DO.
EEEEE!
BUT DO THEY REALIZE HOW MUCH OF A LIA YOU ARE, STEV ROGERS?

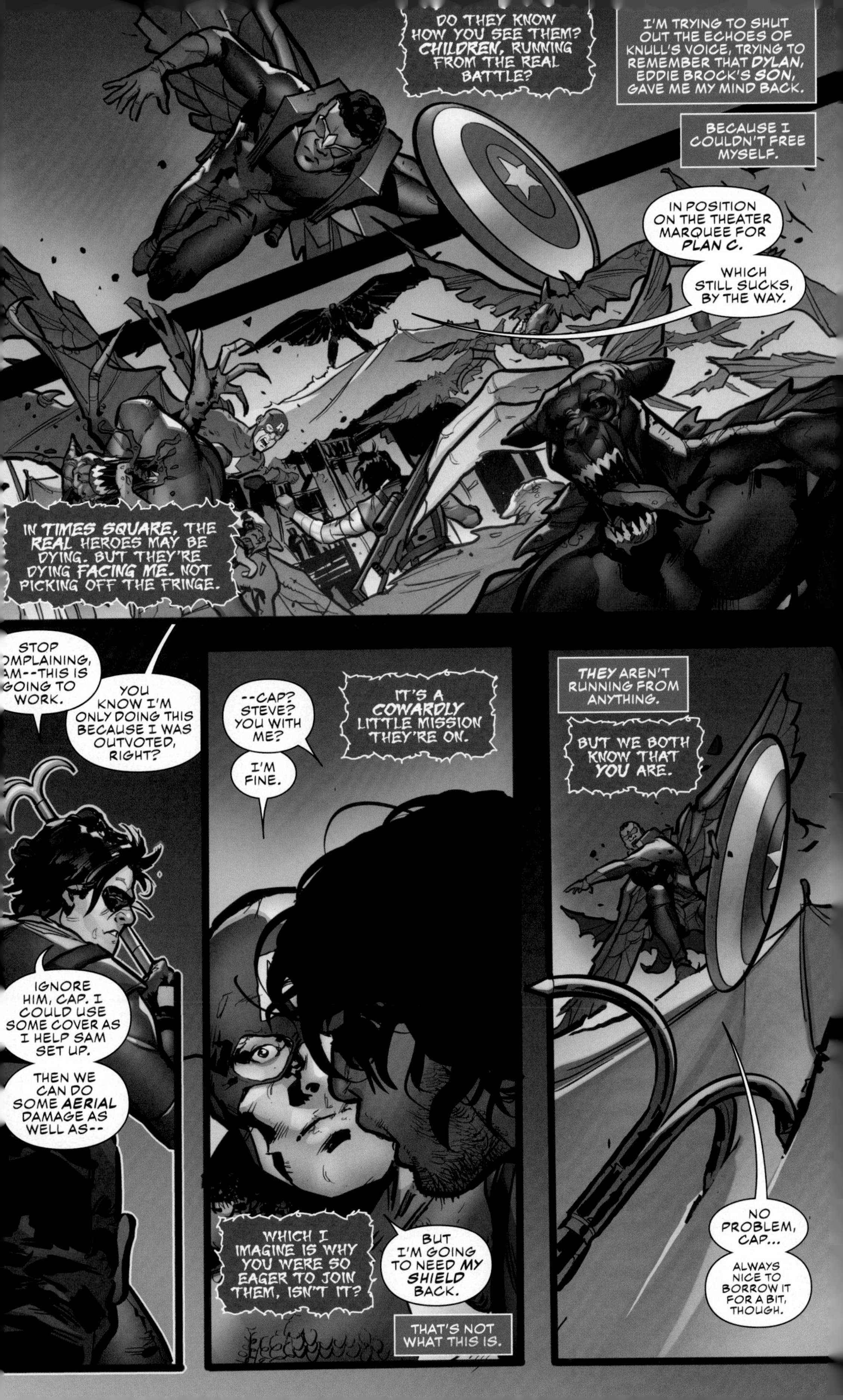
DO THEY KNOW HOW YOU SEE THEM? CHILDREN, RUNNING FROM THE REAL BATTLE?
I'M TRYING TO SHUT OUT THE ECHOES OF KNULL'S VOICE, TRYING TO REMEMBER THAT DYLAN, EDDIE BROCK'S SON, GAVE ME MY MIND BACK.
BECAUSE I COULDN'T FREE MYSELF.
IN POSITION ON THE THEATER MARQUEE FOR PLAN C.
WHICH STILL SUCKS, BY THE WAY.
IN TIMES SQUARE, THE REAL HEROES MAY BE DYING. BUT THEY'RE DYING FACING ME. NOT PICKING OFF THE FRINGE.
STOP OMPLAINING, AM--THIS IS GOING TO WORK.
YOU KNOW I'M ONLY DOING THIS BECAUSE I WAS OUTVOTED, RIGHT?
IGNORE HIM, CAP. I COULD USE SOME COVER AS I HELP SAM SET UP.
THEN WE CAN DO SOME AERIAL DAMAGE AS WELL AS--
IT'S A COWARDLY LITTLE MISSION THEY'RE ON.
--CAP? STEVE? YOU WITH ME?
I'M FINE.
WHICH I IMAGINE IS WHY YOU WERE SO EAGER TO JOIN THEM, ISN'T IT?
BUT I'M GOING TO NEED MY SHIELD BACK.
THAT'S NOT WHAT THIS IS.
THEY AREN'T RUNNING FROM ANYTHING.
BUT WE BOTH KNOW THAT YOU ARE.
NO PROBLEM, CAP...
ALWAYS NICE TO BORROW IT FOR A BIT, THOUGH.

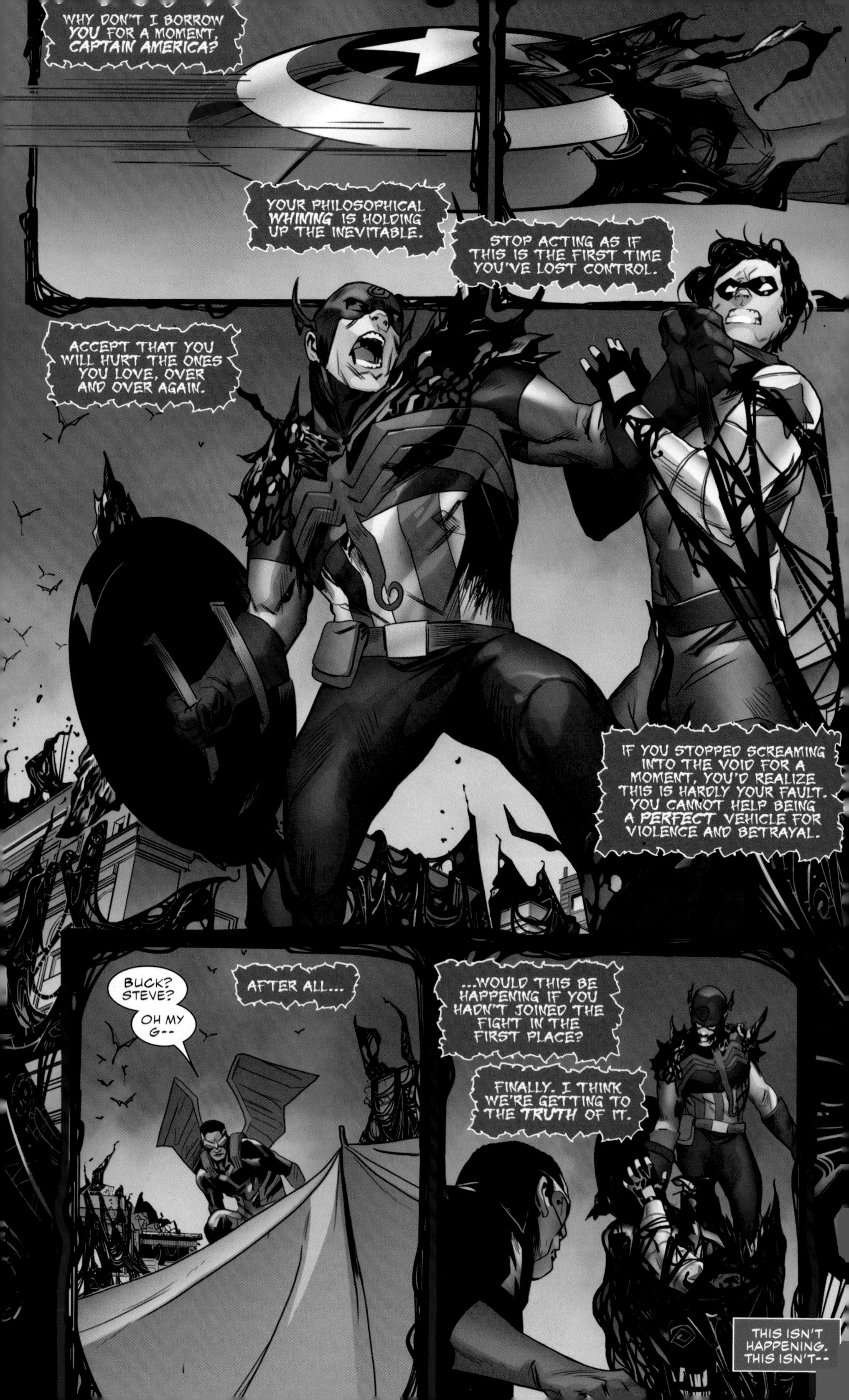
WHY DON'T I BORROW YOU FOR A MOMENT, CAPTAIN AMERICA?
YOUR PHILOSOPHICAL WHINING IS HOLDING UP THE INEVITABLE.
STOP ACTING AS IF THIS IS THE FIRST TIME YOU'VE LOST CONTROL.
ACCEPT THAT YOU WILL HURT THE ONES YOU LOVE, OVER AND OVER AGAIN.
IF YOU STOPPED SCREAMING INTO THE VOID FOR A MOMENT, YOU'D REALIZE THIS IS HARDLY YOUR FAULT. YOU CANNOT HELP BEING A PERFECT VEHICLE FOR VIOLENCE AND BETRAYAL.
BUCK? STEVE?
OH MY G--
AFTER ALL...
...WOULD THIS BE HAPPENING IF YOU HADN'T JOINED THE FIGHT IN THE FIRST PLACE?
FINALLY. I THINK WE'RE GETTING TO THE TRUTH OF IT.
THIS ISN'T HAPPENING. THIS ISN'T--

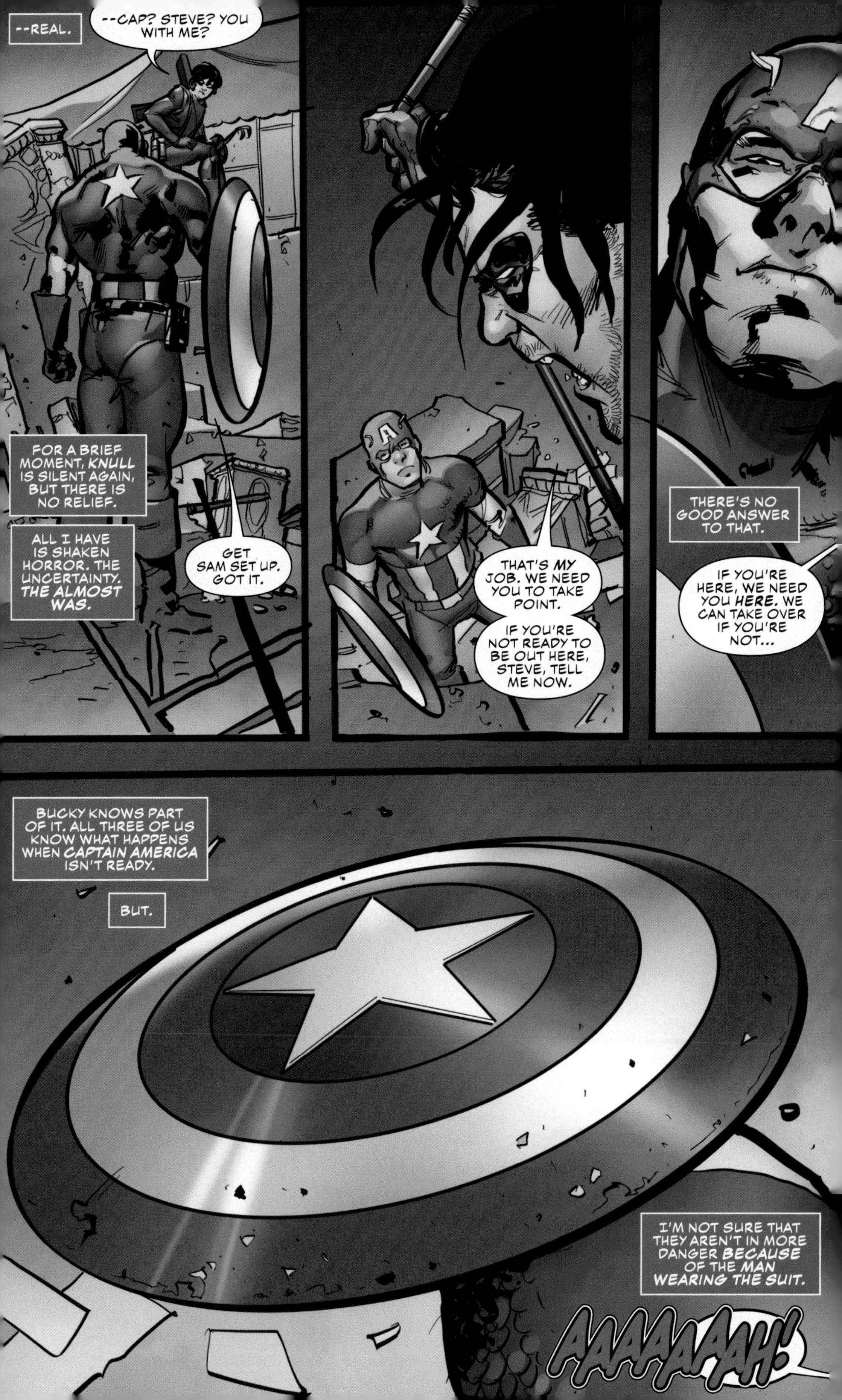
--REAL.
--CAP? STEVE? YOU WITH ME?
FOR A BRIEF MOMENT, KNULL IS SILENT AGAIN, BUT THERE IS NO RELIEF.
ALL I HAVE IS SHAKEN HORROR. THE UNCERTAINTY. THE ALMOST WAS.
GET SAM SET UP. GOT IT.
THAT'S MY JOB. WE NEED YOU TO TAKE POINT.
IF YOU'RE NOT READY TO BE OUT HERE, STEVE, TELL ME NOW.
THERE'S NO GOOD ANSWER TO THAT.
IF YOU'RE HERE, WE NEED YOU HERE. WE CAN TAKE OVER IF YOU'RE NOT...
BUCKY KNOWS PART OF IT. ALL THREE OF US KNOW WHAT HAPPENS WHEN CAPTAIN AMERICA ISN'T READY.
BUT.
I'M NOT SURE THAT THEY AREN'T IN MORE DANGER BECAUSE OF THE MAN WEARING THE SUIT.
AAAAAAAH!

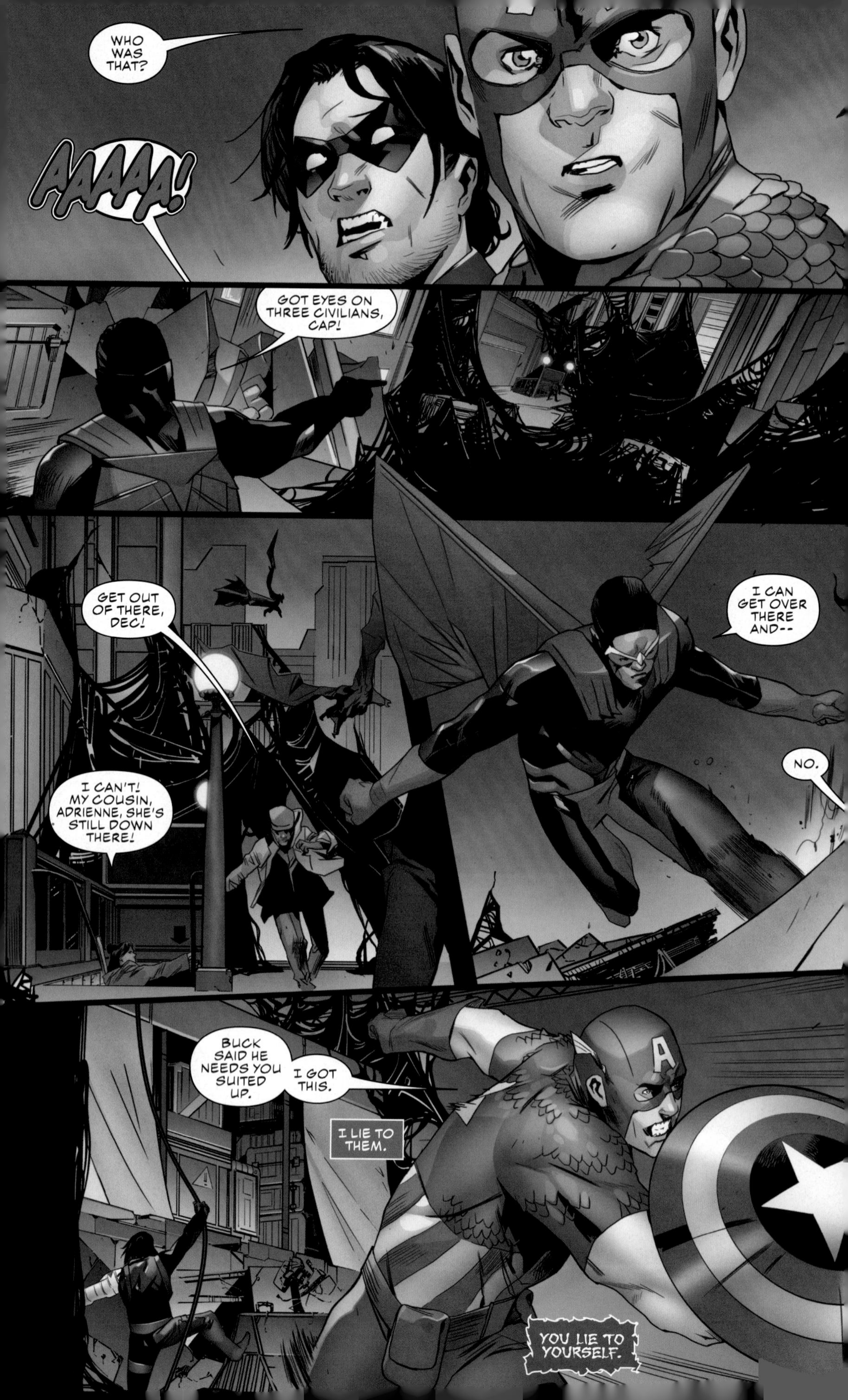
WHO WAS THAT?
AAAAA!
GOT EYES ON THREE CIVILIANS, CAP!
GET OUT OF THERE, DEC!
I CAN GET OVER THERE AND--
I CAN'T! MY COUSIN, ADRIENNE, SHE'S STILL DOWN THERE!
NO.
BUCK SAID HE NEEDS YOU SUITED UP.
I GOT THIS.
I LIE TO THEM.
YOU LIE TO YOURSELF.

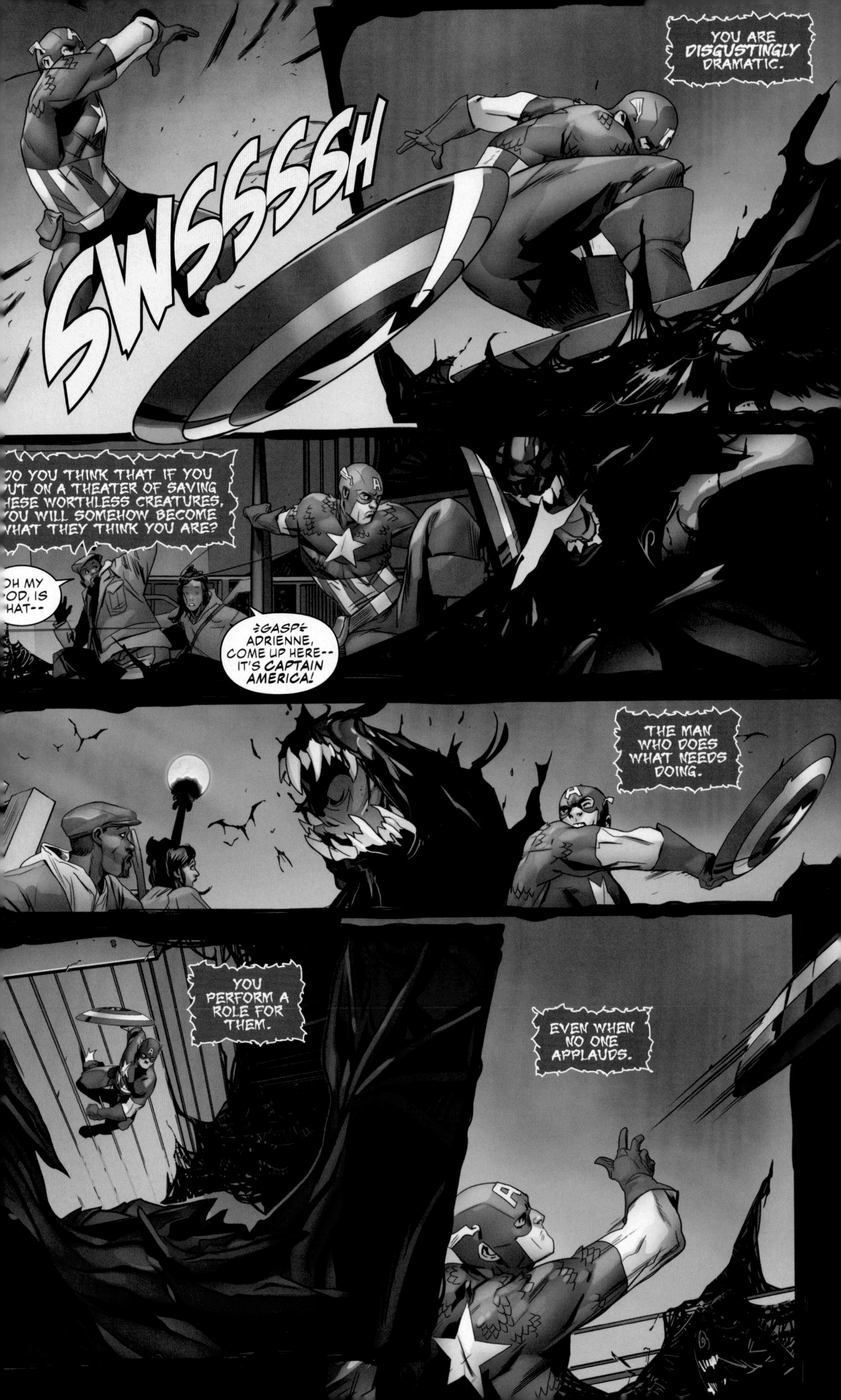

YOU ARE DISGUSTINGLY DRAMATIC.
SWSSSSH
DO YOU THINK THAT IF YOU UT ON A THEATER OF SAVING HESE WORTHLESS CREATURES, YOU WILL SOMEHOW BECOME WHAT THEY THINK YOU ARE?
OH MY OD, IS HAT--
GASP ADRIENNE, COME UP HERE-- IT'S CAPTAIN AMERICA!
THE MAN WHO DOES WHAT NEEDS DOING.
YOU PERFORM A ROLE FOR THEM.
EVEN WHEN NO ONE APPLAUDS.

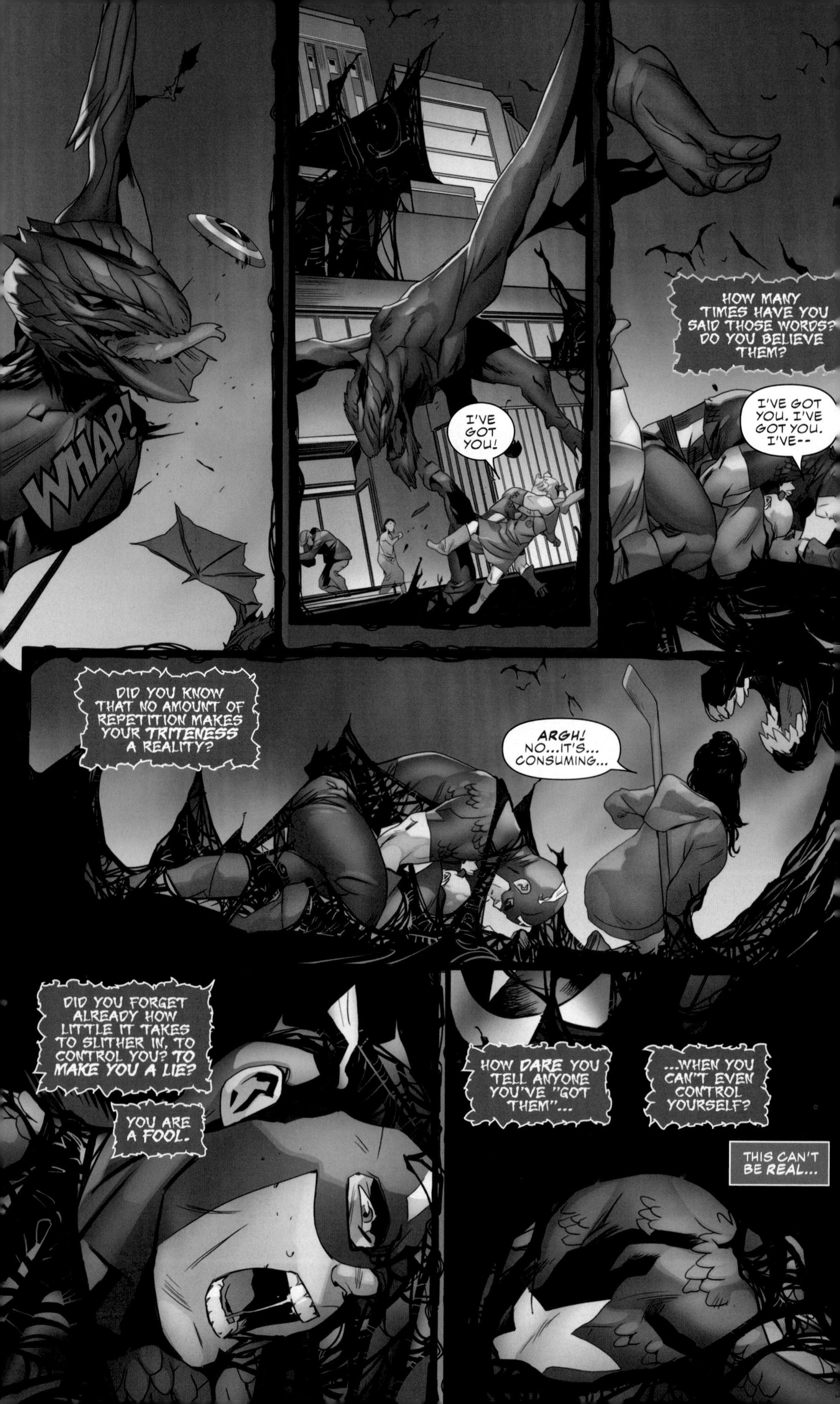
WHAP!
I'VE GOT YOU!
HOW MANY TIMES HAVE YOU SAID THOSE WORDS? DO YOU BELIEVE THEM?
I'VE GOT YOU. I'VE GOT YOU. I'VE--
DID YOU KNOW THAT NO AMOUNT OF REPETITION MAKES YOUR TRITENESS A REALITY?
ARGH! NO...IT'S... CONSUMING...
DID YOU FORGET ALREADY HOW LITTLE IT TAKES TO SLITHER IN, TO CONTROL YOU? TO MAKE YOU A LIE?
YOU ARE A FOOL.
HOW DARE YOU TELL ANYONE YOU'VE "GOT THEM"...
...WHEN YOU CAN'T EVEN CONTROL YOURSELF?
THIS CAN'T BE REAL...

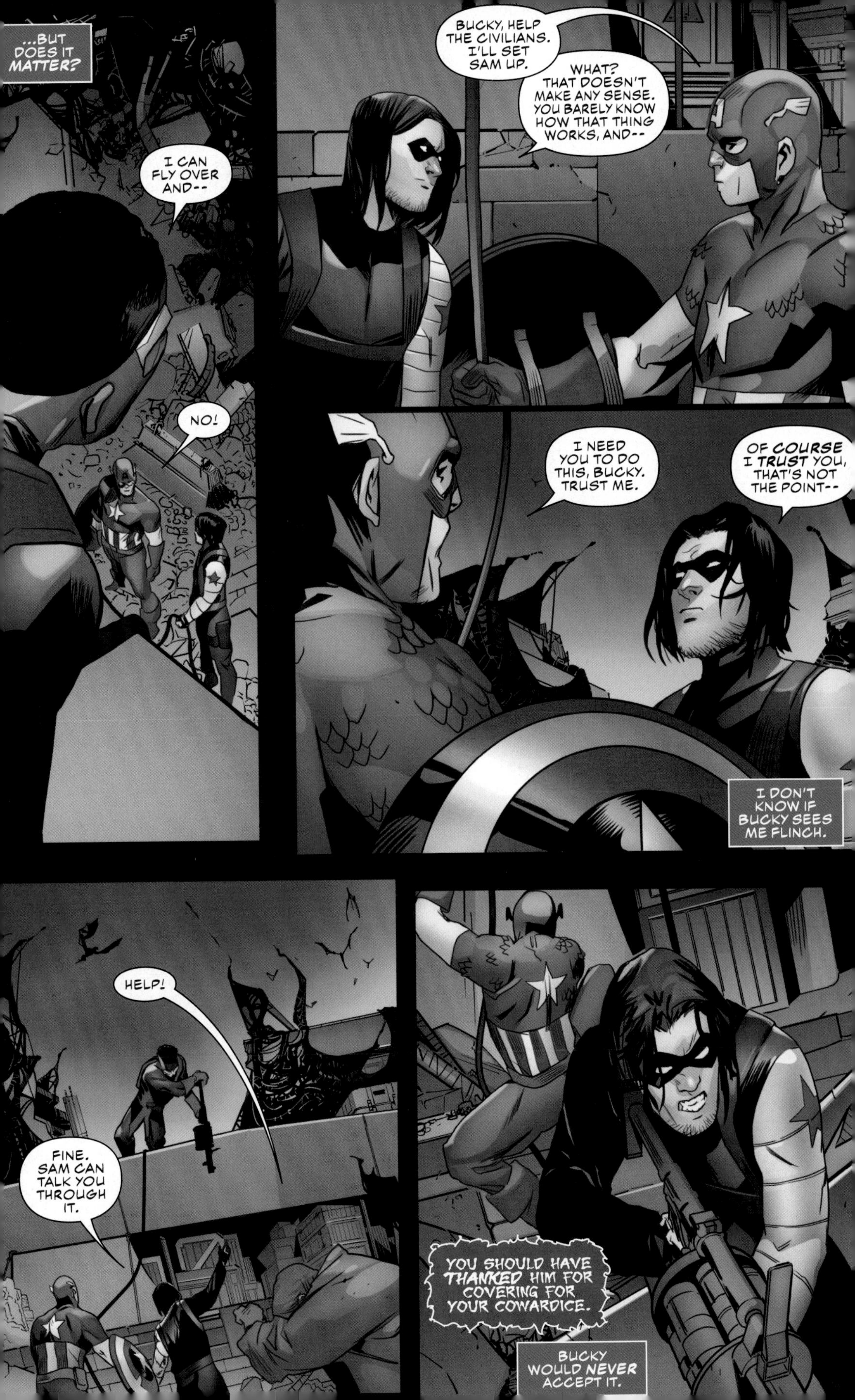
...BUT DOES IT MATTER?
I CAN FLY OVER AND--
NO!
BUCKY, HELP THE CIVILIANS. I'LL SET SAM UP.
WHAT? THAT DOESN'T MAKE ANY SENSE. YOU BARELY KNOW HOW THAT THING WORKS, AND--
I NEED YOU TO DO THIS, BUCKY. TRUST ME.
OF COURSE I TRUST YOU, THAT'S NOT THE POINT--
I DON'T KNOW IF BUCKY SEES ME FLINCH.
HELP!
FINE. SAM CAN TALK YOU THROUGH IT.
YOU SHOULD HAVE THANKED HIM FOR COVERING FOR YOUR COWARDICE.
BUCKY WOULD NEVER ACCEPT IT.

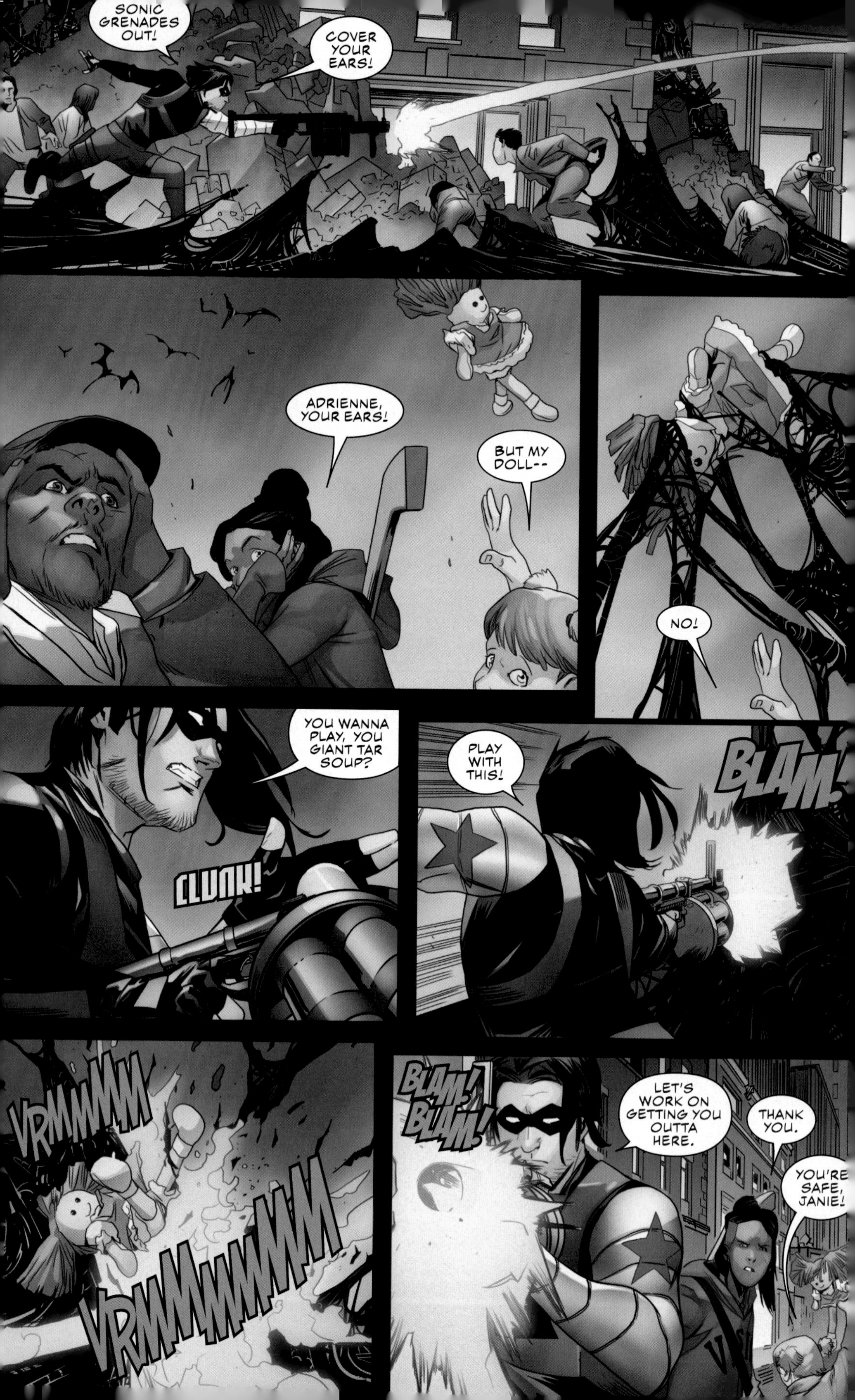
SONIC GRENADES OUT!
COVER YOUR EARS!
ADRIENNE, YOUR EARS!
BUT MY DOLL--
NO!
YOU WANNA PLAY, YOU GIANT TAR SOUP?
CLUNK!
PLAY WITH THIS!
BLAM!
VRMMMMM
VRMMMMMMM
BLAM! BLAM!
LET'S WORK ON GETTING YOU OUTTA HERE.
THANK YOU.
YOU'RE SAFE, JANIE!

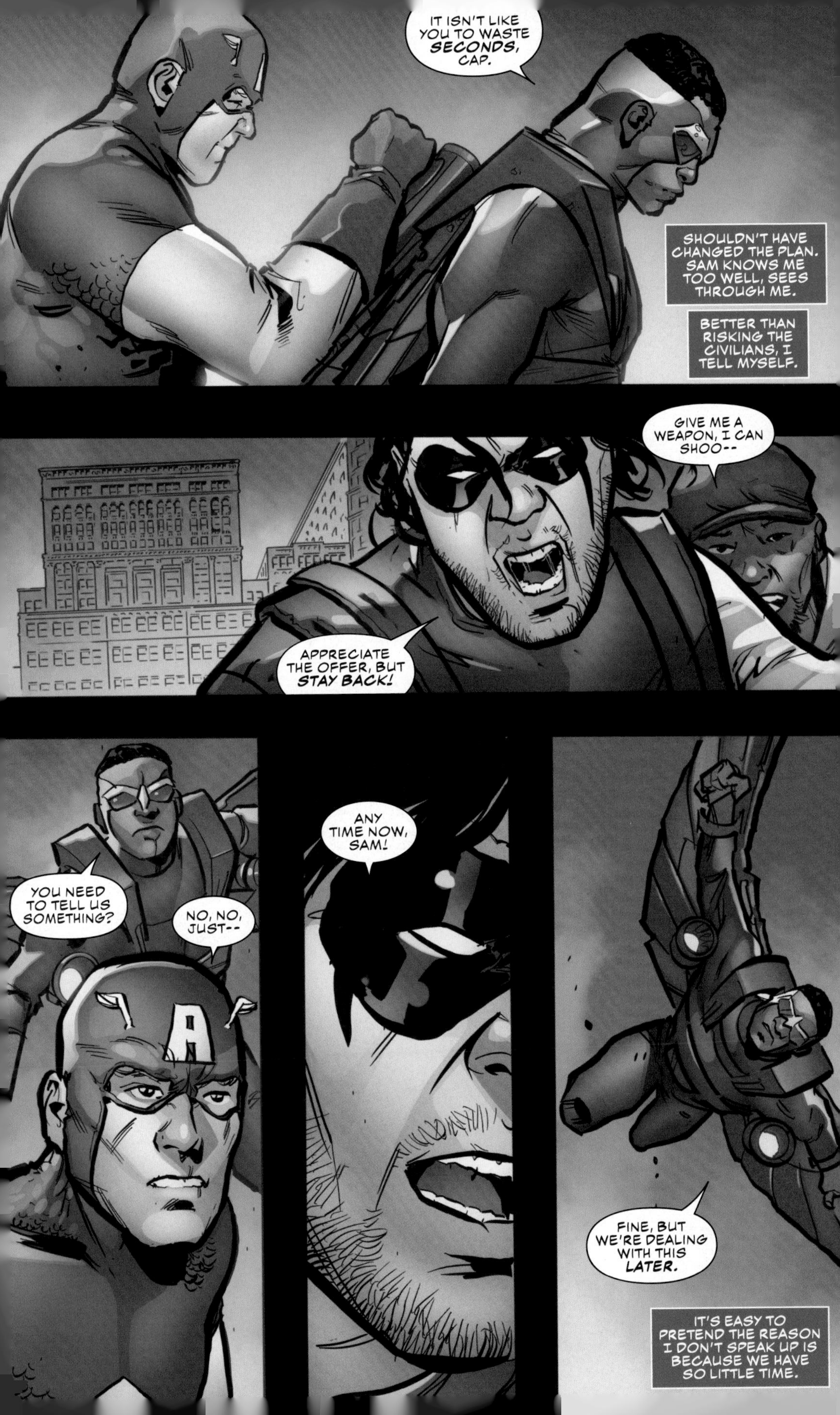
IT ISN'T LIKE YOU TO WASTE SECONDS, CAP.
SHOULDN'T HAVE CHANGED THE PLAN. SAM KNOWS ME TOO WELL, SEES THROUGH ME.
BETTER THAN RISKING THE CIVILIANS, I TELL MYSELF.
GIVE ME A WEAPON, I CAN SHOO--
APPRECIATE THE OFFER, BUT STAY BACK!
YOU NEED TO TELL US SOMETHING?
NO, NO, JUST--
ANY TIME NOW, SAM!
FINE, BUT WE'RE DEALING WITH THIS LATER.
IT'S EASY TO PRETEND THE REASON I DON'T SPEAK UP IS BECAUSE WE HAVE SO LITTLE TIME.

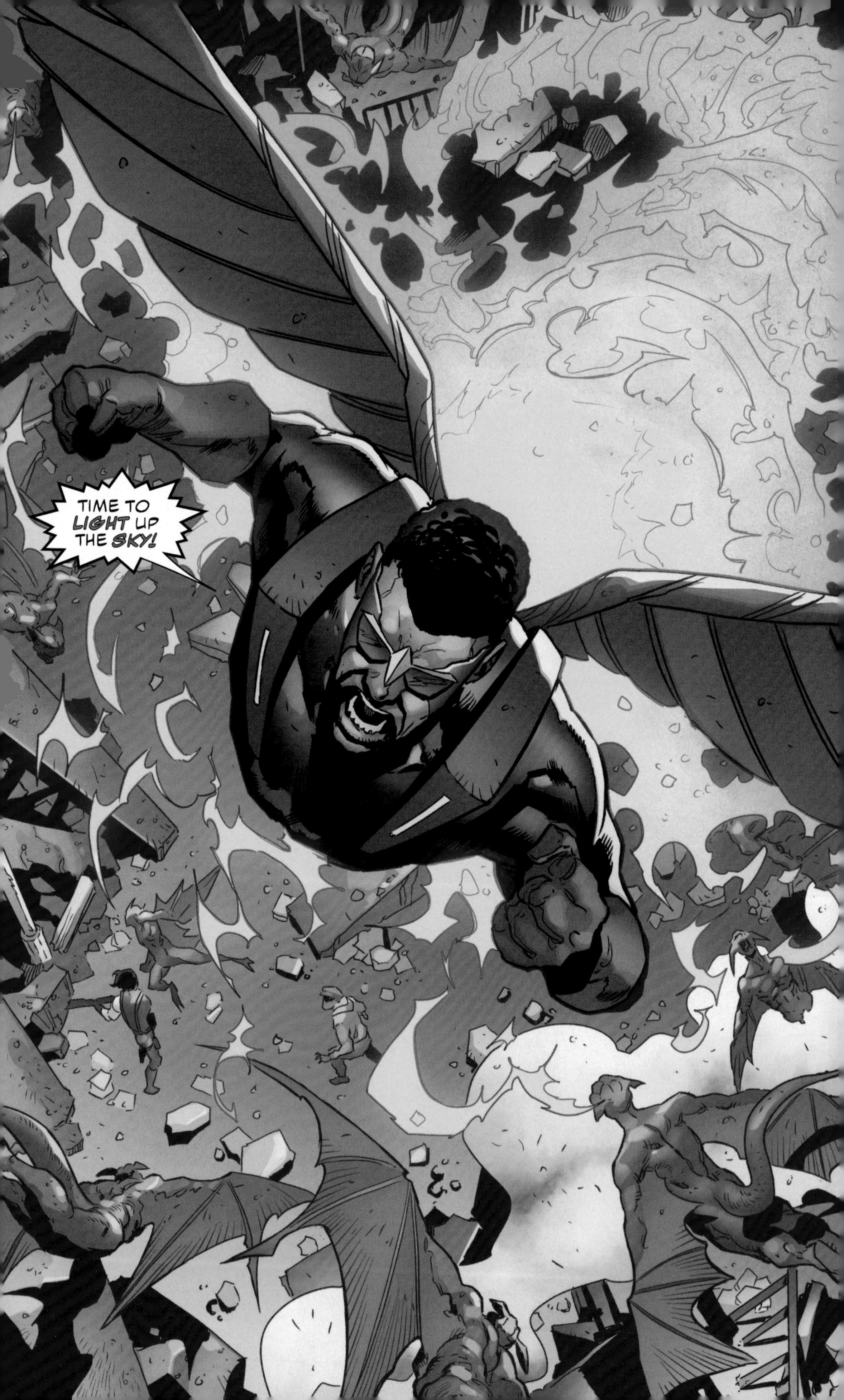
TIME TO LIGHT UP THE SKY!

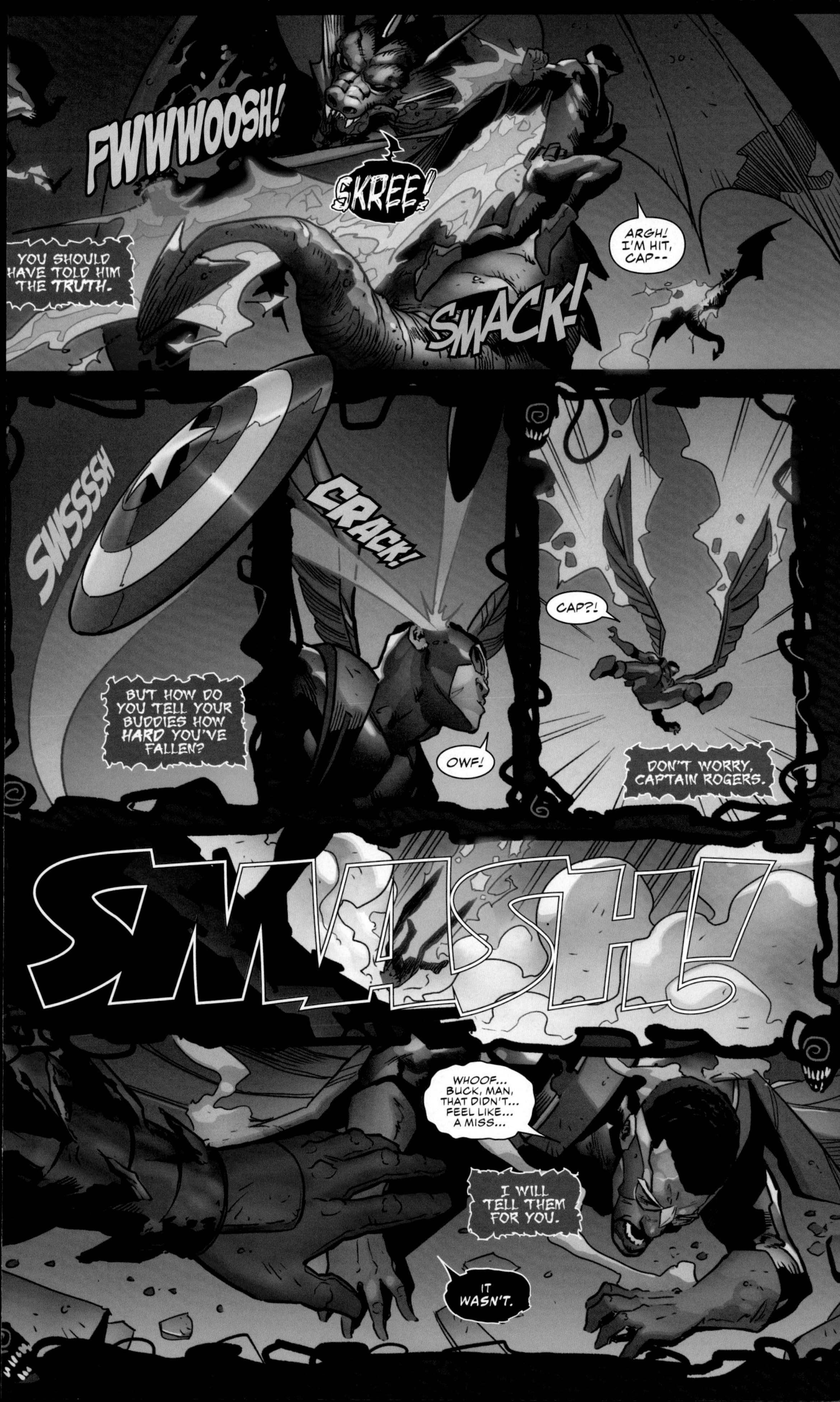
FWWWOOSH!
SKREE!
YOU SHOULD HAVE TOLD HIM THE TRUTH.
ARGH! I'M HIT, CAP--
SMACK!
SWSSSSH
CRACK!
BUT HOW DO YOU TELL YOUR BUDDIES HOW HARD YOU'VE FALLEN?
OWF!
CAP?!
DON'T WORRY, CAPTAIN ROGERS.
SMASH!
WHOOF... BUCK, MAN, THAT DIDN'T... FEEL LIKE... A MISS...
I WILL TELL THEM FOR YOU.
IT WASN'T.

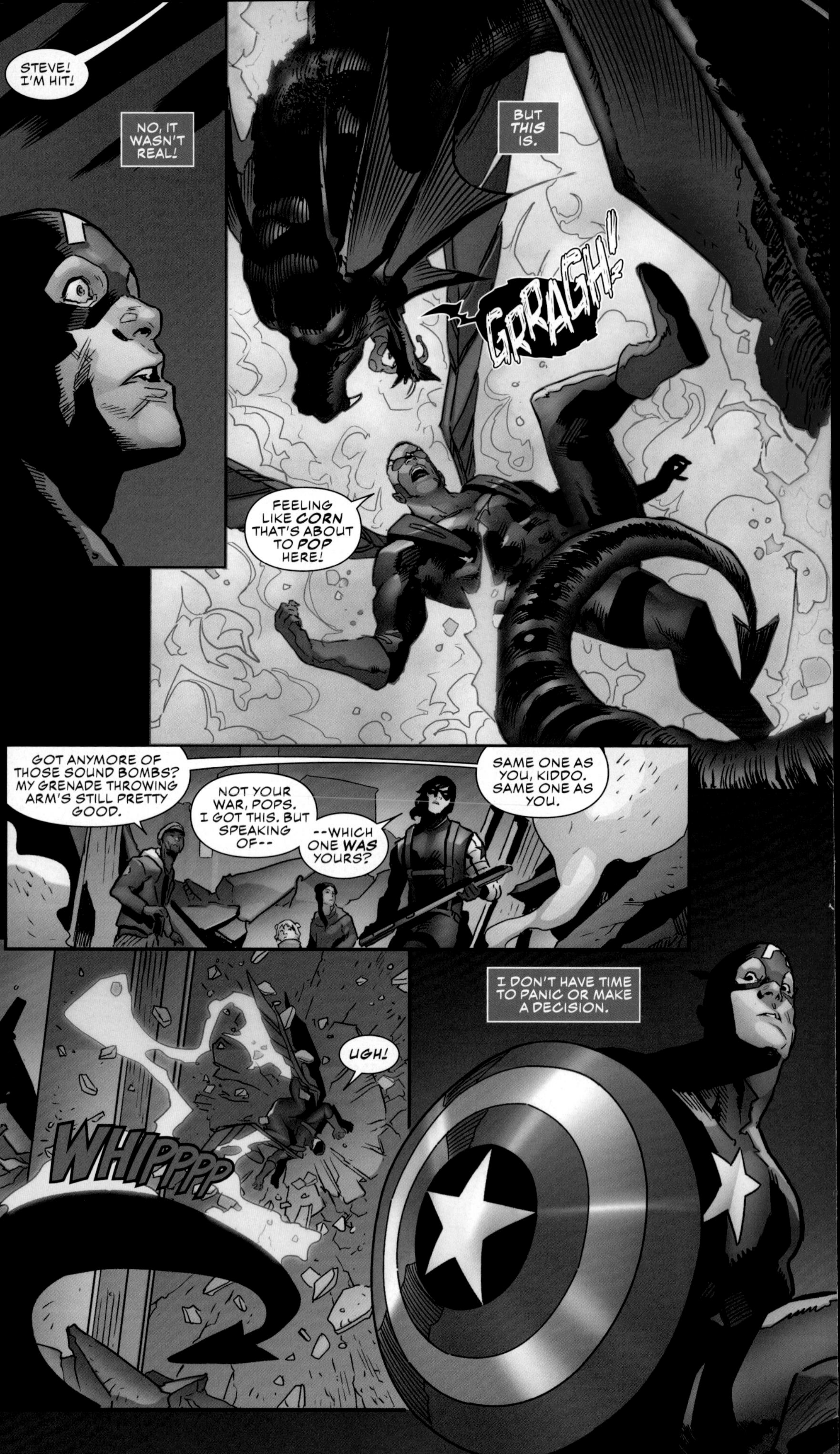
STEVE! I'M HIT!
NO, IT WASN'T REAL!
BUT THIS IS.
GRRAGH!
FEELING LIKE CORN THAT'S ABOUT TO POP HERE!
GOT ANYMORE OF THOSE SOUND BOMBS? MY GRENADE THROWING ARM'S STILL PRETTY GOOD.
NOT YOUR WAR, POPS. I GOT THIS. BUT SPEAKING OF--
--WHICH ONE WAS YOURS?
SAME ONE AS YOU, KIDDO. SAME ONE AS YOU.
UGH!
WHIPPPP
I DON'T HAVE TIME TO PANIC OR MAKE A DECISION.

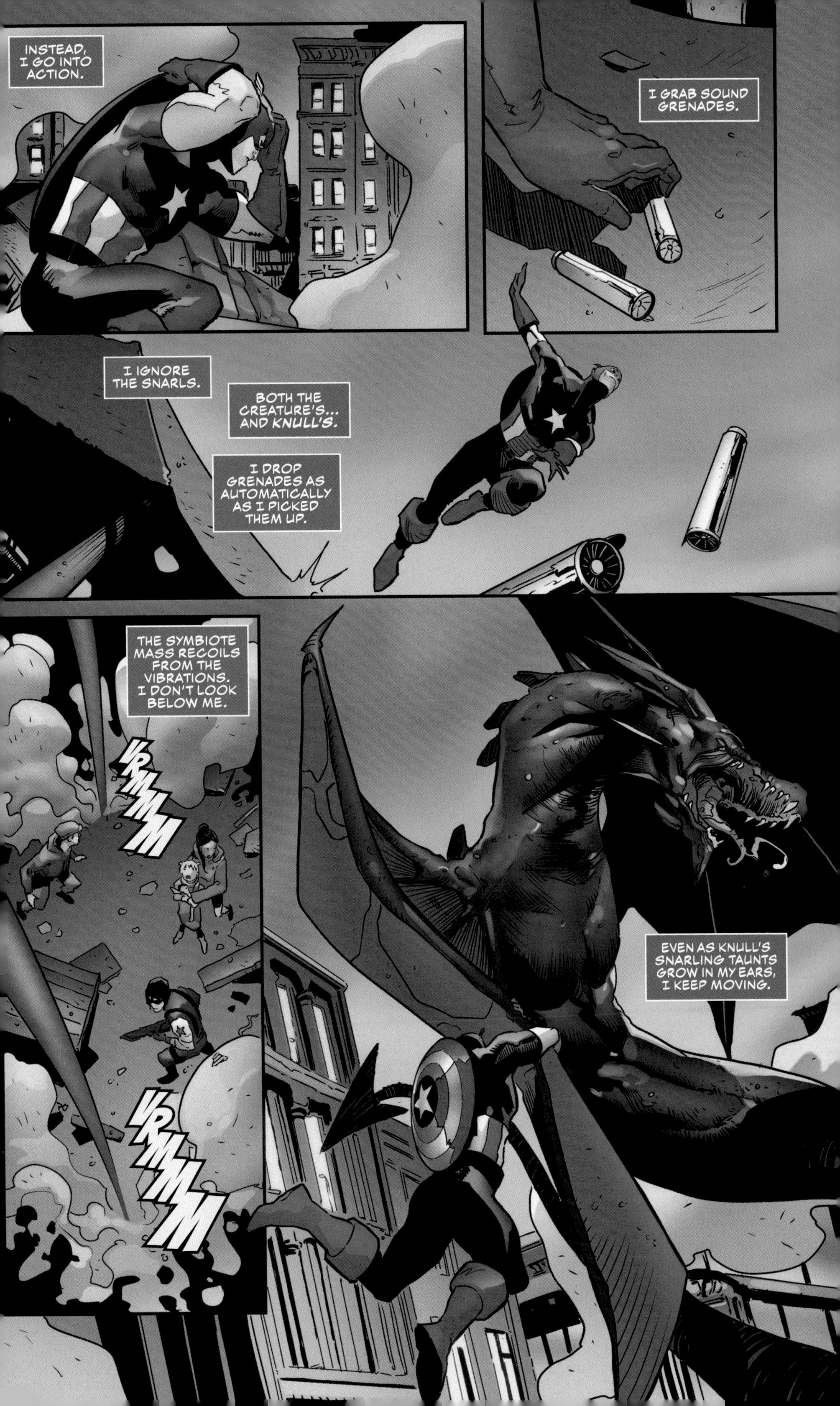

INSTEAD, I GO INTO ACTION.
I GRAB SOUND GRENADES.
I IGNORE THE SNARLS.
BOTH THE CREATURE'S... AND KNULL'S.
I DROP GRENADES AS AUTOMATICALLY AS I PICKED THEM UP.
THE SYMBIOTE MASS RECOILS FROM THE VIBRATIONS. I DON'T LOOK BELOW ME.
VRMMMM
VRMMMM
EVEN AS KNULL'S SNARLING TAUNTS GROW IN MY EARS, I KEEP MOVING.

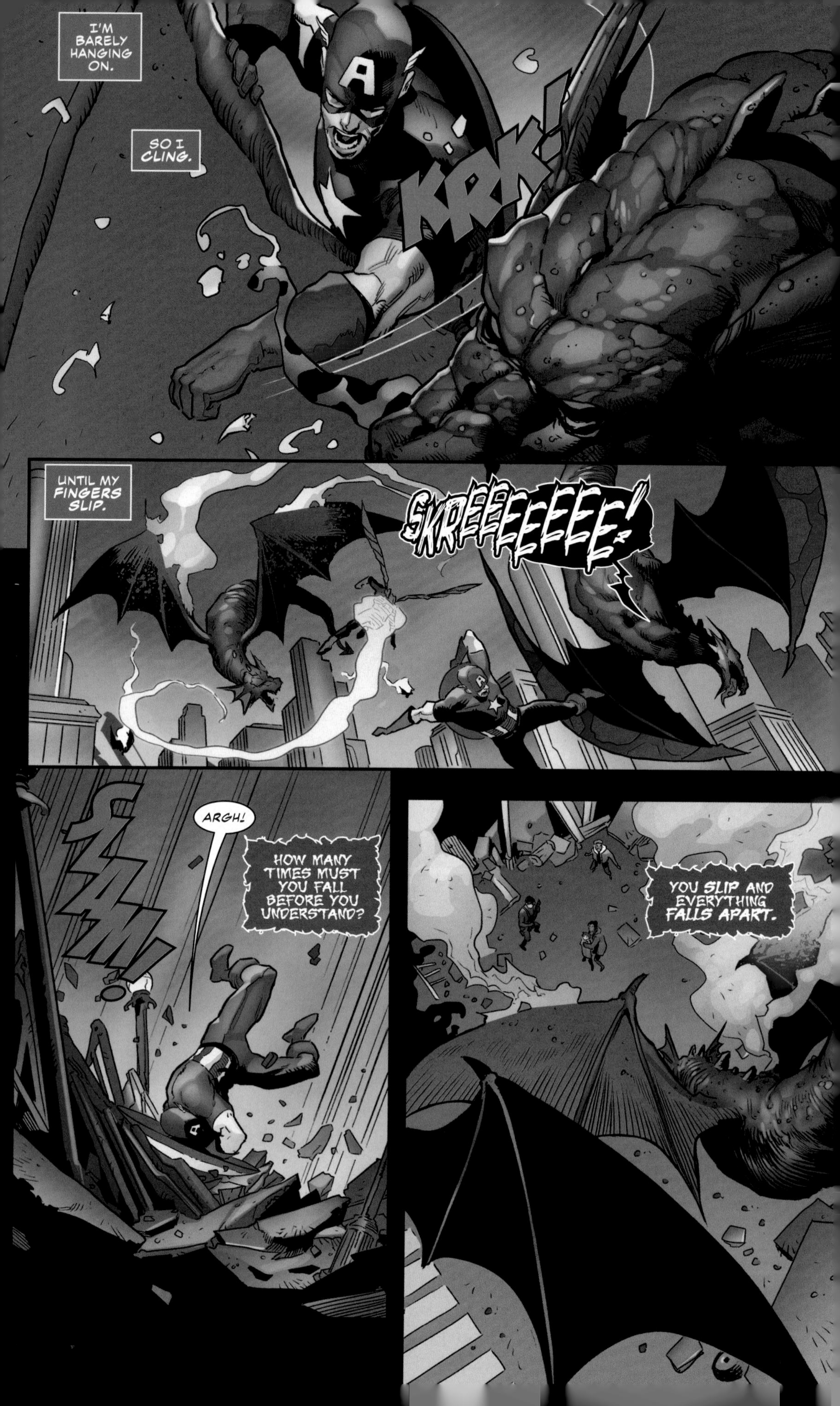

I'M BARELY HANGING ON.
SO I CLING.
KRK!
UNTIL MY FINGERS SLIP.
SKREEEEEEEE!
ARGH!
HOW MANY TIMES MUST YOU FALL BEFORE YOU UNDERSTAND?
YOU SLIP AND EVERYTHING FALLS APART.

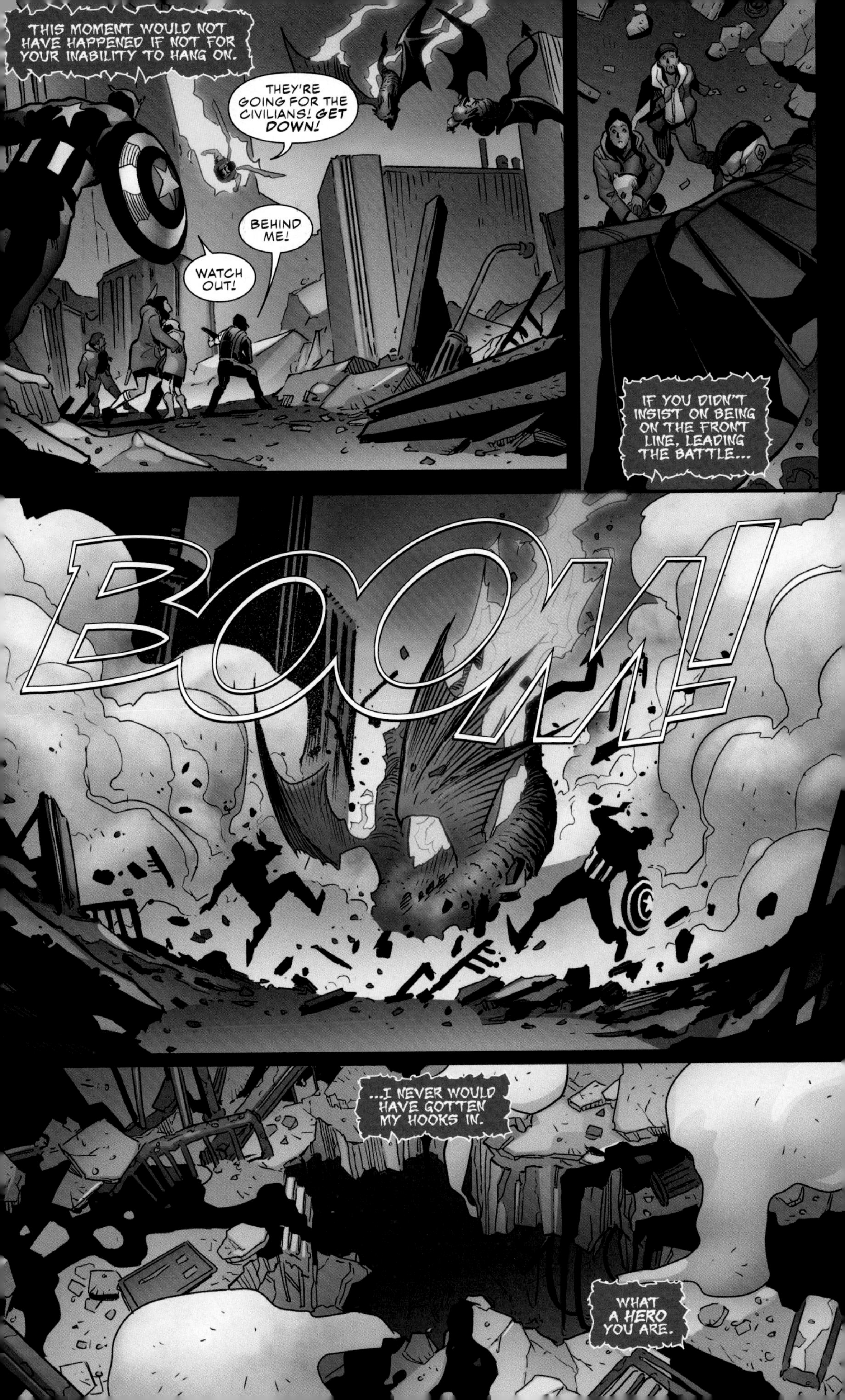
THIS MOMENT WOULD NOT HAVE HAPPENED IF NOT FOR YOUR INABILITY TO HANG ON.
THEY'RE GOING FOR THE CIVILIANS! GET DOWN!
BEHIND ME!
WATCH OUT!
IF YOU DIDN'T INSIST ON BEING ON THE FRONT LINE, LEADING THE BATTLE...
BOOM!
...I NEVER WOULD HAVE GOTTEN MY HOOKS IN.
WHAT A HERO YOU ARE.

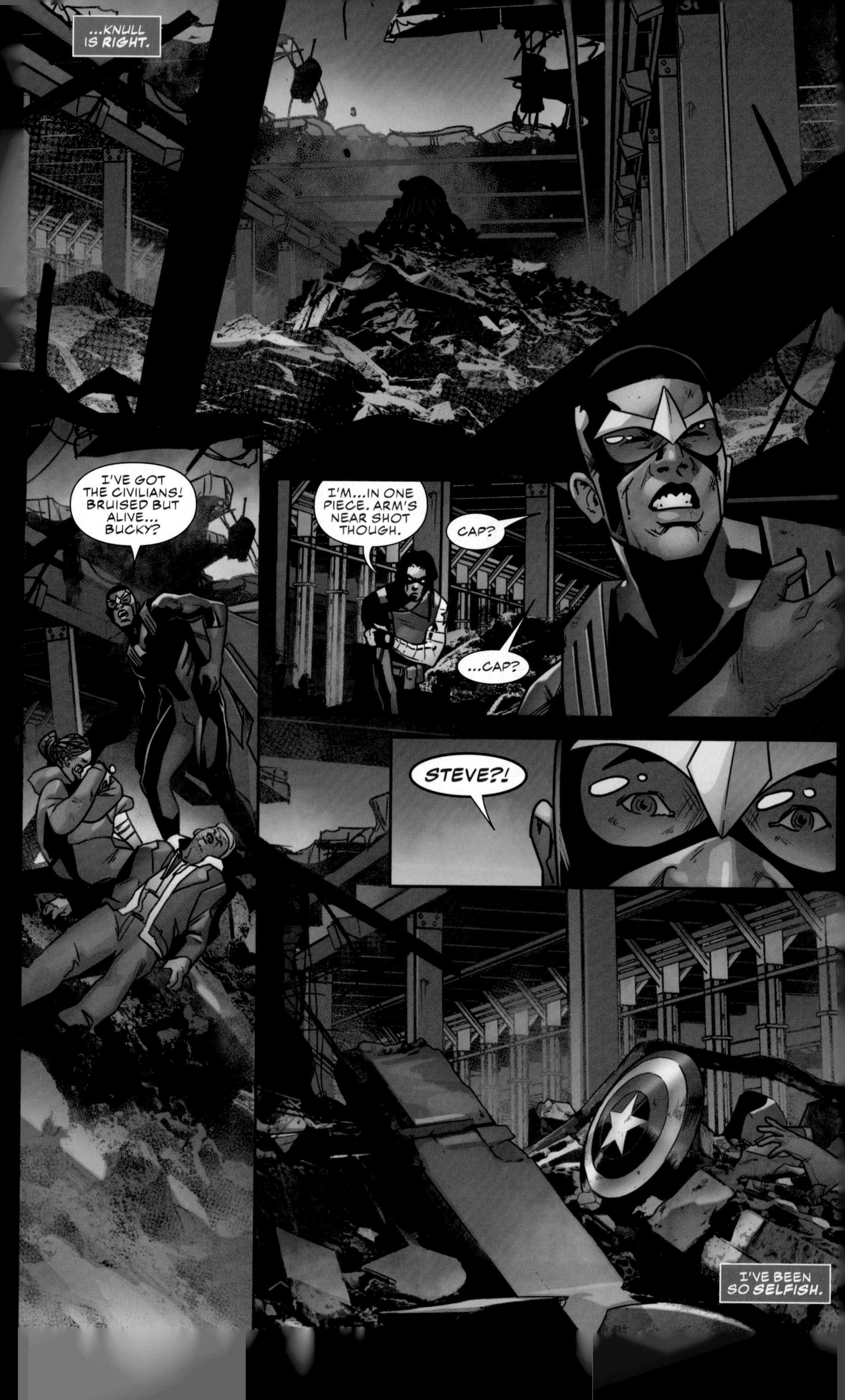
...KNULL IS RIGHT.
I'VE GOT THE CIVILIANS! BRUISED BUT ALIVE... BUCKY?
I'M...IN ONE PIECE. ARM'S NEAR SHOT THOUGH.
CAP?
...CAP?
STEVE?!
I'VE BEEN SO SELFISH.

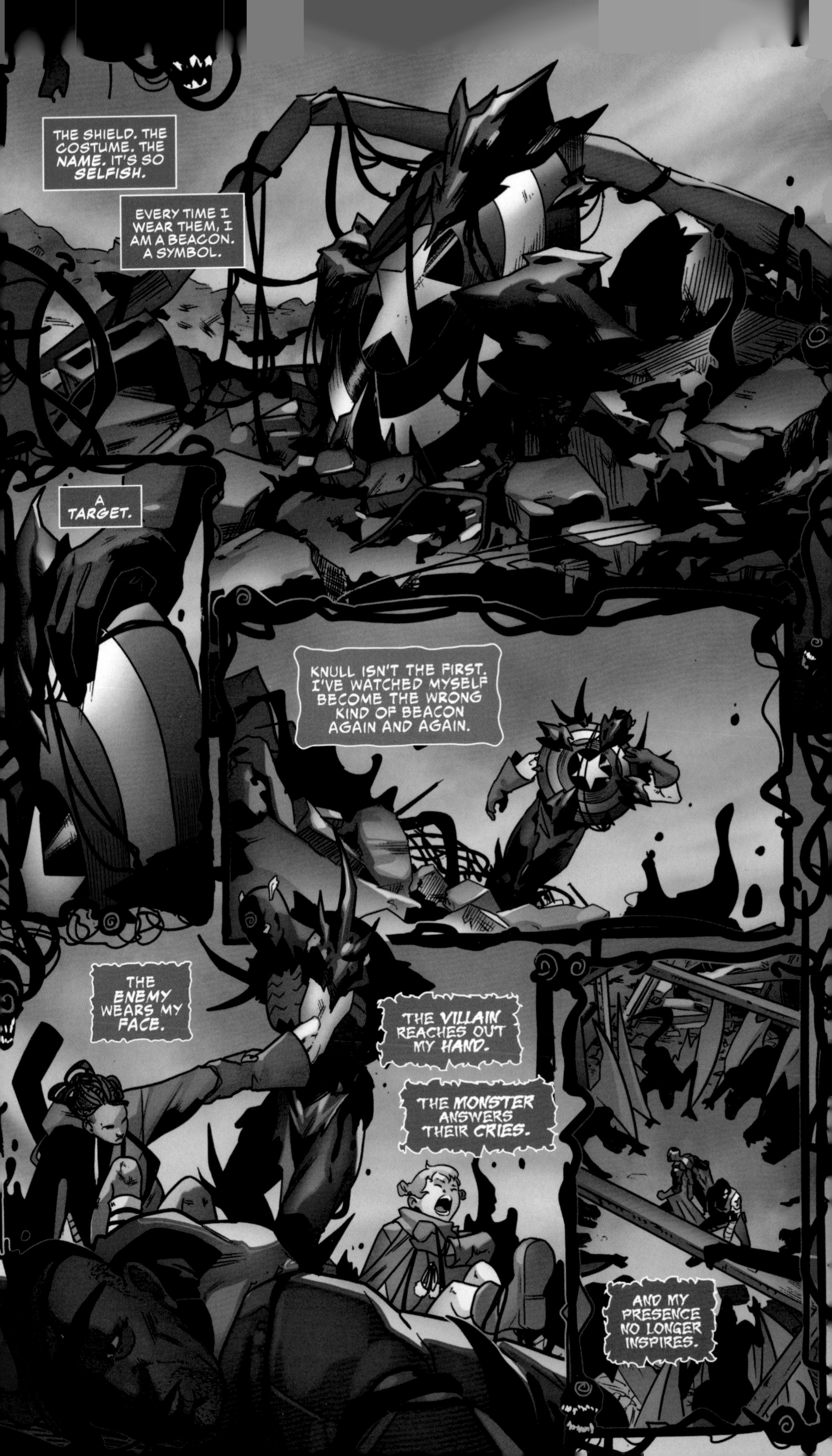
THE SHIELD. THE COSTUME. THE NAME. IT'S SO SELFISH.
EVERY TIME I WEAR THEM, I AM A BEACON. A SYMBOL.
A TARGET.
KNULL ISN'T THE FIRST. I'VE WATCHED MYSELF BECOME THE WRONG KIND OF BEACON AGAIN AND AGAIN.
THE ENEMY WEARS MY FACE.
THE VILLAIN REACHES OUT MY HAND.
THE MONSTER ANSWERS THEIR CRIES.
AND MY PRESENCE NO LONGER INSPIRES.

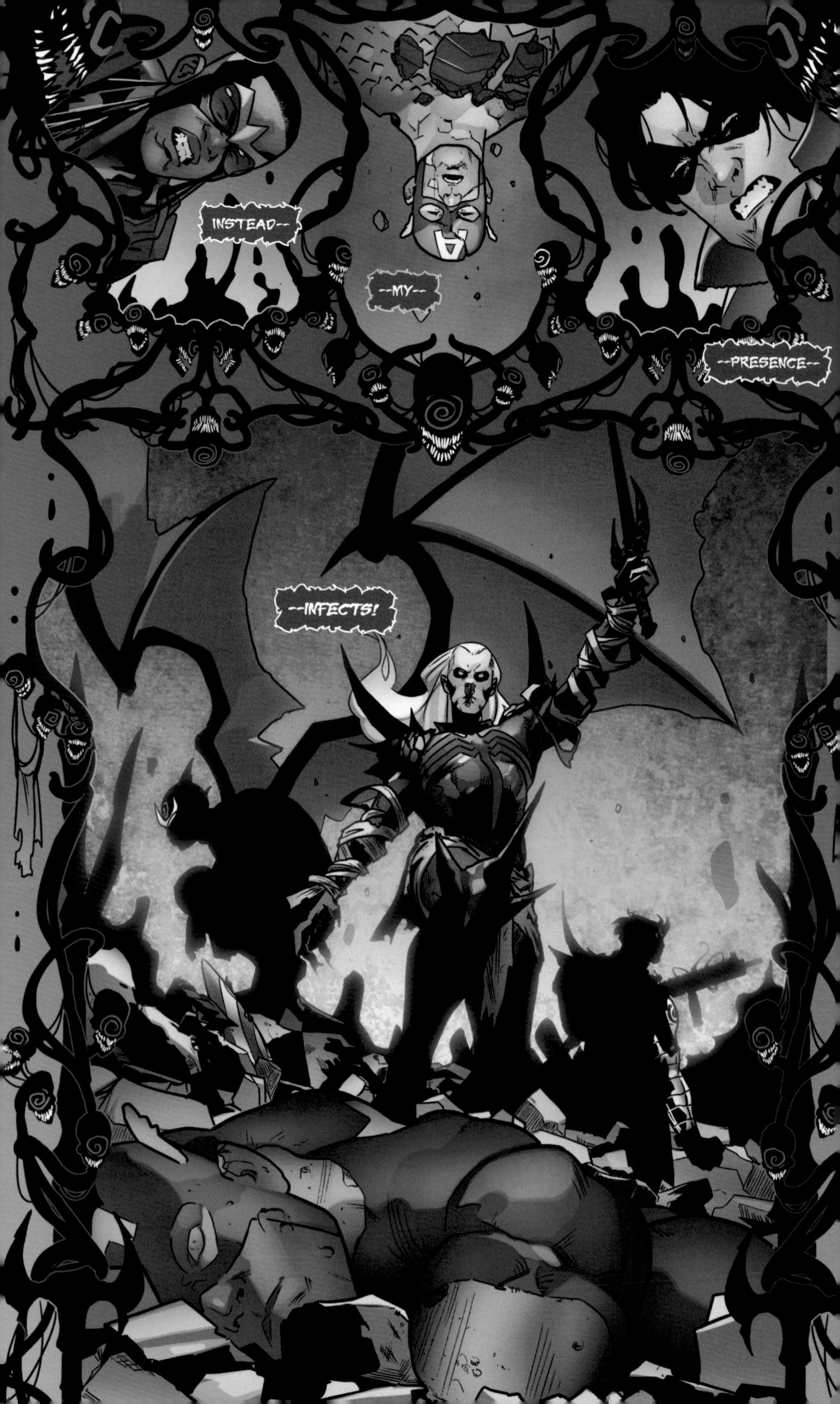
INSTEAD--
--MY--
--PRESENCE--
--INFECTS!

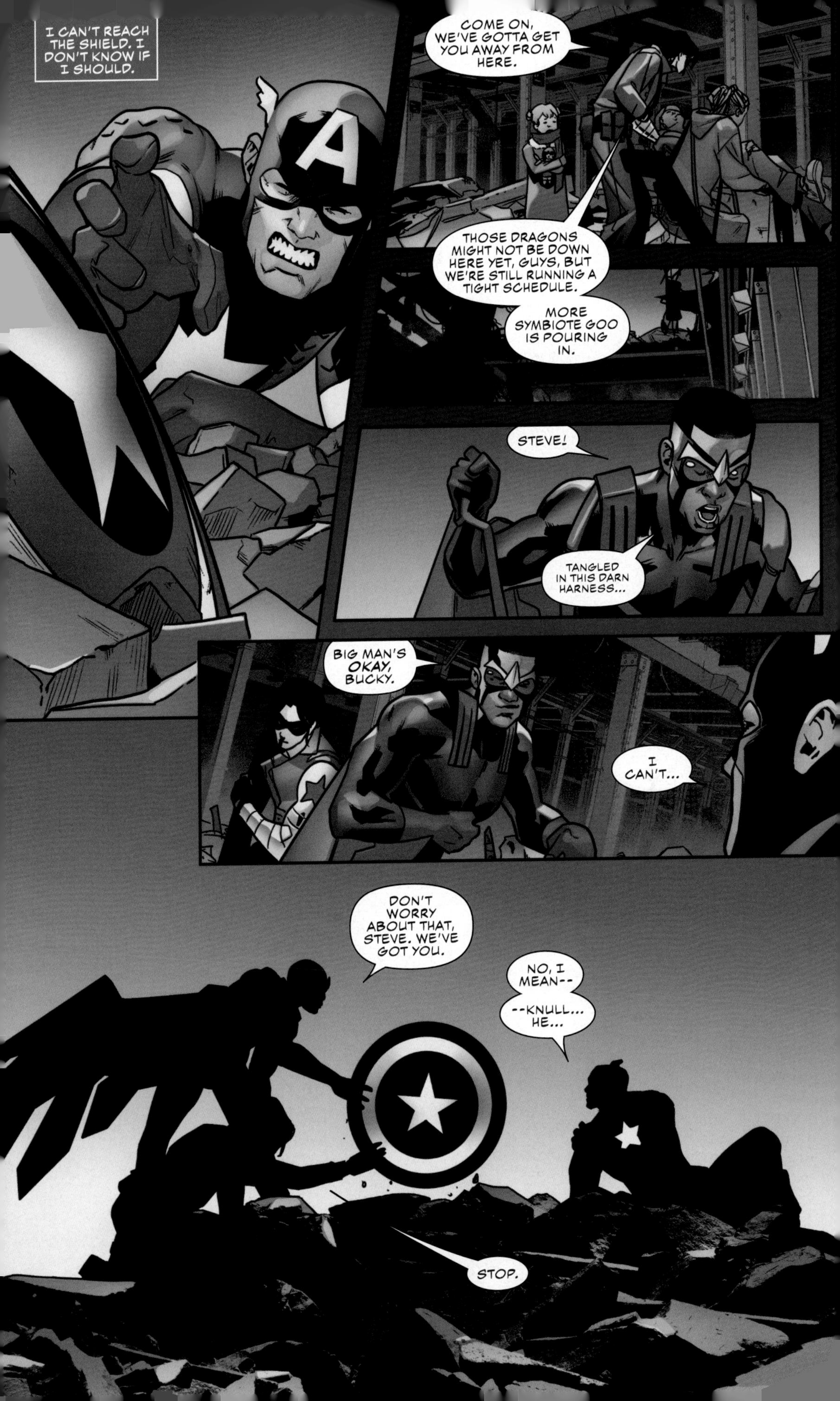
I CAN'T REACH THE SHIELD. I DON'T KNOW IF I SHOULD.
COME ON, WE'VE GOTTA GET YOU AWAY FROM HERE.
THOSE DRAGONS MIGHT NOT BE DOWN HERE YET, GUYS, BUT WE'RE STILL RUNNING A TIGHT SCHEDULE.
MORE SYMBIOTE GOO IS POURING IN.
STEVE!
TANGLED IN THIS DARN HARNESS...
BIG MAN'S OKAY, BUCKY.
I CAN'T...
DON'T WORRY ABOUT THAT, STEVE. WE'VE GOT YOU.
NO, I MEAN--
--KNULL... HE...
STOP.

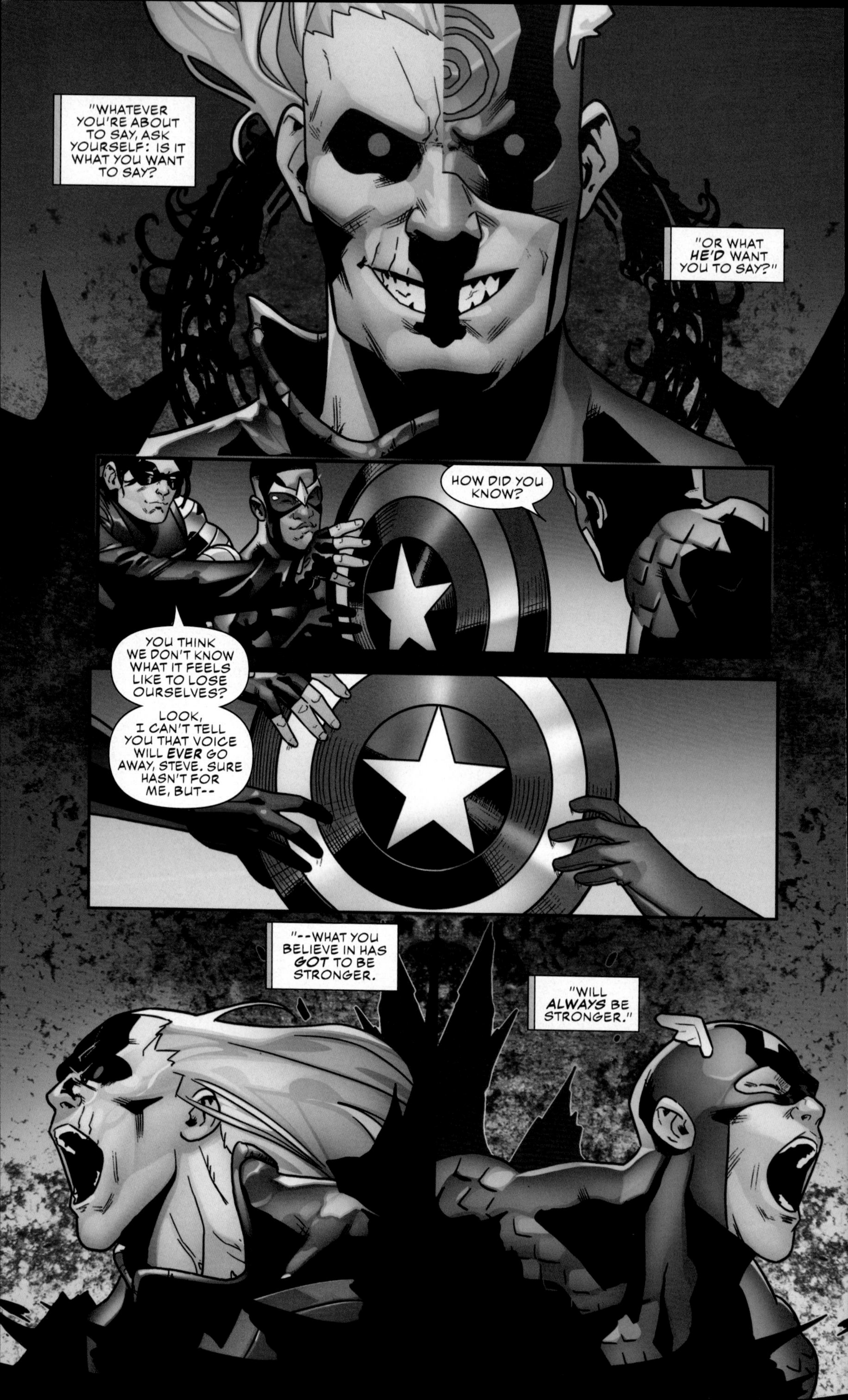
"WHATEVER YOU'RE ABOUT TO SAY, ASK YOURSELF: IS IT WHAT YOU WANT TO SAY?
"OR WHAT HE'D WANT YOU TO SAY?"
HOW DID YOU KNOW?
YOU THINK WE DON'T KNOW WHAT IT FEELS LIKE TO LOSE OURSELVES?
LOOK, I CAN'T TELL YOU THAT VOICE WILL EVER GO AWAY, STEVE. SURE HASN'T FOR ME, BUT--
"--WHAT YOU BELIEVE IN HAS GOT TO BE STRONGER.
"WILL ALWAYS BE STRONGER."

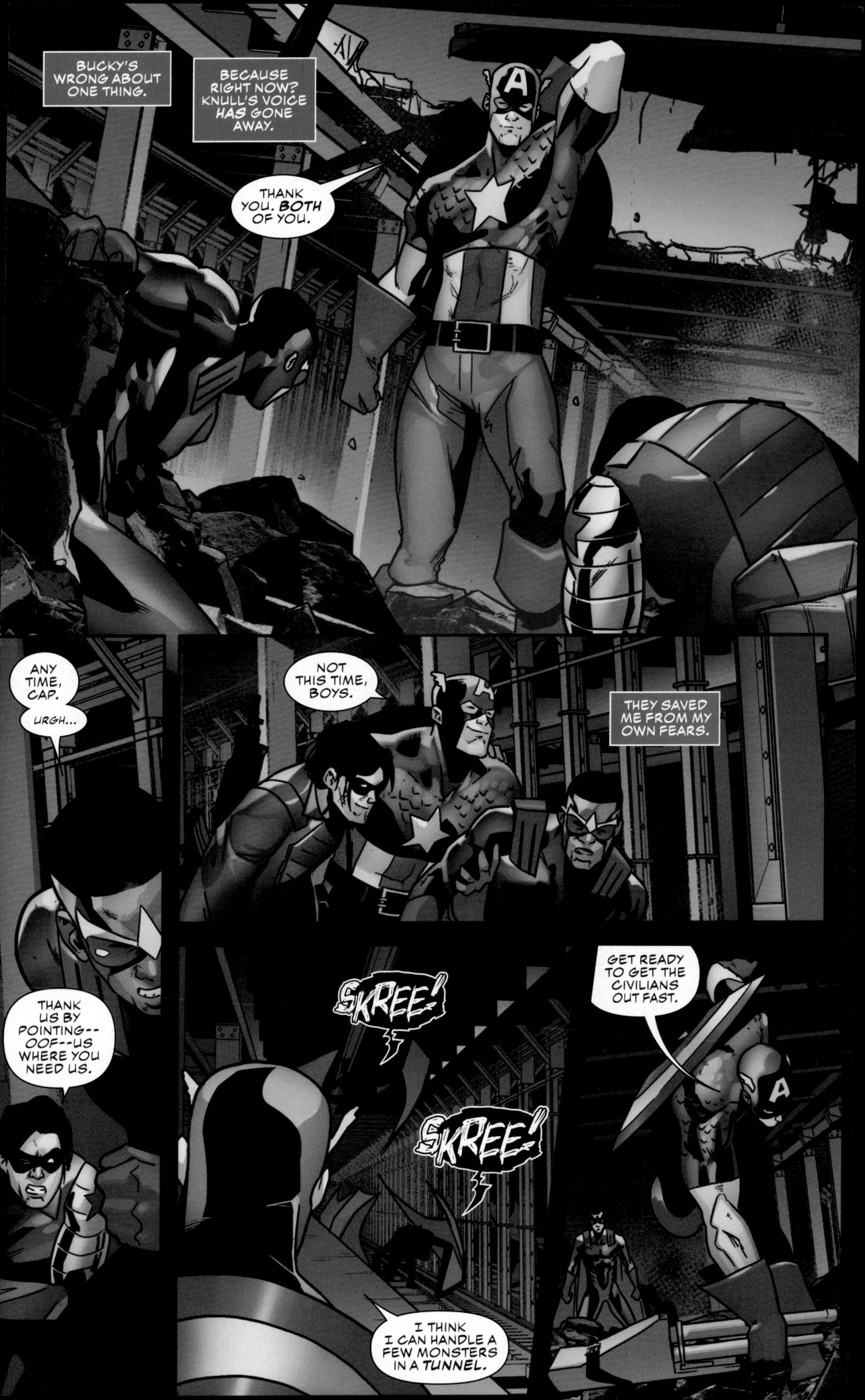
BUCKY'S WRONG ABOUT ONE THING.
BECAUSE RIGHT NOW? KNULL'S VOICE HAS GONE AWAY.
THANK YOU. BOTH OF YOU.
ANY TIME, CAP.
URGH...
NOT THIS TIME, BOYS.
THEY SAVED ME FROM MY OWN FEARS.
THANK US BY POINTING--OOF--US WHERE YOU NEED US.
SKREE!
SKREE!
GET READY TO GET THE CIVILIANS OUT FAST.
I THINK I CAN HANDLE A FEW MONSTERS IN A TUNNEL.

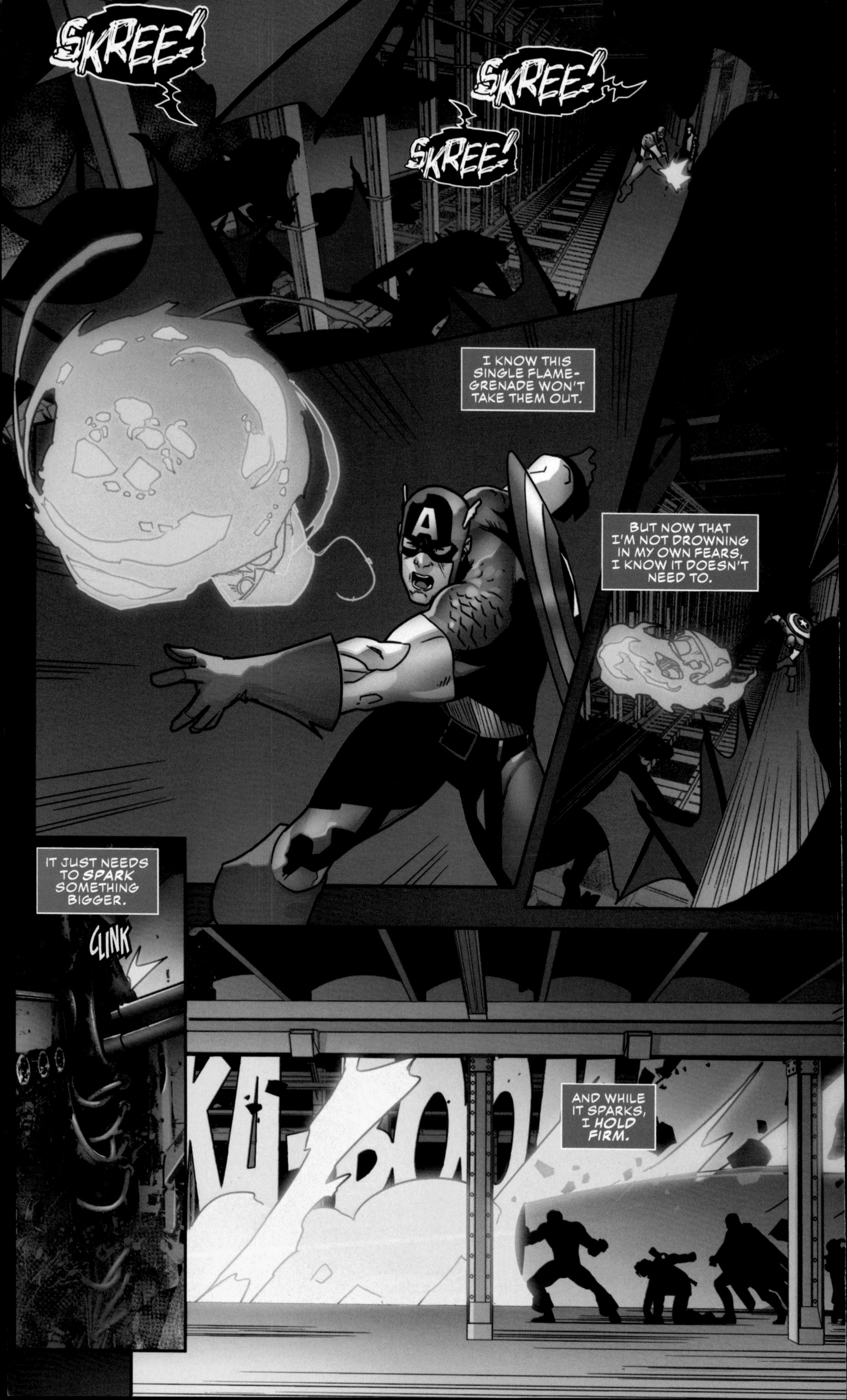
SKREE!
SKREE!
SKREE!
I KNOW THIS SINGLE FLAME-GRENADE WON'T TAKE THEM OUT.
BUT NOW THAT I'M NOT DROWNING IN MY OWN FEARS, I KNOW IT DOESN'T NEED TO.
IT JUST NEEDS TO SPARK SOMETHING BIGGER.
CLINK
AND WHILE IT SPARKS, I HOLD FIRM.

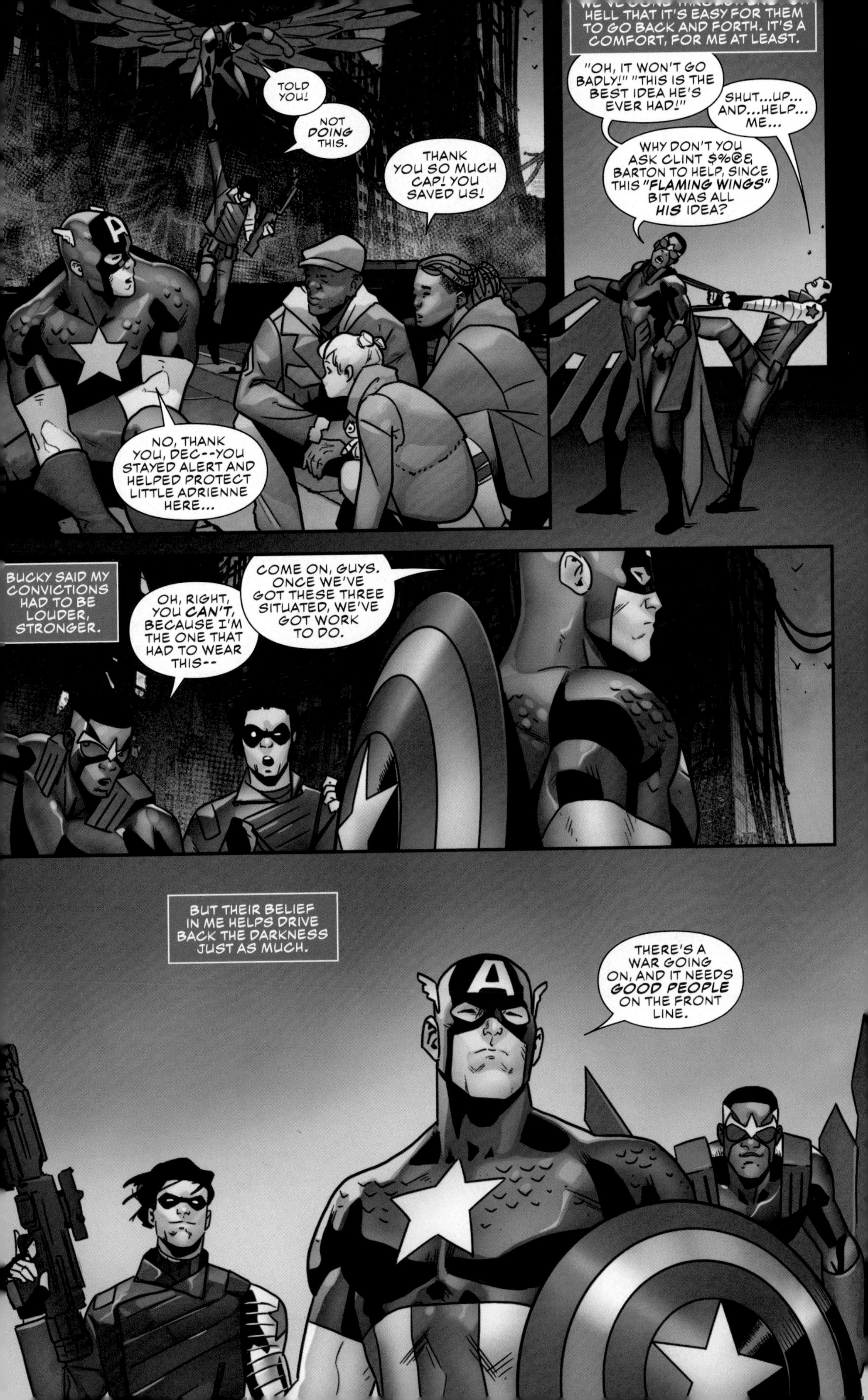
TOLD YOU!
NOT DOING THIS.
THANK YOU SO MUCH CAP! YOU SAVED US!
NO, THANK YOU, DEC--YOU STAYED ALERT AND HELPED PROTECT LITTLE ADRIENNE HERE...
HELL THAT IT'S EASY FOR THEM TO GO BACK AND FORTH. IT'S A COMFORT, FOR ME AT LEAST.
"OH, IT WON'T GO BADLY!" "THIS IS THE BEST IDEA HE'S EVER HAD!"
SHUT...UP... AND...HELP... ME...
WHY DON'T YOU ASK CLINT $%@& BARTON TO HELP, SINCE THIS "FLAMING WINGS" BIT WAS ALL HIS IDEA?
BUCKY SAID MY CONVICTIONS HAD TO BE LOUDER, STRONGER.
OH, RIGHT, YOU CAN'T, BECAUSE I'M THE ONE THAT HAD TO WEAR THIS--
COME ON, GUYS. ONCE WE'VE GOT THESE THREE SITUATED, WE'VE GOT WORK TO DO.
BUT THEIR BELIEF IN ME HELPS DRIVE BACK THE DARKNESS JUST AS MUCH.
THERE'S A WAR GOING ON, AND IT NEEDS GOOD PEOPLE ON THE FRONT LINE.

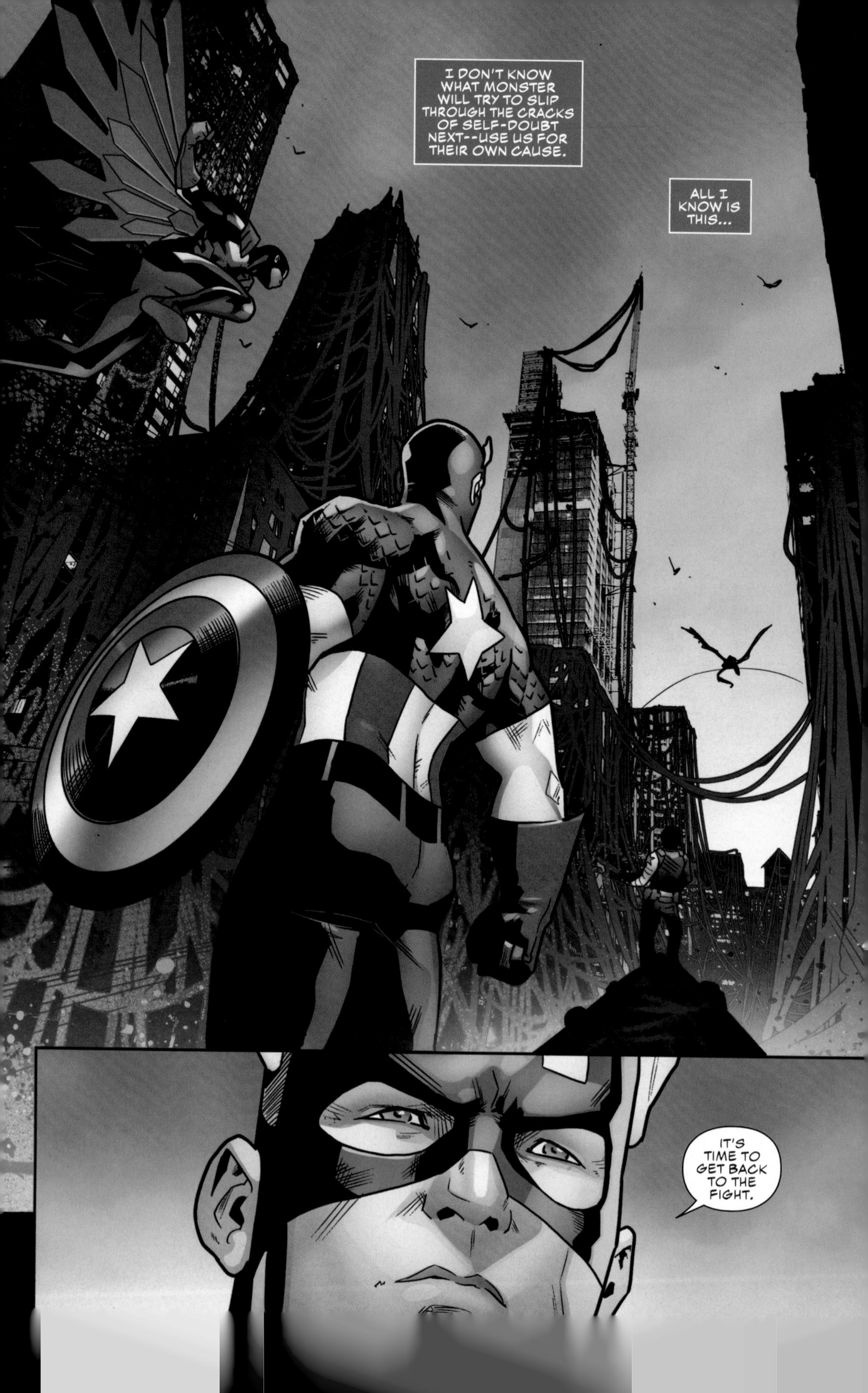
I DON'T KNOW WHAT MONSTER WILL TRY TO SLIP THROUGH THE CRACKS OF SELF-DOUBT NEXT--USE US FOR THEIR OWN CAUSE.
ALL I KNOW IS THIS...
IT'S TIME TO GET BACK TO THE FIGHT.

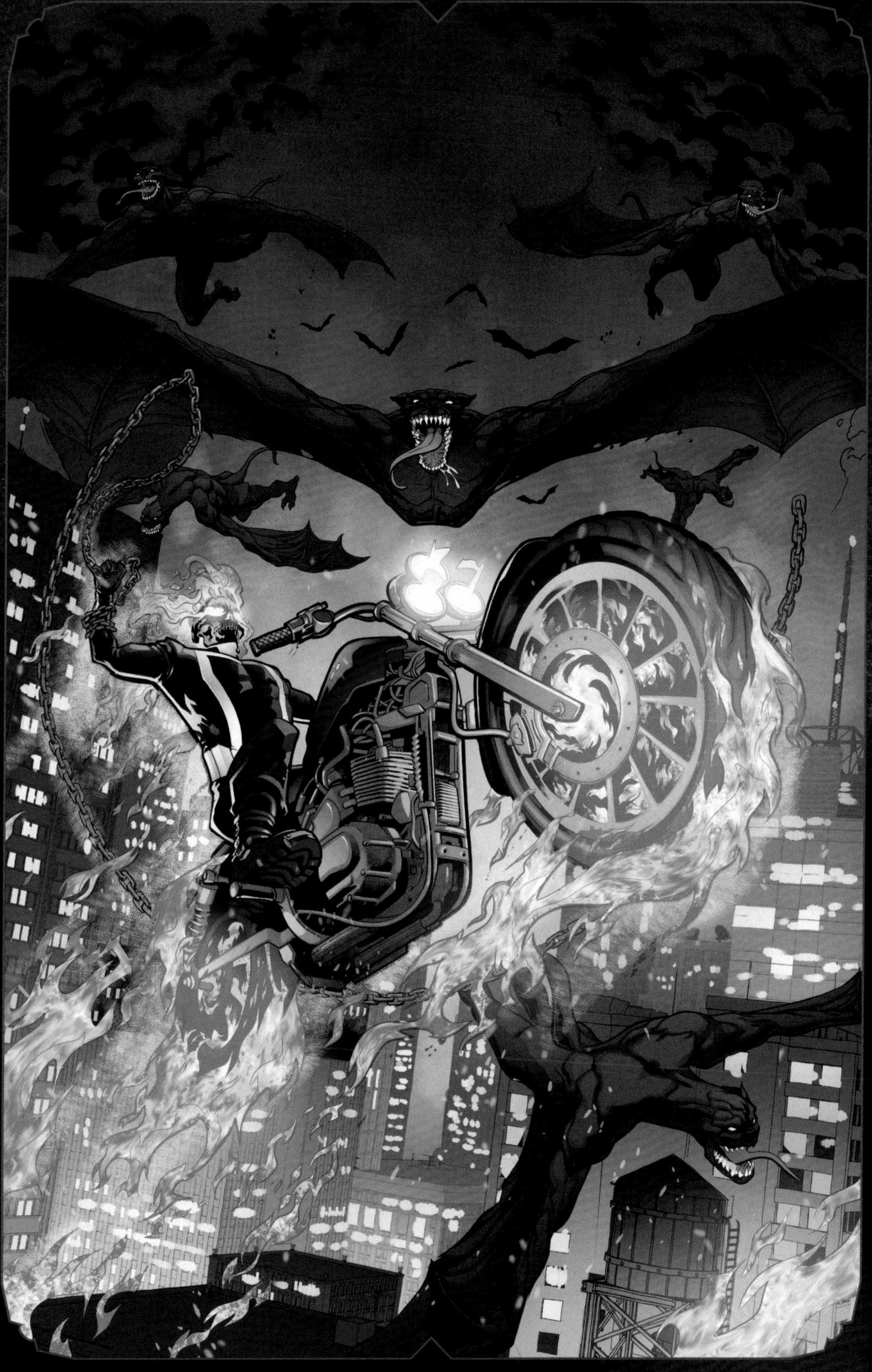

GHOST RIDER

Recently, JOHNNY BLAZE (A.K.A. GHOST RIDER
and THE CURRENT RULER OF HELL) has not been himself.
Under his rule, demons have escaped hell and wreaked
havoc on Earth. Johnny's been rounding up all the demonic
jail breakers, but it seems every demon he sends back to
hell leaves behind a piece of evil within him. That's a fight
no one could withstand unscathed, but thanks to Danny
Ketch and DOCTOR STRANGE, the demonic hold over
Johnny has finally been broken.

Now Johnny's ready to continue his mission: save
humanity from hell on Earth! But what if hell has already
arrived? Enter KNULL, the symbiote god who has brought
his black-goo army to take over the world...

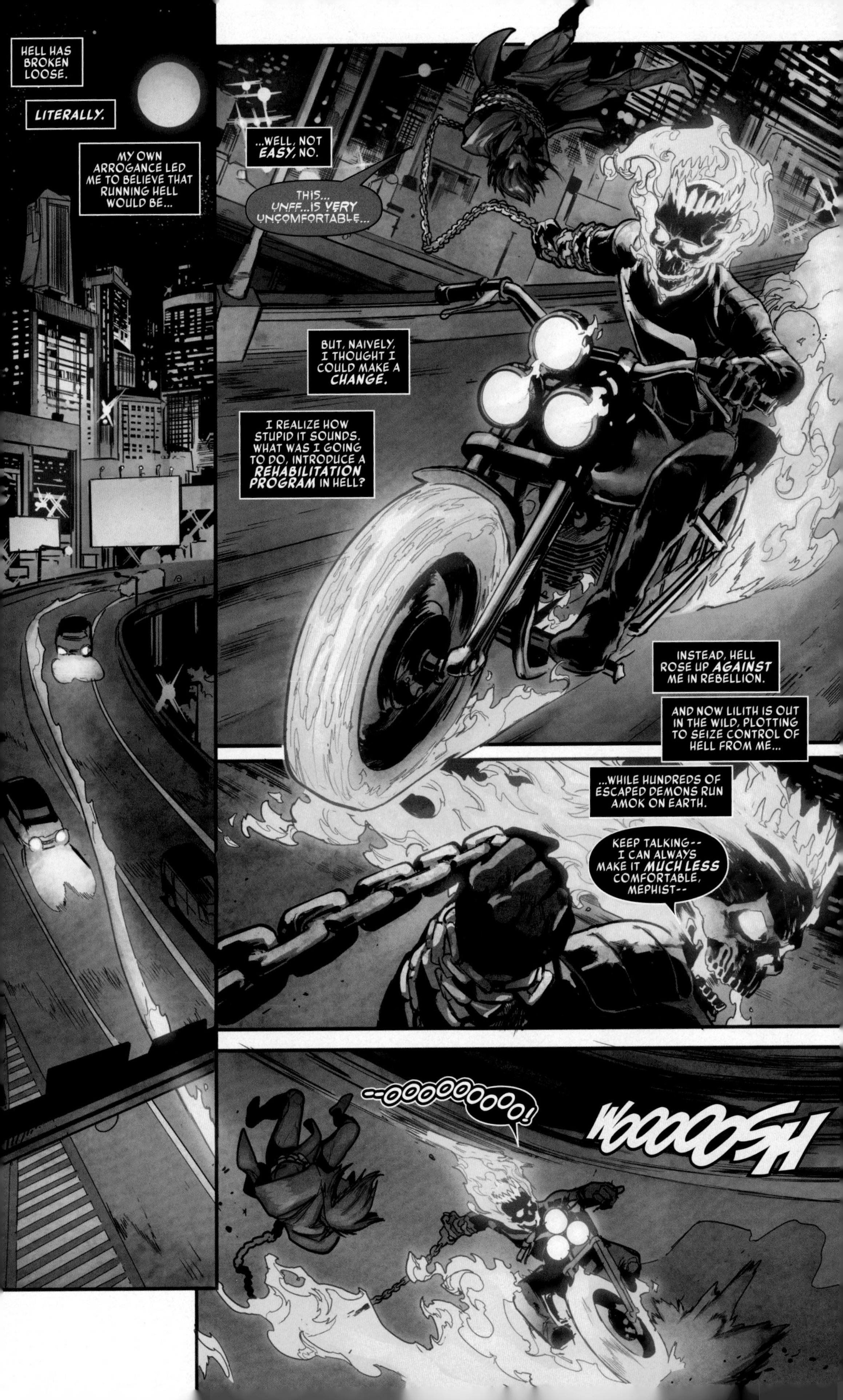
HELL HAS BROKEN LOOSE.
LITERALLY.
MY OWN ARROGANCE LED ME TO BELIEVE THAT RUNNING HELL WOULD BE...
...WELL, NOT EASY, NO.
THIS... UNFF...IS VERY UNCOMFORTABLE...
BUT, NAIVELY, I THOUGHT I COULD MAKE A CHANGE.
I REALIZE HOW STUPID IT SOUNDS. WHAT WAS I GOING TO DO, INTRODUCE A REHABILITATION PROGRAM IN HELL?
INSTEAD, HELL ROSE UP AGAINST ME IN REBELLION.
AND NOW LILITH IS OUT IN THE WILD, PLOTTING TO SEIZE CONTROL OF HELL FROM ME...
...WHILE HUNDREDS OF ESCAPED DEMONS RUN AMOK ON EARTH.
KEEP TALKING-- I CAN ALWAYS MAKE IT MUCH LESS COMFORTABLE, MEPHIST--
--OOOOOOOOO!
WOOOOSH

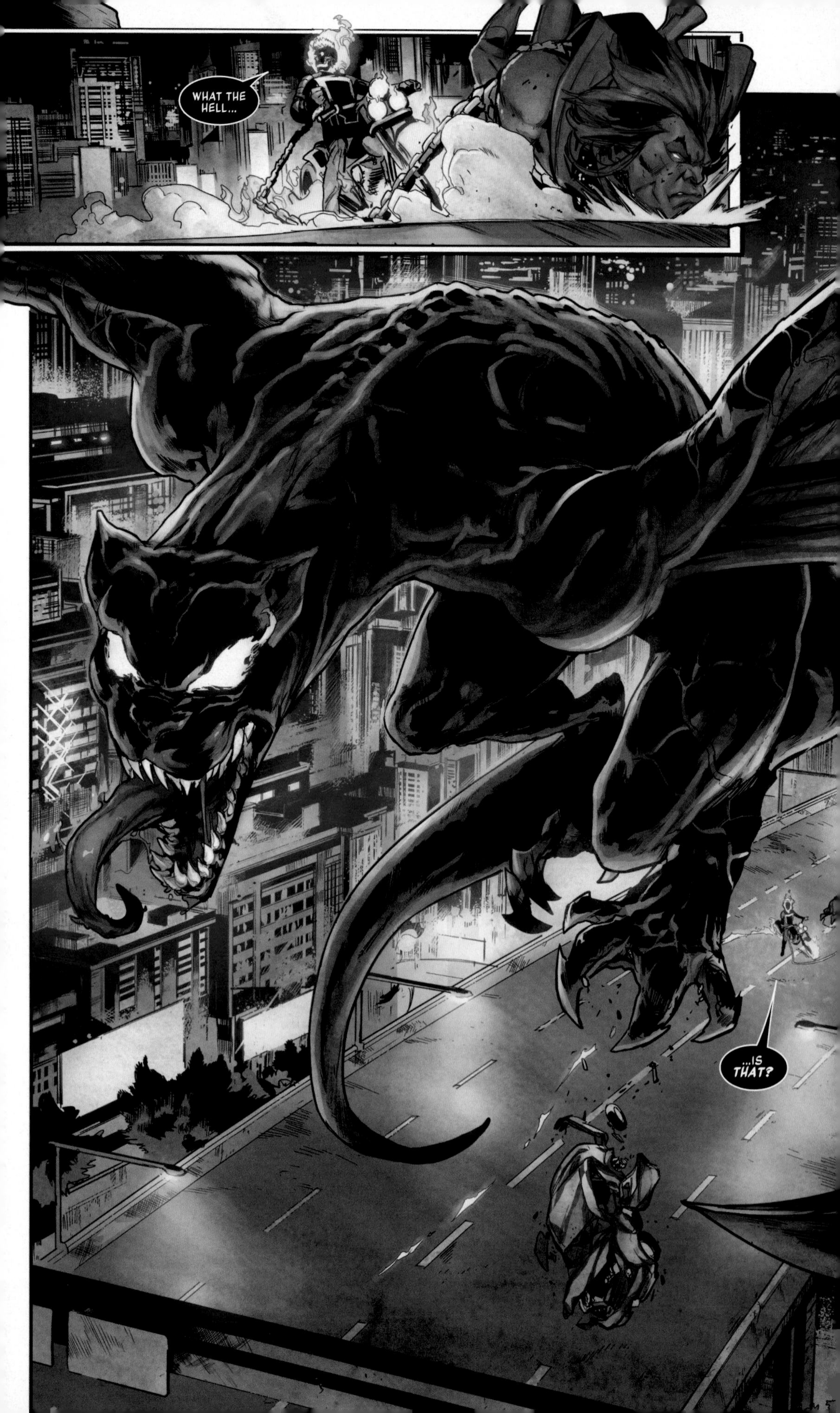
WHAT THE HELL...
...IS THAT?

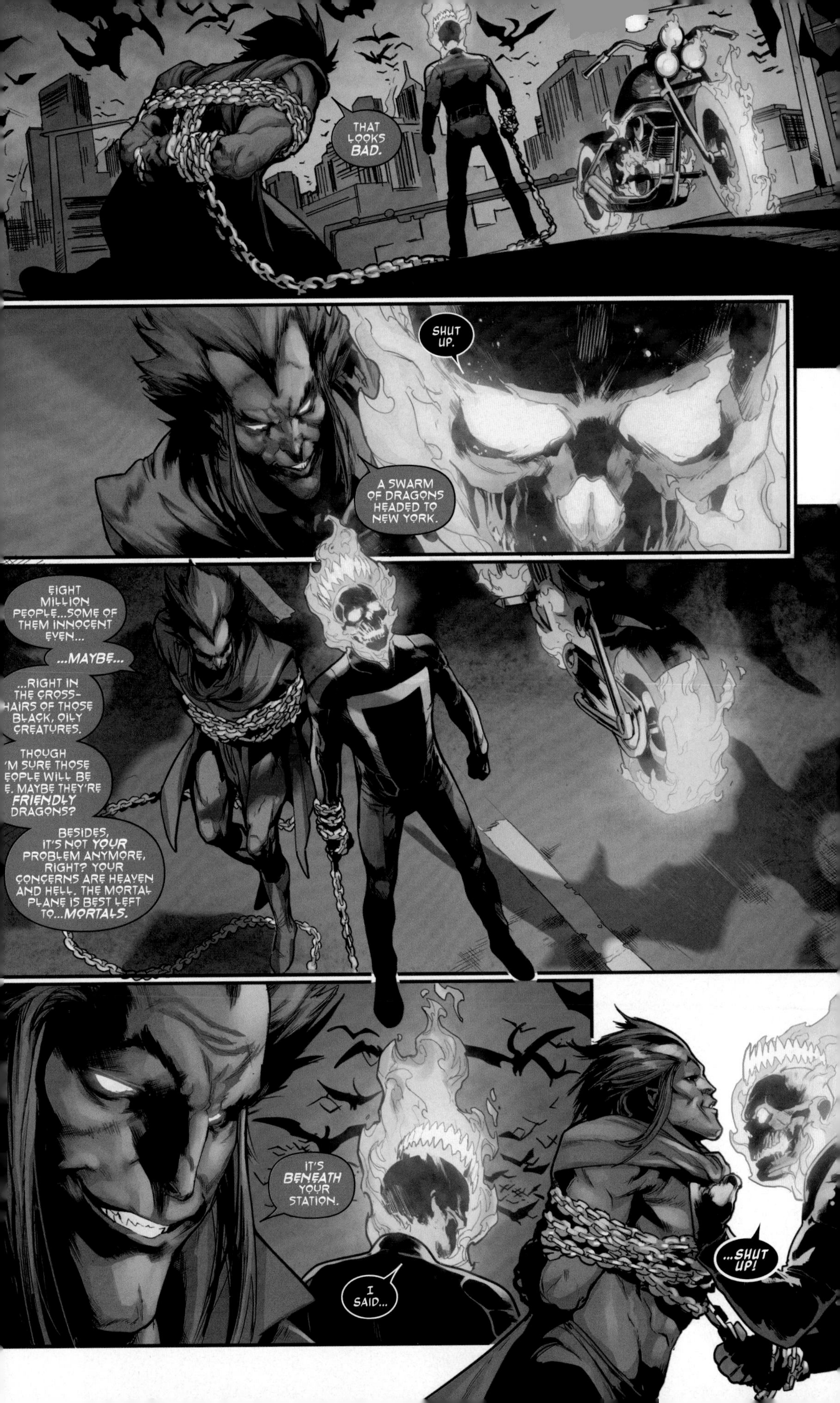

THAT LOOKS *BAD.*
SHUT UP.
A SWARM OF DRAGONS HEADED TO NEW YORK.
EIGHT MILLION PEOPLE...SOME OF THEM INNOCENT EVEN...
...*MAYBE*...
...RIGHT IN THE CROSS-HAIRS OF THOSE BLACK, OILY CREATURES.
THOUGH 'M SURE THOSE EOPLE WILL BE E. MAYBE THEY'RE *FRIENDLY* DRAGONS?
BESIDES, IT'S NOT *YOUR* PROBLEM ANYMORE, RIGHT? YOUR CONCERNS ARE HEAVEN AND HELL. THE MORTAL PLANE IS BEST LEFT TO...*MORTALS.*
IT'S *BENEATH* YOUR STATION.
I SAID...
...*SHUT UP!*

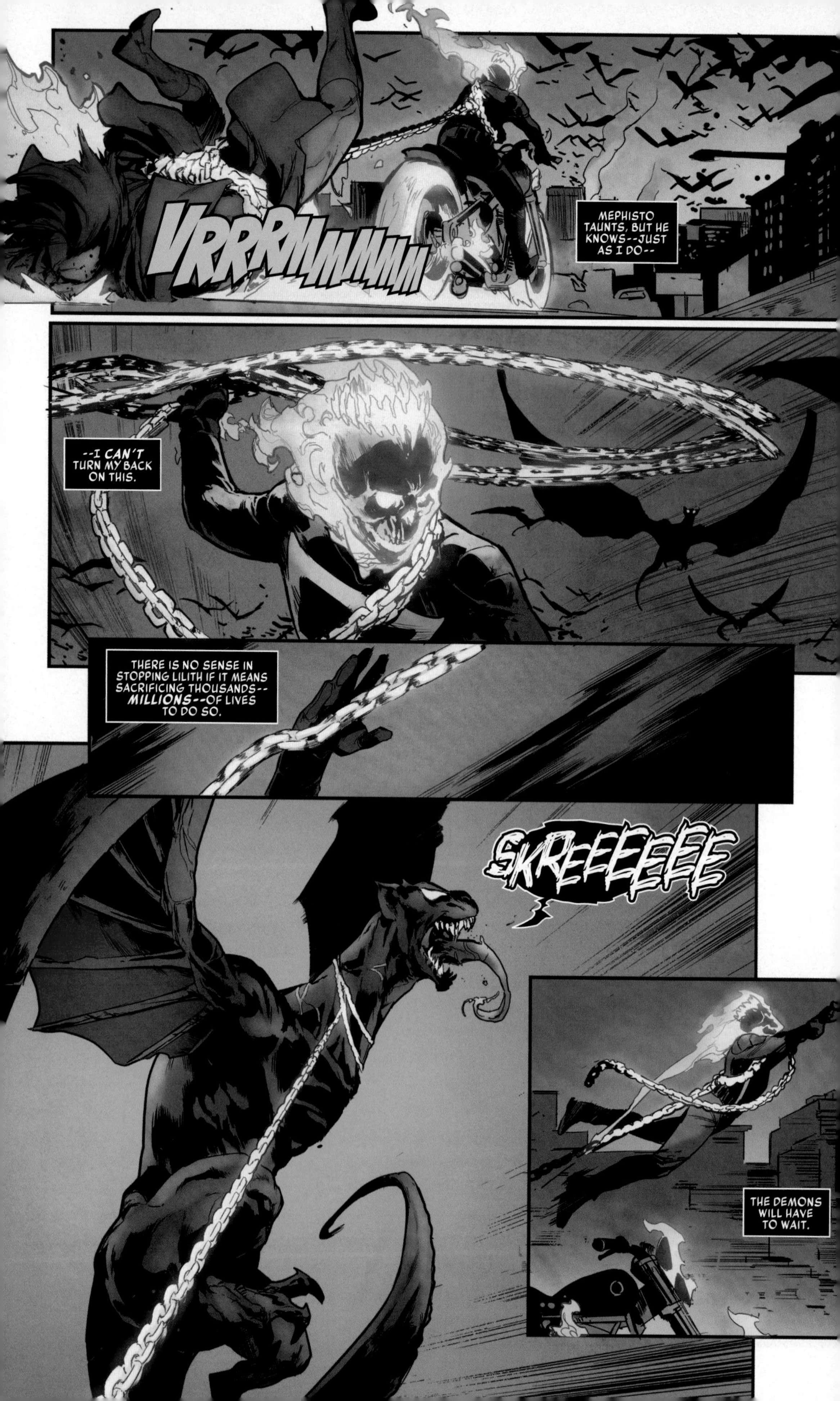
VRRRMMMMMM
MEPHISTO TAUNTS, BUT HE KNOWS--JUST AS I DO--
--I CAN'T TURN MY BACK ON THIS.
THERE IS NO SENSE IN STOPPING LILITH IF IT MEANS SACRIFICING THOUSANDS--MILLIONS--OF LIVES TO DO SO.
SKREEEEEEE
THE DEMONS WILL HAVE TO WAIT.

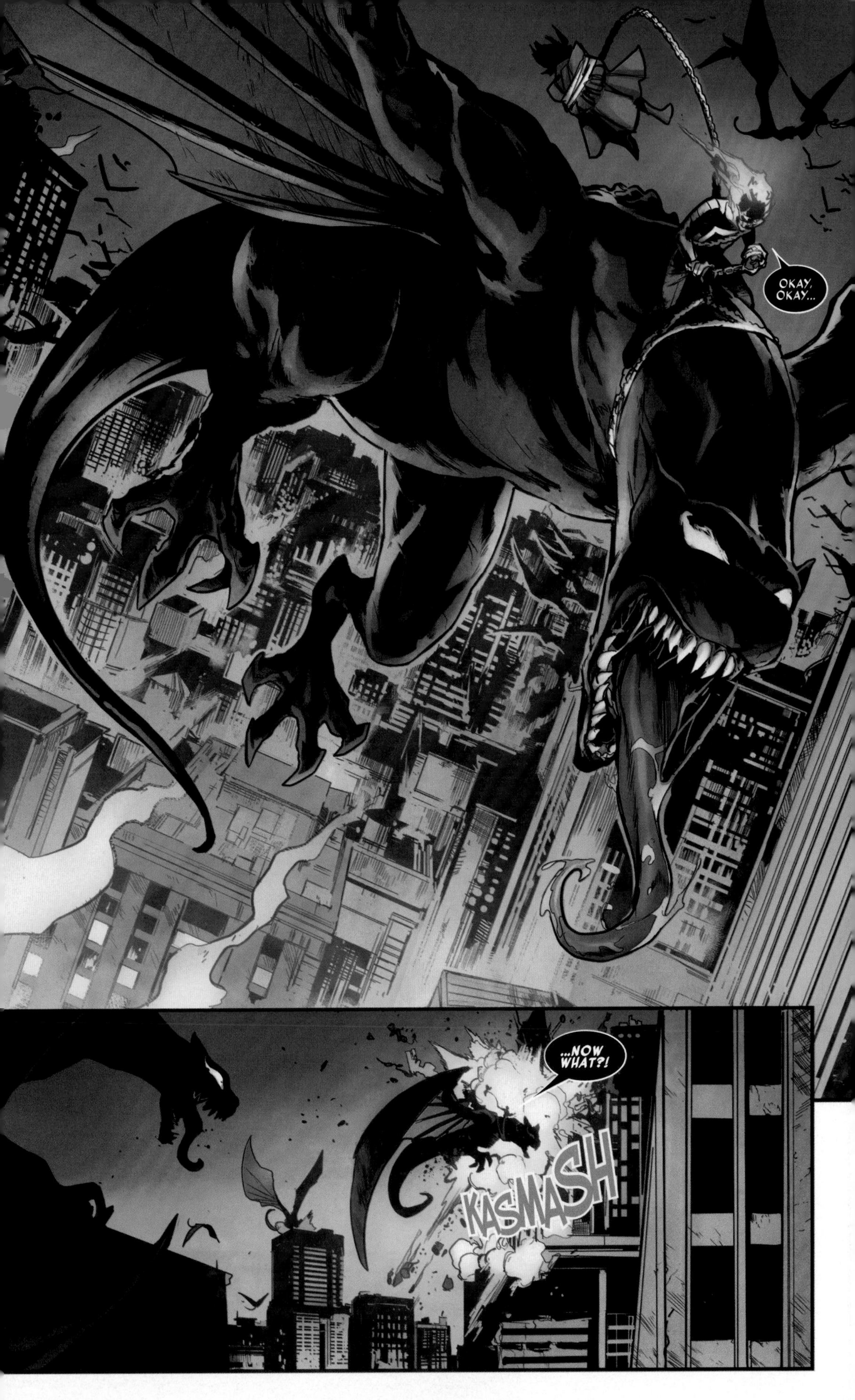
OKAY, OKAY...
...NOW WHAT?!
KASMASH

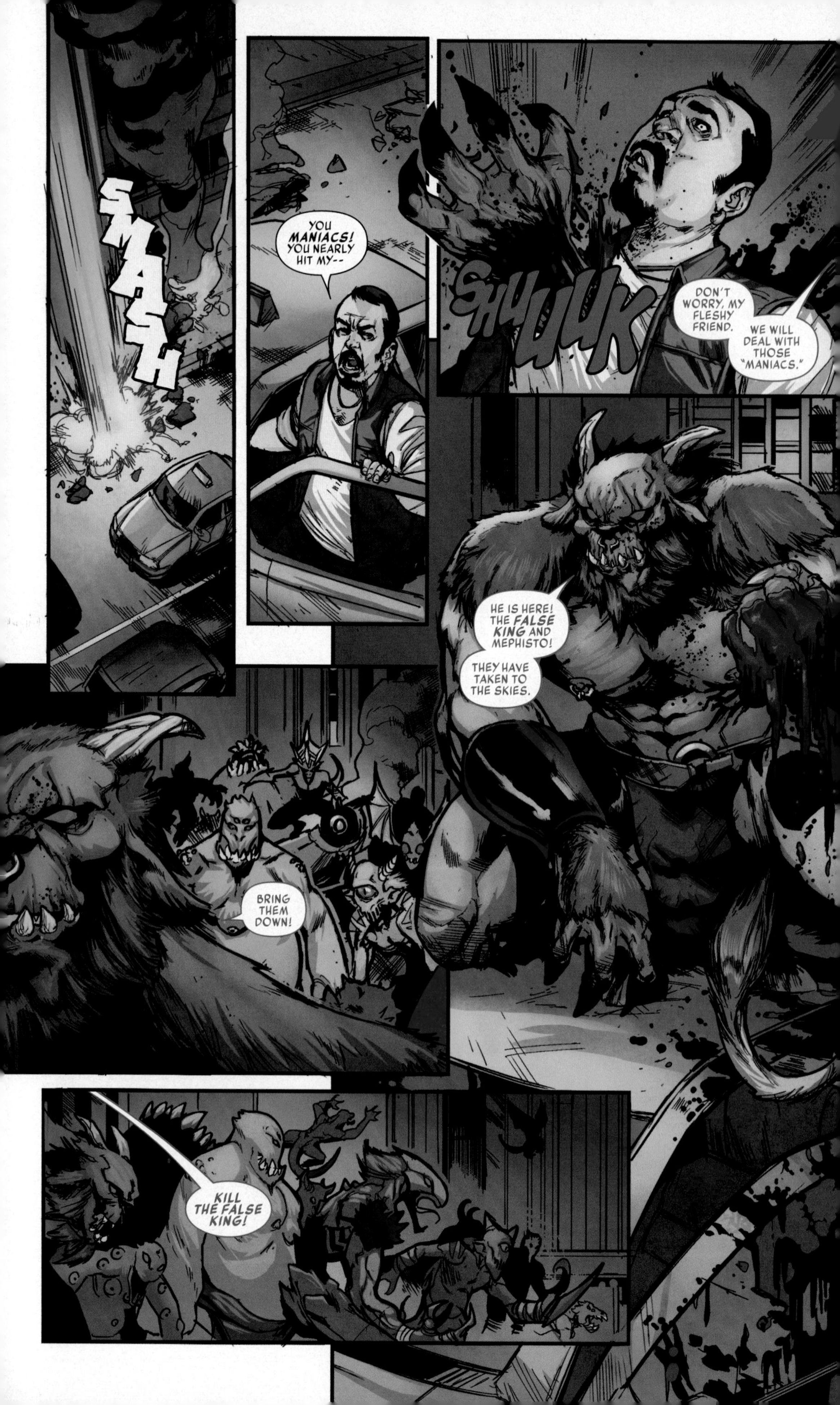
SMASH
YOU MANIACS! YOU NEARLY HIT MY--
SHUUUK
DON'T WORRY, MY FLESHY FRIEND.
WE WILL DEAL WITH THOSE "MANIACS."
HE IS HERE! THE FALSE KING AND MEPHISTO!
THEY HAVE TAKEN TO THE SKIES.
BRING THEM DOWN!
KILL THE FALSE KING!

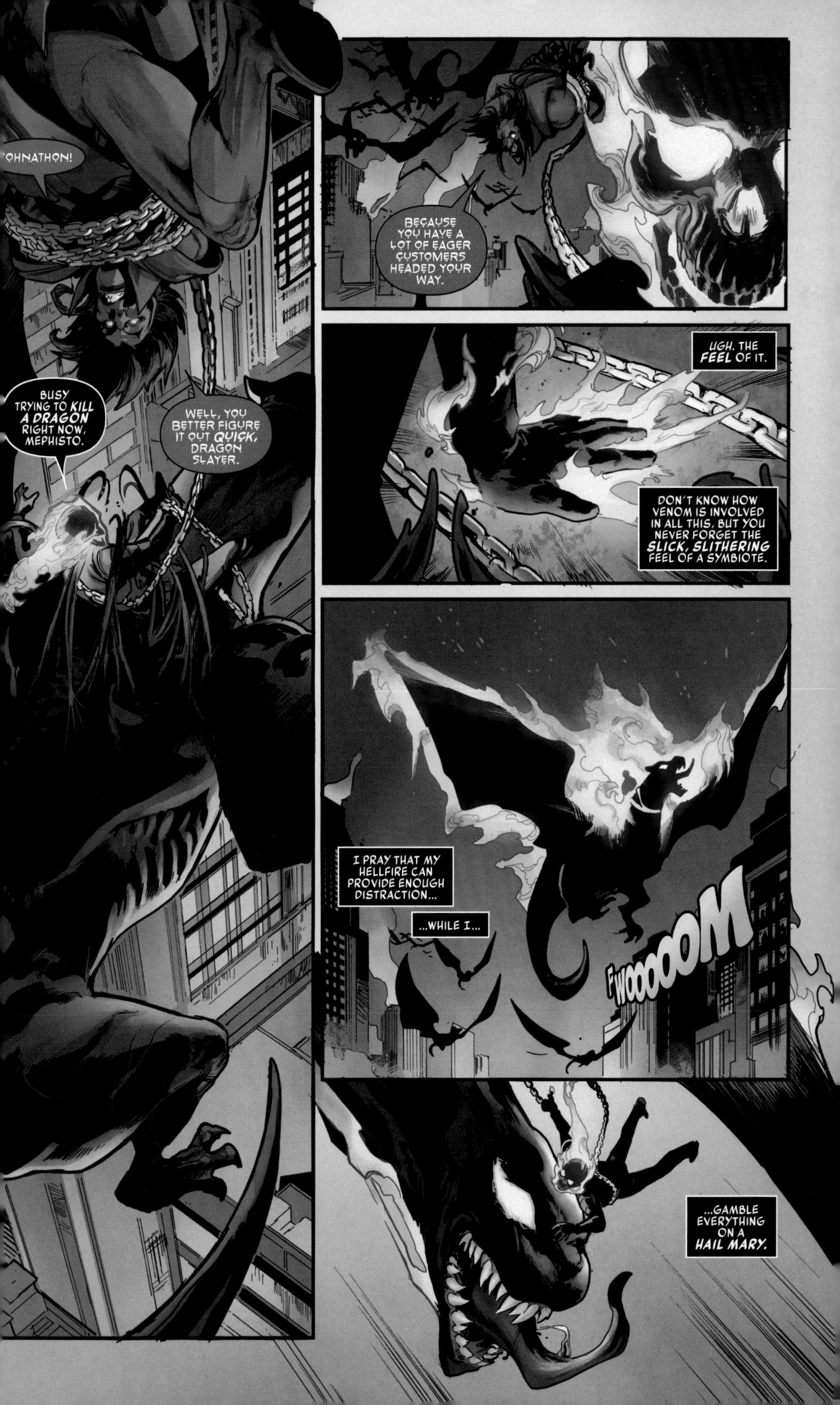

OHNATHON!
BECAUSE YOU HAVE A LOT OF EAGER CUSTOMERS HEADED YOUR WAY.
BUSY TRYING TO KILL A DRAGON RIGHT NOW, MEPHISTO.
WELL, YOU BETTER FIGURE IT OUT QUICK, DRAGON SLAYER.
UGH. THE FEEL OF IT.
DON'T KNOW HOW VENOM IS INVOLVED IN ALL THIS, BUT YOU NEVER FORGET THE SLICK, SLITHERING FEEL OF A SYMBIOTE.
I PRAY THAT MY HELLFIRE CAN PROVIDE ENOUGH DISTRACTION...
...WHILE I...
FWOOOOOM
...GAMBLE EVERYTHING ON A HAIL MARY.

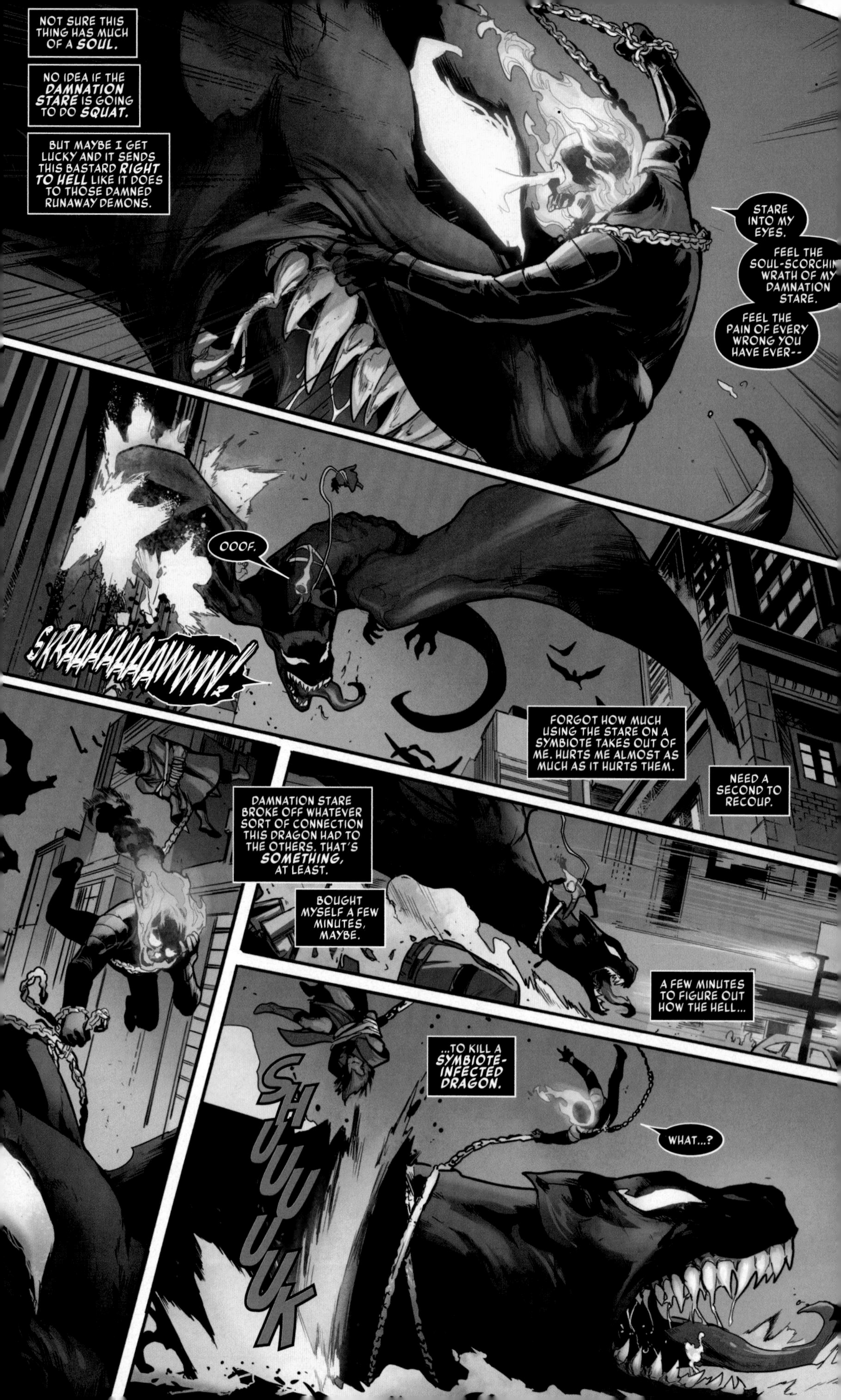
NOT SURE THIS THING HAS MUCH OF A **SOUL.**
NO IDEA IF THE ***DAMNATION STARE*** IS GOING TO DO ***SQUAT.***
BUT MAYBE I GET LUCKY AND IT SENDS THIS BASTARD ***RIGHT TO HELL*** LIKE IT DOES TO THOSE DAMNED RUNAWAY DEMONS.
STARE INTO MY EYES.
FEEL THE SOUL-SCORCHIN WRATH OF MY DAMNATION STARE.
FEEL THE PAIN OF EVERY WRONG YOU HAVE EVER--
OOOF.
SKRAAAAAAAWWW!
FORGOT HOW MUCH USING THE STARE ON A SYMBIOTE TAKES OUT OF ME. HURTS ME ALMOST AS MUCH AS IT HURTS THEM.
NEED A SECOND TO RECOUP.
DAMNATION STARE BROKE OFF WHATEVER SORT OF CONNECTION THIS DRAGON HAD TO THE OTHERS. THAT'S ***SOMETHING,*** AT LEAST.
BOUGHT MYSELF A FEW MINUTES, MAYBE.
A FEW MINUTES TO FIGURE OUT HOW THE HELL...
...TO KILL A ***SYMBIOTE-INFECTED DRAGON.***
SHUUUUUK
WHAT...?

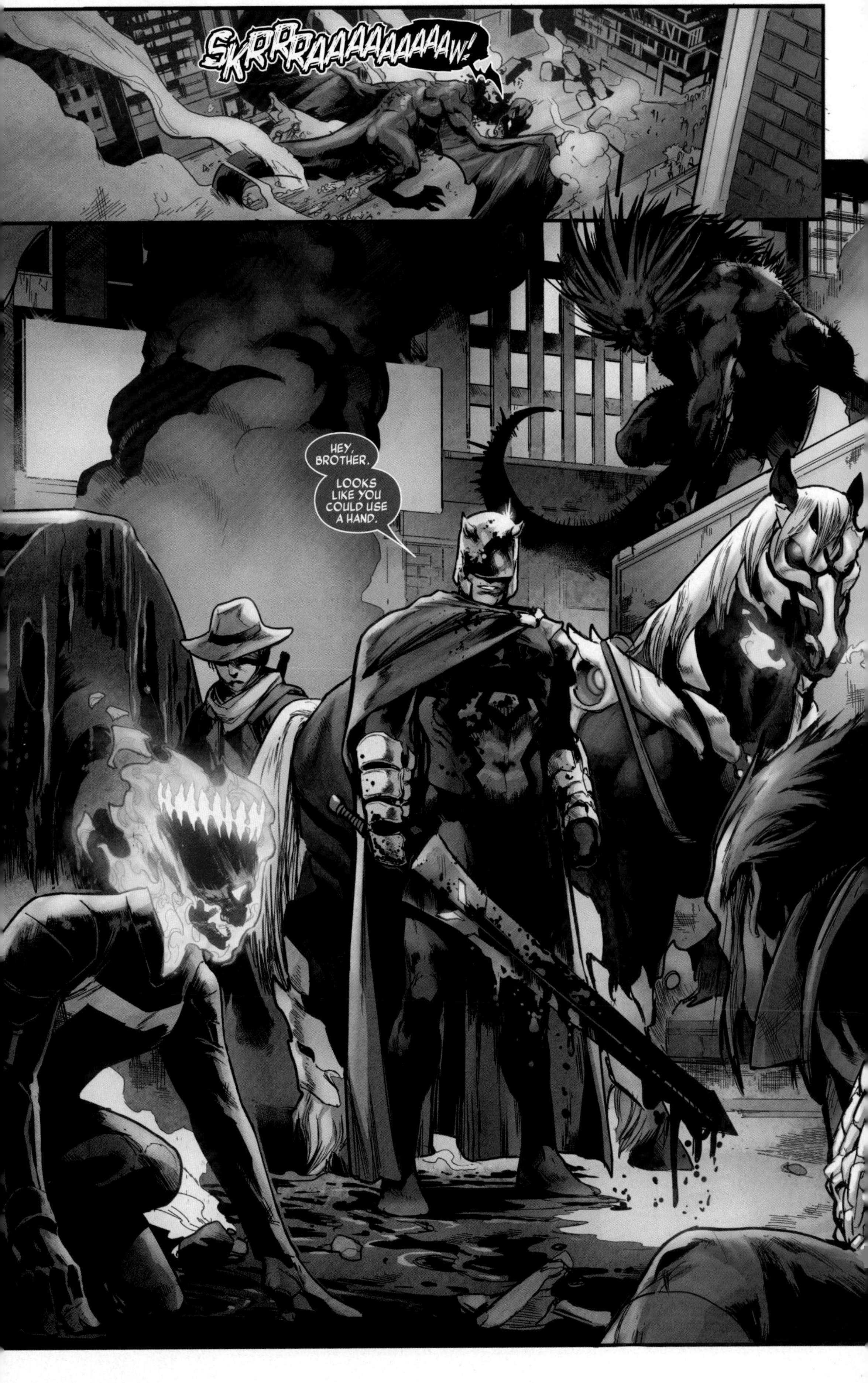
SKRRRAAAAAAAAAW!
HEY, BROTHER.
LOOKS LIKE YOU COULD USE A HAND.

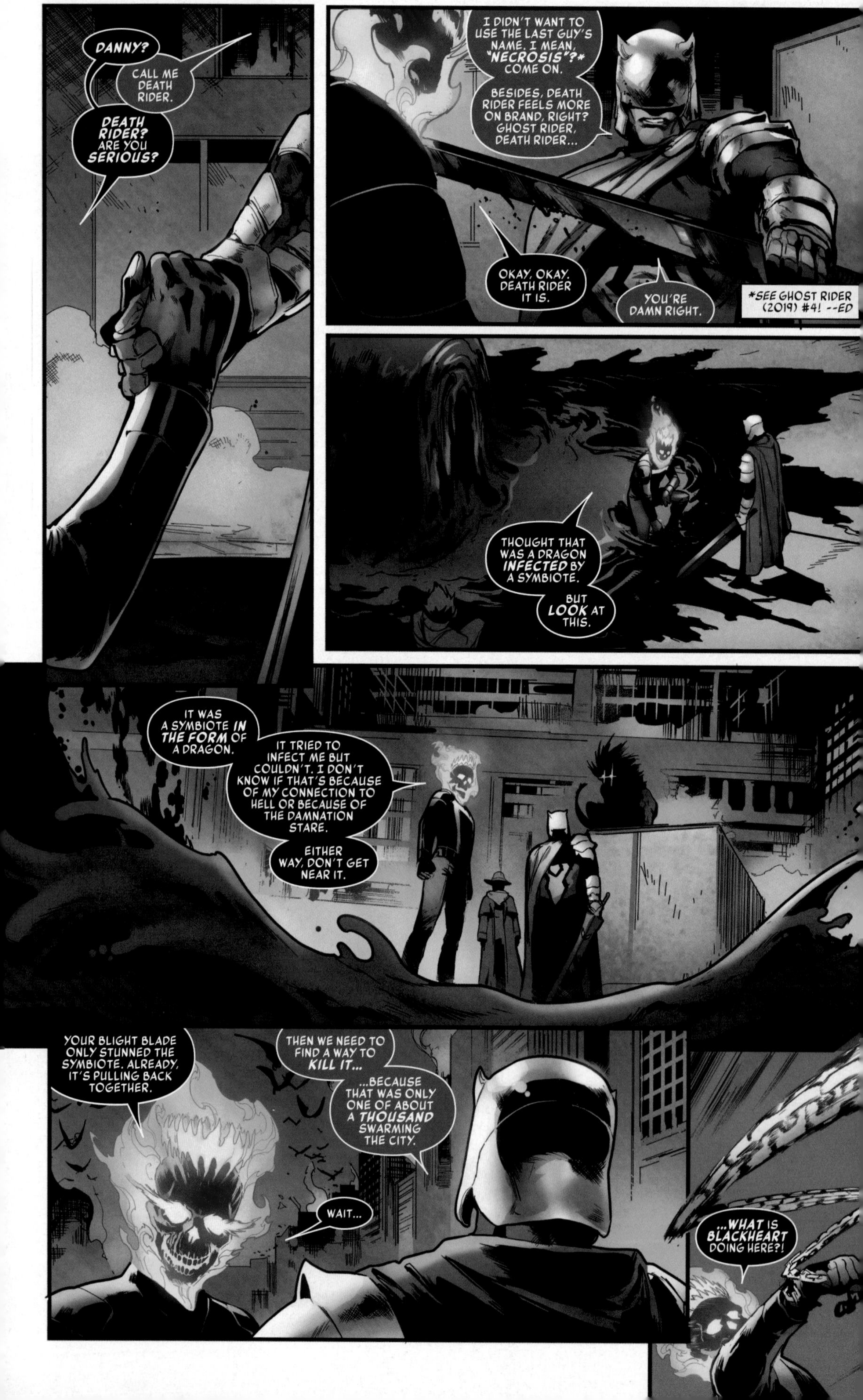
DANNY?
CALL ME DEATH RIDER.
DEATH RIDER? ARE YOU SERIOUS?
I DIDN'T WANT TO USE THE LAST GUY'S NAME. I MEAN, "NECROSIS"?* COME ON.
BESIDES, DEATH RIDER FEELS MORE ON BRAND, RIGHT? GHOST RIDER, DEATH RIDER...
OKAY, OKAY. DEATH RIDER IT IS.
YOU'RE DAMN RIGHT.
*SEE GHOST RIDER (2019) #4! --ED
THOUGHT THAT WAS A DRAGON INFECTED BY A SYMBIOTE.
BUT LOOK AT THIS.
IT WAS A SYMBIOTE IN THE FORM OF A DRAGON.
IT TRIED TO INFECT ME BUT COULDN'T. I DON'T KNOW IF THAT'S BECAUSE OF MY CONNECTION TO HELL OR BECAUSE OF THE DAMNATION STARE.
EITHER WAY, DON'T GET NEAR IT.
YOUR BLIGHT BLADE ONLY STUNNED THE SYMBIOTE. ALREADY, IT'S PULLING BACK TOGETHER.
THEN WE NEED TO FIND A WAY TO KILL IT...
...BECAUSE THAT WAS ONLY ONE OF ABOUT A THOUSAND SWARMING THE CITY.
WAIT...
...WHAT IS BLACKHEART DOING HERE?!

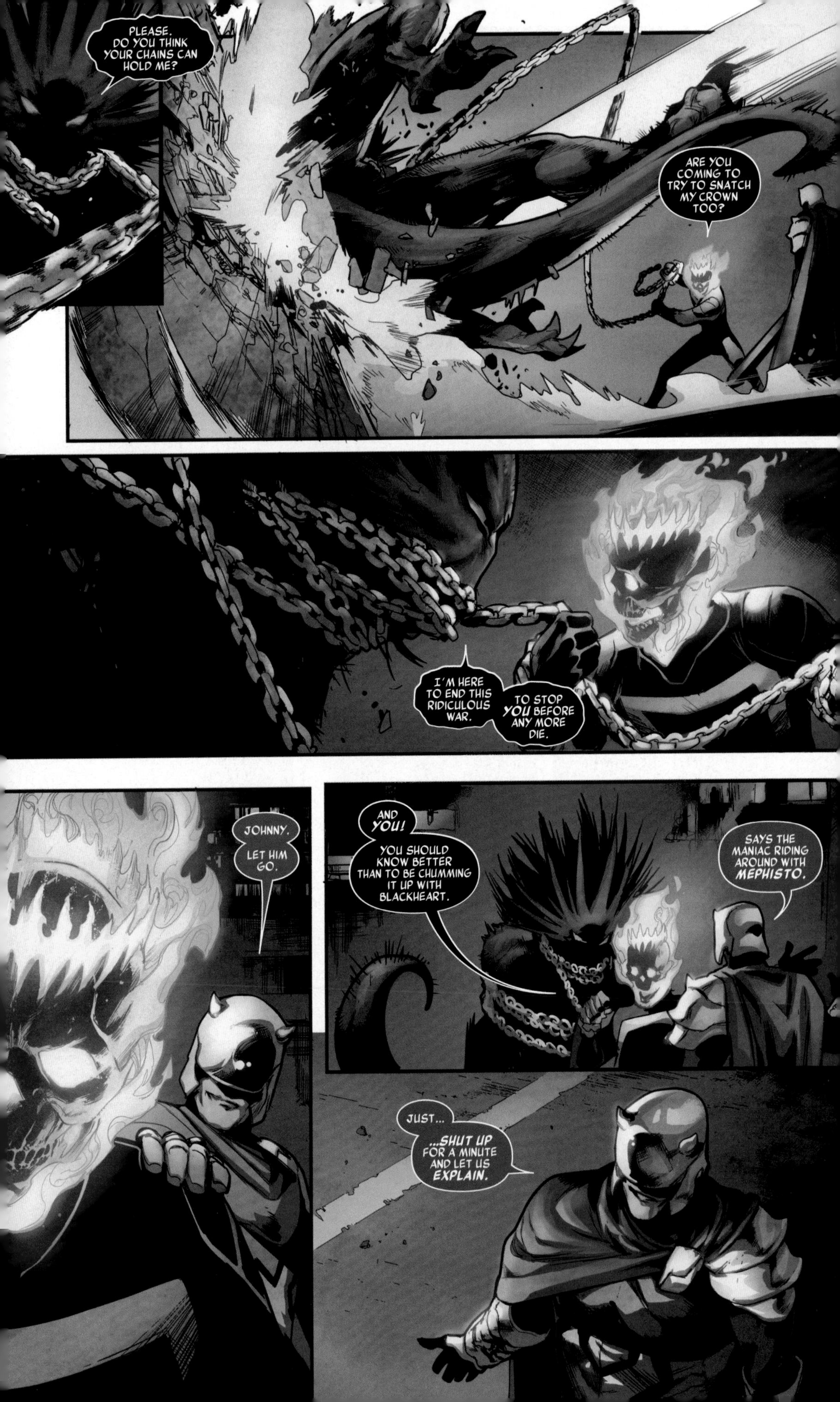
PLEASE. DO YOU THINK YOUR CHAINS CAN HOLD ME?
ARE YOU COMING TO TRY TO SNATCH MY CROWN TOO?
I'M HERE TO END THIS RIDICULOUS WAR.
TO STOP YOU BEFORE ANY MORE DIE.
JOHNNY.
LET HIM GO.
AND YOU!
YOU SHOULD KNOW BETTER THAN TO BE CHUMMING IT UP WITH BLACKHEART.
SAYS THE MANIAC RIDING AROUND WITH MEPHISTO.
JUST...
...SHUT UP FOR A MINUTE AND LET US EXPLAIN.

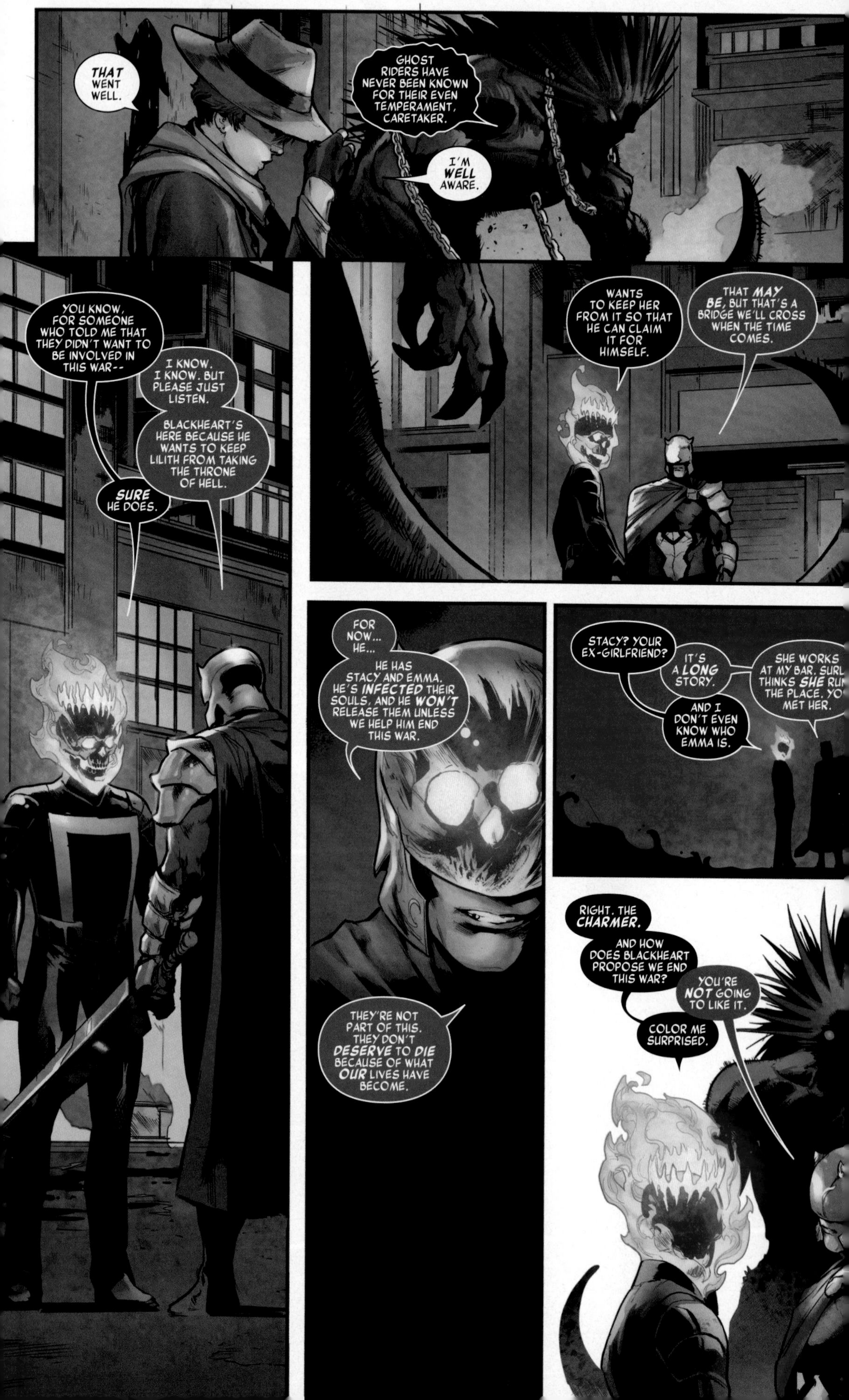

THAT WENT WELL.
GHOST RIDERS HAVE NEVER BEEN KNOWN FOR THEIR EVEN TEMPERAMENT, CARETAKER.
I'M WELL AWARE.
YOU KNOW, FOR SOMEONE WHO TOLD ME THAT THEY DIDN'T WANT TO BE INVOLVED IN THIS WAR--
I KNOW, I KNOW. BUT PLEASE JUST LISTEN.
BLACKHEART'S HERE BECAUSE HE WANTS TO KEEP LILITH FROM TAKING THE THRONE OF HELL.
SURE HE DOES.
WANTS TO KEEP HER FROM IT SO THAT HE CAN CLAIM IT FOR HIMSELF.
THAT MAY BE, BUT THAT'S A BRIDGE WE'LL CROSS WHEN THE TIME COMES.
FOR NOW... HE...
HE HAS STACY AND EMMA. HE'S INFECTED THEIR SOULS, AND HE WON'T RELEASE THEM UNLESS WE HELP HIM END THIS WAR.
THEY'RE NOT PART OF THIS. THEY DON'T DESERVE TO DIE BECAUSE OF WHAT OUR LIVES HAVE BECOME.
STACY? YOUR EX-GIRLFRIEND?
IT'S A LONG STORY.
AND I DON'T EVEN KNOW WHO EMMA IS.
SHE WORKS AT MY BAR. SURL THINKS SHE RU THE PLACE. YO MET HER.
RIGHT. THE CHARMER.
AND HOW DOES BLACKHEART PROPOSE WE END THIS WAR?
YOU'RE NOT GOING TO LIKE IT.
COLOR ME SURPRISED.

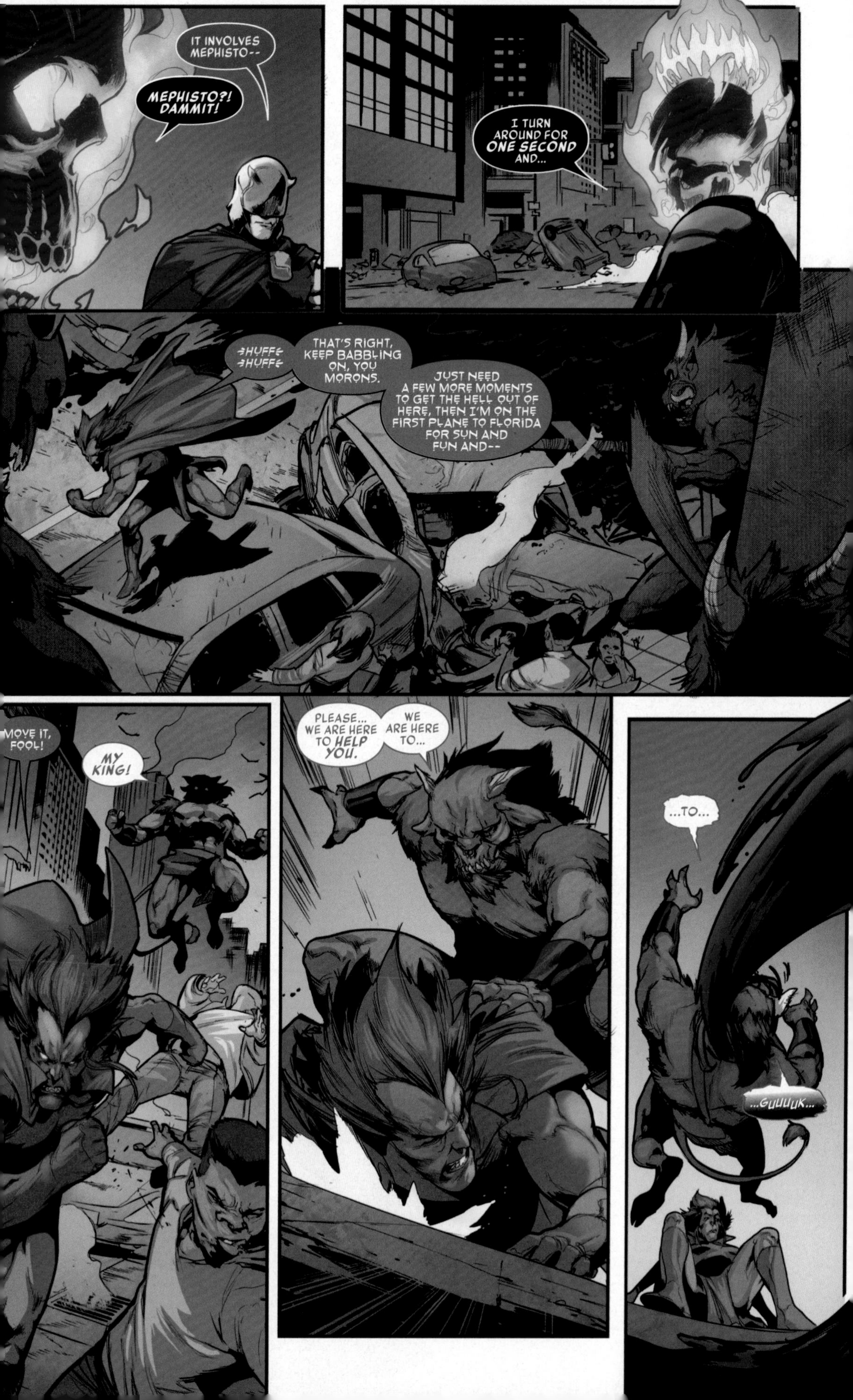
IT INVOLVES MEPHISTO--
MEPHISTO?! DAMMIT!
I TURN AROUND FOR ONE SECOND AND...
HUFF HUFF
THAT'S RIGHT, KEEP BABBLING ON, YOU MORONS.
JUST NEED A FEW MORE MOMENTS TO GET THE HELL OUT OF HERE, THEN I'M ON THE FIRST PLANE TO FLORIDA FOR SUN AND FUN AND--
MOVE IT, FOOL!
MY KING!
PLEASE... WE ARE HERE TO HELP YOU.
WE ARE HERE TO...
...TO...
...GUUUUK...

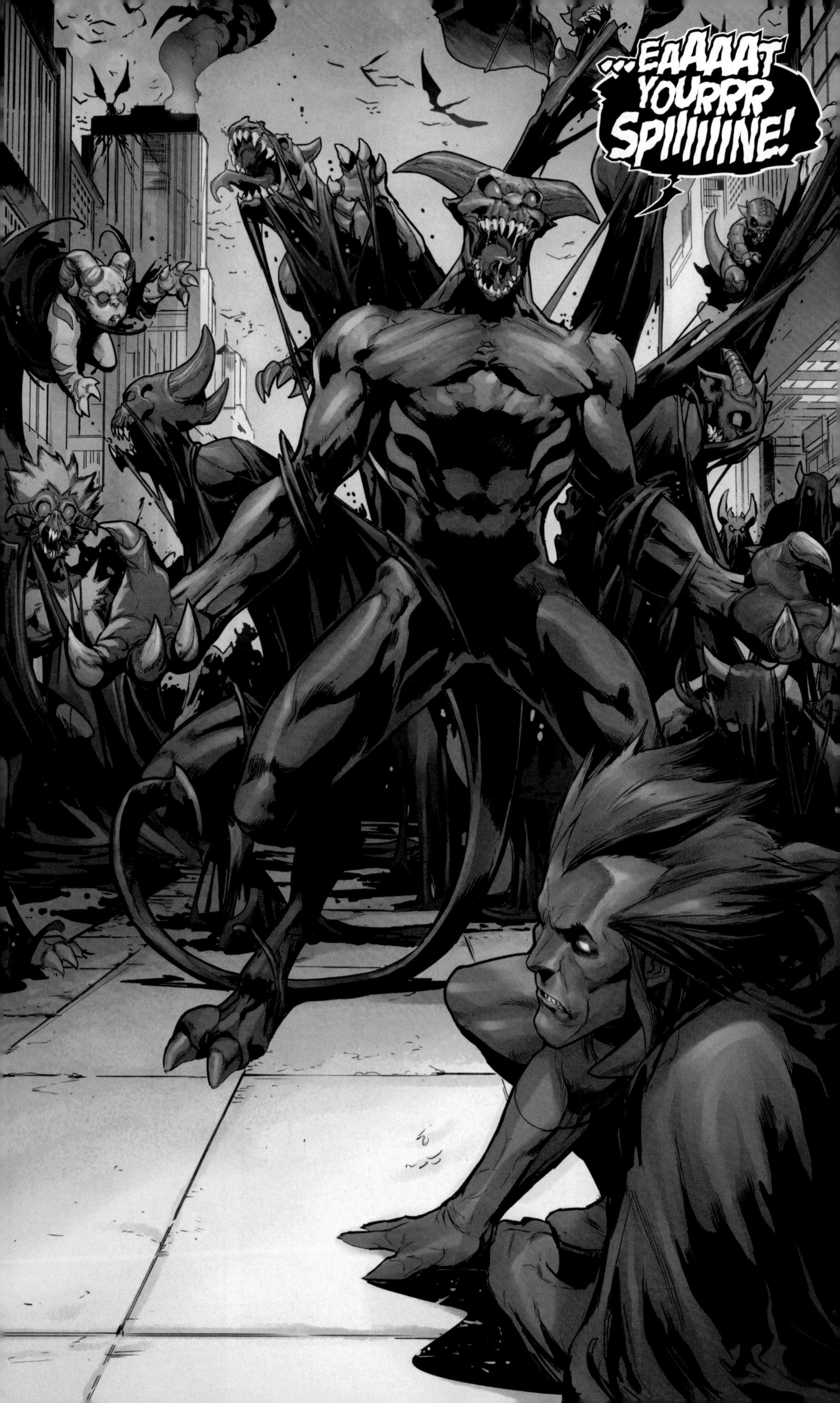
...EAAAAT YOURRR SPIIIIIINE!

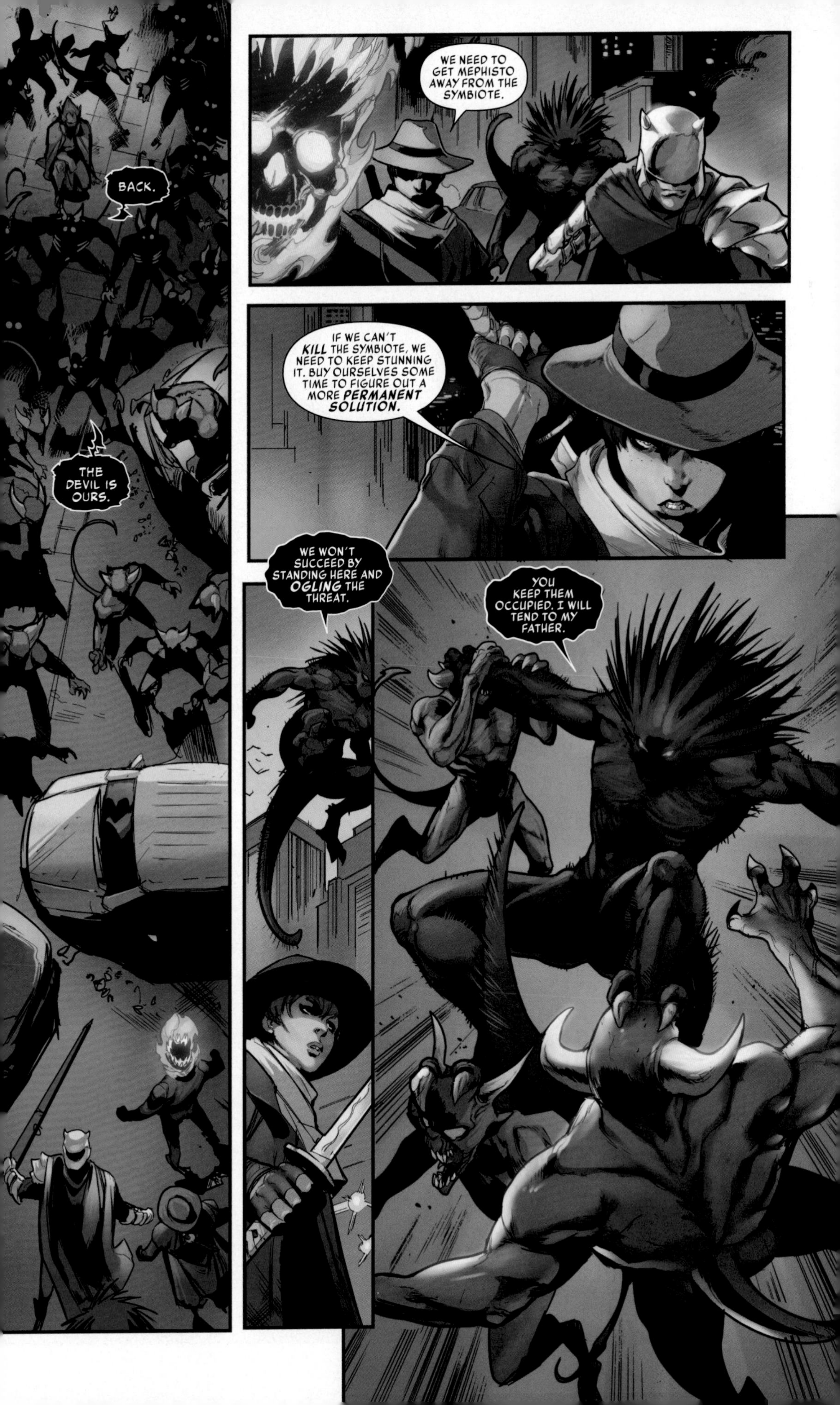
BACK.
THE DEVIL IS OURS.
WE NEED TO GET MEPHISTO AWAY FROM THE SYMBIOTE.
IF WE CAN'T KILL THE SYMBIOTE, WE NEED TO KEEP STUNNING IT. BUY OURSELVES SOME TIME TO FIGURE OUT A MORE PERMANENT SOLUTION.
WE WON'T SUCCEED BY STANDING HERE AND OGLING THE THREAT.
YOU KEEP THEM OCCUPIED. I WILL TEND TO MY FATHER.

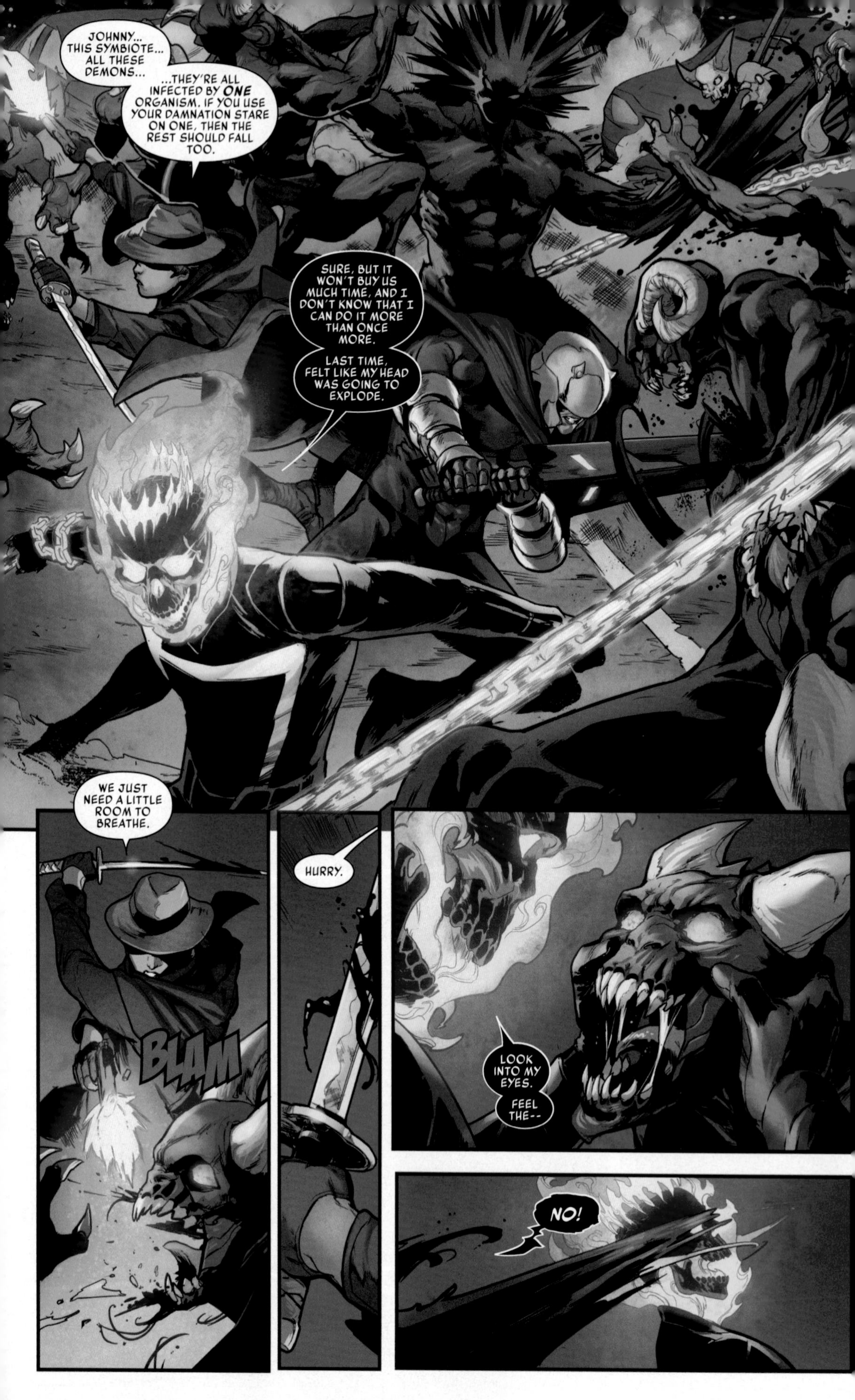
JOHNNY... THIS SYMBIOTE... ALL THESE DEMONS...
...THEY'RE ALL INFECTED BY ONE ORGANISM. IF YOU USE YOUR DAMNATION STARE ON ONE, THEN THE REST SHOULD FALL TOO.
SURE, BUT IT WON'T BUY US MUCH TIME, AND I DON'T KNOW THAT I CAN DO IT MORE THAN ONCE MORE.
LAST TIME, FELT LIKE MY HEAD WAS GOING TO EXPLODE.
WE JUST NEED A LITTLE ROOM TO BREATHE.
BLAM
HURRY.
LOOK INTO MY EYES.
FEEL THE--
NO!

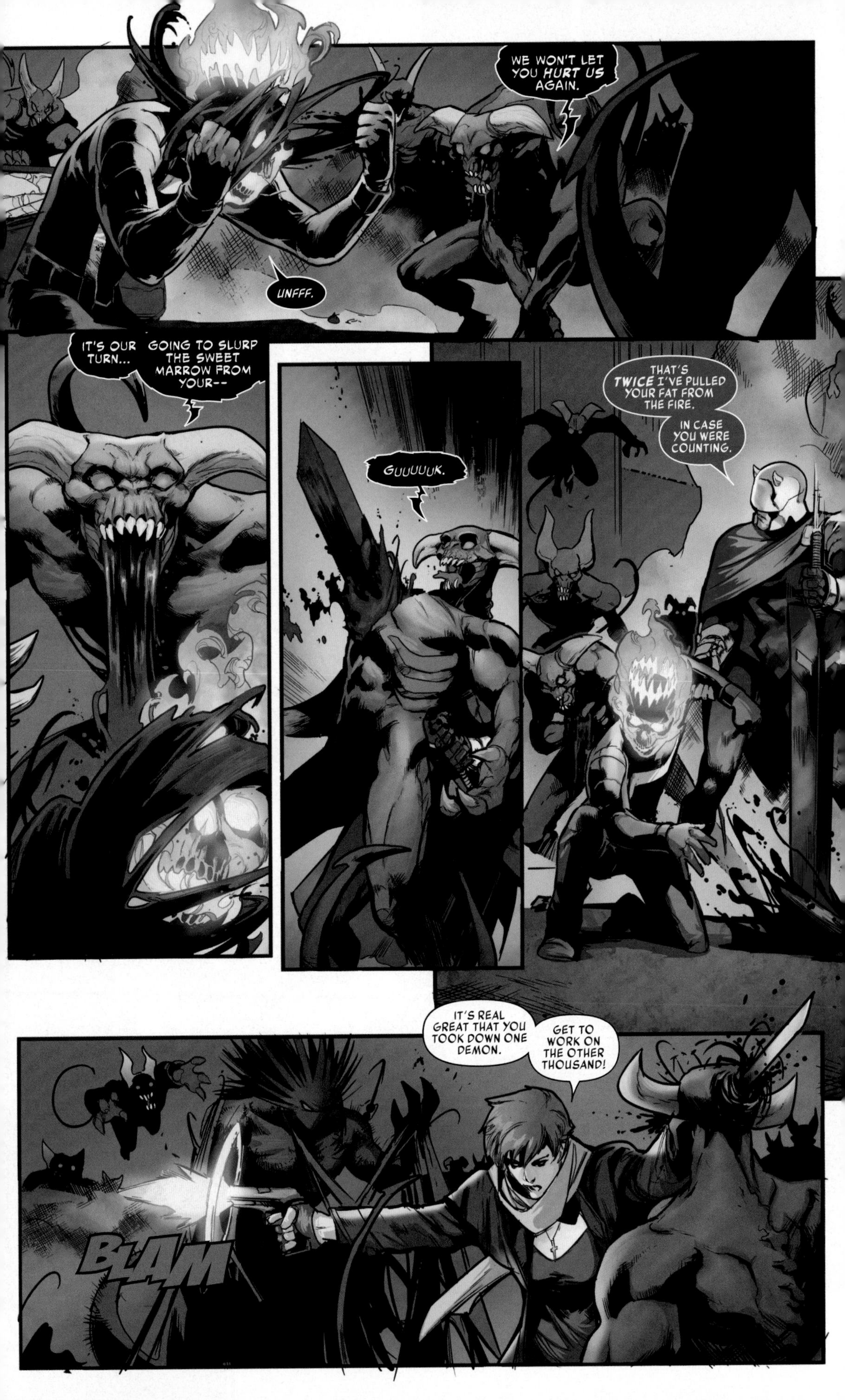
WE WON'T LET YOU HURT US AGAIN.
UNFFF.
IT'S OUR TURN...
GOING TO SLURP THE SWEET MARROW FROM YOUR--
GUUUUUK.
THAT'S TWICE I'VE PULLED YOUR FAT FROM THE FIRE.
IN CASE YOU WERE COUNTING.
IT'S REAL GREAT THAT YOU TOOK DOWN ONE DEMON.
GET TO WORK ON THE OTHER THOUSAND!
BLAM

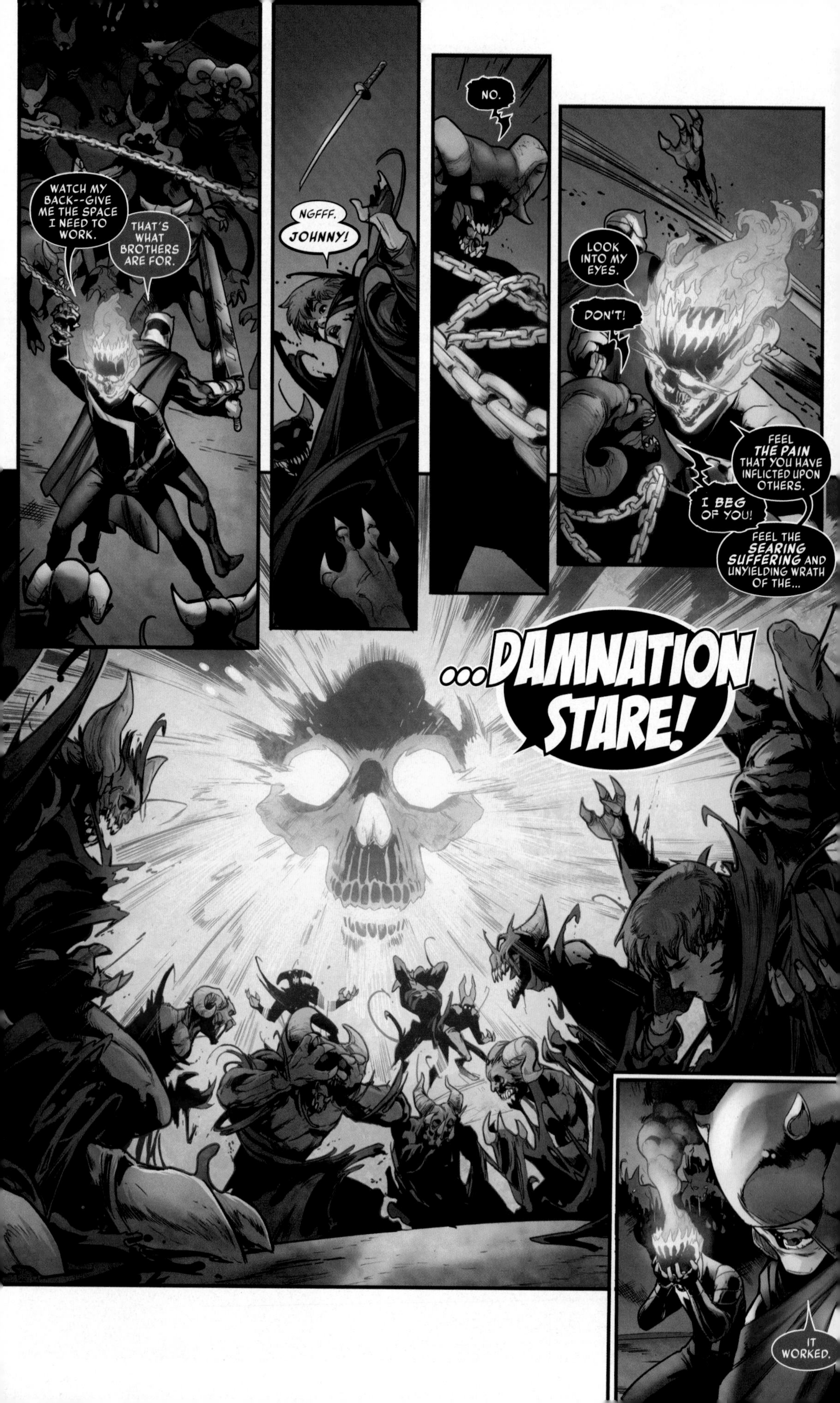

WATCH MY BACK--GIVE ME THE SPACE I NEED TO WORK.
THAT'S WHAT BROTHERS ARE FOR.
NGFFF.
JOHNNY!
NO.
LOOK INTO MY EYES.
DON'T!
FEEL THE PAIN THAT YOU HAVE INFLICTED UPON OTHERS.
I BEG OF YOU!
FEEL THE SEARING SUFFERING AND UNYIELDING WRATH OF THE...
...DAMNATION STARE!
IT WORKED.

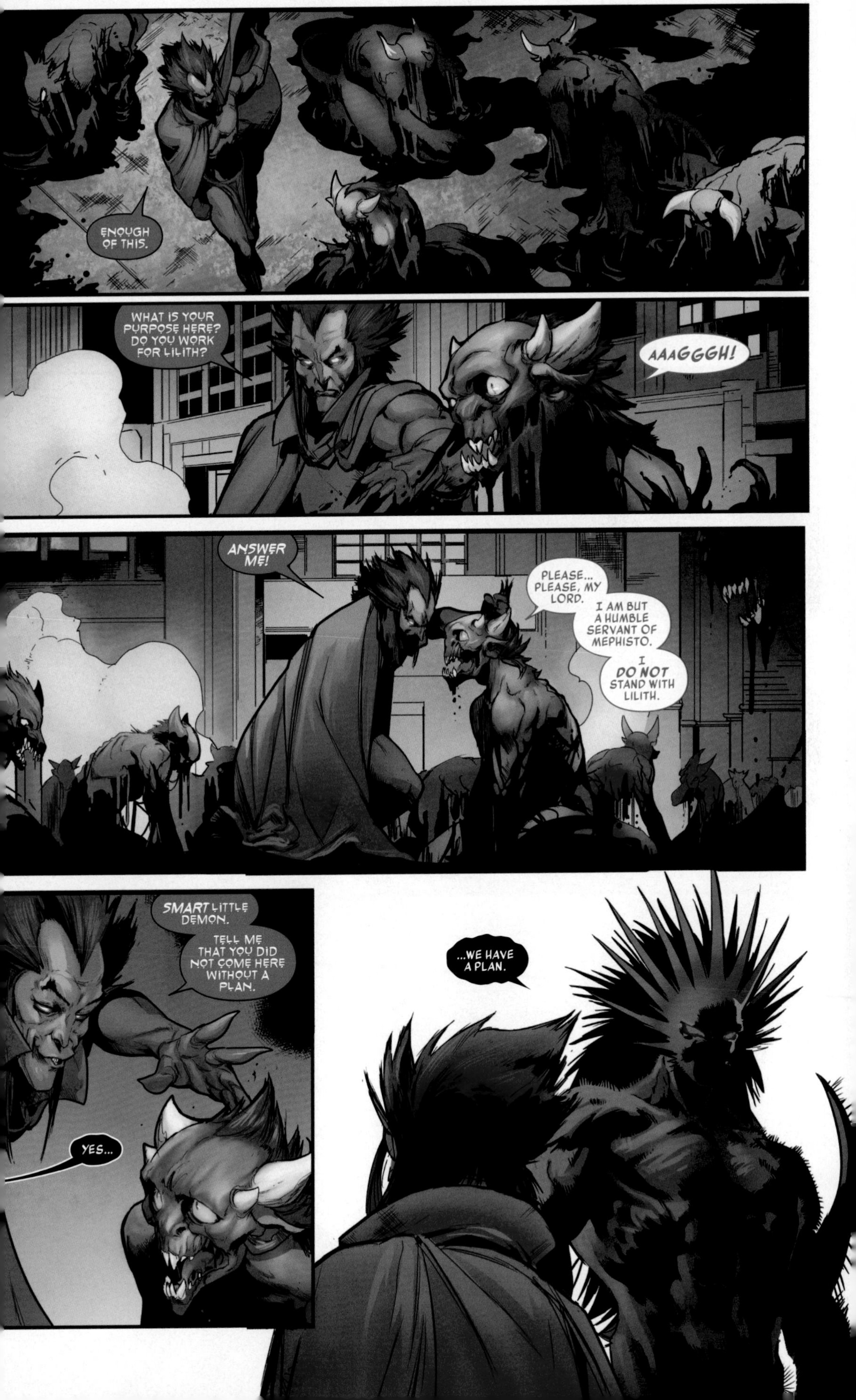
ENOUGH OF THIS.
WHAT IS YOUR PURPOSE HERE? DO YOU WORK FOR LILITH?
AAAGGGH!
ANSWER ME!
PLEASE... PLEASE, MY LORD.
I AM BUT A HUMBLE SERVANT OF MEPHISTO.
I DO NOT STAND WITH LILITH.
SMART LITTLE DEMON.
TELL ME THAT YOU DID NOT COME HERE WITHOUT A PLAN.
YES...
...WE HAVE A PLAN.

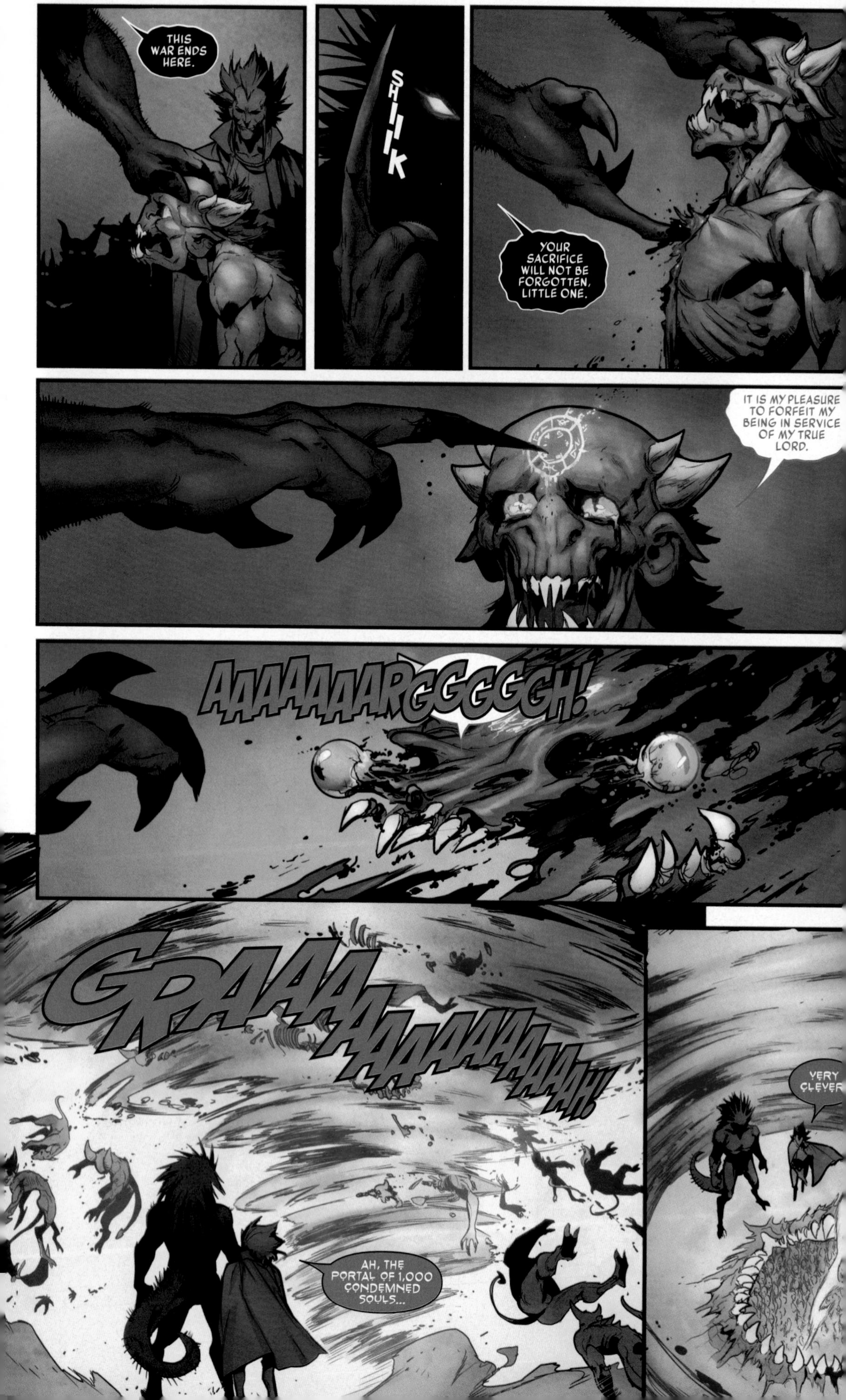

THIS WAR ENDS HERE.
SHHIIK
YOUR SACRIFICE WILL NOT BE FORGOTTEN, LITTLE ONE.
IT IS MY PLEASURE TO FORFEIT MY BEING IN SERVICE OF MY TRUE LORD.
AAAAAAARGGGGGH!
GRAAAAAAAAAAAAAAAH!
AH, THE PORTAL OF 1,000 CONDEMNED SOULS...
VERY CLEVER

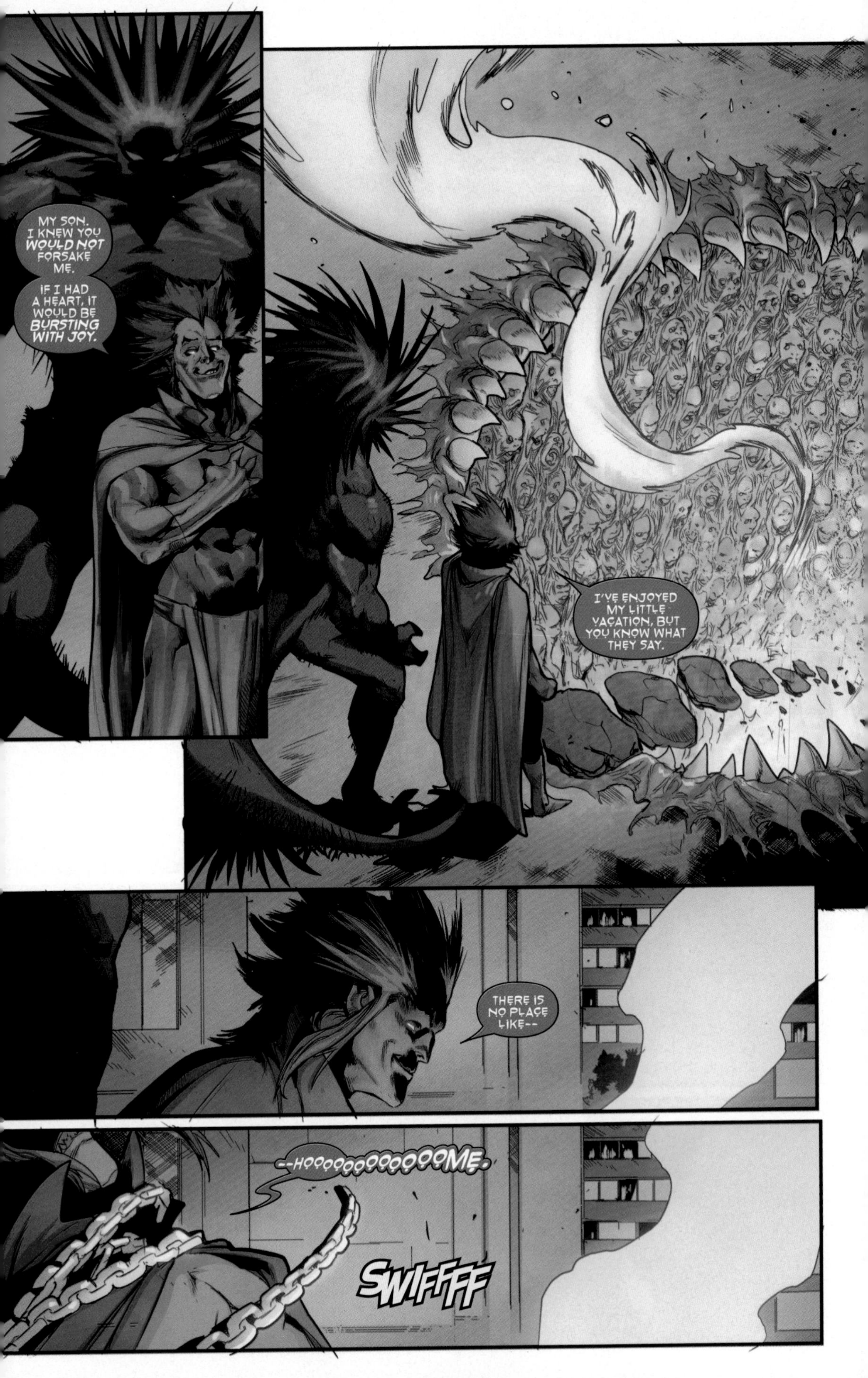
MY SON. I KNEW YOU WOULD NOT FORSAKE ME.
IF I HAD A HEART, IT WOULD BE BURSTING WITH JOY.
I'VE ENJOYED MY LITTLE VACATION, BUT YOU KNOW WHAT THEY SAY.
THERE IS NO PLACE LIKE--
--HOOOOOOOOOOOOME.
SWIFFFF

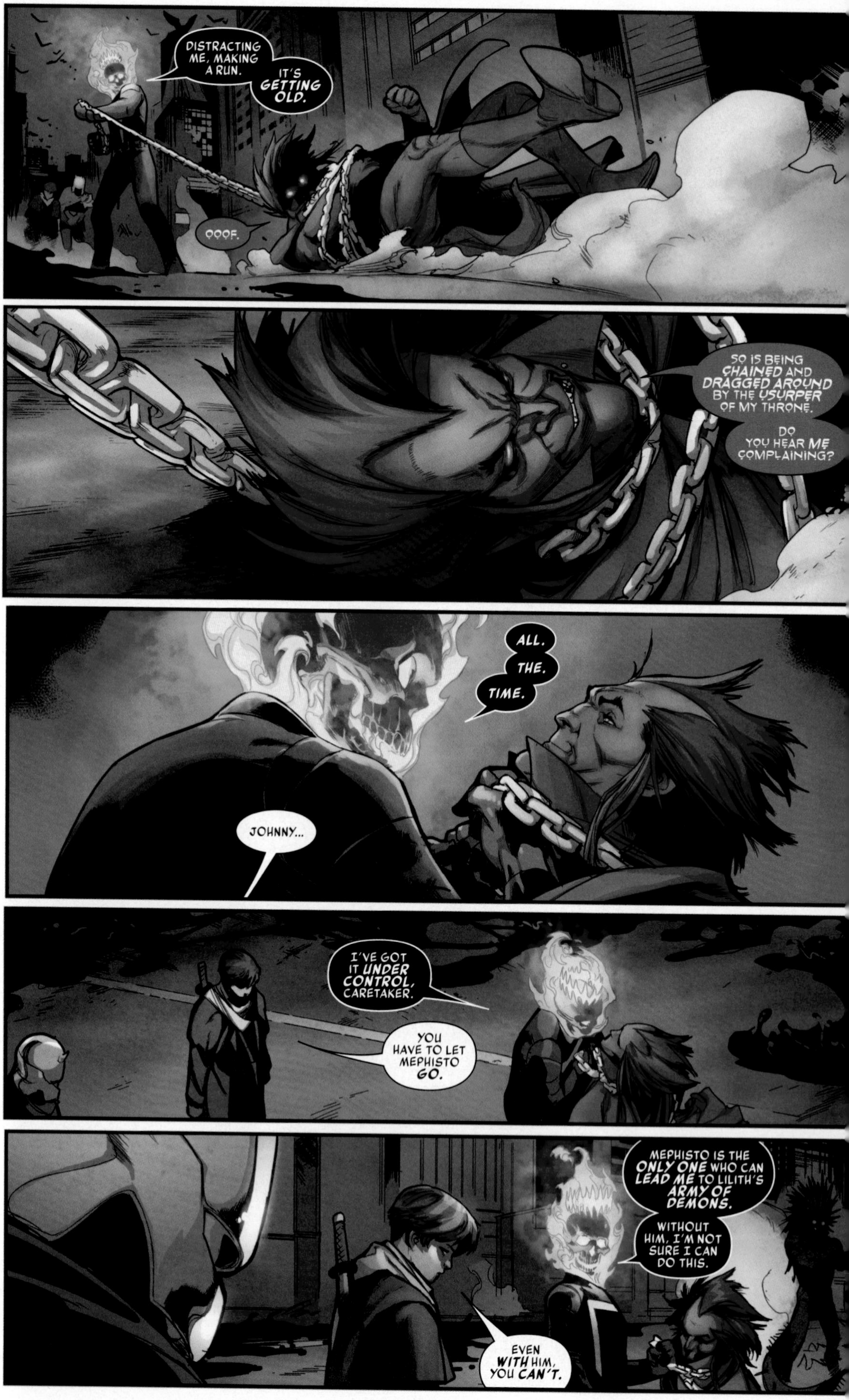

DISTRACTING ME, MAKING A RUN.
IT'S GETTING OLD.
OOOF.
SO IS BEING CHAINED AND DRAGGED AROUND BY THE USURPER OF MY THRONE.
DO YOU HEAR ME COMPLAINING?
ALL.
THE.
TIME.
JOHNNY...
I'VE GOT IT UNDER CONTROL, CARETAKER.
YOU HAVE TO LET MEPHISTO GO.
MEPHISTO IS THE ONLY ONE WHO CAN LEAD ME TO LILITH'S ARMY OF DEMONS.
WITHOUT HIM, I'M NOT SURE I CAN DO THIS.
EVEN WITH HIM, YOU CAN'T.

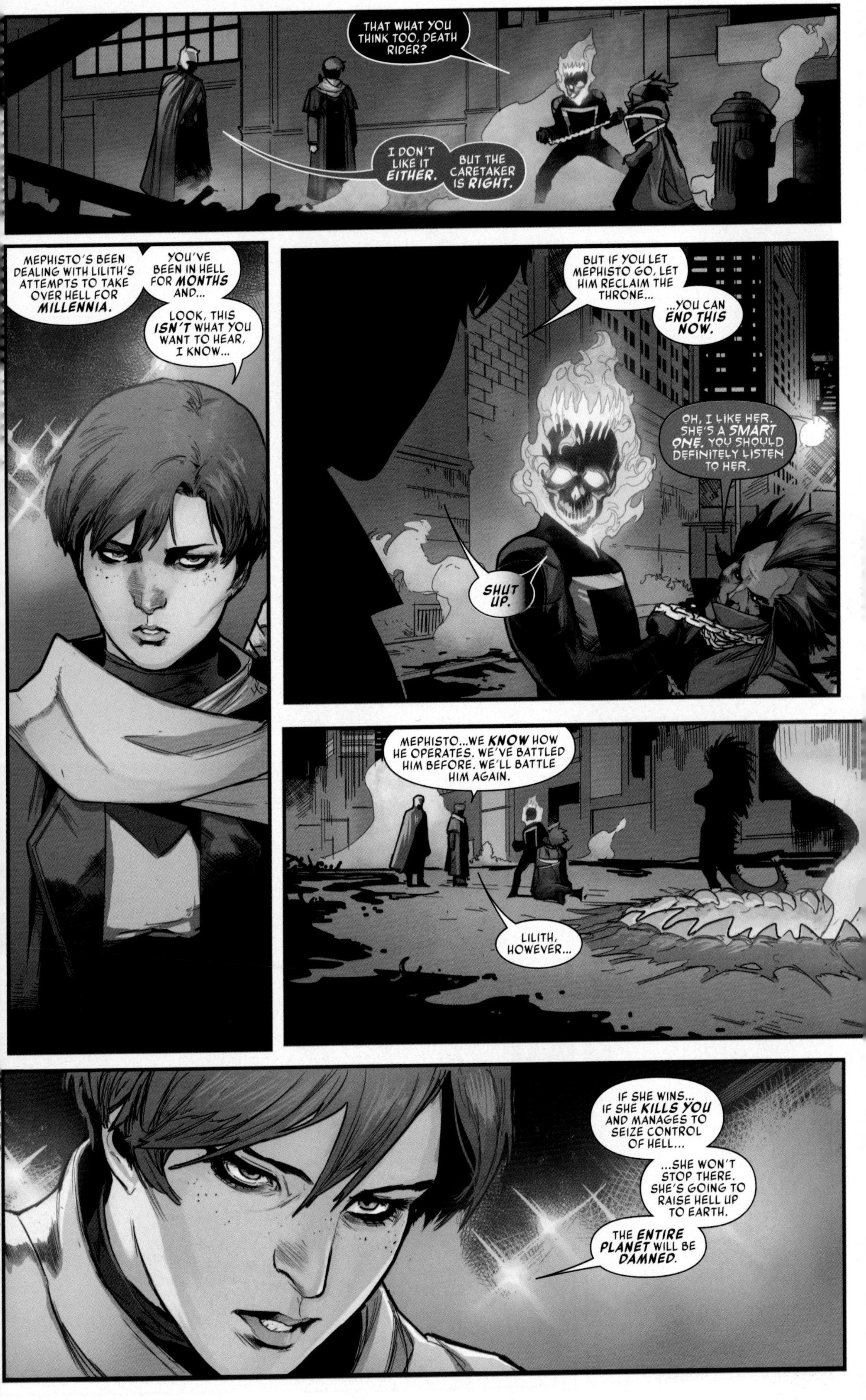

THAT WHAT YOU THINK TOO, DEATH RIDER?
I DON'T LIKE IT EITHER.
BUT THE CARETAKER IS RIGHT.
MEPHISTO'S BEEN DEALING WITH LILITH'S ATTEMPTS TO TAKE OVER HELL FOR MILLENNIA.
YOU'VE BEEN IN HELL FOR MONTHS AND...
LOOK, THIS ISN'T WHAT YOU WANT TO HEAR, I KNOW...
BUT IF YOU LET MEPHISTO GO, LET HIM RECLAIM THE THRONE...
...YOU CAN END THIS NOW.
OH, I LIKE HER. SHE'S A SMART ONE. YOU SHOULD DEFINITELY LISTEN TO HER.
SHUT UP.
MEPHISTO...WE KNOW HOW HE OPERATES. WE'VE BATTLED HIM BEFORE. WE'LL BATTLE HIM AGAIN.
LILITH, HOWEVER...
IF SHE WINS... IF SHE KILLS YOU AND MANAGES TO SEIZE CONTROL OF HELL...
...SHE WON'T STOP THERE. SHE'S GOING TO RAISE HELL UP TO EARTH.
THE ENTIRE PLANET WILL BE DAMNED.

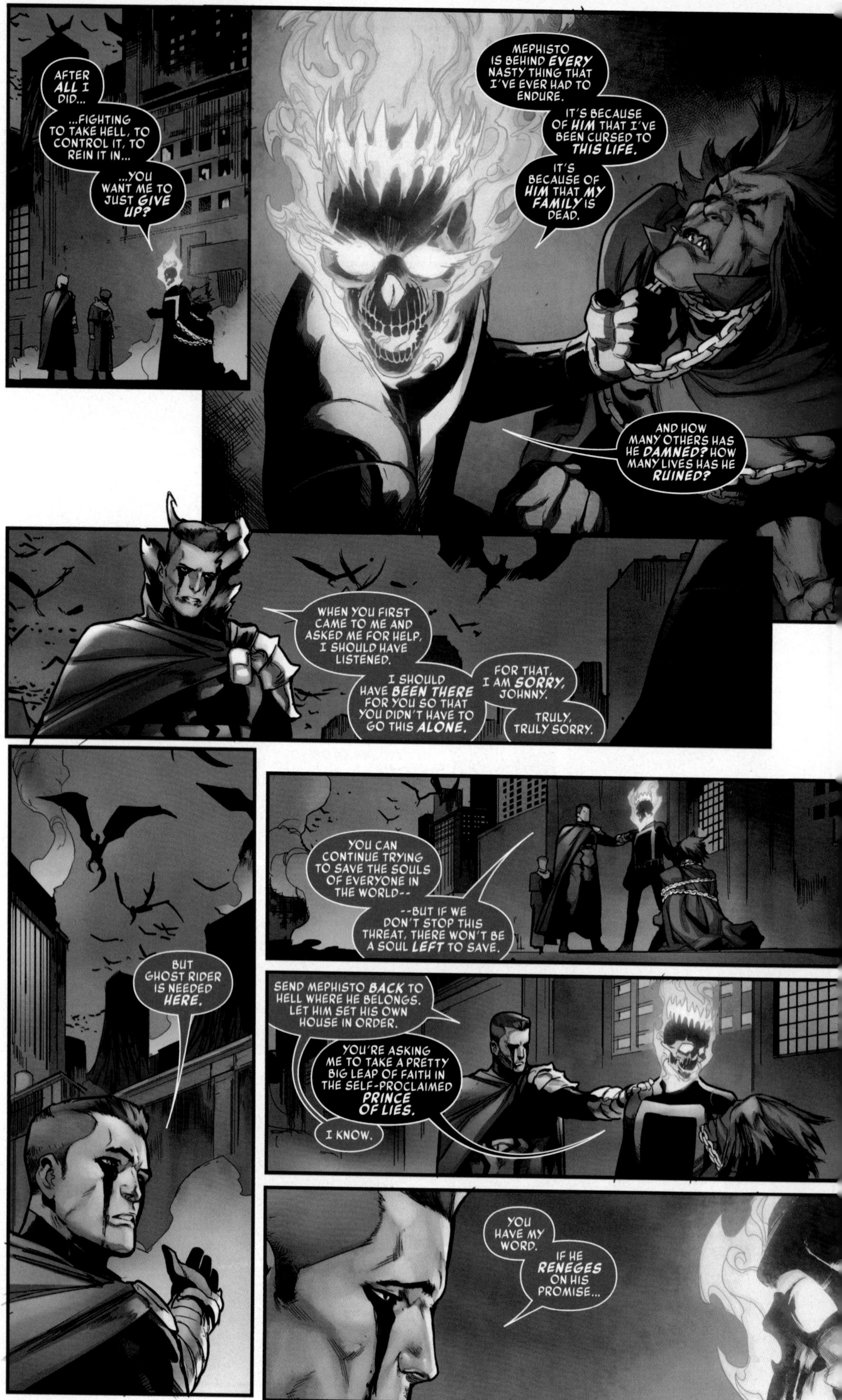
AFTER ALL I DID...
...FIGHTING TO TAKE HELL, TO CONTROL IT, TO REIN IT IN...
...YOU WANT ME TO JUST GIVE UP?
MEPHISTO IS BEHIND EVERY NASTY THING THAT I'VE EVER HAD TO ENDURE.
IT'S BECAUSE OF HIM THAT I'VE BEEN CURSED TO THIS LIFE.
IT'S BECAUSE OF HIM THAT MY FAMILY IS DEAD.
AND HOW MANY OTHERS HAS HE DAMNED? HOW MANY LIVES HAS HE RUINED?
WHEN YOU FIRST CAME TO ME AND ASKED ME FOR HELP, I SHOULD HAVE LISTENED.
I SHOULD HAVE BEEN THERE FOR YOU SO THAT YOU DIDN'T HAVE TO GO THIS ALONE.
FOR THAT, I AM SORRY, JOHNNY.
TRULY, TRULY SORRY.
BUT GHOST RIDER IS NEEDED HERE.
YOU CAN CONTINUE TRYING TO SAVE THE SOULS OF EVERYONE IN THE WORLD--
--BUT IF WE DON'T STOP THIS THREAT, THERE WON'T BE A SOUL LEFT TO SAVE.
SEND MEPHISTO BACK TO HELL WHERE HE BELONGS. LET HIM SET HIS OWN HOUSE IN ORDER.
YOU'RE ASKING ME TO TAKE A PRETTY BIG LEAP OF FAITH IN THE SELF-PROCLAIMED PRINCE OF LIES.
I KNOW.
YOU HAVE MY WORD.
IF HE RENEGES ON HIS PROMISE...

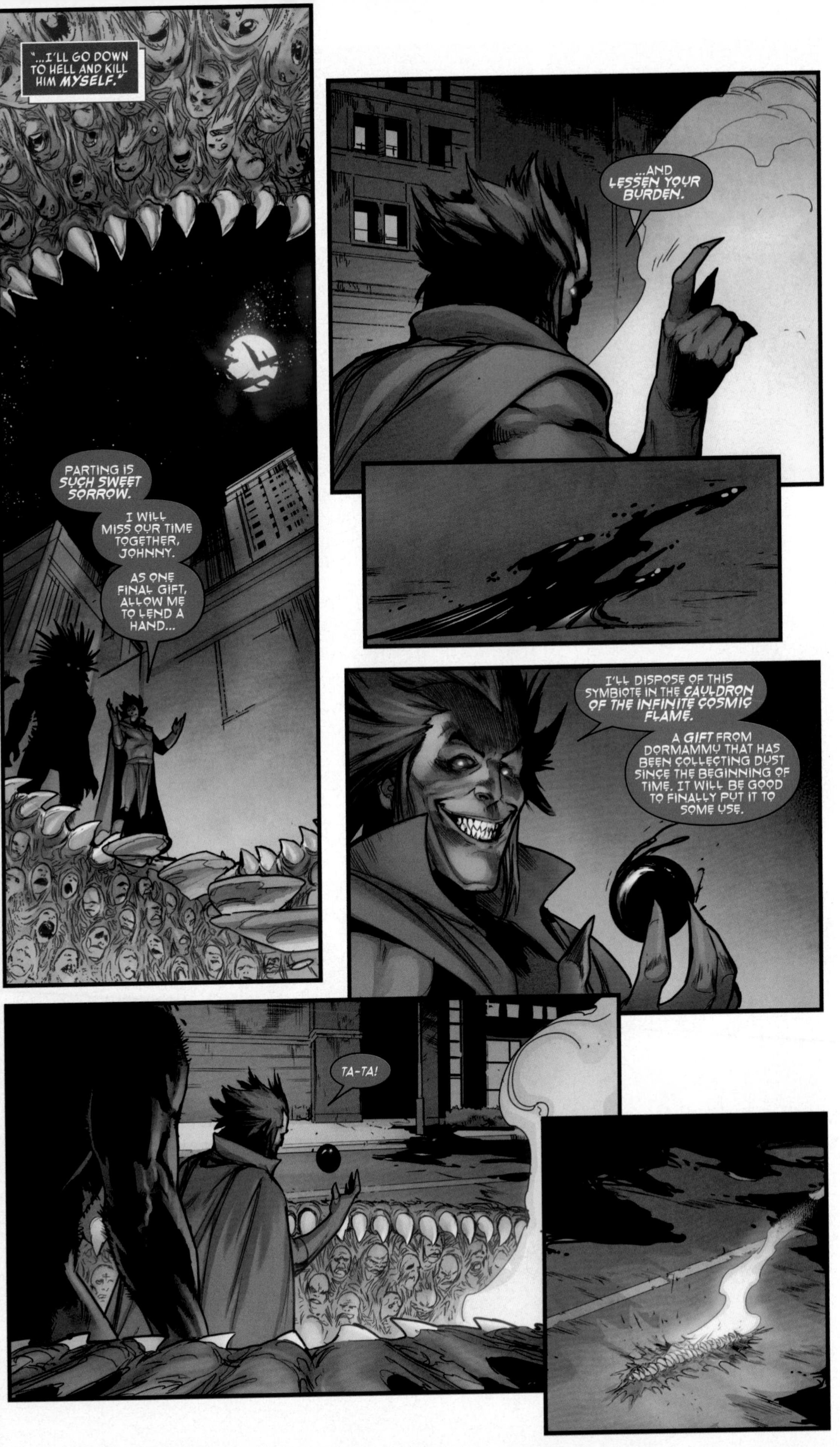
"...I'LL GO DOWN TO HELL AND KILL HIM MYSELF."
PARTING IS SUCH SWEET SORROW.
I WILL MISS OUR TIME TOGETHER, JOHNNY.
AS ONE FINAL GIFT, ALLOW ME TO LEND A HAND...
...AND LESSEN YOUR BURDEN.
I'LL DISPOSE OF THIS SYMBIOTE IN THE CAULDRON OF THE INFINITE COSMIC FLAME.
A GIFT FROM DORMAMMU THAT HAS BEEN COLLECTING DUST SINCE THE BEGINNING OF TIME. IT WILL BE GOOD TO FINALLY PUT IT TO SOME USE.
TA-TA!

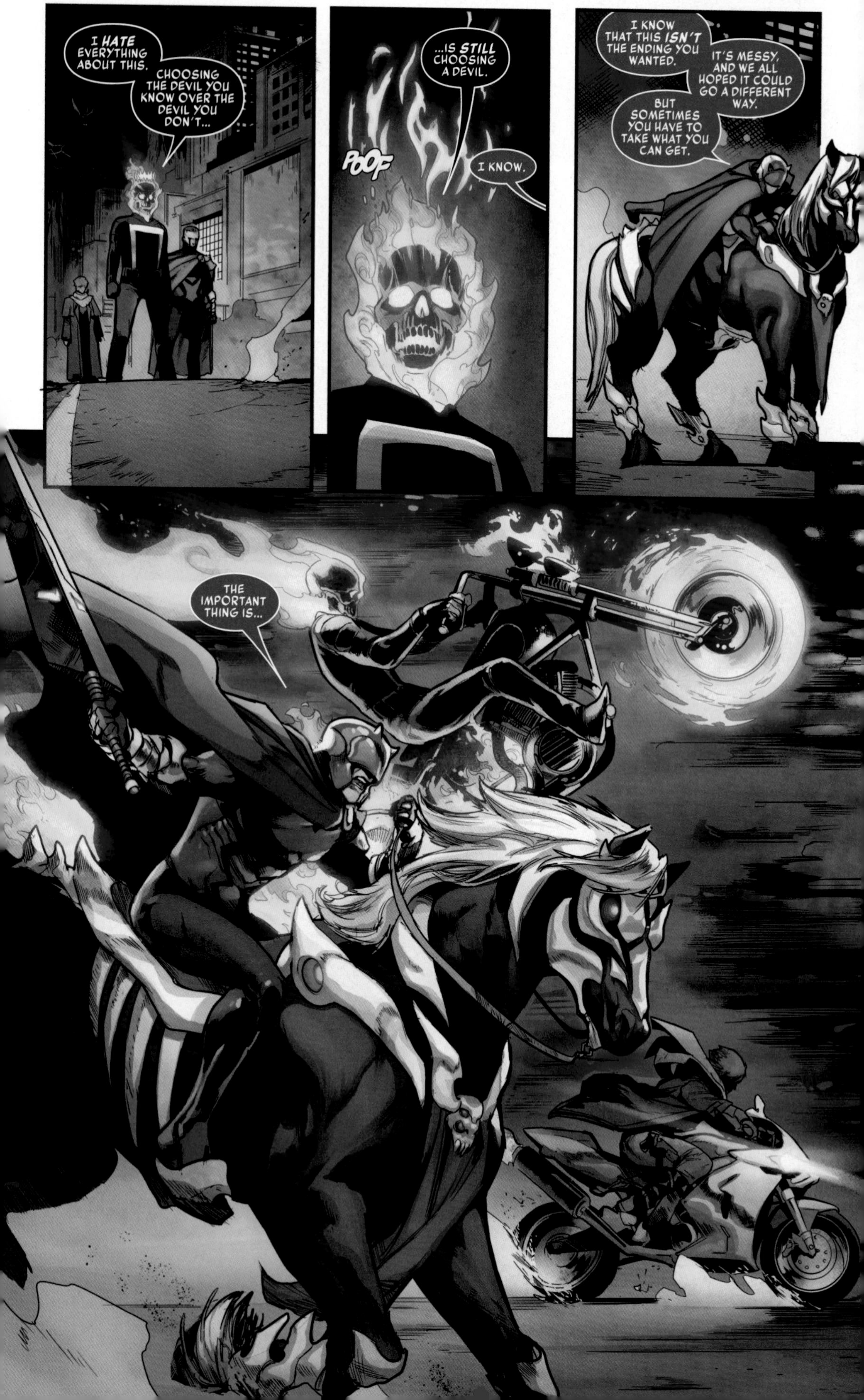
I HATE EVERYTHING ABOUT THIS.
CHOOSING THE DEVIL YOU KNOW OVER THE DEVIL YOU DON'T...
...IS STILL CHOOSING A DEVIL.
POOF
I KNOW.
I KNOW THAT THIS ISN'T THE ENDING YOU WANTED.
IT'S MESSY, AND WE ALL HOPED IT COULD GO A DIFFERENT WAY.
BUT SOMETIMES YOU HAVE TO TAKE WHAT YOU CAN GET.
THE IMPORTANT THING IS...

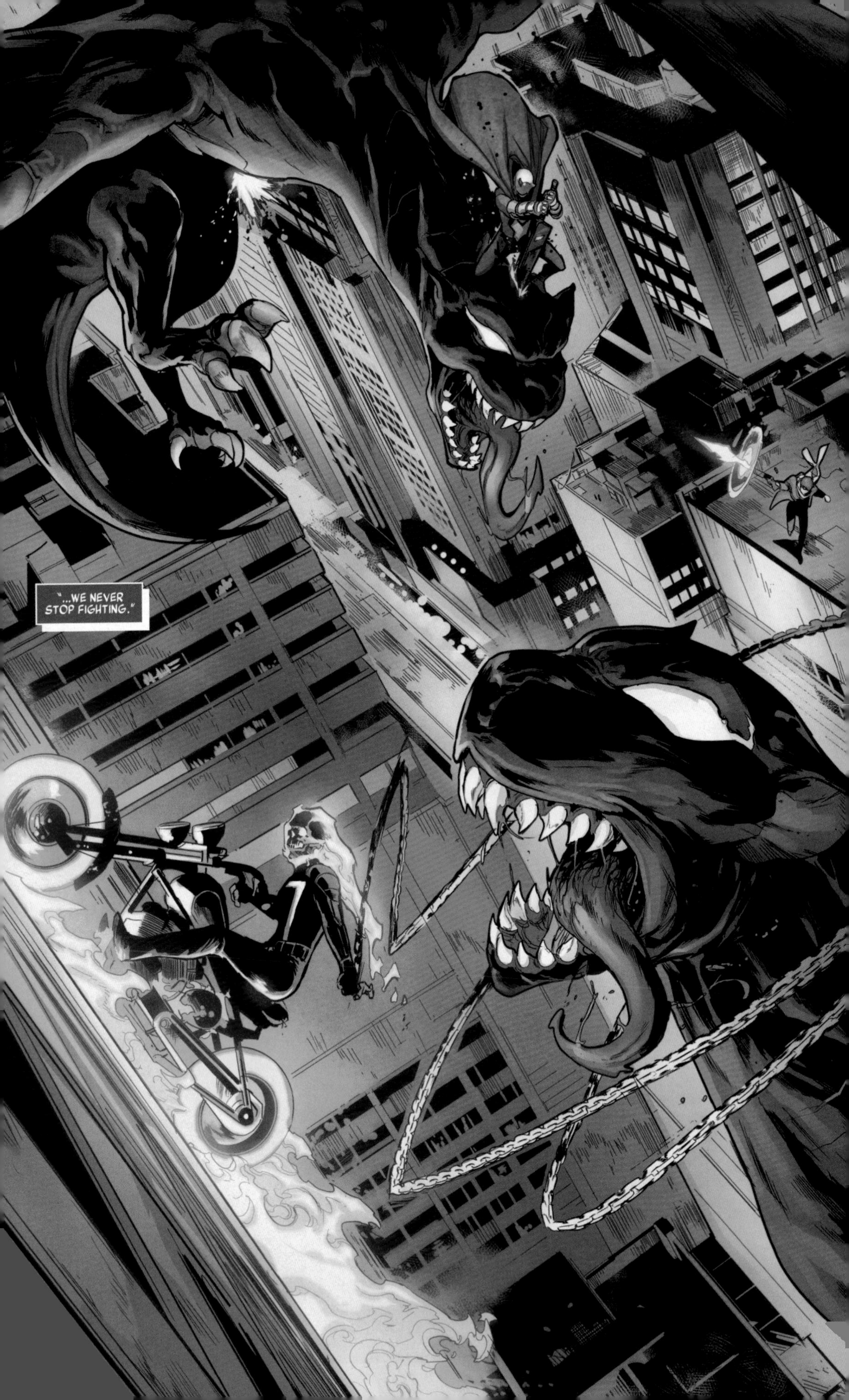
"...WE NEVER STOP FIGHTING."

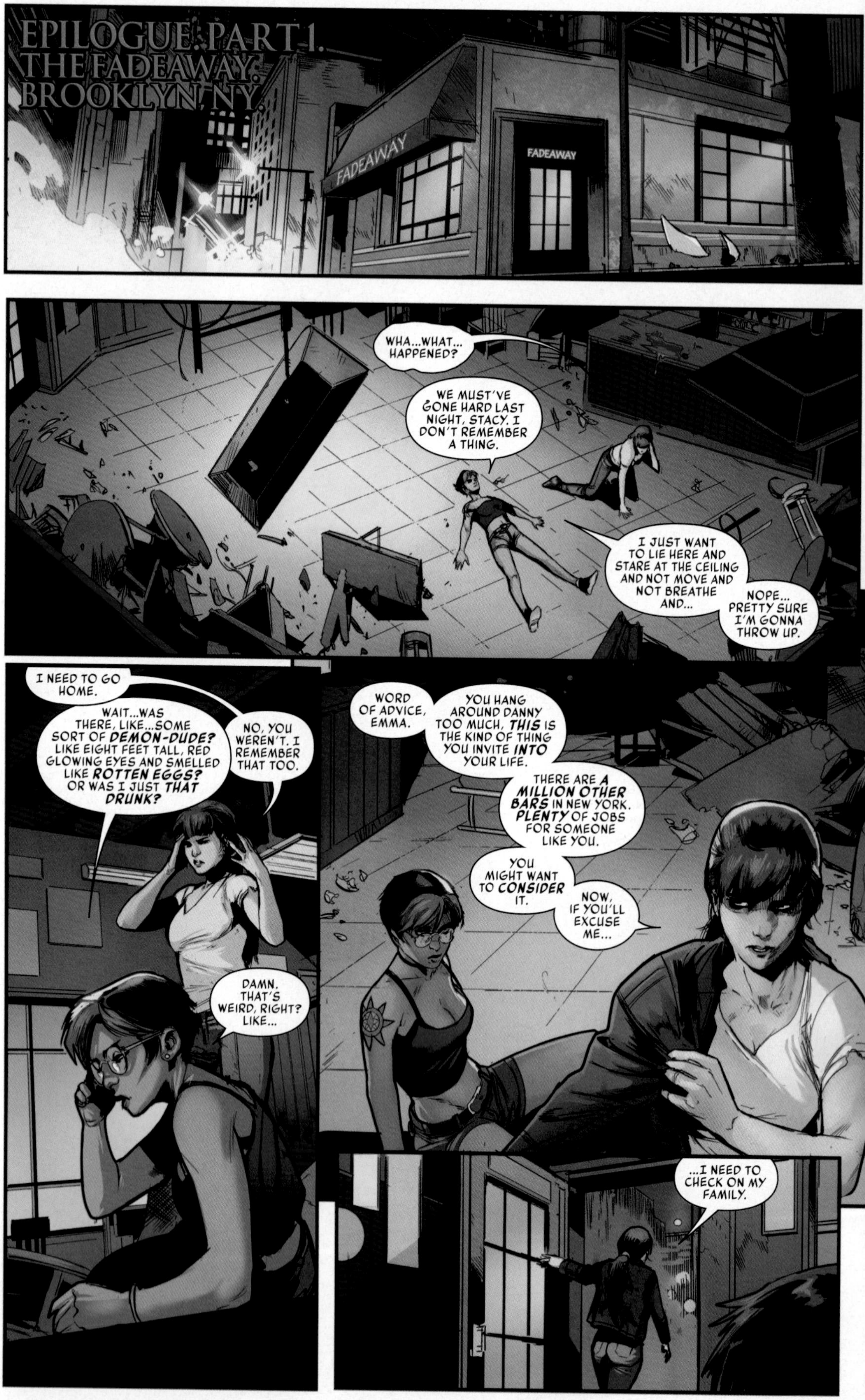
EPILOGUE PART 1. THE FADEAWAY. BROOKLYN, NY.
FADEAWAY
FADEAWAY
WHA...WHAT... HAPPENED?
WE MUST'VE GONE HARD LAST NIGHT, STACY. I DON'T REMEMBER A THING.
I JUST WANT TO LIE HERE AND STARE AT THE CEILING AND NOT MOVE AND NOT BREATHE AND...
NOPE... PRETTY SURE I'M GONNA THROW UP.
I NEED TO GO HOME.
WAIT...WAS THERE, LIKE...SOME SORT OF DEMON-DUDE? LIKE EIGHT FEET TALL, RED GLOWING EYES AND SMELLED LIKE ROTTEN EGGS? OR WAS I JUST THAT DRUNK?
NO, YOU WEREN'T. I REMEMBER THAT TOO.
DAMN. THAT'S WEIRD, RIGHT? LIKE...
WORD OF ADVICE, EMMA.
YOU HANG AROUND DANNY TOO MUCH, THIS IS THE KIND OF THING YOU INVITE INTO YOUR LIFE.
THERE ARE A MILLION OTHER BARS IN NEW YORK. PLENTY OF JOBS FOR SOMEONE LIKE YOU.
YOU MIGHT WANT TO CONSIDER IT.
NOW, IF YOU'LL EXCUSE ME...
...I NEED TO CHECK ON MY FAMILY.

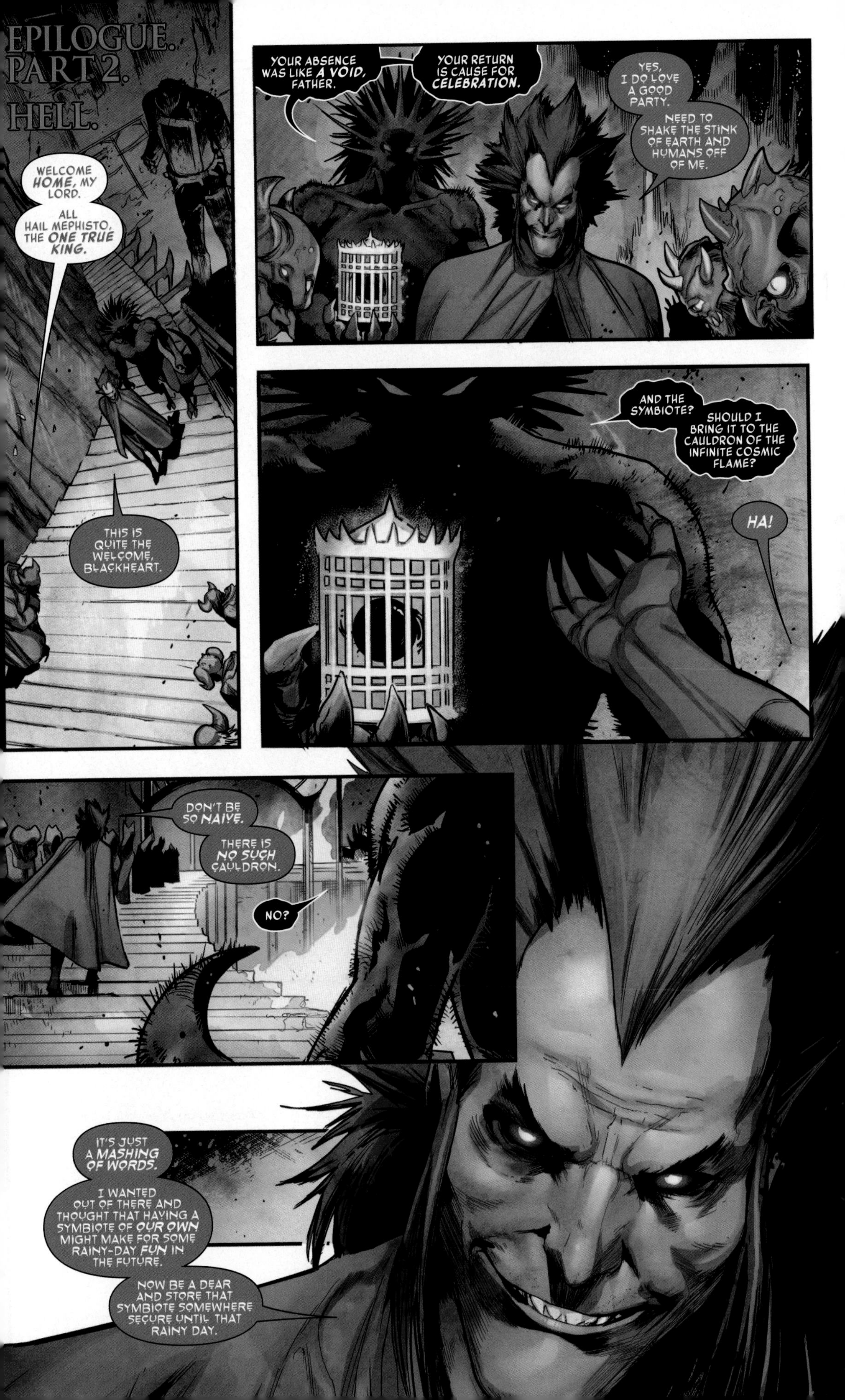
EPILOGUE. PART 2. HELL.
WELCOME HOME, MY LORD.
ALL HAIL MEPHISTO, THE ONE TRUE KING.
THIS IS QUITE THE WELCOME, BLACKHEART.
YOUR ABSENCE WAS LIKE A VOID, FATHER.
YOUR RETURN IS CAUSE FOR CELEBRATION.
YES, I DO LOVE A GOOD PARTY.
NEED TO SHAKE THE STINK OF EARTH AND HUMANS OFF OF ME.
AND THE SYMBIOTE?
SHOULD I BRING IT TO THE CAULDRON OF THE INFINITE COSMIC FLAME?
HA!
DON'T BE SO NAIVE.
THERE IS NO SUCH CAULDRON.
NO?
IT'S JUST A MASHING OF WORDS.
I WANTED OUT OF THERE AND THOUGHT THAT HAVING A SYMBIOTE OF OUR OWN MIGHT MAKE FOR SOME RAINY-DAY FUN IN THE FUTURE.
NOW BE A DEAR AND STORE THAT SYMBIOTE SOMEWHERE SECURE UNTIL THAT RAINY DAY.

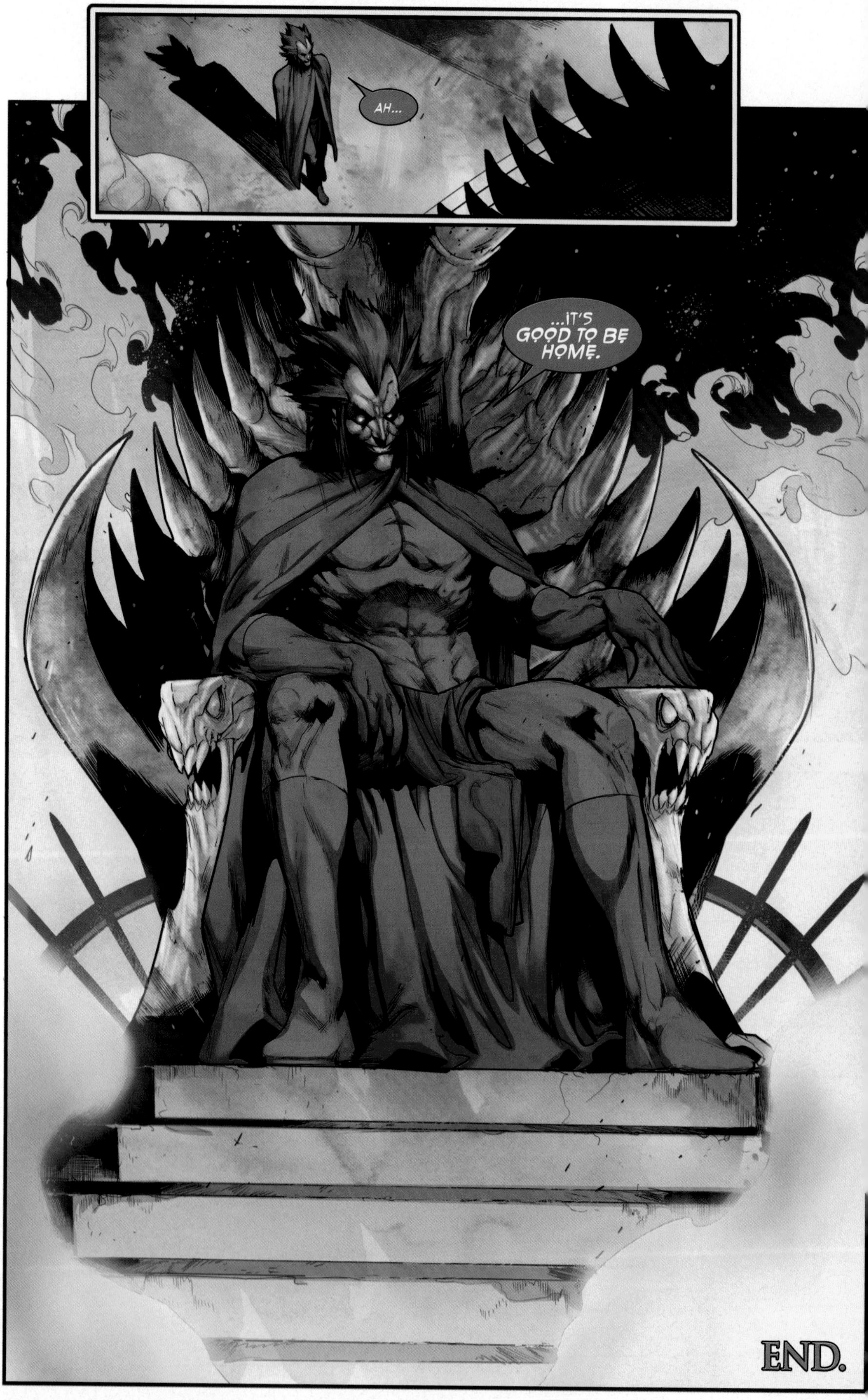
AH...
...IT'S GOOD TO BE HOME.
END.

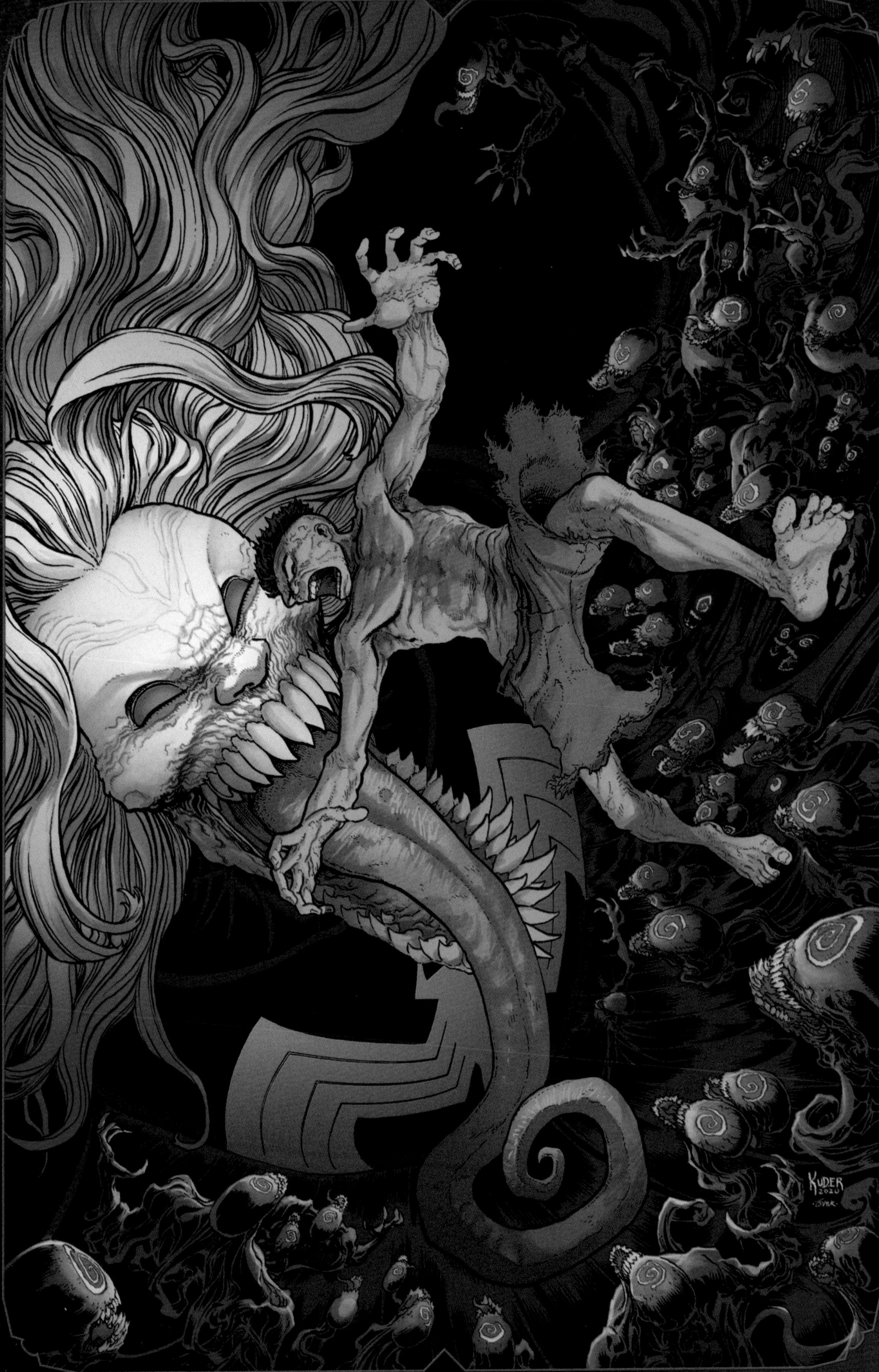
KUDER
2020

IMMORTAL HULK

THE IMMORTAL HULK

BLACK CHRISTMAS

The HULK is in bad shape.

Devil Hulk, the lovingly violent persona that has
sought to protect both Hulk and Banner for decades,
is dead. And BRUCE BANNER is gone — dragged out
of his own mindscape by the leader, who cracked
the code to the Hulk's complex personalities.

Now all that's left is the childlike savage Hulk —
drained of so much gamma that he can barely walk
— and JOE FIXIT, the former gray Hulk who now
manifests in Banner's body. Savage, Joe...any way
you cut it, the Hulk's a wanted man. And he's in no
shape to face the demonic army of a mad god.

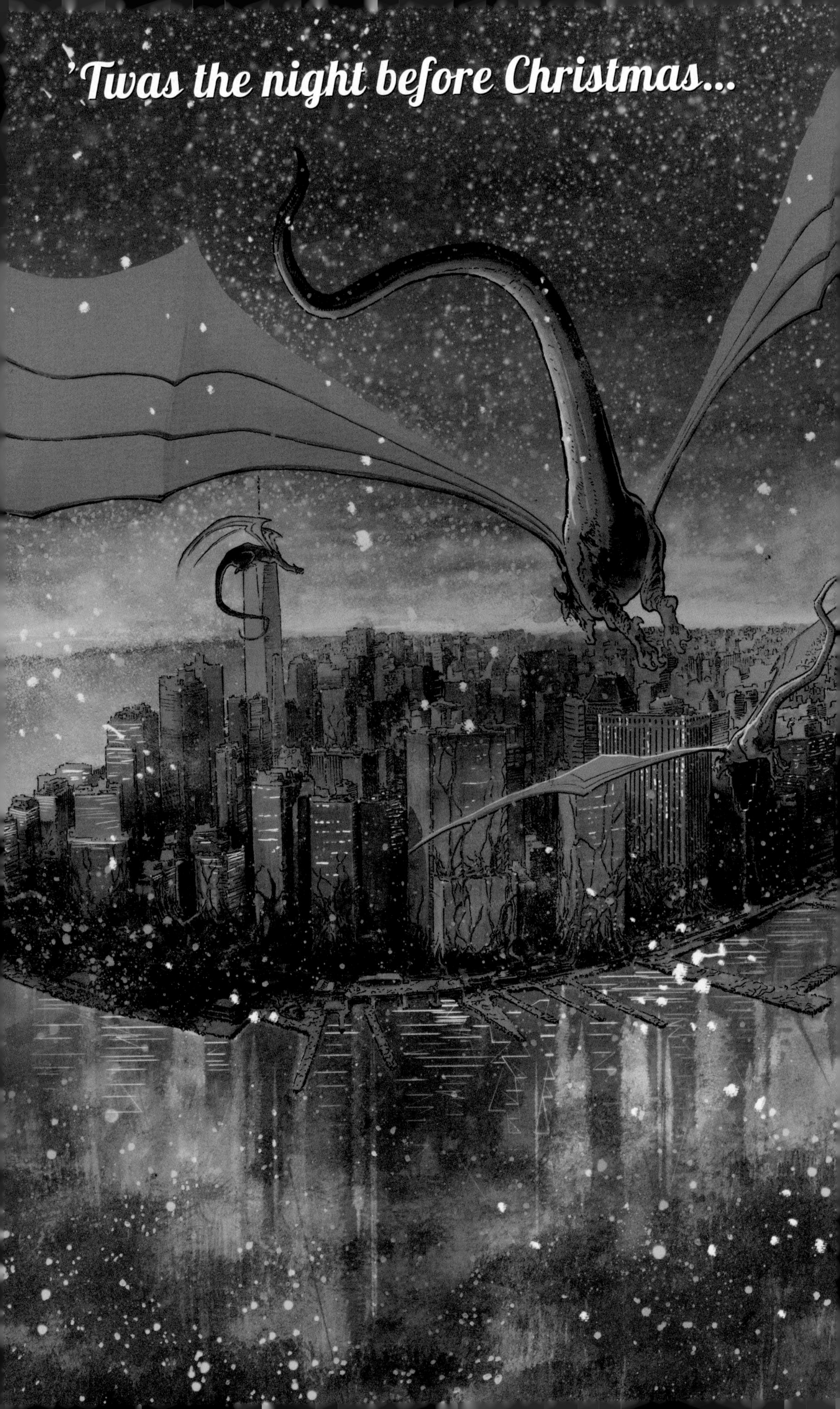
'Twas the night before Christmas...

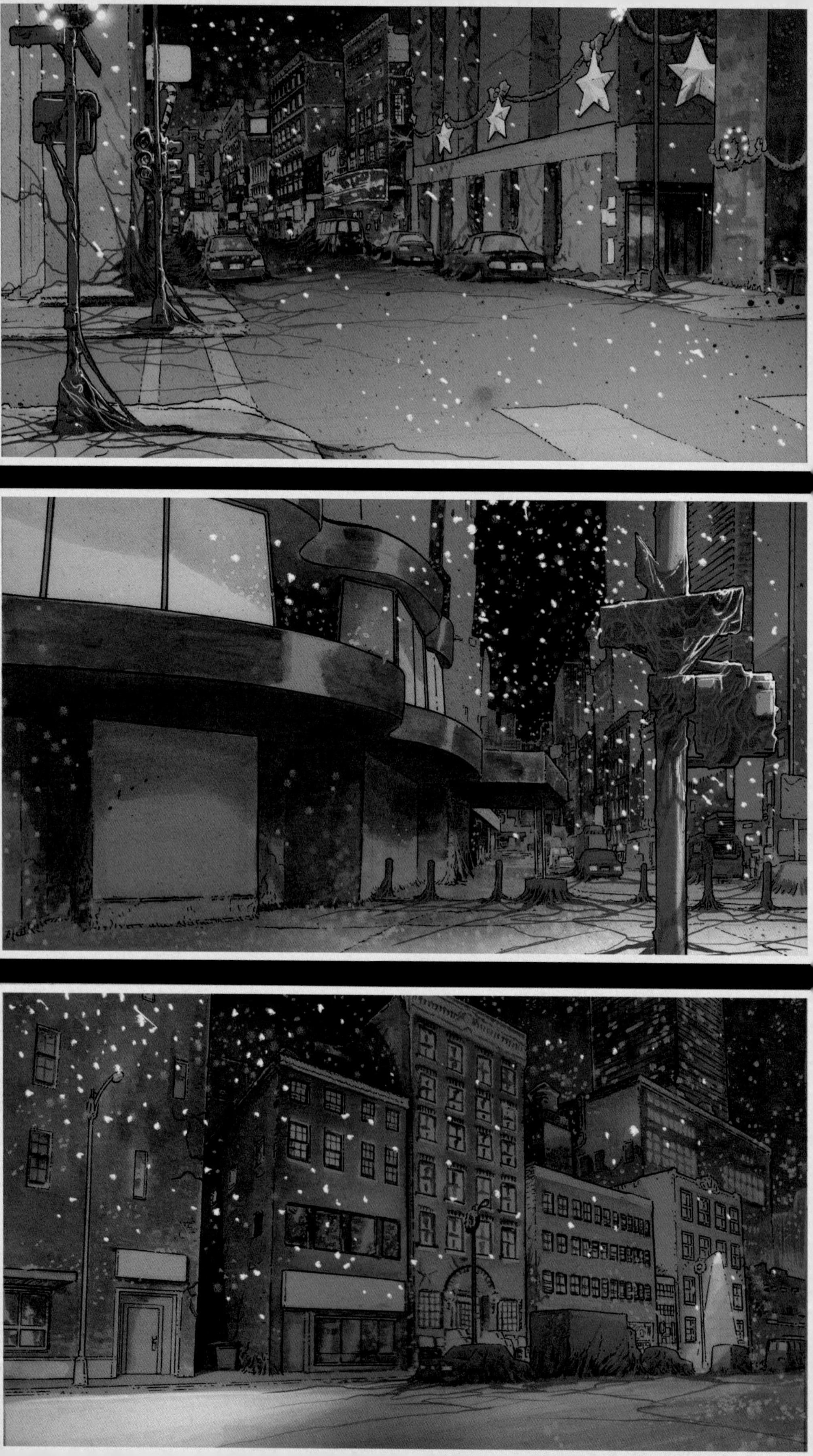

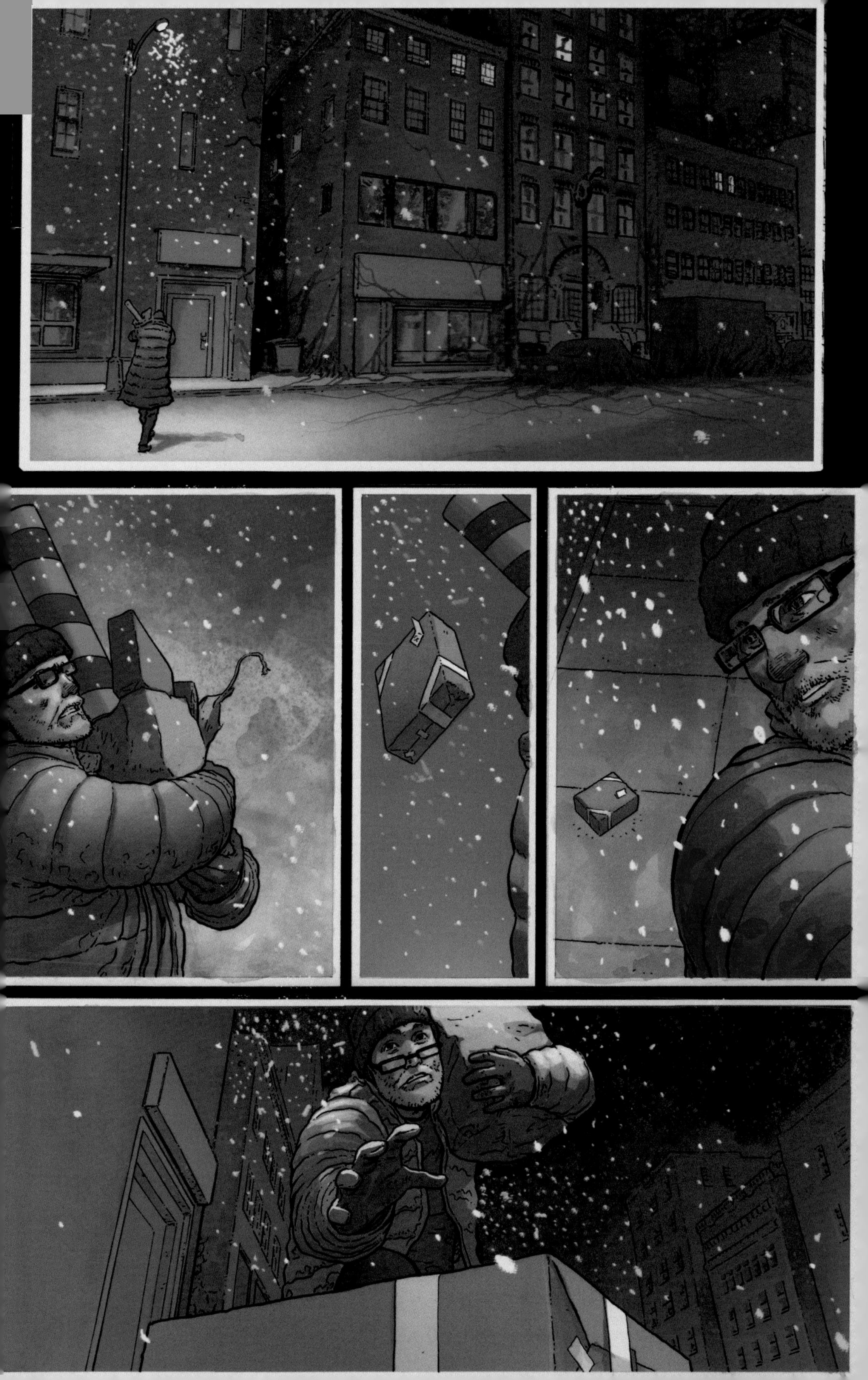

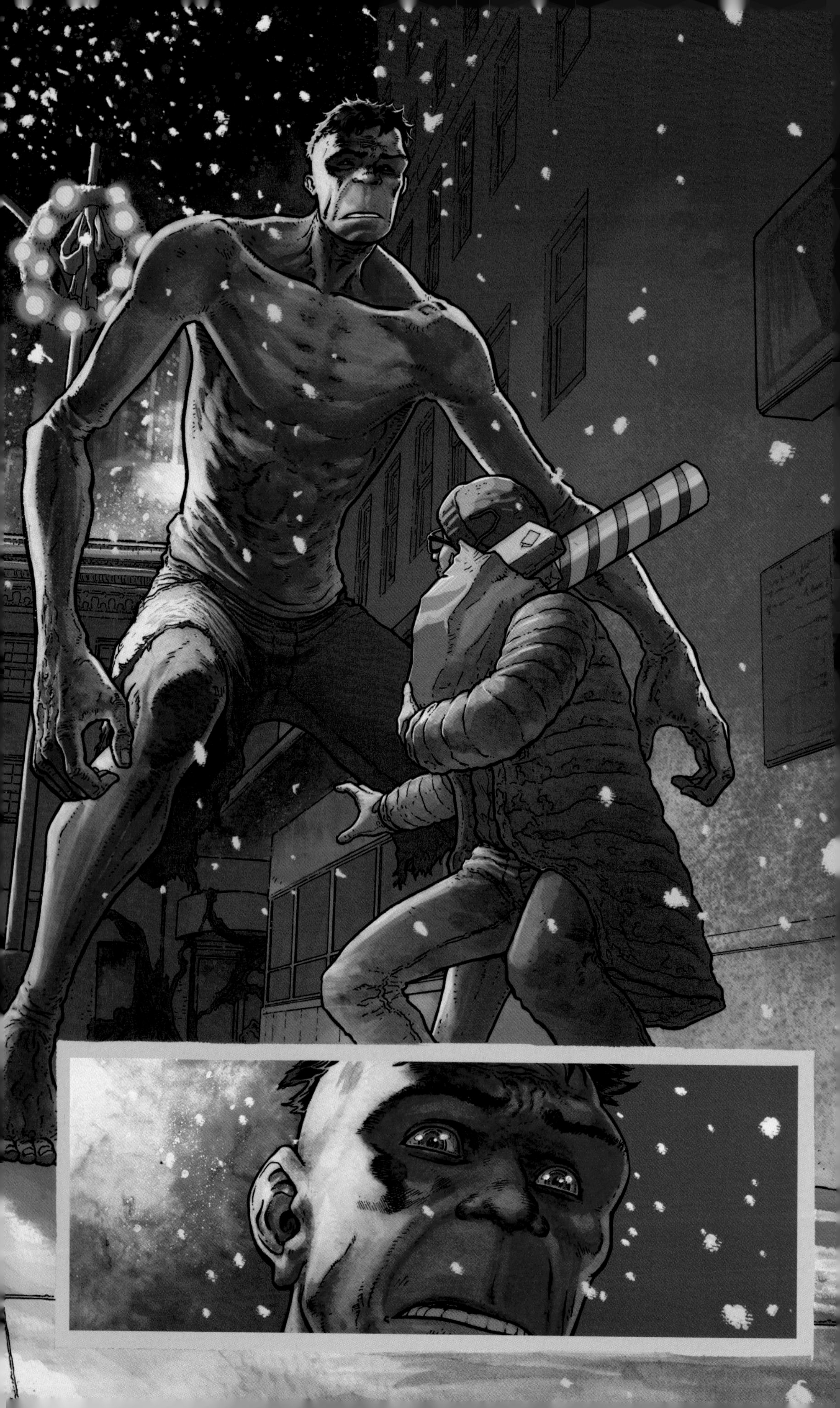

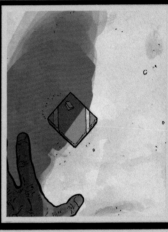

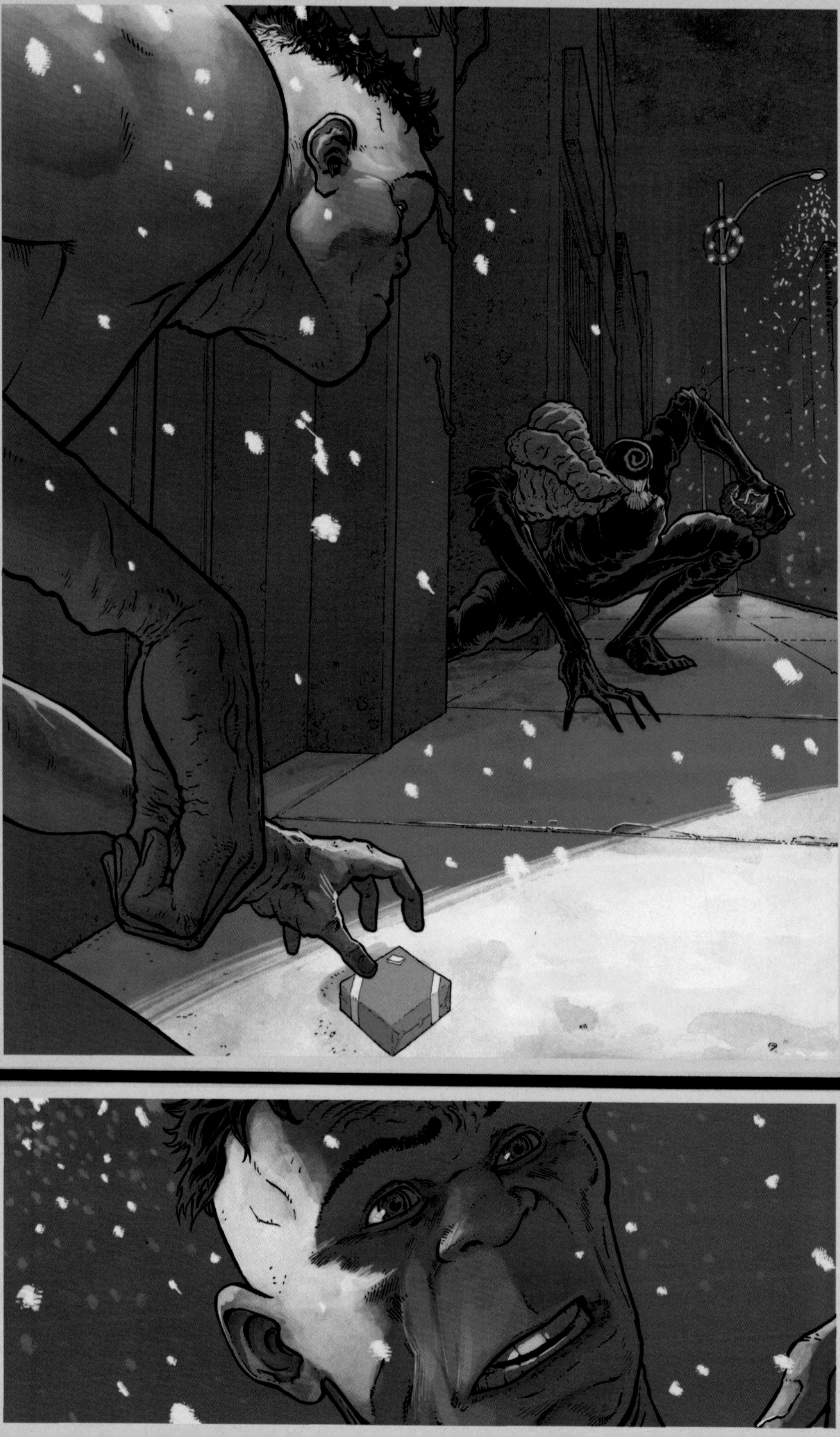

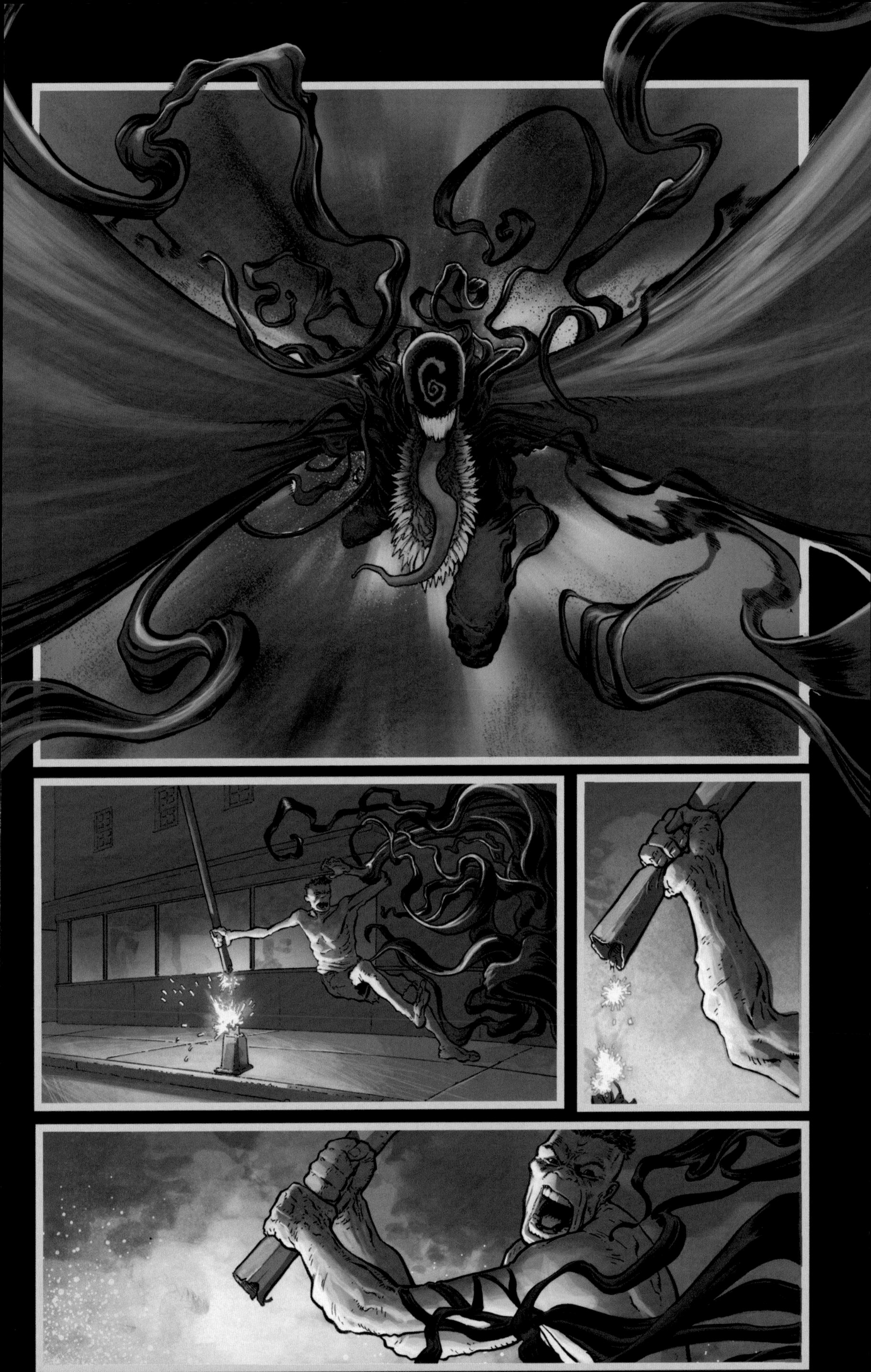

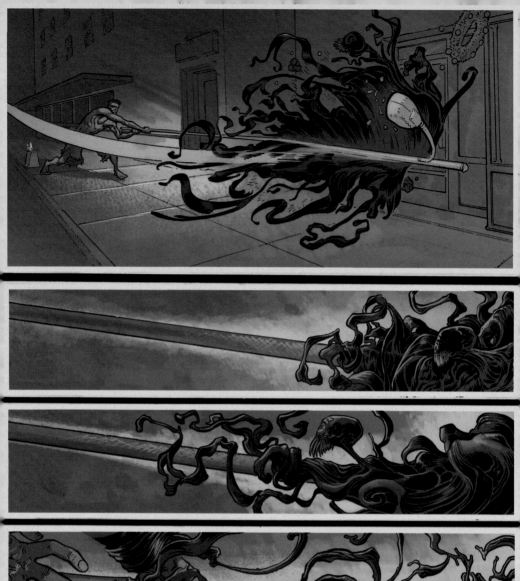

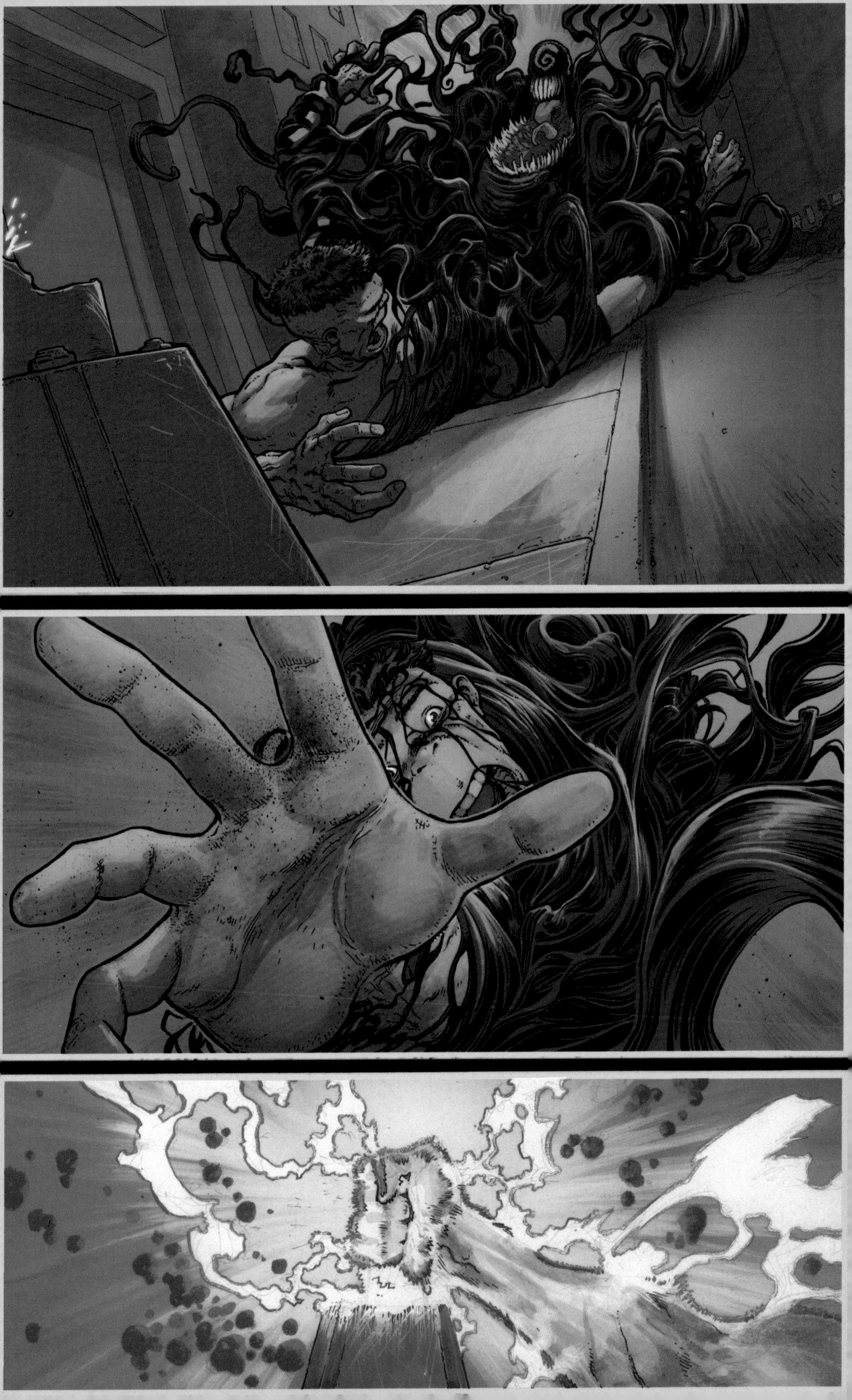

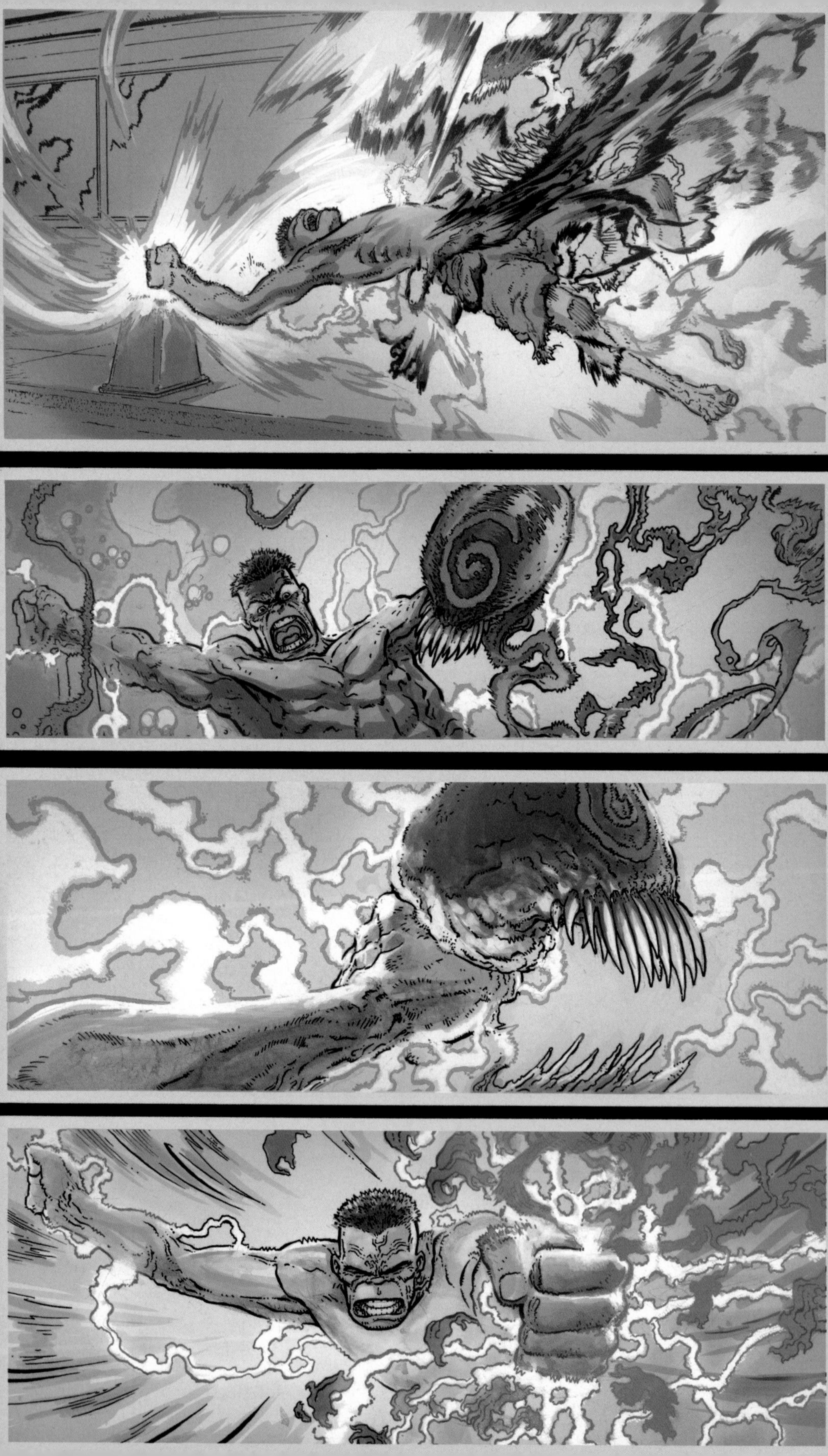

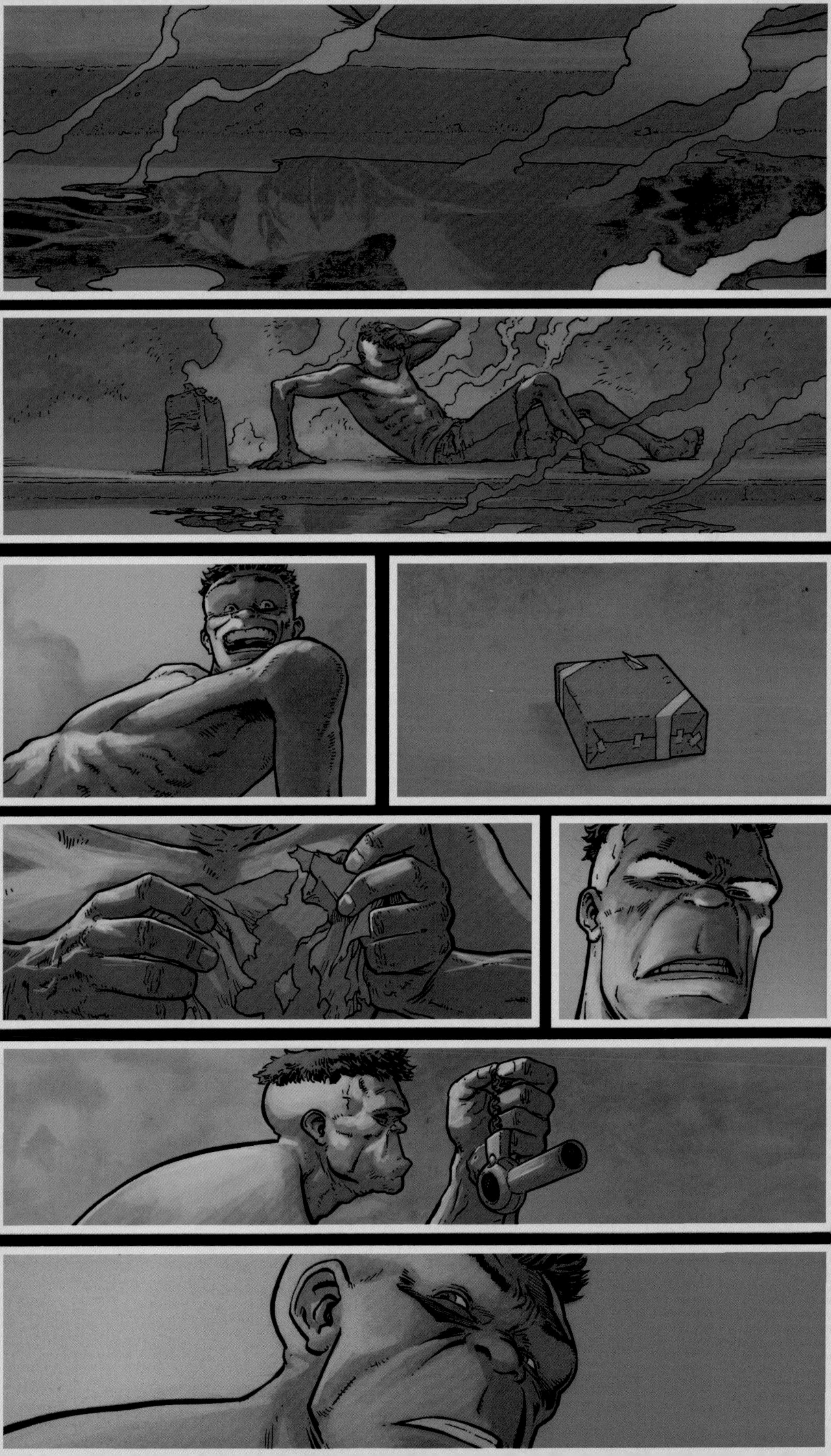

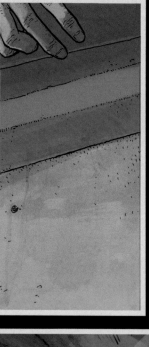

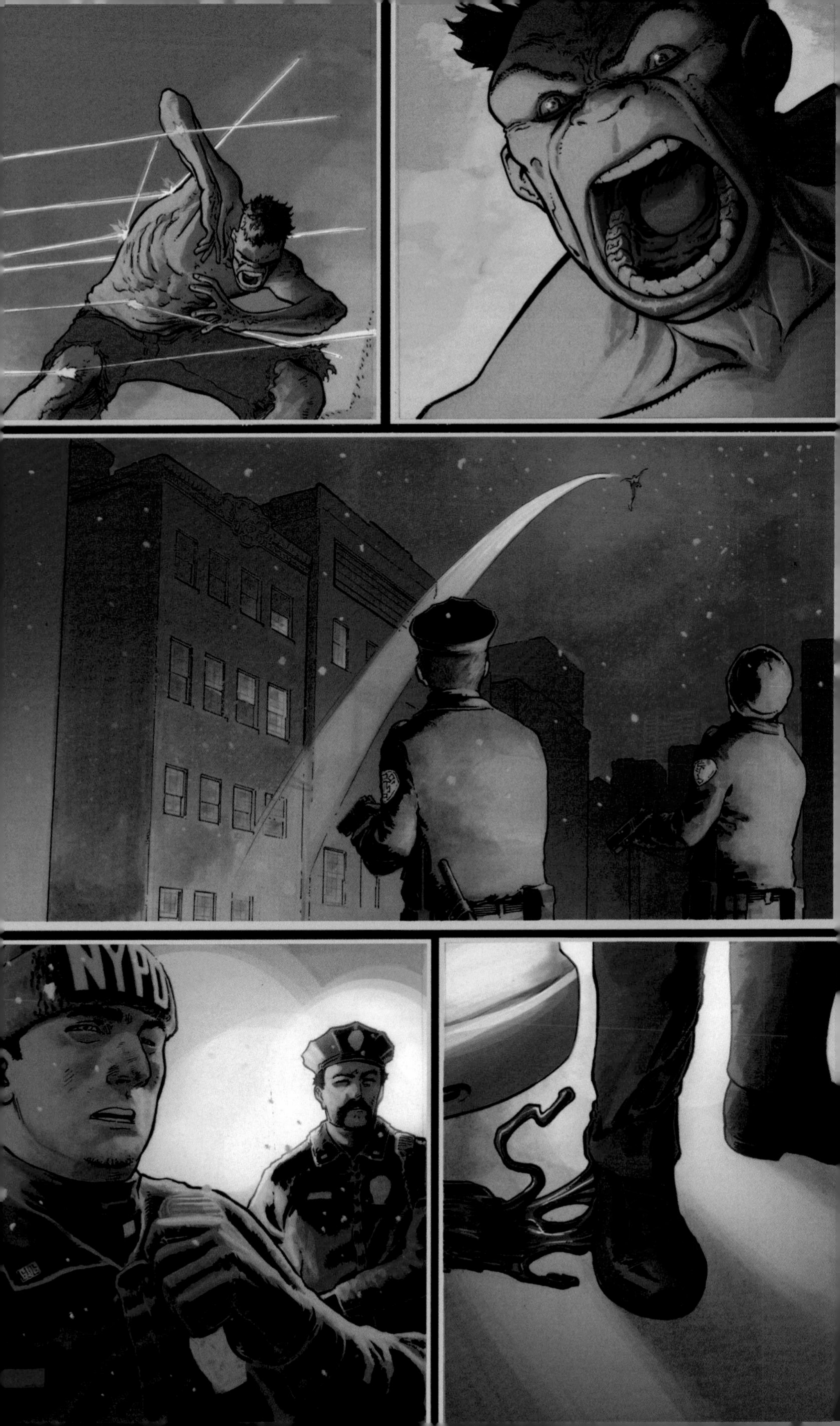
NYPD

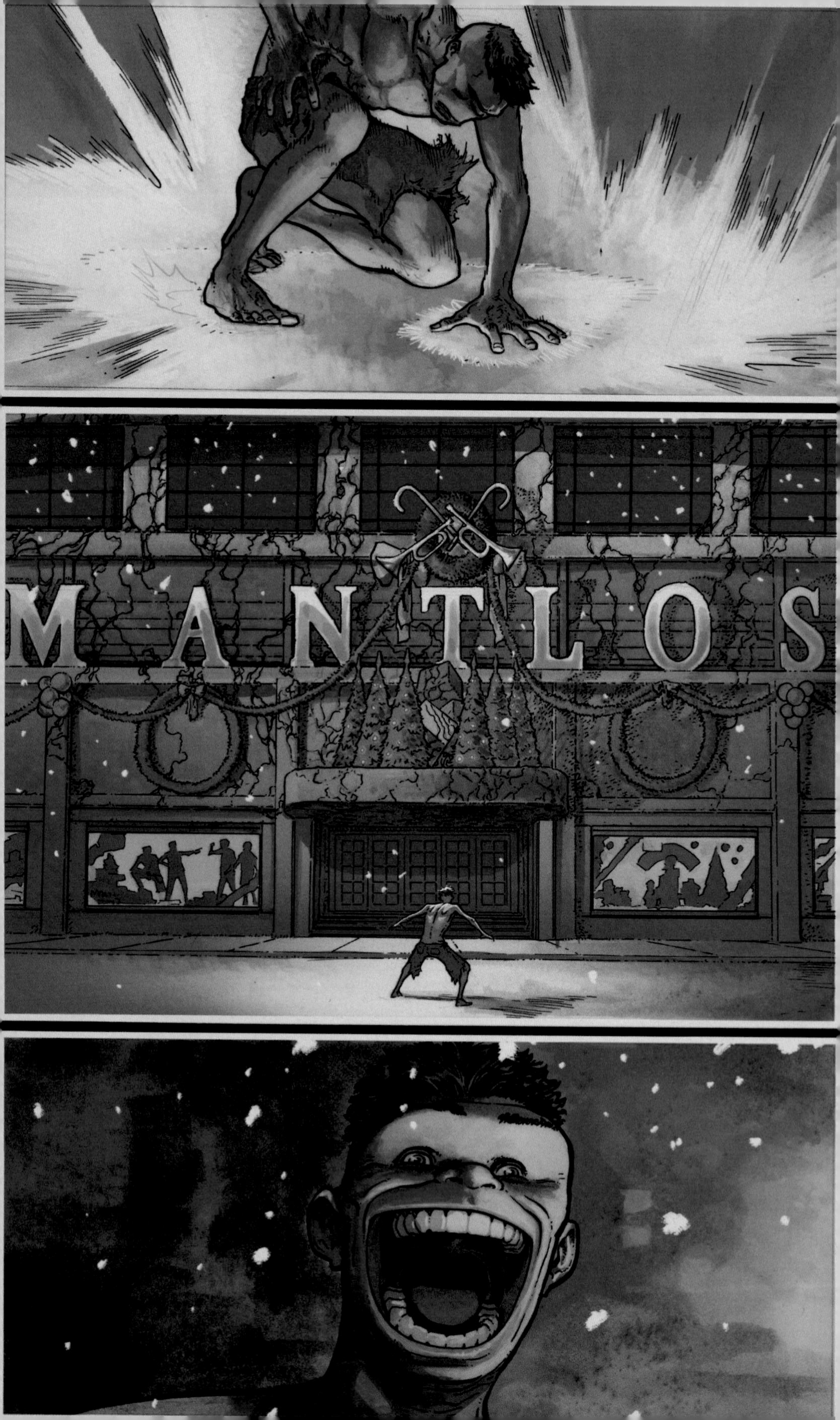
MANTLOS

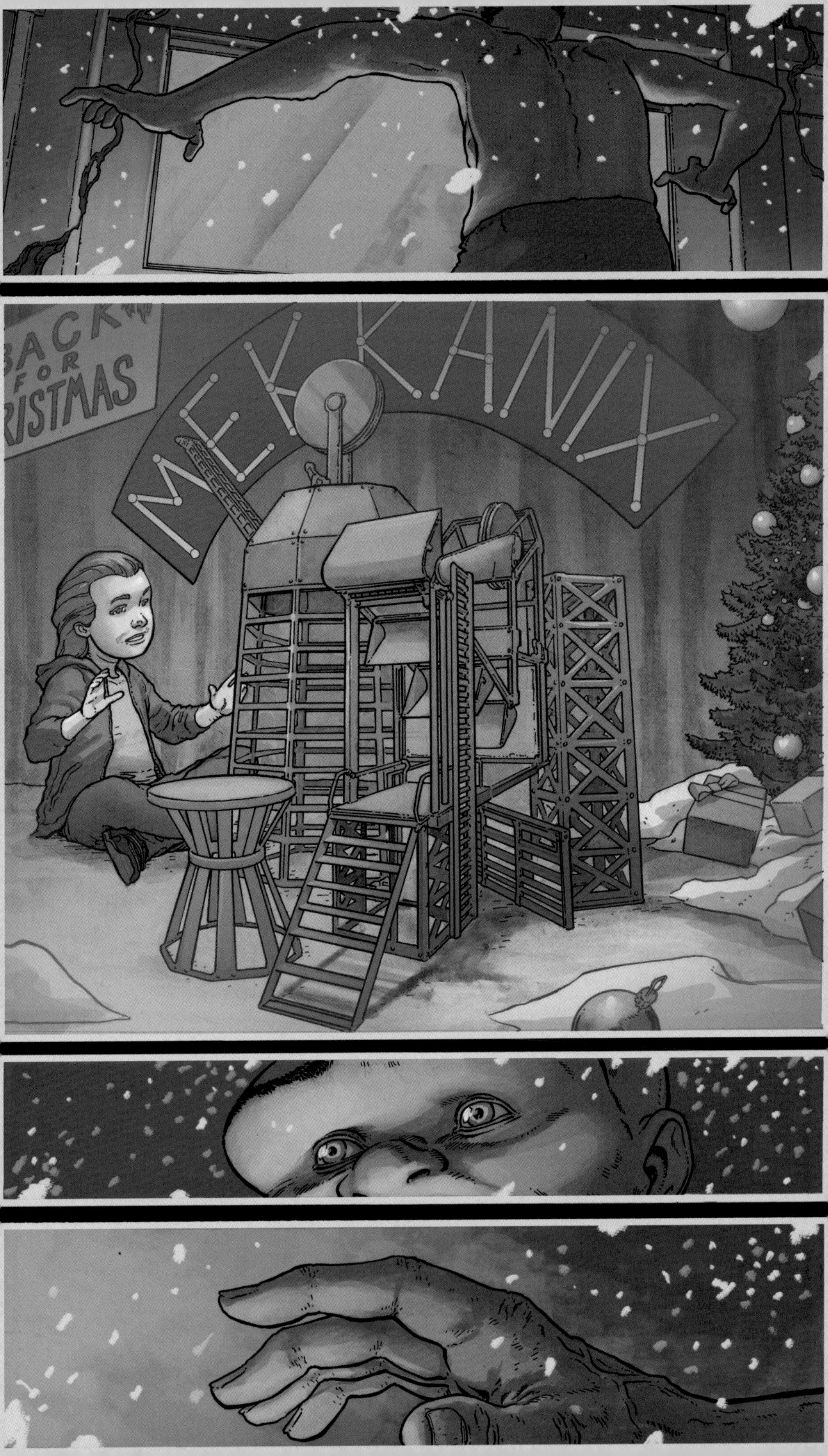

BACK
FOR
RISTMAS
MEKKANIX

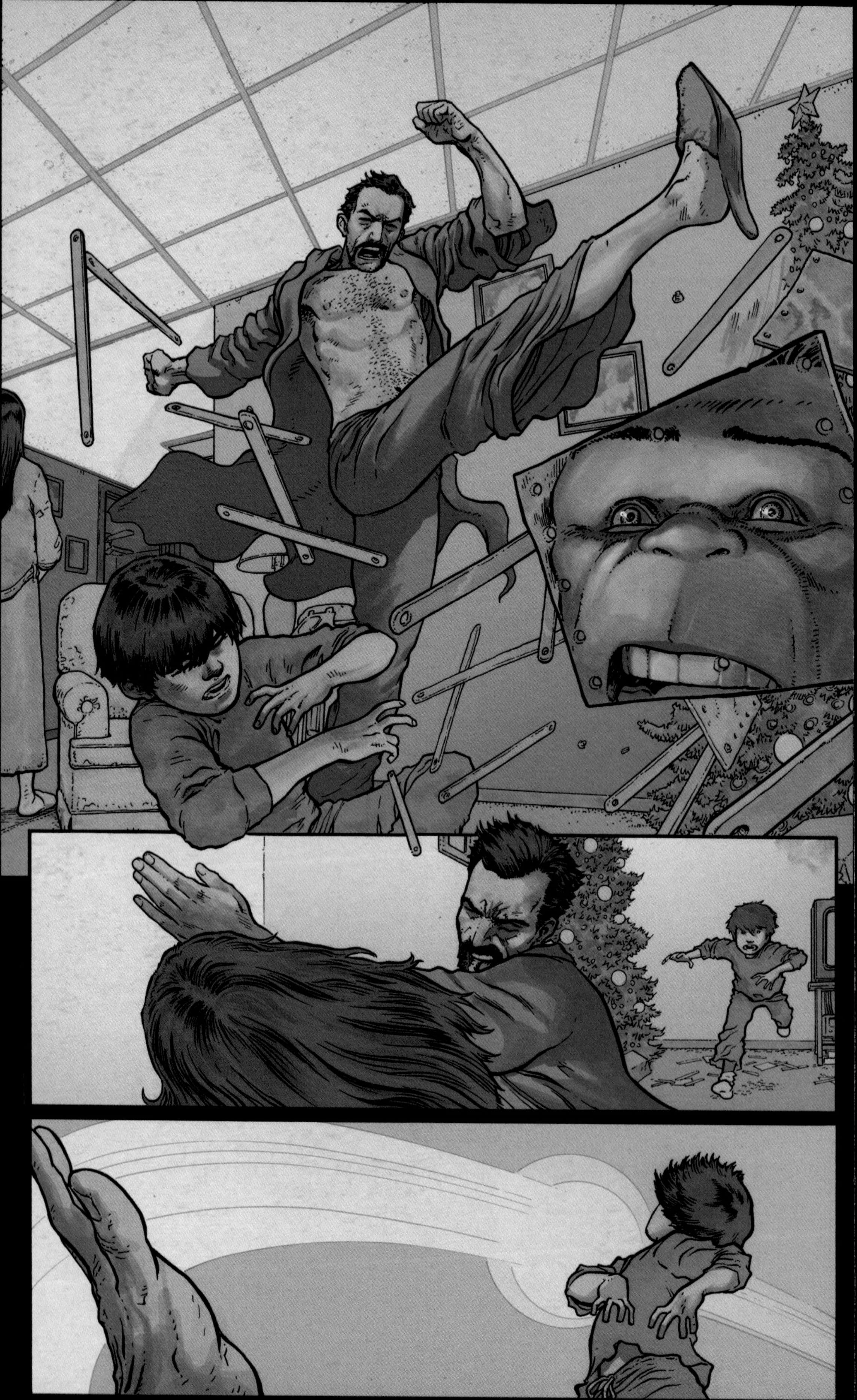

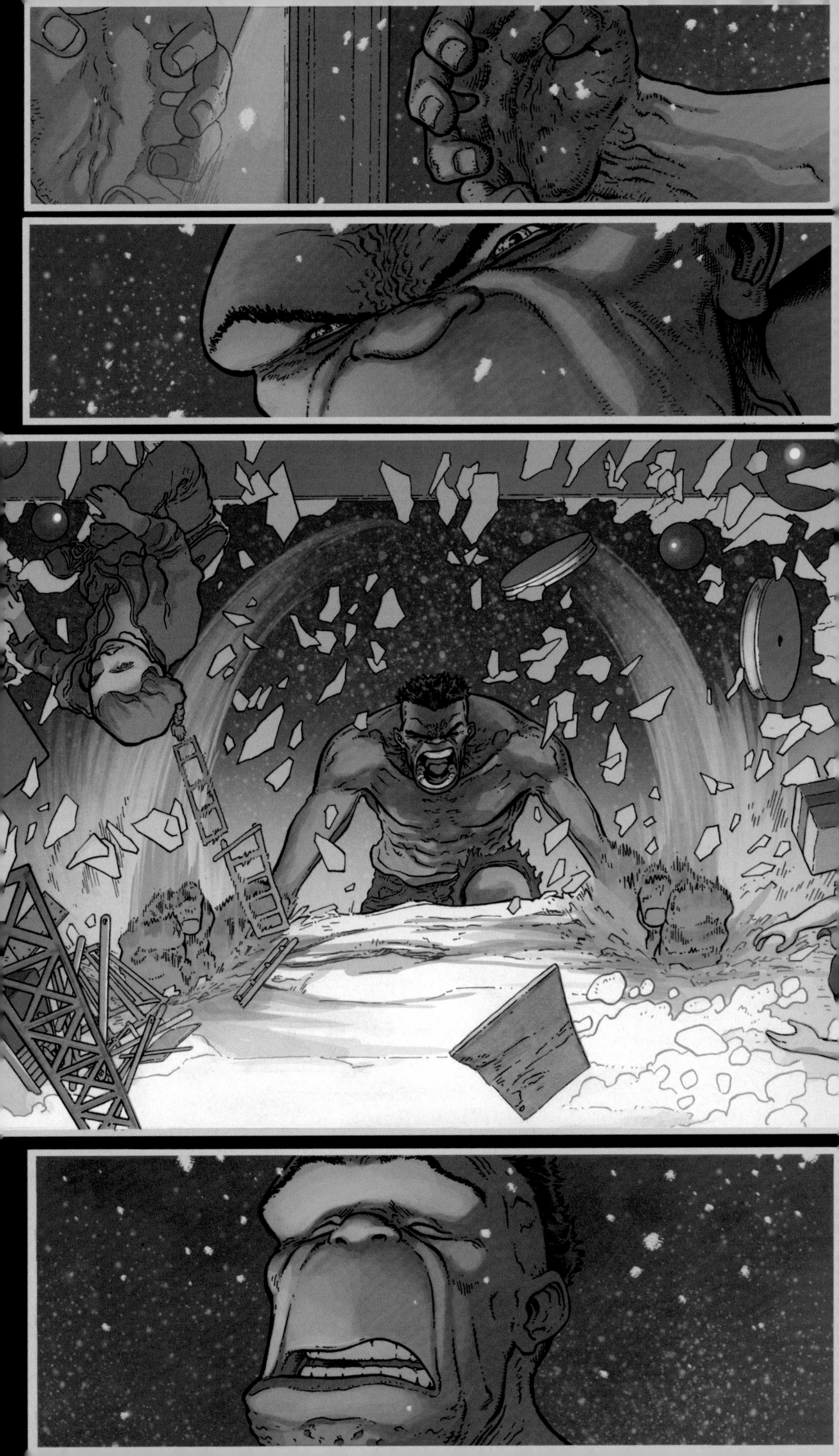

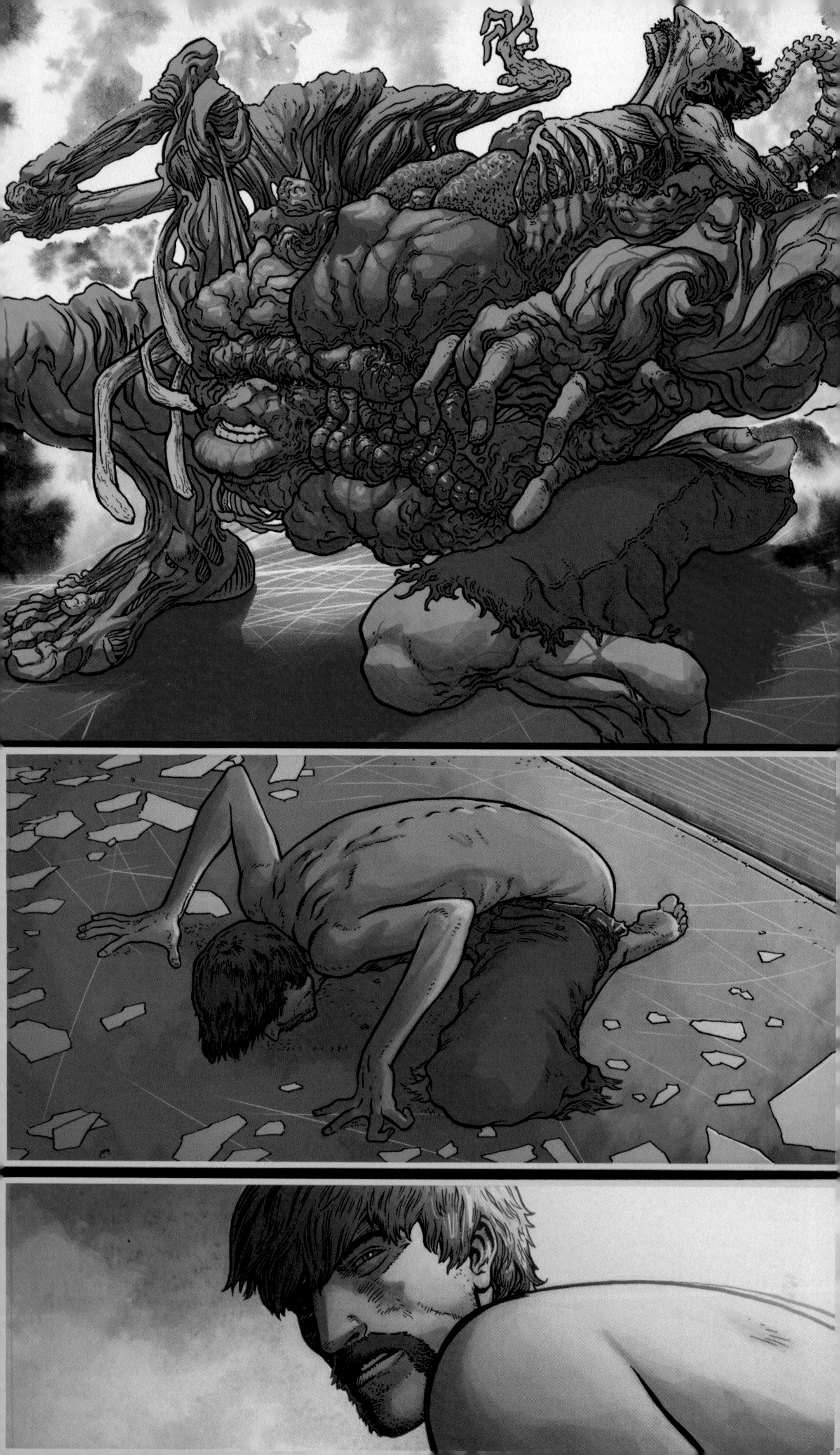

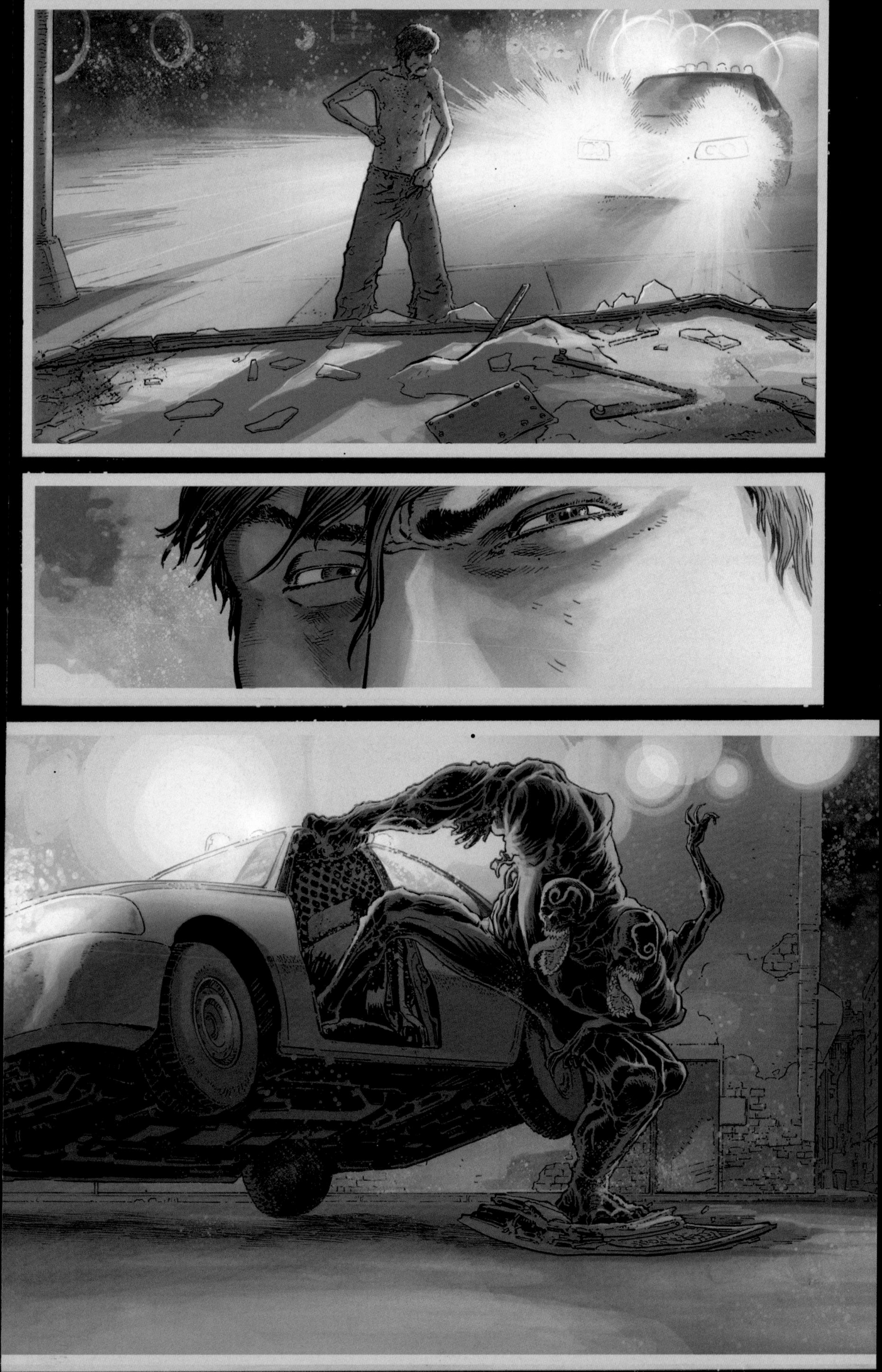

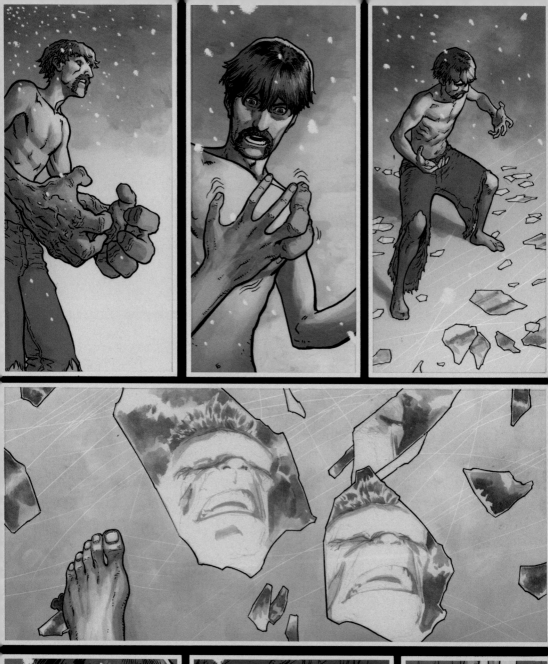

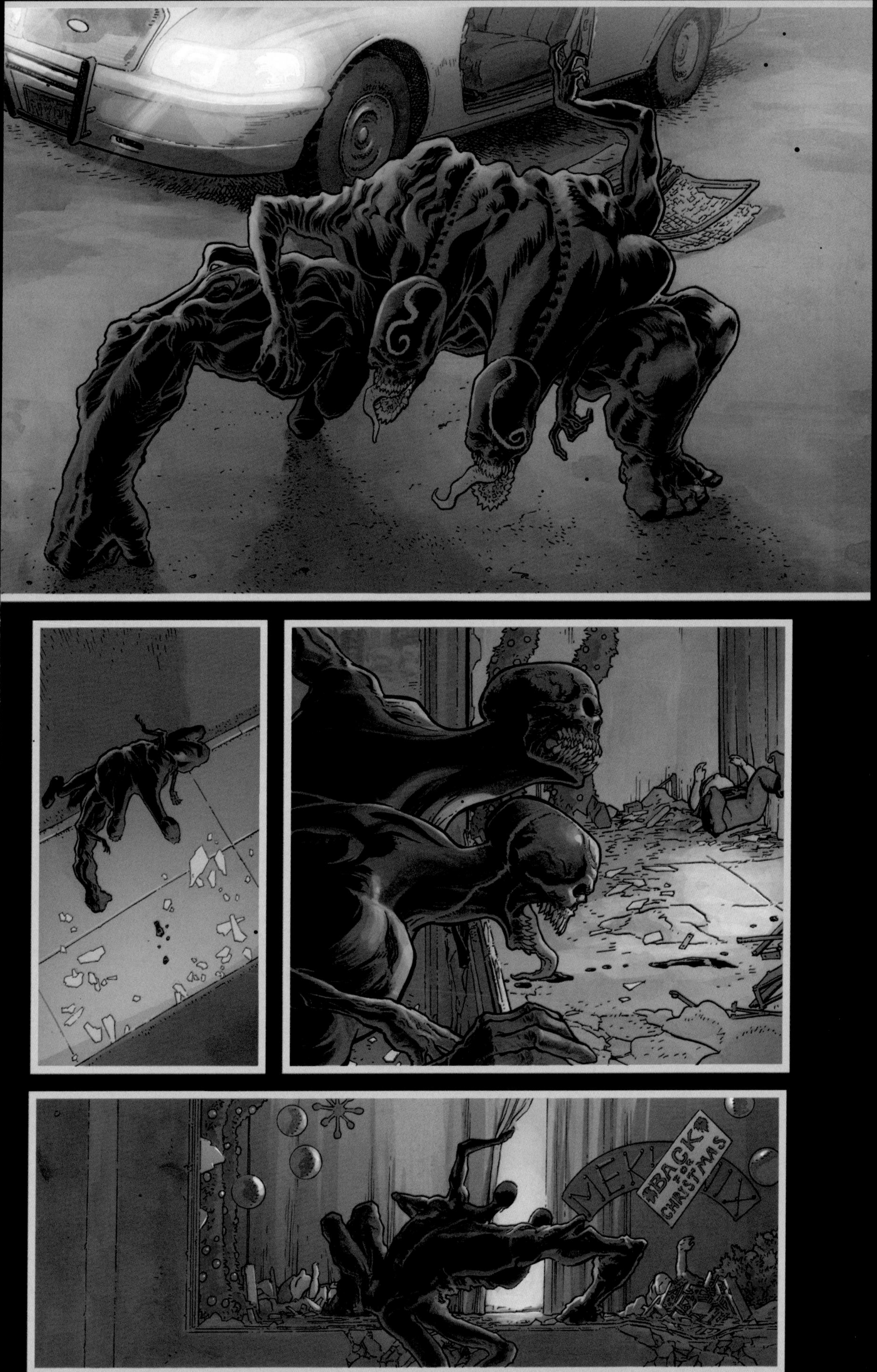
BACK FOR CHRISTMAS

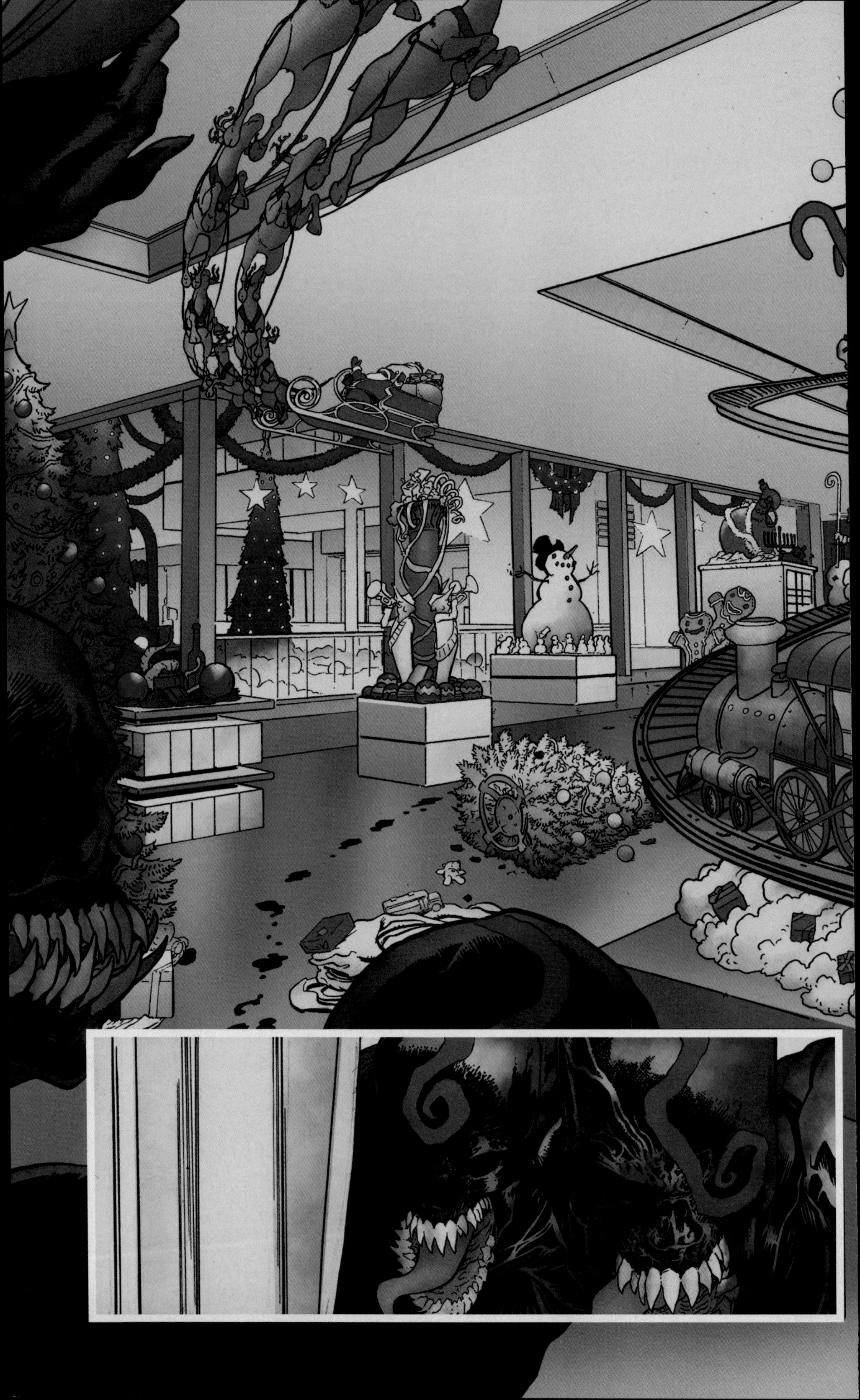

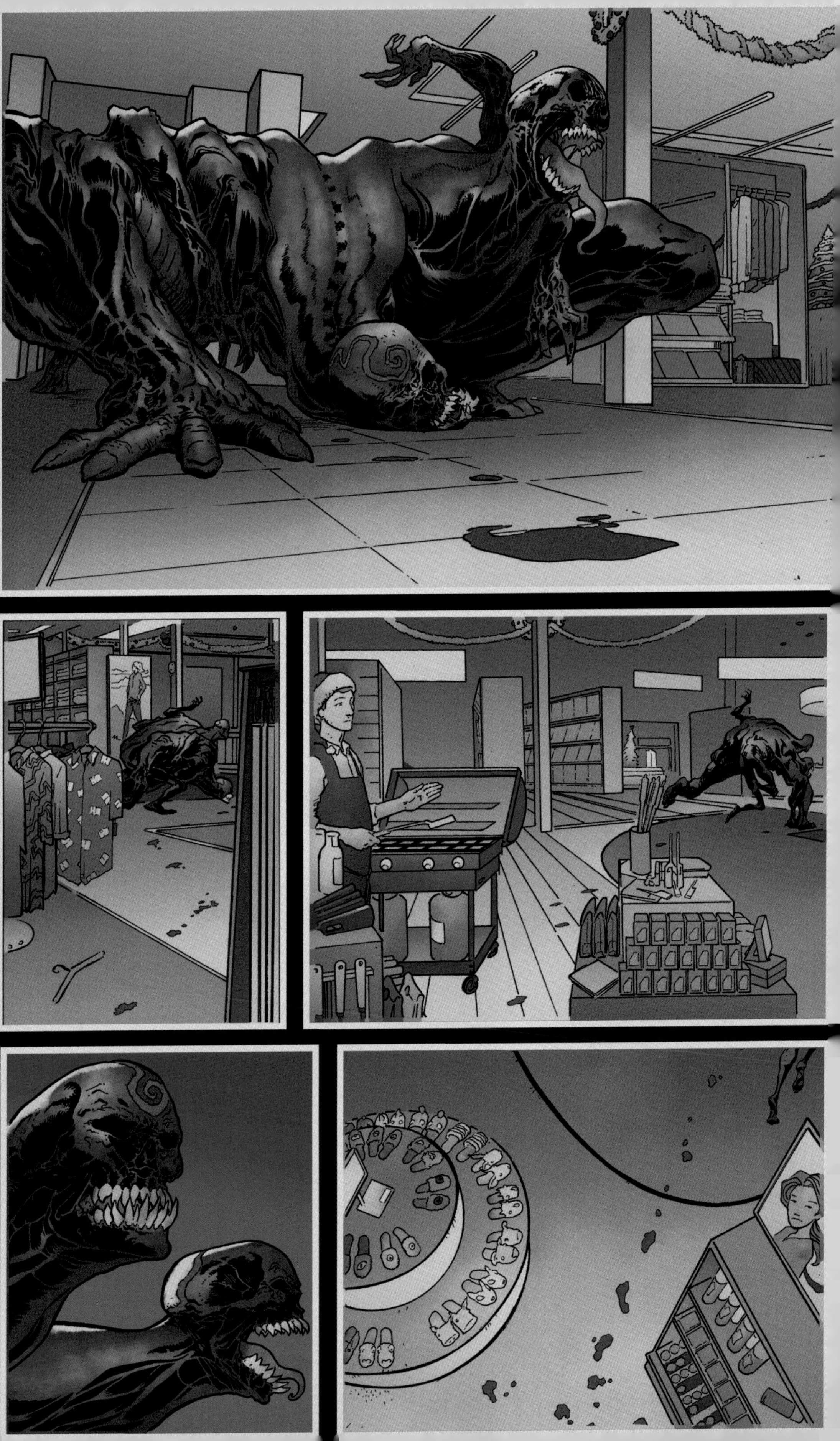

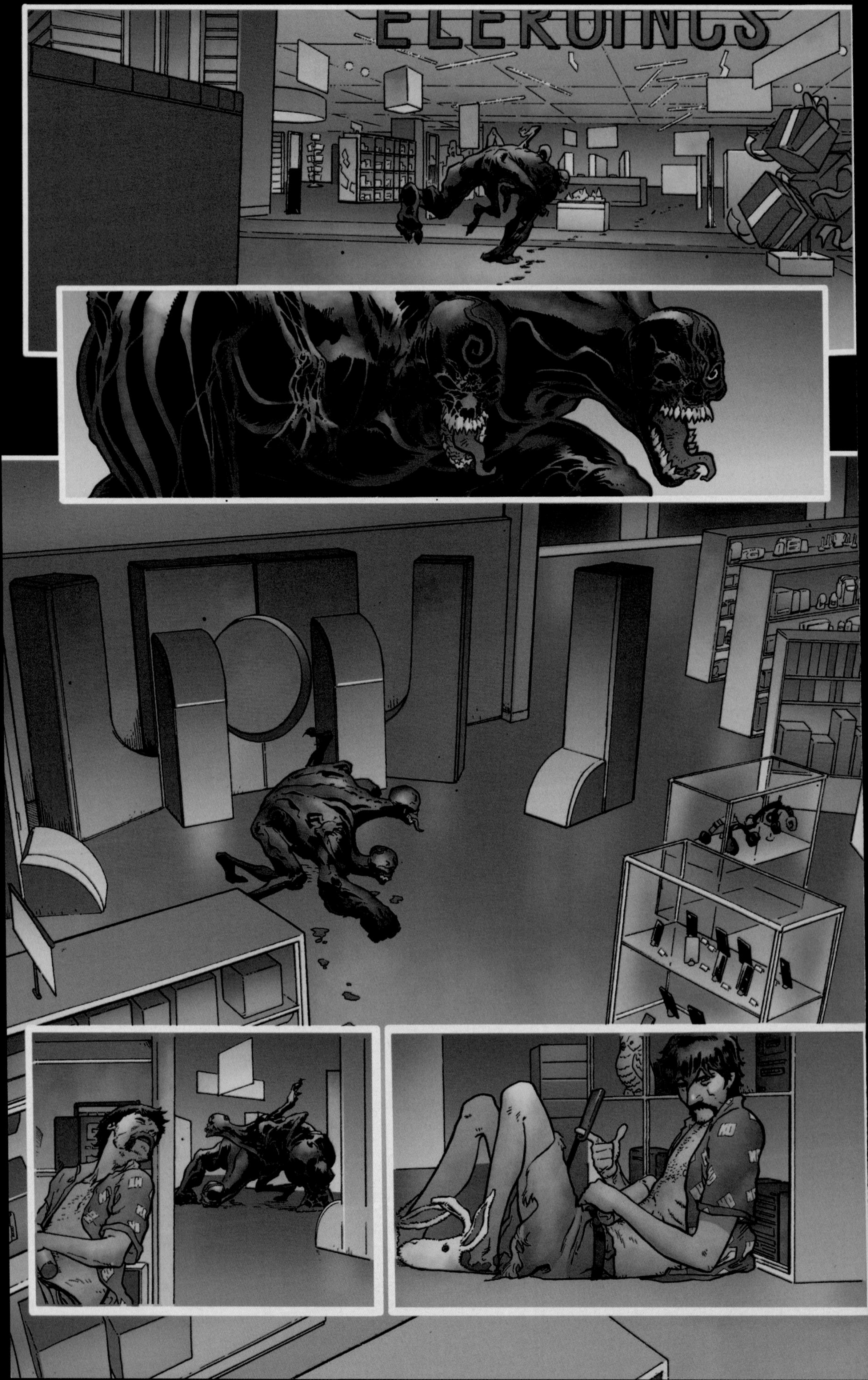

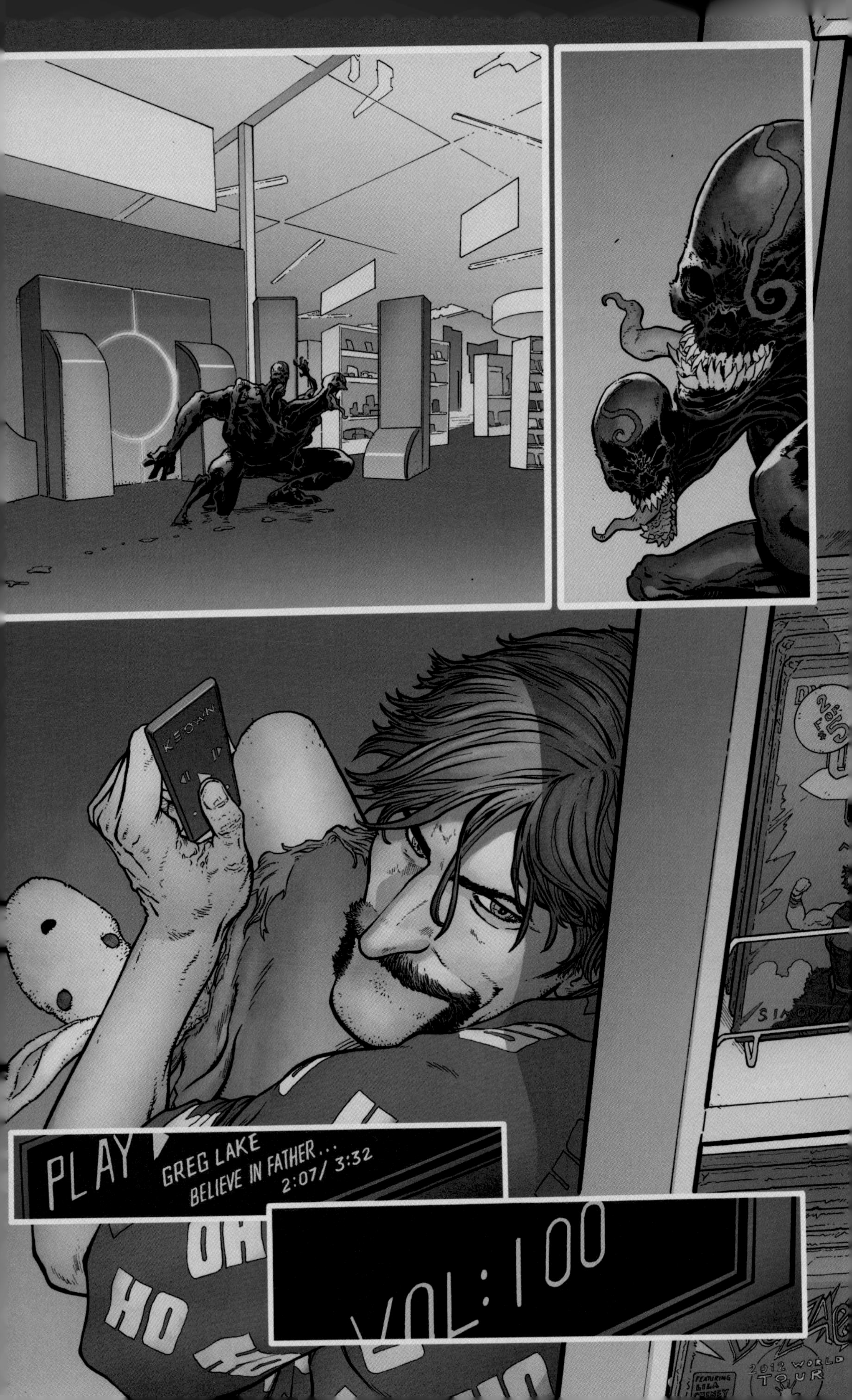
PLAY
GREG LAKE
BELIEVE IN FATHER...
2:07/ 3:32
VOL: 100
2012 WORLD TOUR

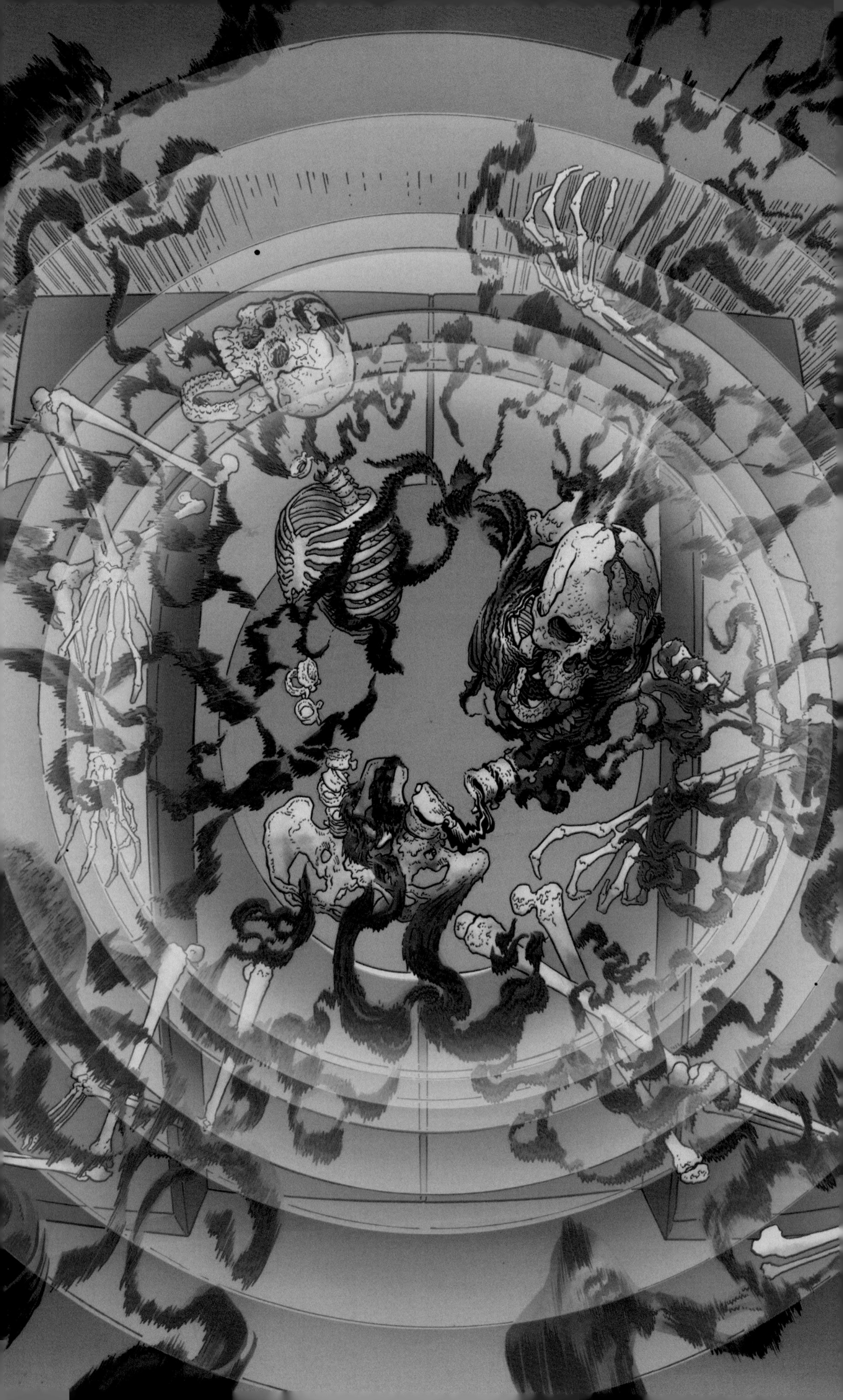

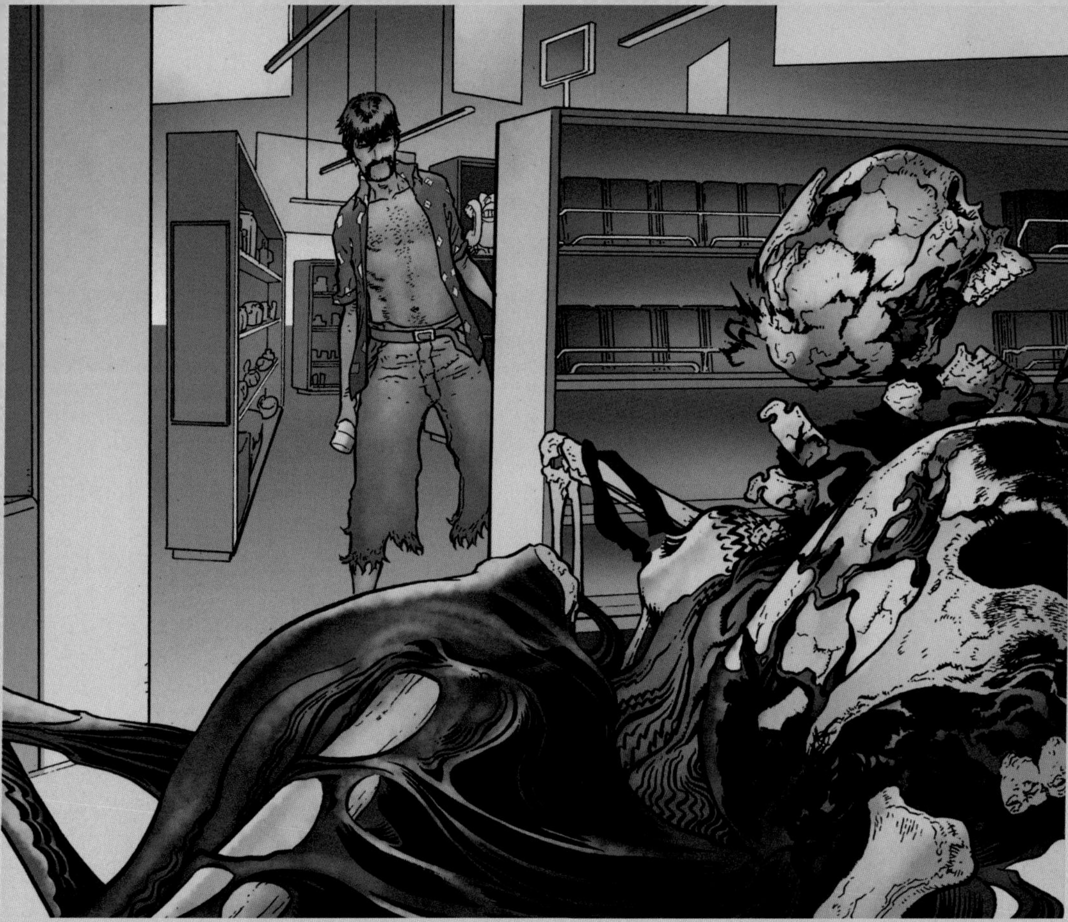
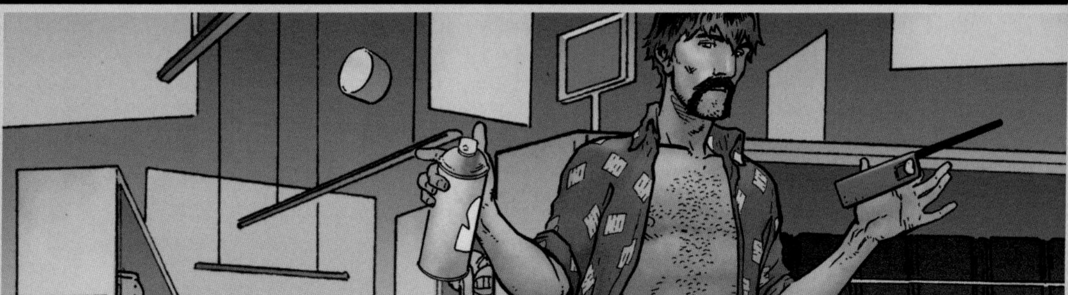
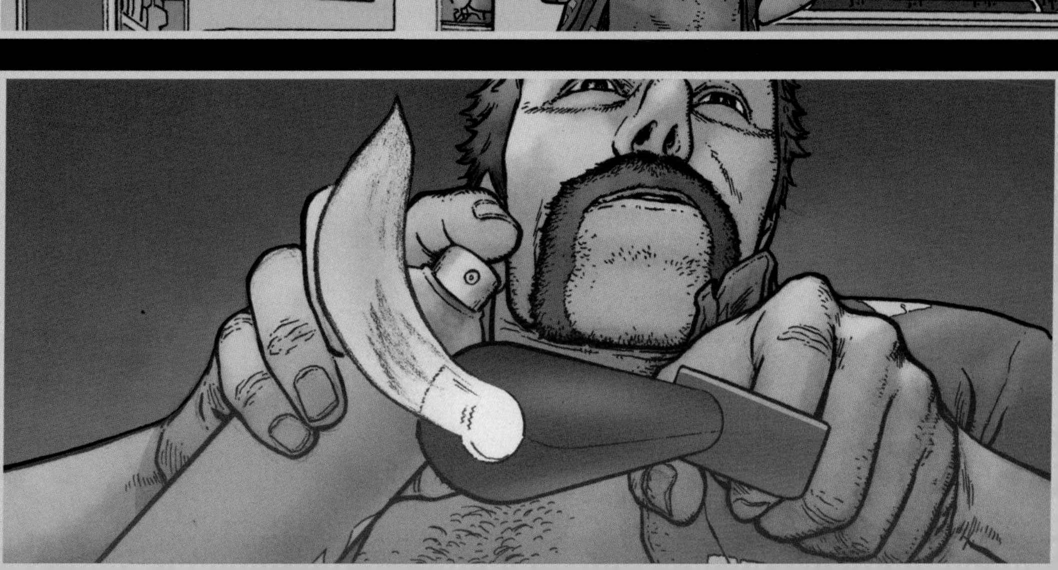

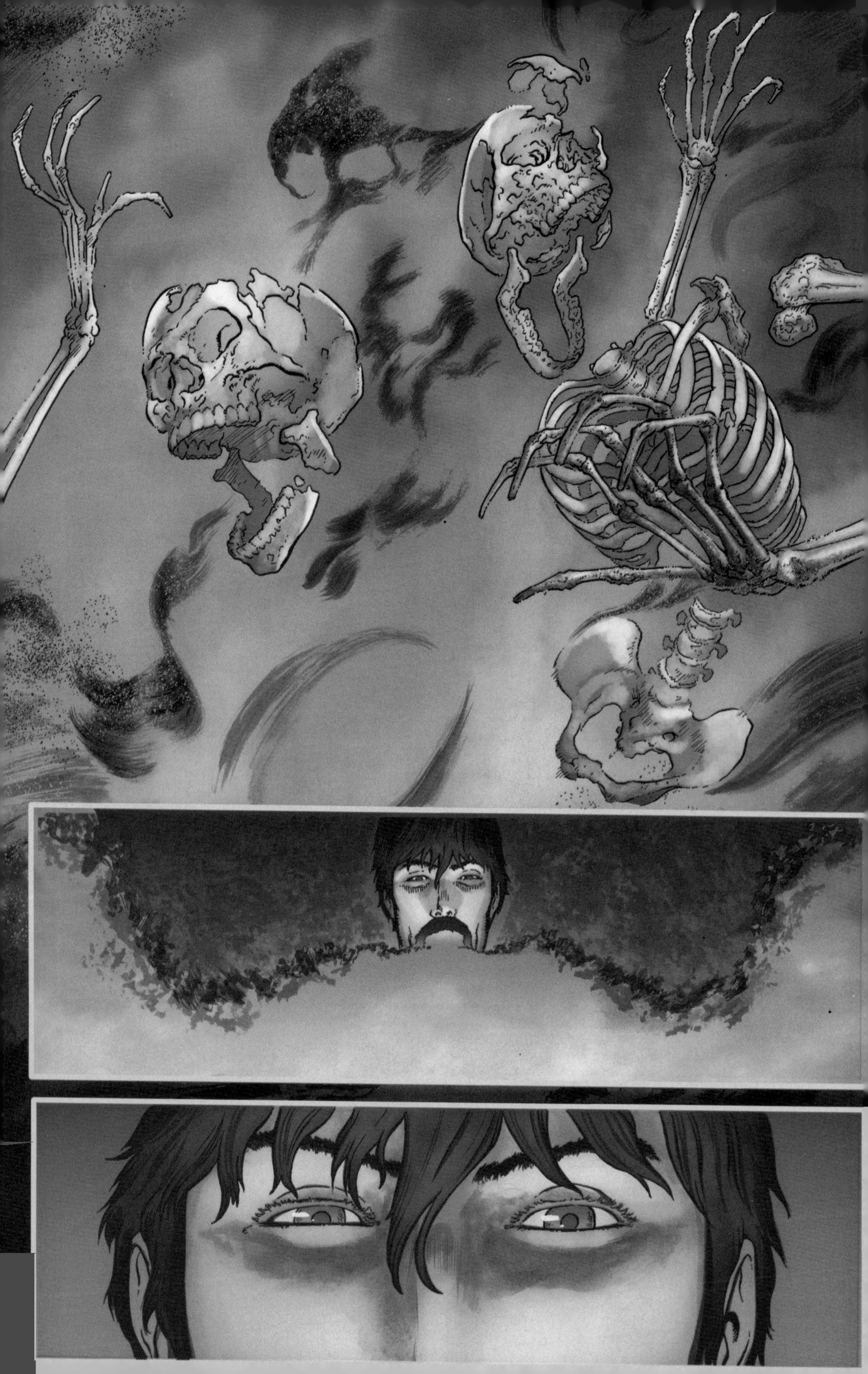

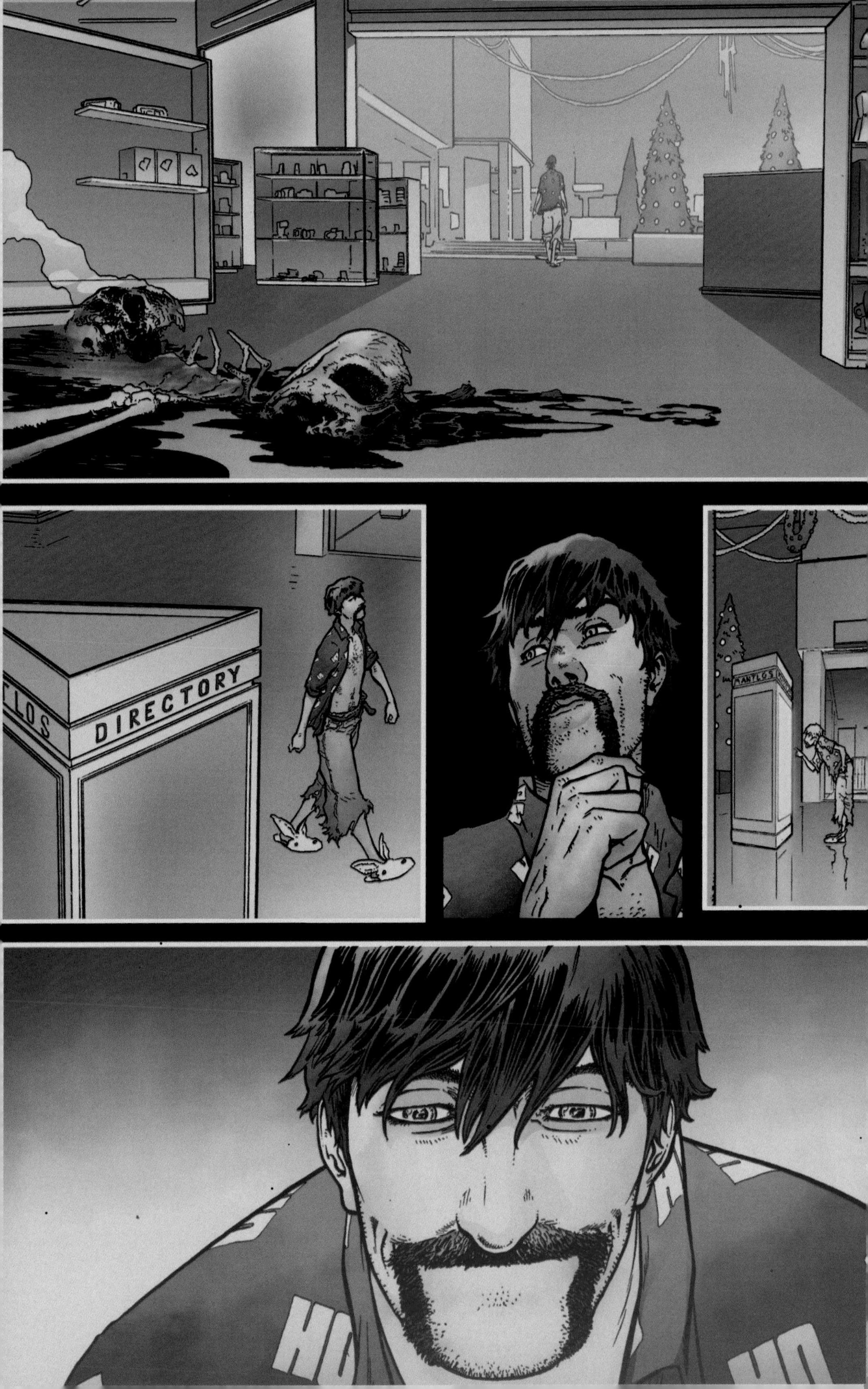
DIRECTORY

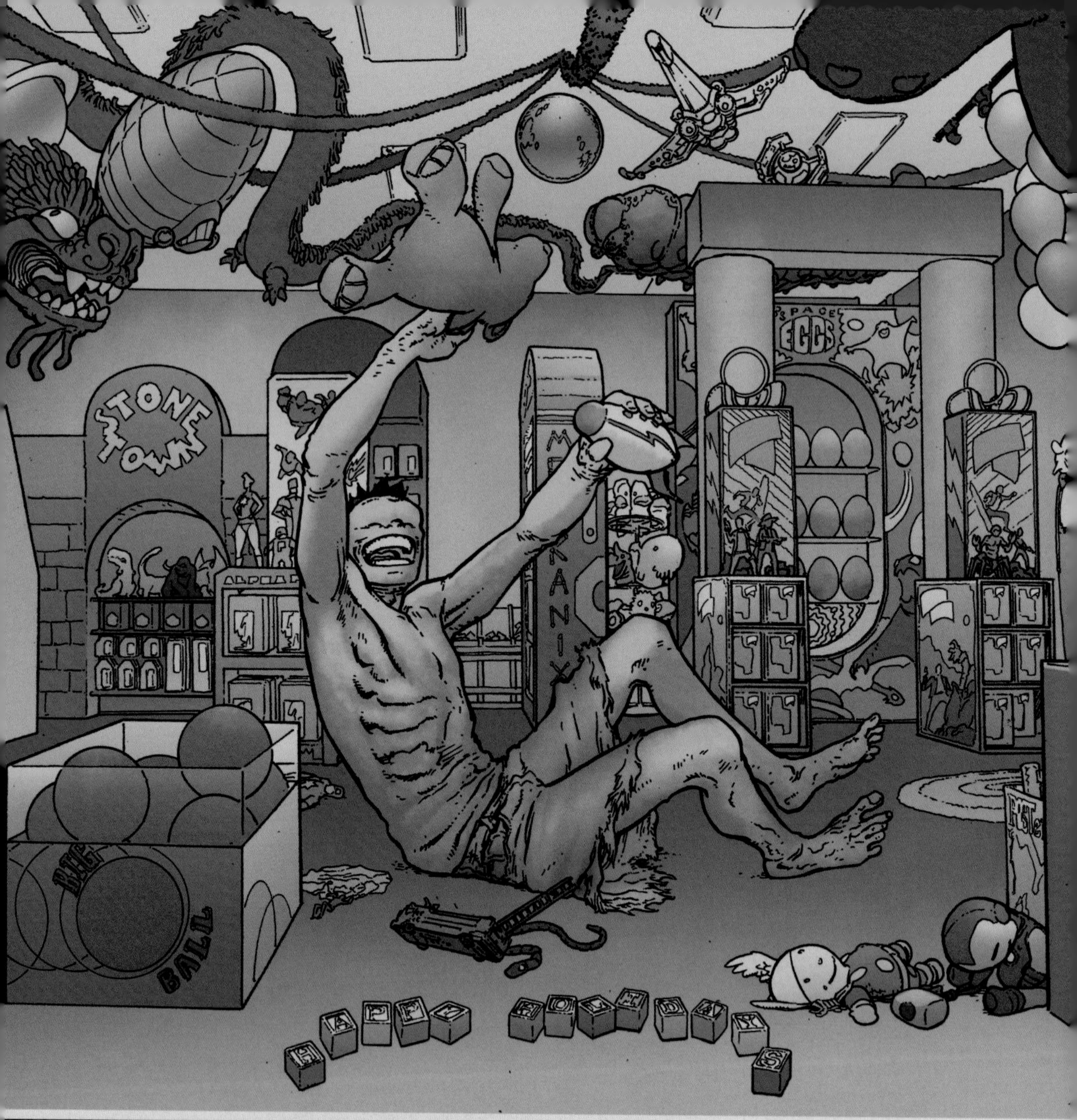
STONE TOWN
BIG BALL
SPACE EGGS

...and to all a

GOOD NIGHT.

"IF THESE SHADOWS REMAIN
UNALTERED BY THE FUTURE,
THE CHILD WILL DIE."

— CHARLES DICKENS,
A CHRISTMAS CAROL

IRON MAN / DOCTOR DOOM

Genius industrialist **TONY STARK** protects humanity as the armored avenger **IRON MAN**.

DOCTOR VICTOR VON DOOM has long used his talents for sorcery and technology for both great good and great evil.

In the midst of battling **KNULL**'s dragons, **IRON MAN** created a new version of his Extremis armor that combines his tech with a symbiote, though seemingly at the cost Of **EDDIE BROCK**'s life.

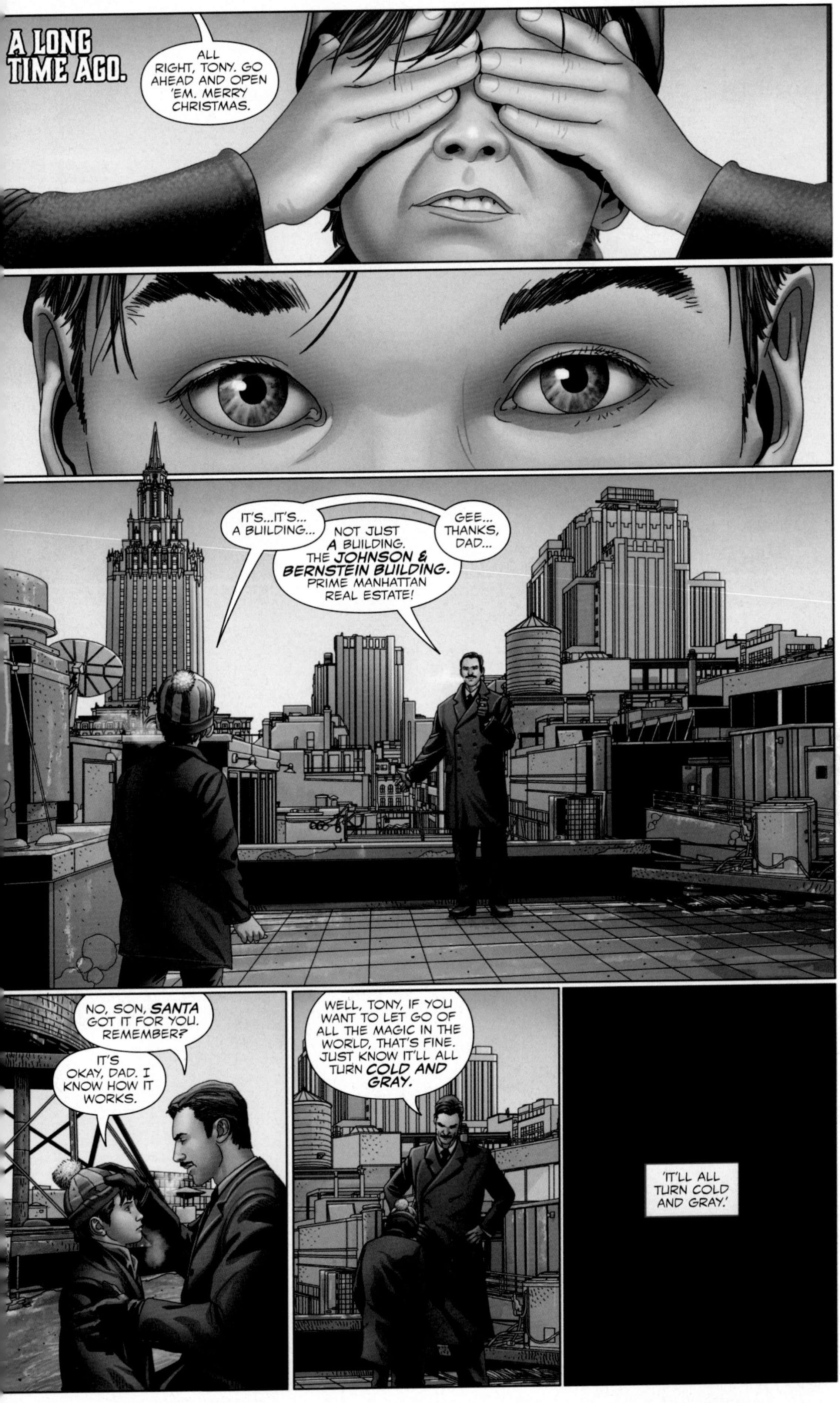
A LONG TIME AGO.
ALL RIGHT, TONY. GO AHEAD AND OPEN 'EM. MERRY CHRISTMAS.
IT'S...IT'S... A BUILDING...
NOT JUST A BUILDING. THE JOHNSON & BERNSTEIN BUILDING. PRIME MANHATTAN REAL ESTATE!
GEE... THANKS, DAD...
NO, SON, SANTA GOT IT FOR YOU. REMEMBER?
IT'S OKAY, DAD. I KNOW HOW IT WORKS.
WELL, TONY, IF YOU WANT TO LET GO OF ALL THE MAGIC IN THE WORLD, THAT'S FINE. JUST KNOW IT'LL ALL TURN COLD AND GRAY.
'IT'LL ALL TURN COLD AND GRAY.'

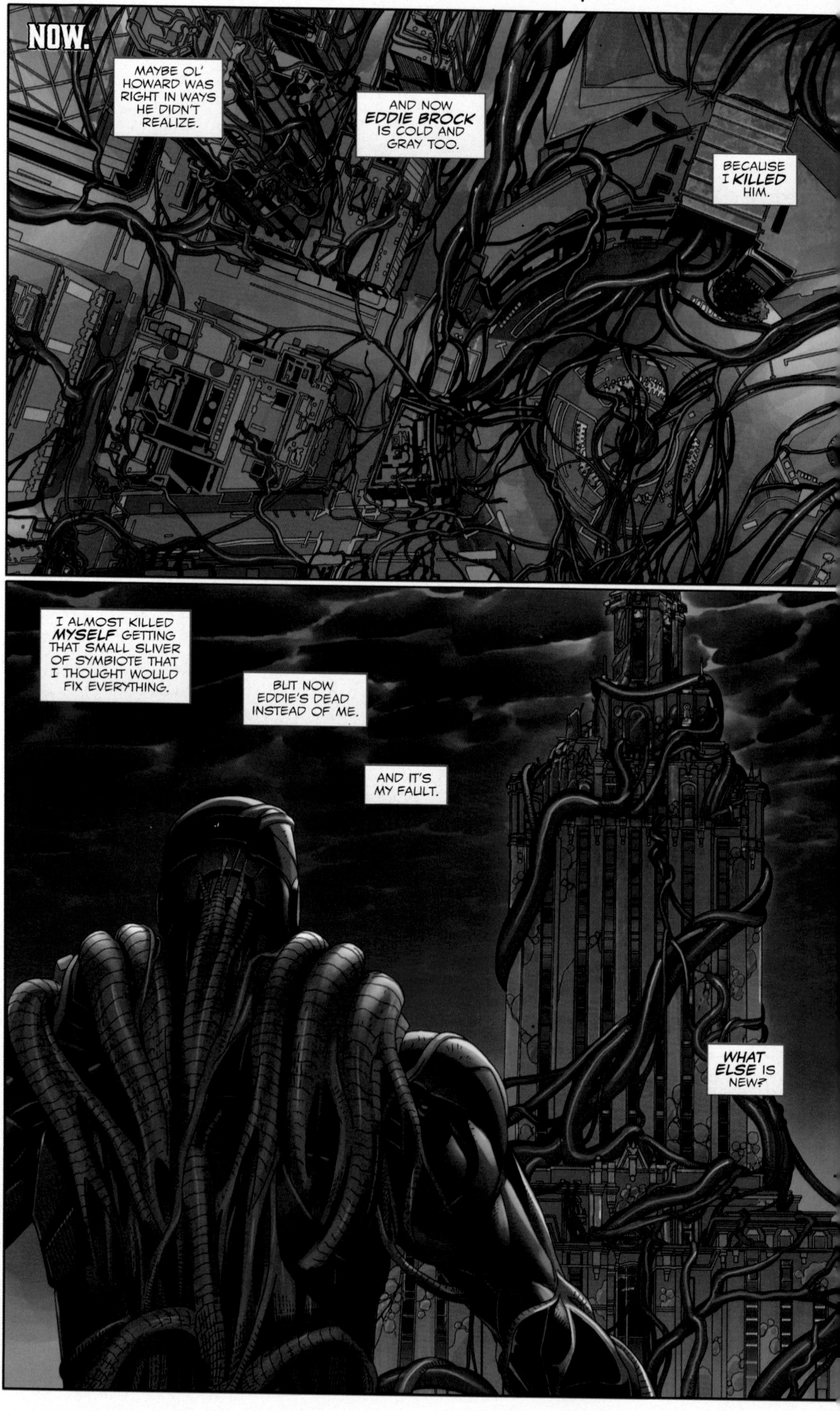
NOW.
MAYBE OL' HOWARD WAS RIGHT IN WAYS HE DIDN'T REALIZE.
AND NOW EDDIE BROCK IS COLD AND GRAY TOO.
BECAUSE I KILLED HIM.
I ALMOST KILLED MYSELF GETTING THAT SMALL SLIVER OF SYMBIOTE THAT I THOUGHT WOULD FIX EVERYTHING.
BUT NOW EDDIE'S DEAD INSTEAD OF ME.
AND IT'S MY FAULT.
WHAT ELSE IS NEW?

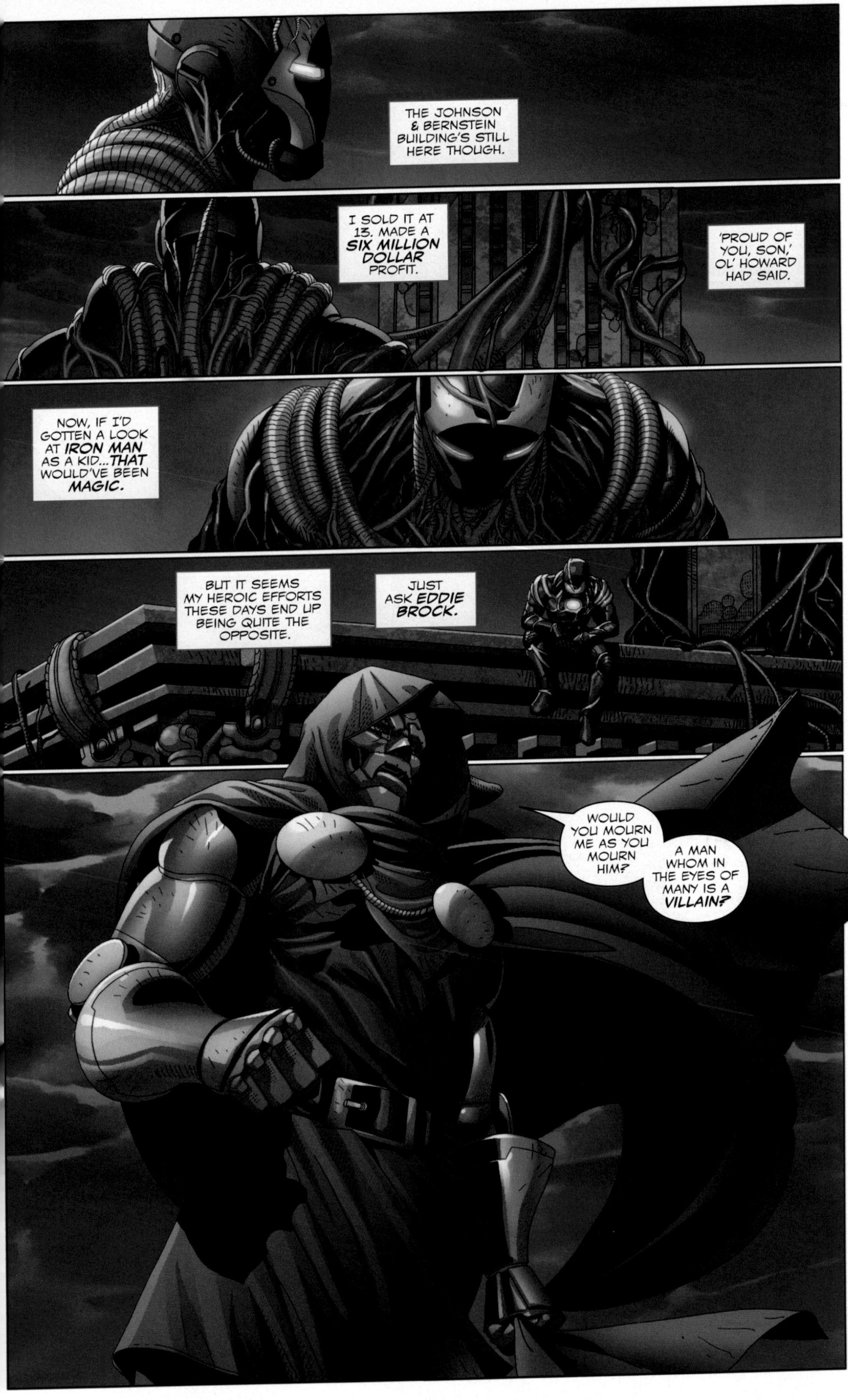
THE JOHNSON & BERNSTEIN BUILDING'S STILL HERE THOUGH.
I SOLD IT AT 13. MADE A **SIX MILLION DOLLAR** PROFIT.
'PROUD OF YOU, SON,' OL' HOWARD HAD SAID.
NOW, IF I'D GOTTEN A LOOK AT **IRON MAN** AS A KID...**THAT** WOULD'VE BEEN **MAGIC.**
BUT IT SEEMS MY HEROIC EFFORTS THESE DAYS END UP BEING QUITE THE OPPOSITE.
JUST ASK **EDDIE BROCK.**
WOULD YOU MOURN ME AS YOU MOURN HIM?
A MAN WHOM IN THE EYES OF MANY IS A **VILLAIN?**

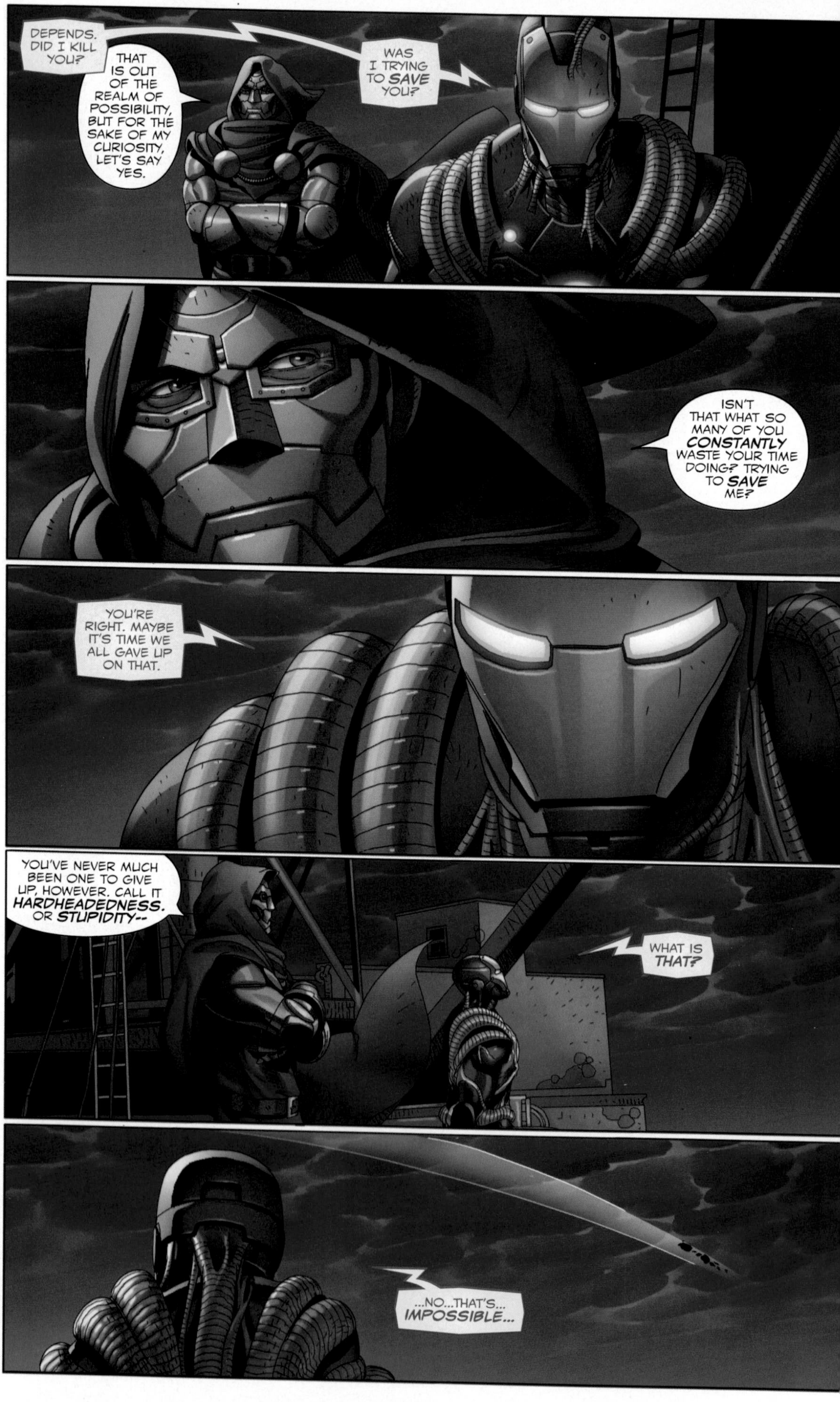
DEPENDS. DID I KILL YOU?
WAS I TRYING TO SAVE YOU?
THAT IS OUT OF THE REALM OF POSSIBILITY, BUT FOR THE SAKE OF MY CURIOSITY, LET'S SAY YES.
ISN'T THAT WHAT SO MANY OF YOU CONSTANTLY WASTE YOUR TIME DOING? TRYING TO SAVE ME?
YOU'RE RIGHT. MAYBE IT'S TIME WE ALL GAVE UP ON THAT.
YOU'VE NEVER MUCH BEEN ONE TO GIVE UP, HOWEVER. CALL IT HARDHEADEDNESS. OR STUPIDITY--
WHAT IS THAT?
...NO...THAT'S... IMPOSSIBLE...

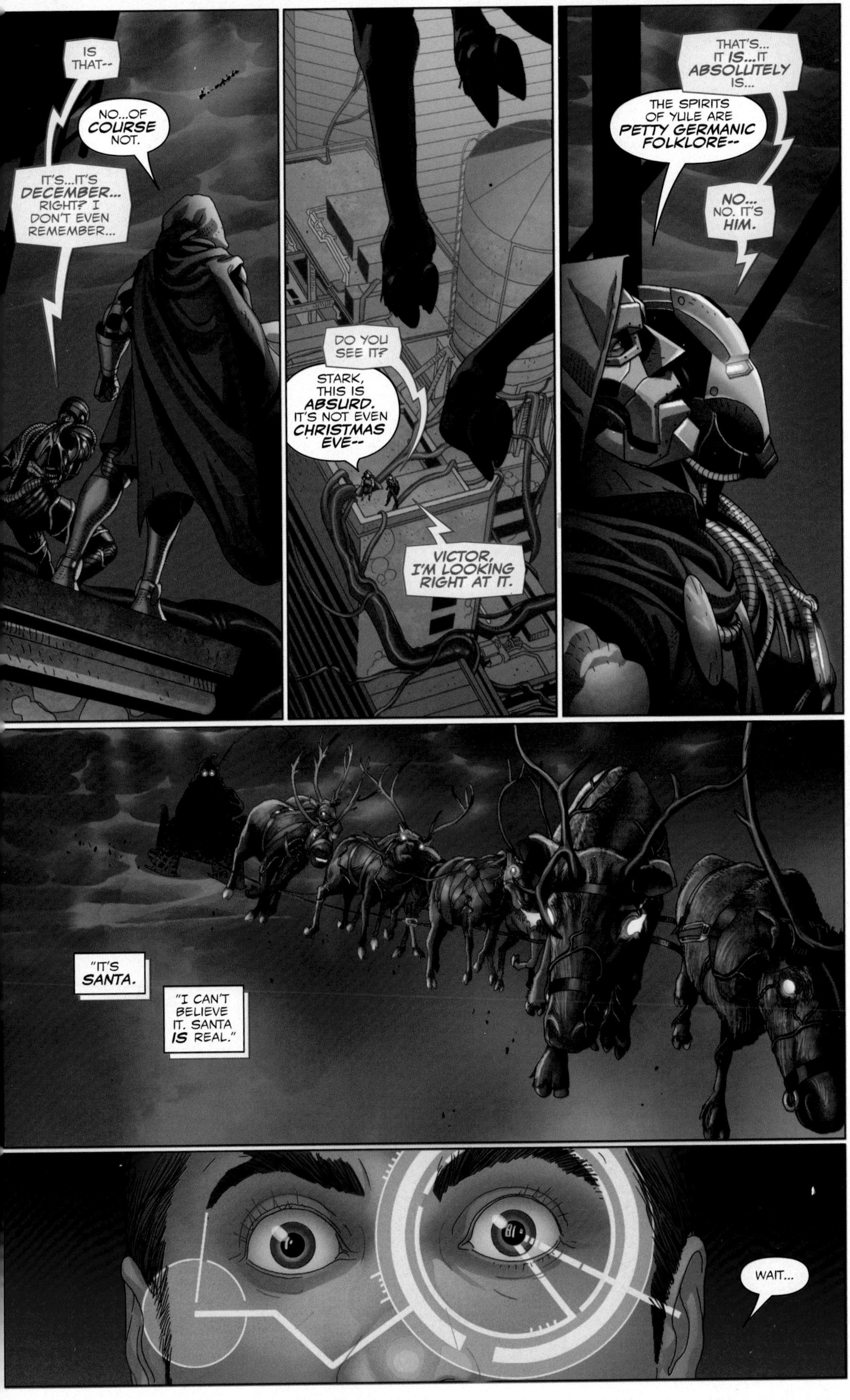
IS THAT--
NO...OF COURSE NOT.
IT'S...IT'S DECEMBER... RIGHT? I DON'T EVEN REMEMBER...
DO YOU SEE IT?
STARK, THIS IS ABSURD. IT'S NOT EVEN CHRISTMAS EVE--
VICTOR, I'M LOOKING RIGHT AT IT.
THAT'S... IT IS...IT ABSOLUTELY IS...
THE SPIRITS OF YULE ARE PETTY GERMANIC FOLKLORE--
NO... NO. IT'S HIM.
"IT'S SANTA.
"I CAN'T BELIEVE IT. SANTA IS REAL."
WAIT...

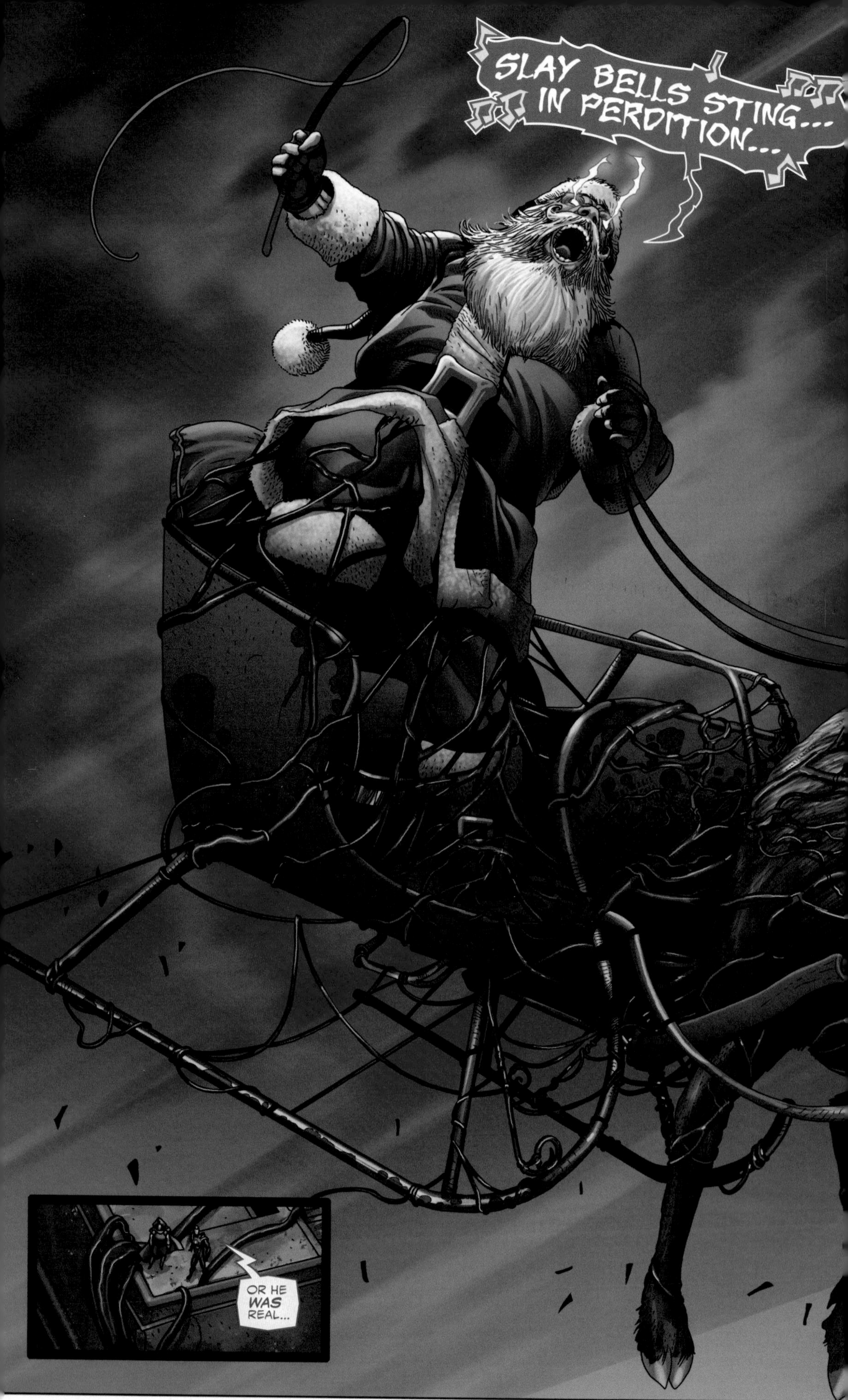
SLAY BELLS STING... IN PERDITION...
OR HE WAS REAL...

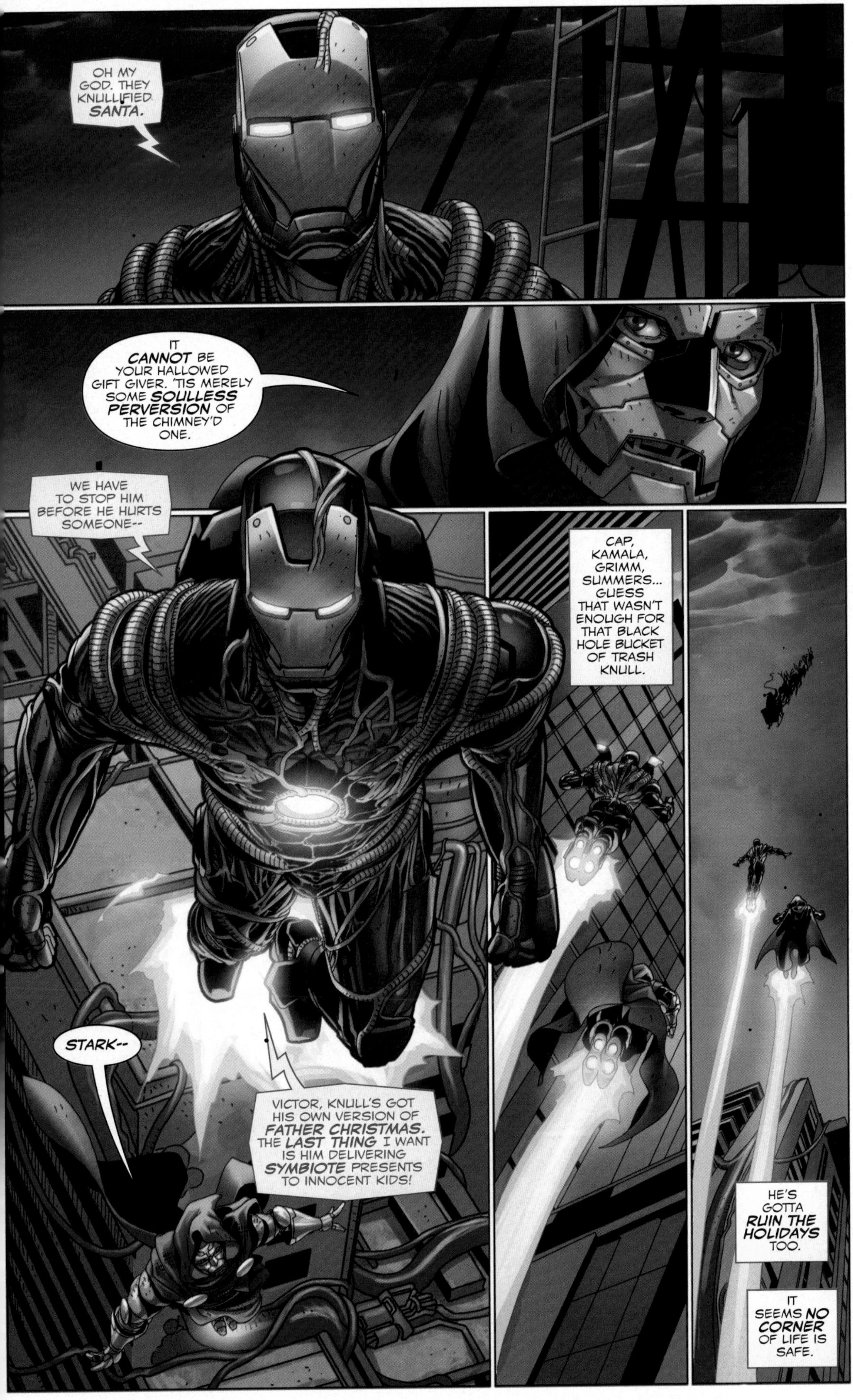
OH MY GOD. THEY KNULLIFIED SANTA.
IT CANNOT BE YOUR HALLOWED GIFT GIVER. 'TIS MERELY SOME SOULLESS PERVERSION OF THE CHIMNEY'D ONE.
WE HAVE TO STOP HIM BEFORE HE HURTS SOMEONE--
STARK--
VICTOR, KNULL'S GOT HIS OWN VERSION OF FATHER CHRISTMAS. THE LAST THING I WANT IS HIM DELIVERING SYMBIOTE PRESENTS TO INNOCENT KIDS!
CAP, KAMALA, GRIMM, SUMMERS... GUESS THAT WASN'T ENOUGH FOR THAT BLACK HOLE BUCKET OF TRASH KNULL.
HE'S GOTTA RUIN THE HOLIDAYS TOO.
IT SEEMS NO CORNER OF LIFE IS SAFE.

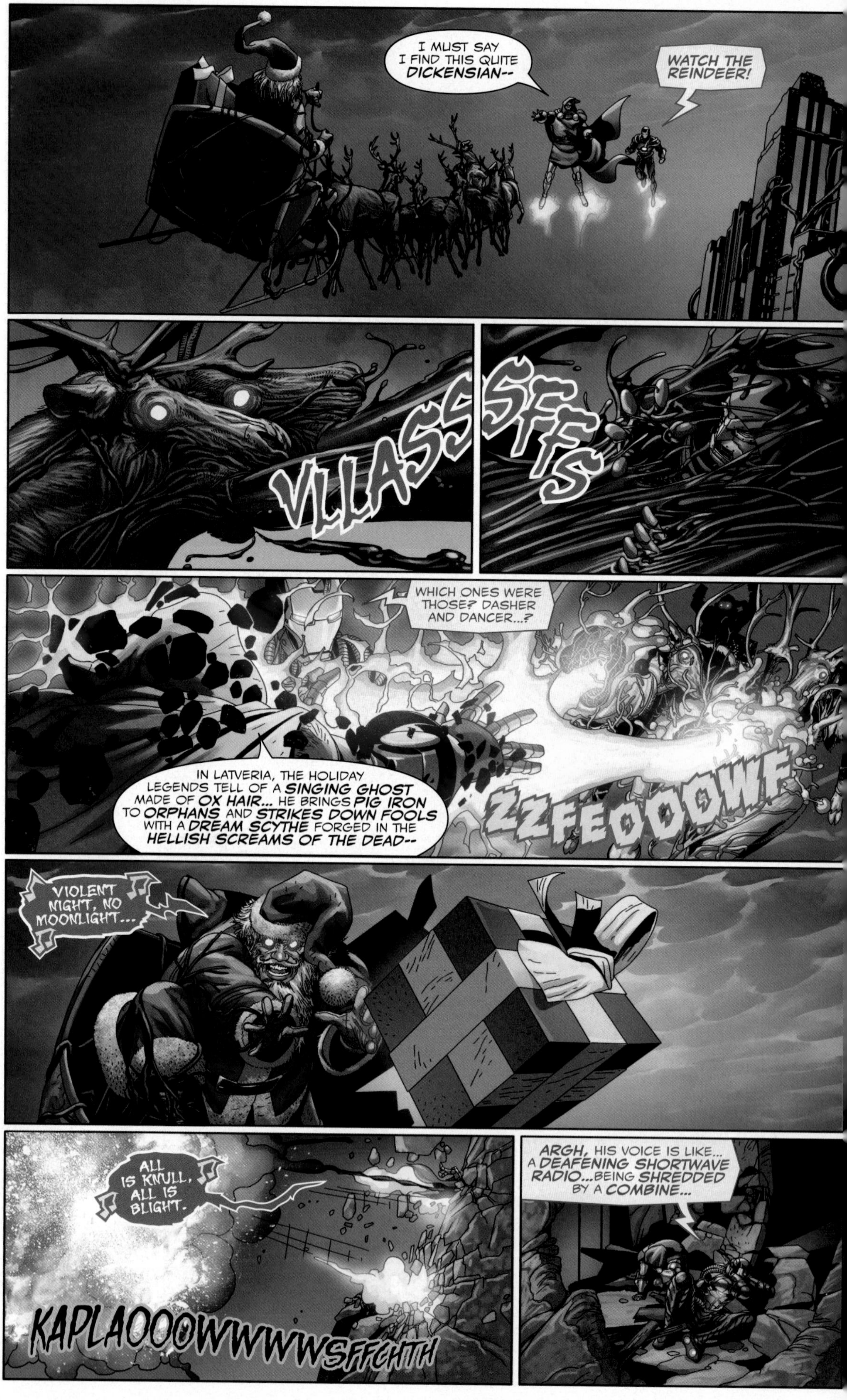

I MUST SAY I FIND THIS QUITE DICKENSIAN--
WATCH THE REINDEER!
VLLASSSFFS
WHICH ONES WERE THOSE? DASHER AND DANCER...?
IN LATVERIA, THE HOLIDAY LEGENDS TELL OF A SINGING GHOST MADE OF OX HAIR... HE BRINGS PIG IRON TO ORPHANS AND STRIKES DOWN FOOLS WITH A DREAM SCYTHE FORGED IN THE HELLISH SCREAMS OF THE DEAD--
ZZFEOOOWF
VIOLENT NIGHT, NO MOONLIGHT...
ALL IS KNULL, ALL IS BLIGHT.
KAPLAOOOWWWWWSFFCHTH
ARGH, HIS VOICE IS LIKE... A DEAFENING SHORTWAVE RADIO...BEING SHREDDED BY A COMBINE...

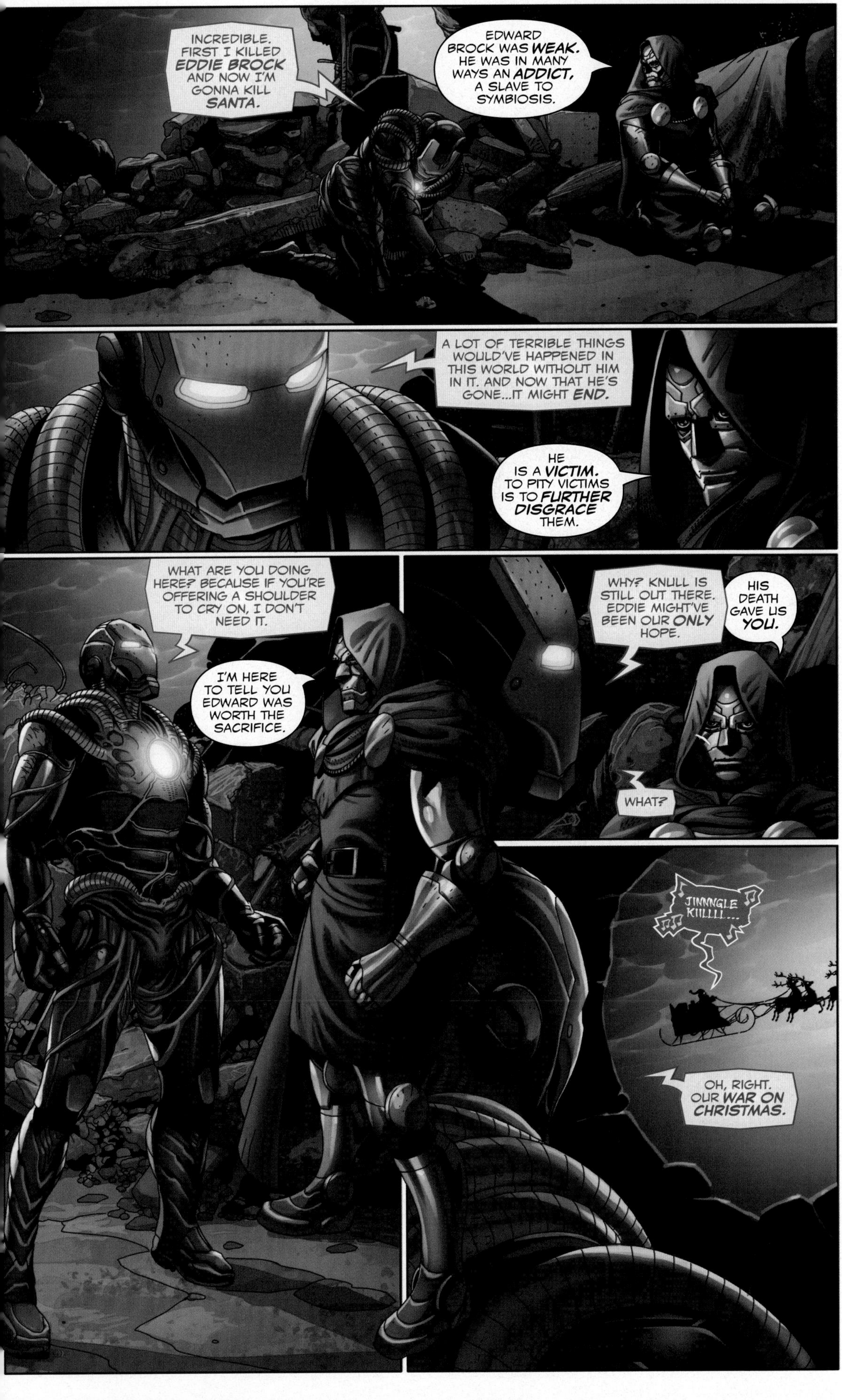
INCREDIBLE. FIRST I KILLED EDDIE BROCK AND NOW I'M GONNA KILL SANTA.
EDWARD BROCK WAS WEAK. HE WAS IN MANY WAYS AN ADDICT, A SLAVE TO SYMBIOSIS.
A LOT OF TERRIBLE THINGS WOULD'VE HAPPENED IN THIS WORLD WITHOUT HIM IN IT. AND NOW THAT HE'S GONE...IT MIGHT END.
HE IS A VICTIM. TO PITY VICTIMS IS TO FURTHER DISGRACE THEM.
WHAT ARE YOU DOING HERE? BECAUSE IF YOU'RE OFFERING A SHOULDER TO CRY ON, I DON'T NEED IT.
I'M HERE TO TELL YOU EDWARD WAS WORTH THE SACRIFICE.
WHY? KNULL IS STILL OUT THERE. EDDIE MIGHT'VE BEEN OUR ONLY HOPE.
HIS DEATH GAVE US YOU.
WHAT?
JINNNGLE KIIllll...
OH, RIGHT. OUR WAR ON CHRISTMAS.

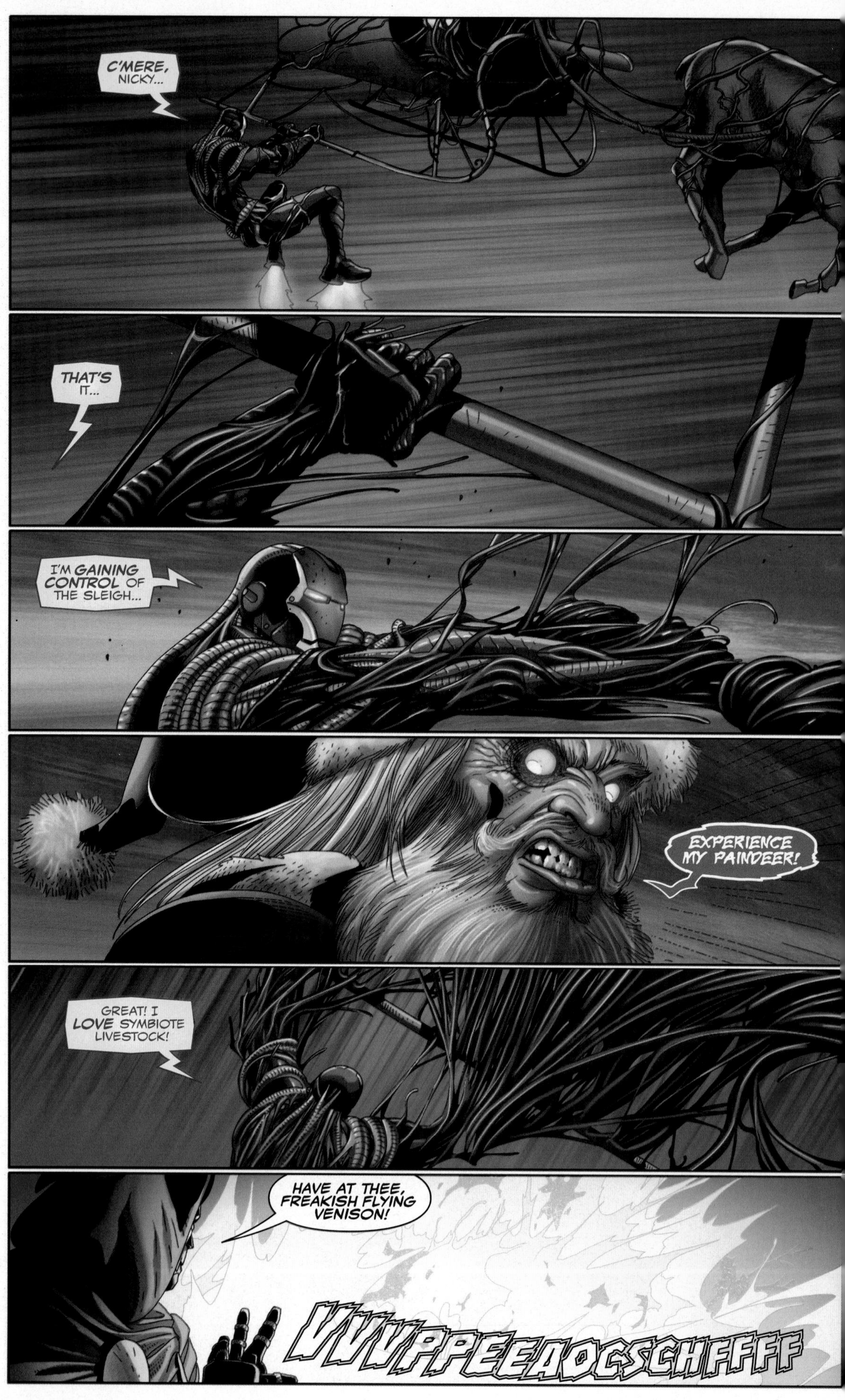
C'MERE, NICKY...
THAT'S IT...
I'M GAINING CONTROL OF THE SLEIGH...
EXPERIENCE MY PAINDEER!
GREAT! I LOVE SYMBIOTE LIVESTOCK!
HAVE AT THEE, FREAKISH FLYING VENISON!
VVVPPEEAOCSCHFFFF

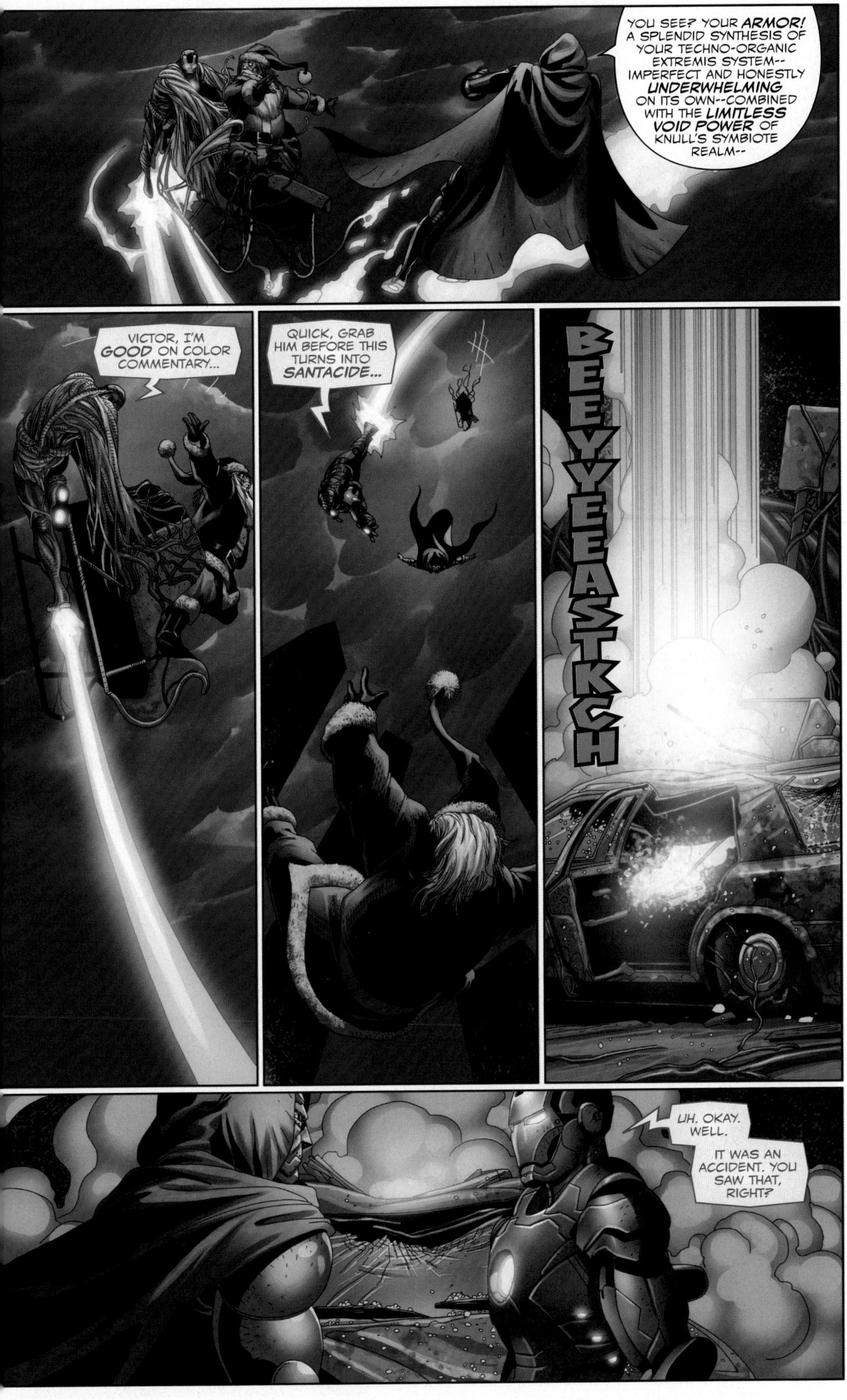
YOU SEE? YOUR ARMOR! A SPLENDID SYNTHESIS OF YOUR TECHNO-ORGANIC EXTREMIS SYSTEM--IMPERFECT AND HONESTLY UNDERWHELMING ON ITS OWN--COMBINED WITH THE LIMITLESS VOID POWER OF KNULL'S SYMBIOTE REALM--
VICTOR, I'M GOOD ON COLOR COMMENTARY...
QUICK, GRAB HIM BEFORE THIS TURNS INTO SANTACIDE...
BEEYYEEASTKCH
UH. OKAY. WELL.
IT WAS AN ACCIDENT. YOU SAW THAT, RIGHT?

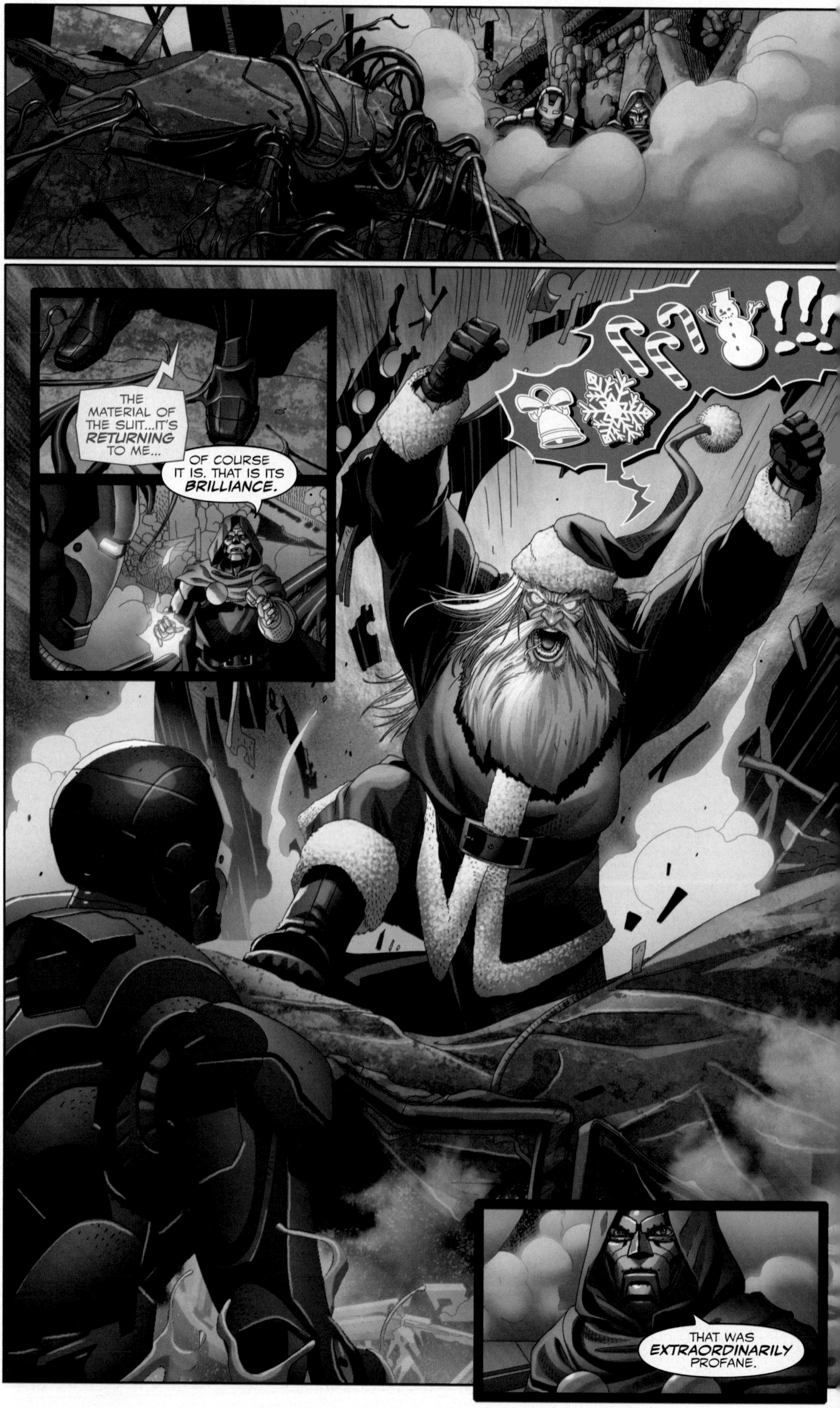
THE MATERIAL OF THE SUIT...IT'S RETURNING TO ME...
OF COURSE IT IS. THAT IS ITS BRILLIANCE.
!!!
THAT WAS EXTRAORDINARILY PROFANE.

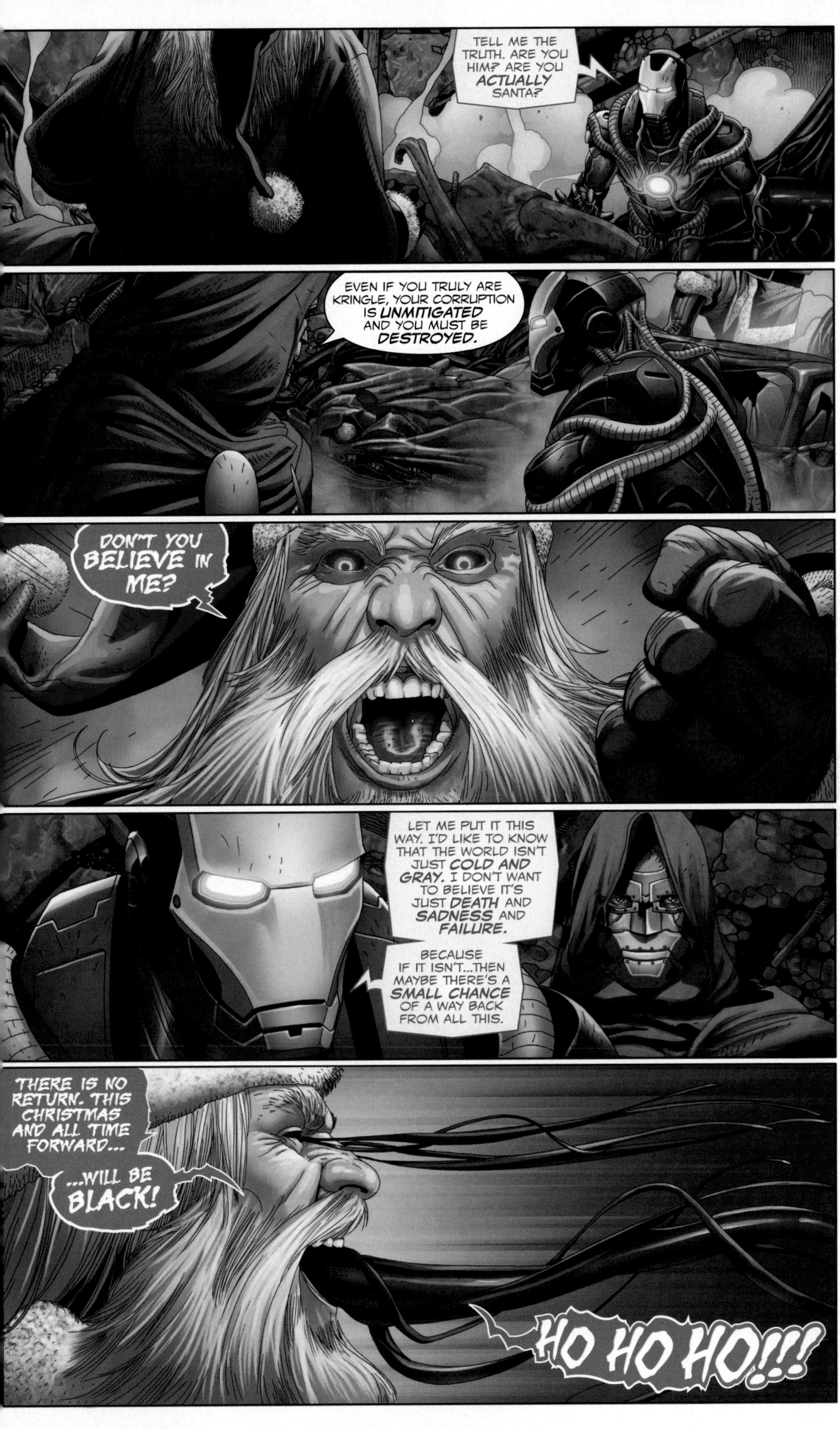

TELL ME THE TRUTH. ARE YOU HIM? ARE YOU ACTUALLY SANTA?
EVEN IF YOU TRULY ARE KRINGLE, YOUR CORRUPTION IS UNMITIGATED AND YOU MUST BE DESTROYED.
DON'T YOU BELIEVE IN ME?
LET ME PUT IT THIS WAY. I'D LIKE TO KNOW THAT THE WORLD ISN'T JUST COLD AND GRAY. I DON'T WANT TO BELIEVE IT'S JUST DEATH AND SADNESS AND FAILURE.
BECAUSE IF IT ISN'T...THEN MAYBE THERE'S A SMALL CHANCE OF A WAY BACK FROM ALL THIS.
THERE IS NO RETURN. THIS CHRISTMAS AND ALL TIME FORWARD...
...WILL BE BLACK!
HO HO HO!!!

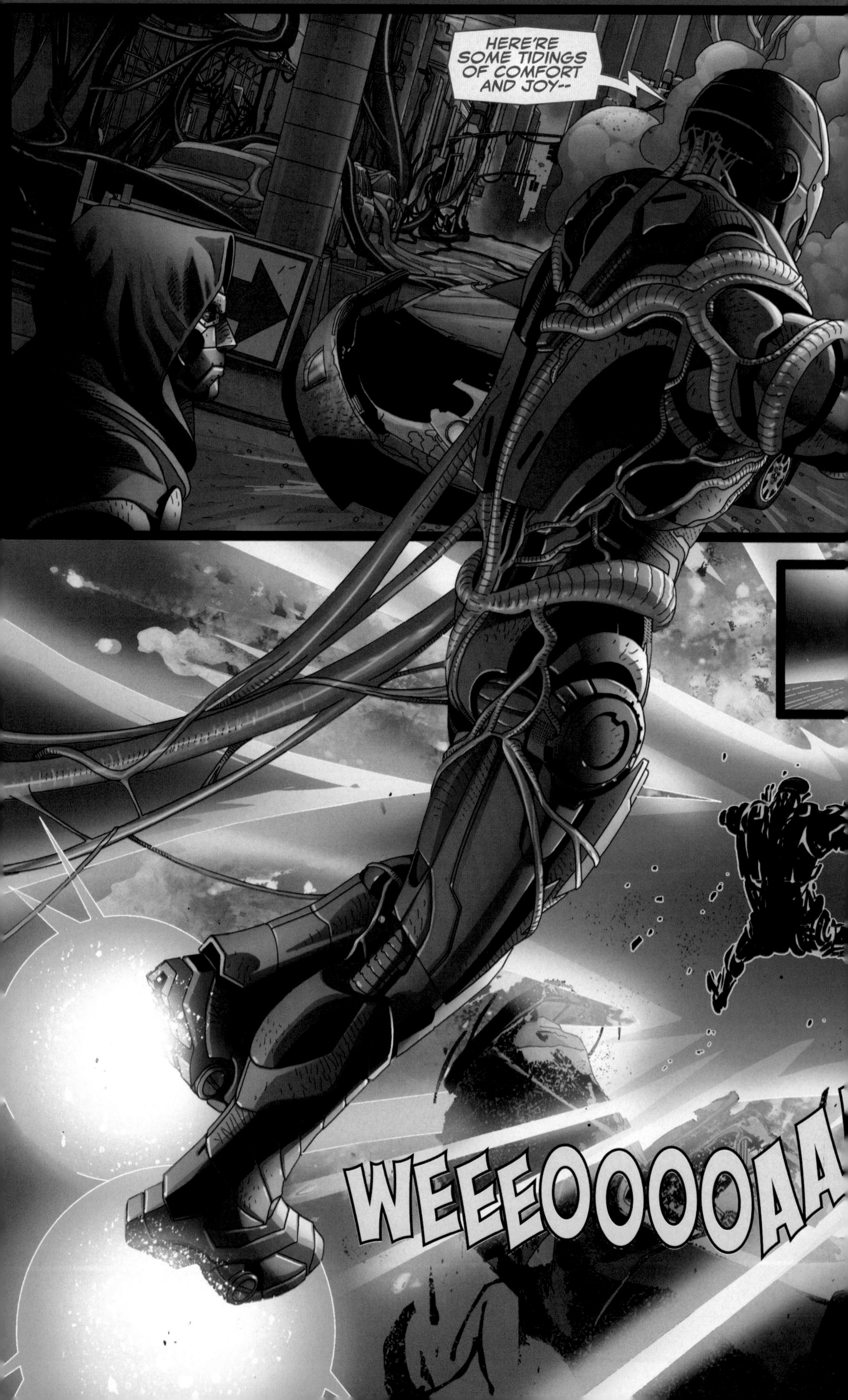
HERE'RE SOME TIDINGS OF COMFORT AND JOY--
WEEEOOOOAA

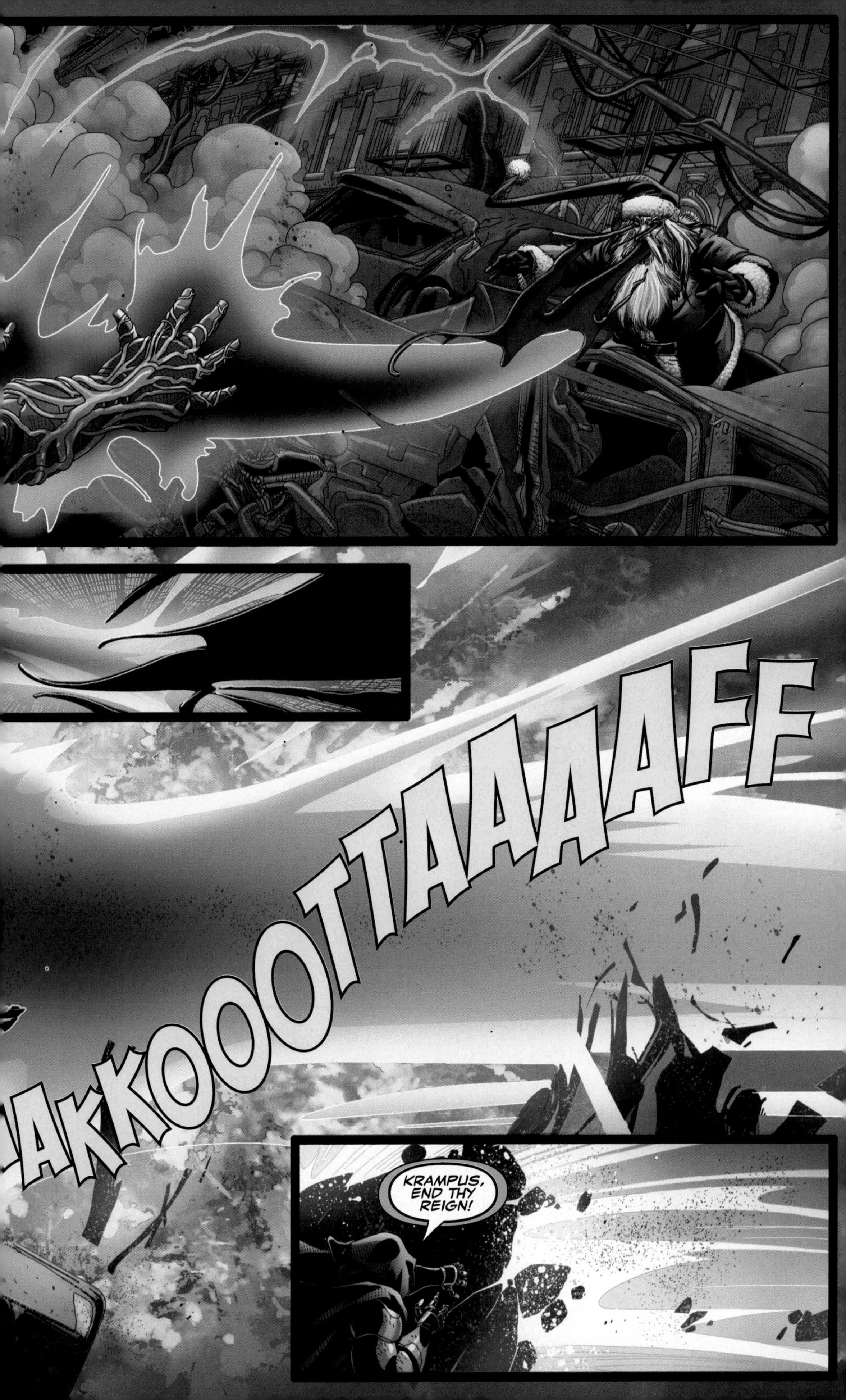

KAKKOOOOTTAAAAFF
KRAMPUS, END THY REIGN!

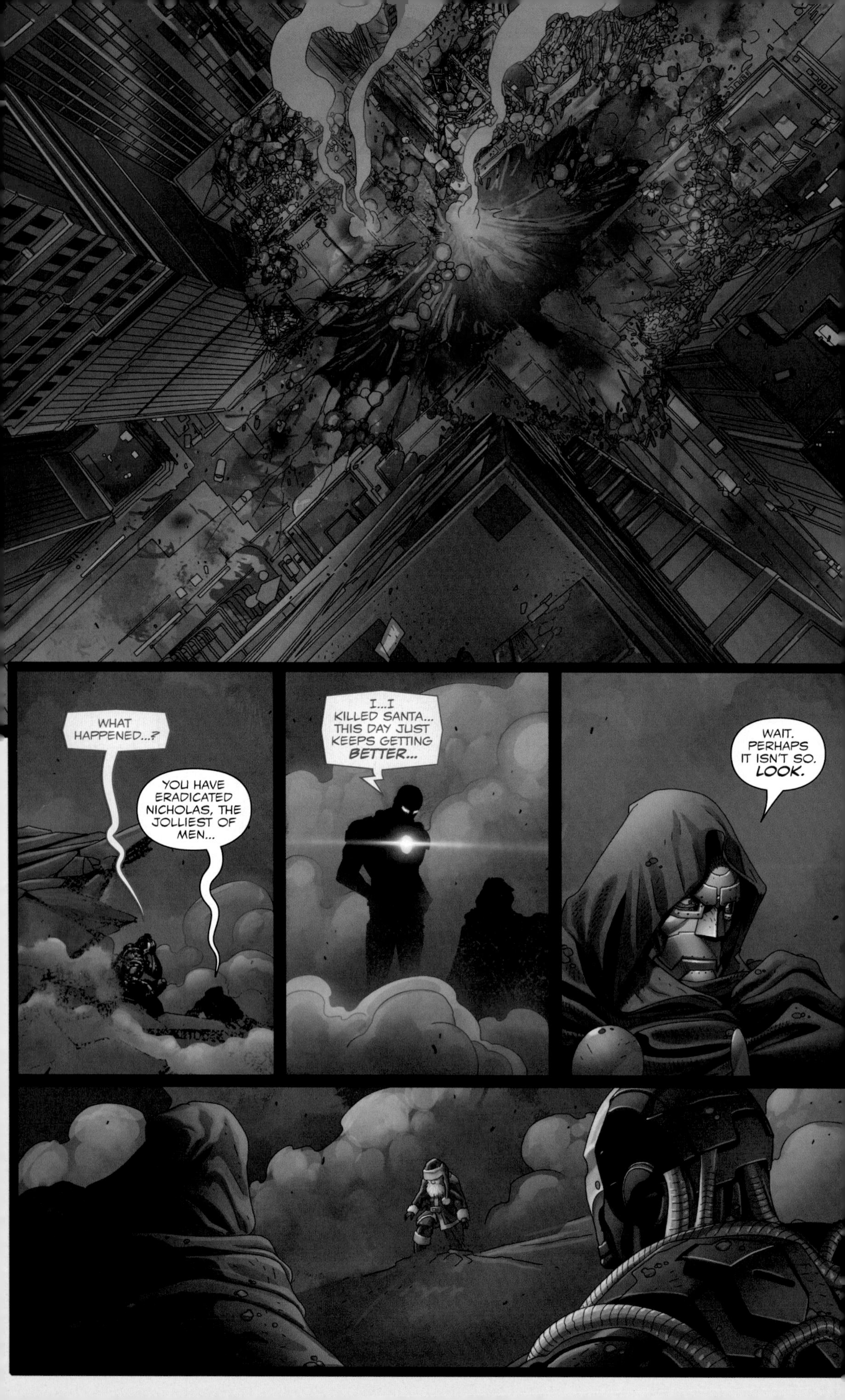
WHAT HAPPENED...?
YOU HAVE ERADICATED NICHOLAS, THE JOLLIEST OF MEN...
I...I KILLED SANTA... THIS DAY JUST KEEPS GETTING BETTER...
WAIT. PERHAPS IT ISN'T SO. LOOK.

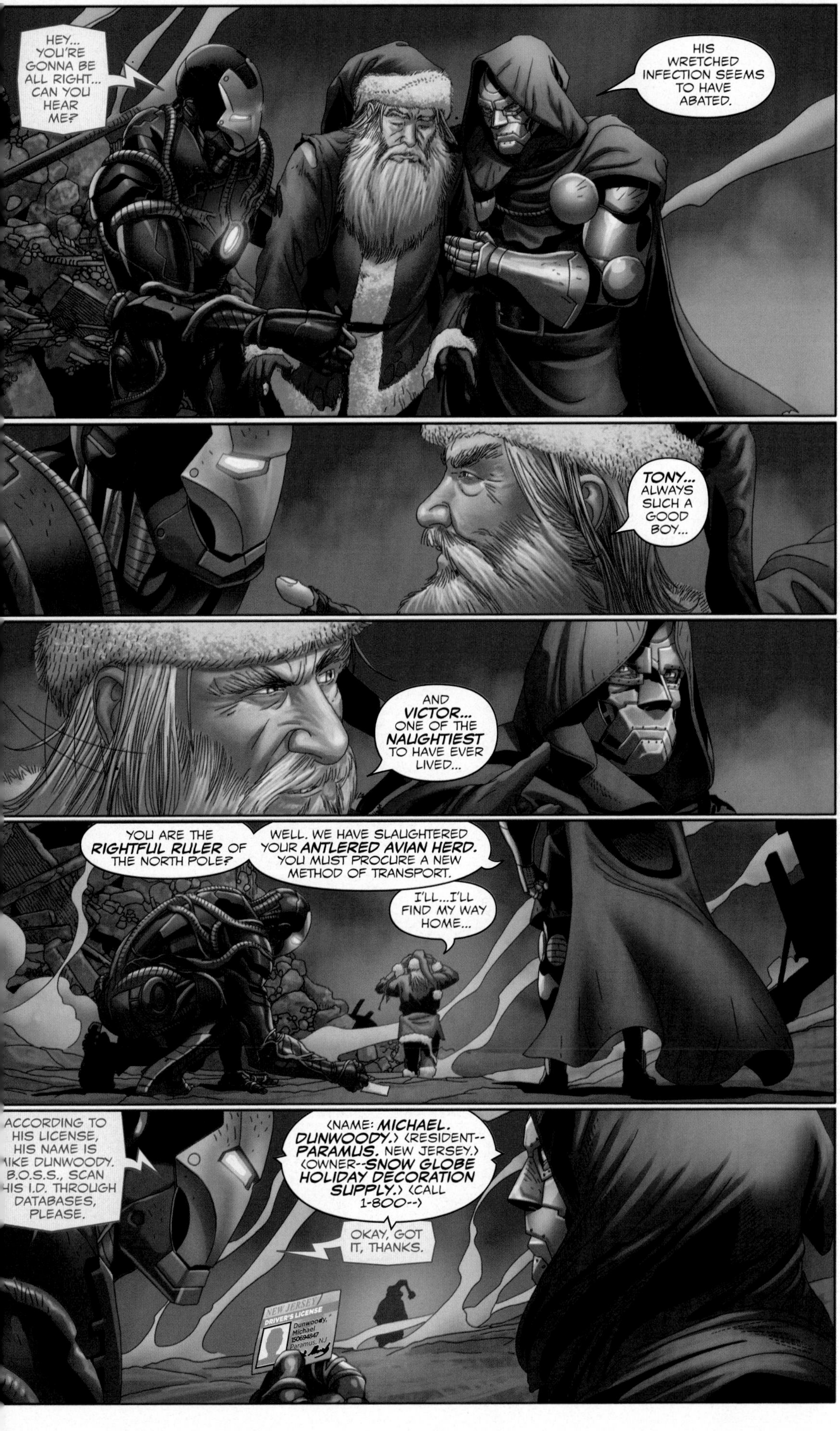

HEY... YOU'RE GONNA BE ALL RIGHT... CAN YOU HEAR ME?
HIS WRETCHED INFECTION SEEMS TO HAVE ABATED.
TONY... ALWAYS SUCH A GOOD BOY...
AND VICTOR... ONE OF THE NAUGHTIEST TO HAVE EVER LIVED...
YOU ARE THE RIGHTFUL RULER OF THE NORTH POLE?
WELL. WE HAVE SLAUGHTERED YOUR ANTLERED AVIAN HERD. YOU MUST PROCURE A NEW METHOD OF TRANSPORT.
I'LL...I'LL FIND MY WAY HOME...
ACCORDING TO HIS LICENSE, HIS NAME IS IKE DUNWOODY. B.O.S.S., SCAN HIS I.D. THROUGH DATABASES, PLEASE.
<NAME: MICHAEL. DUNWOODY.> <RESIDENT--PARAMUS. NEW JERSEY.> <OWNER--SNOW GLOBE HOLIDAY DECORATION SUPPLY.> <CALL 1-800-->
OKAY, GOT IT, THANKS.
NEW JERSEY
DRIVER'S LICENSE
Dunwoody, Michael
150694847
Paramus, NJ

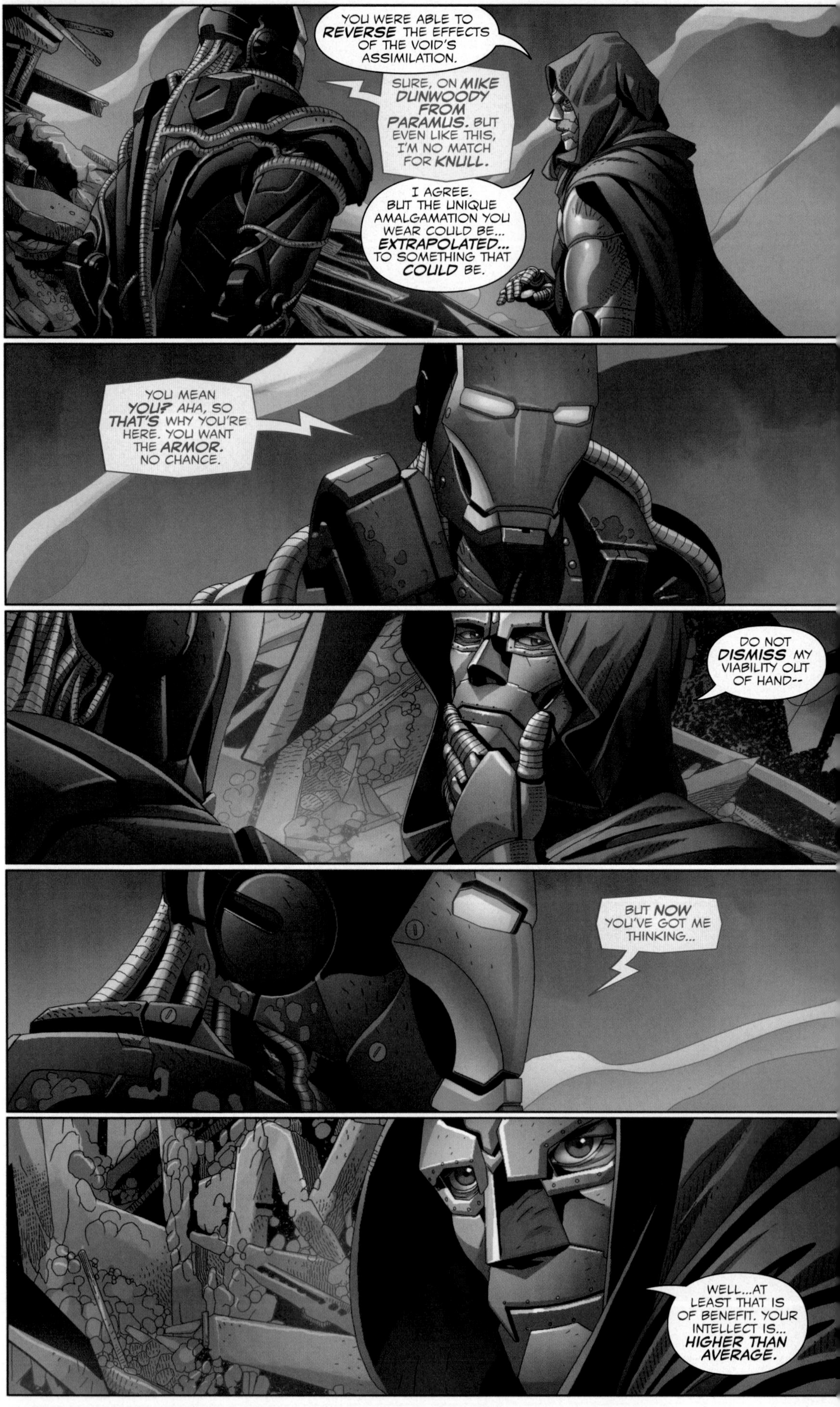

YOU WERE ABLE TO REVERSE THE EFFECTS OF THE VOID'S ASSIMILATION.
SURE, ON MIKE DUNWOODY FROM PARAMUS. BUT EVEN LIKE THIS, I'M NO MATCH FOR KNULL.
I AGREE. BUT THE UNIQUE AMALGAMATION YOU WEAR COULD BE... EXTRAPOLATED... TO SOMETHING THAT COULD BE.
YOU MEAN YOU? AHA, SO THAT'S WHY YOU'RE HERE. YOU WANT THE ARMOR. NO CHANCE.
DO NOT DISMISS MY VIABILITY OUT OF HAND--
BUT NOW YOU'VE GOT ME THINKING...
WELL...AT LEAST THAT IS OF BENEFIT. YOUR INTELLECT IS... HIGHER THAN AVERAGE.

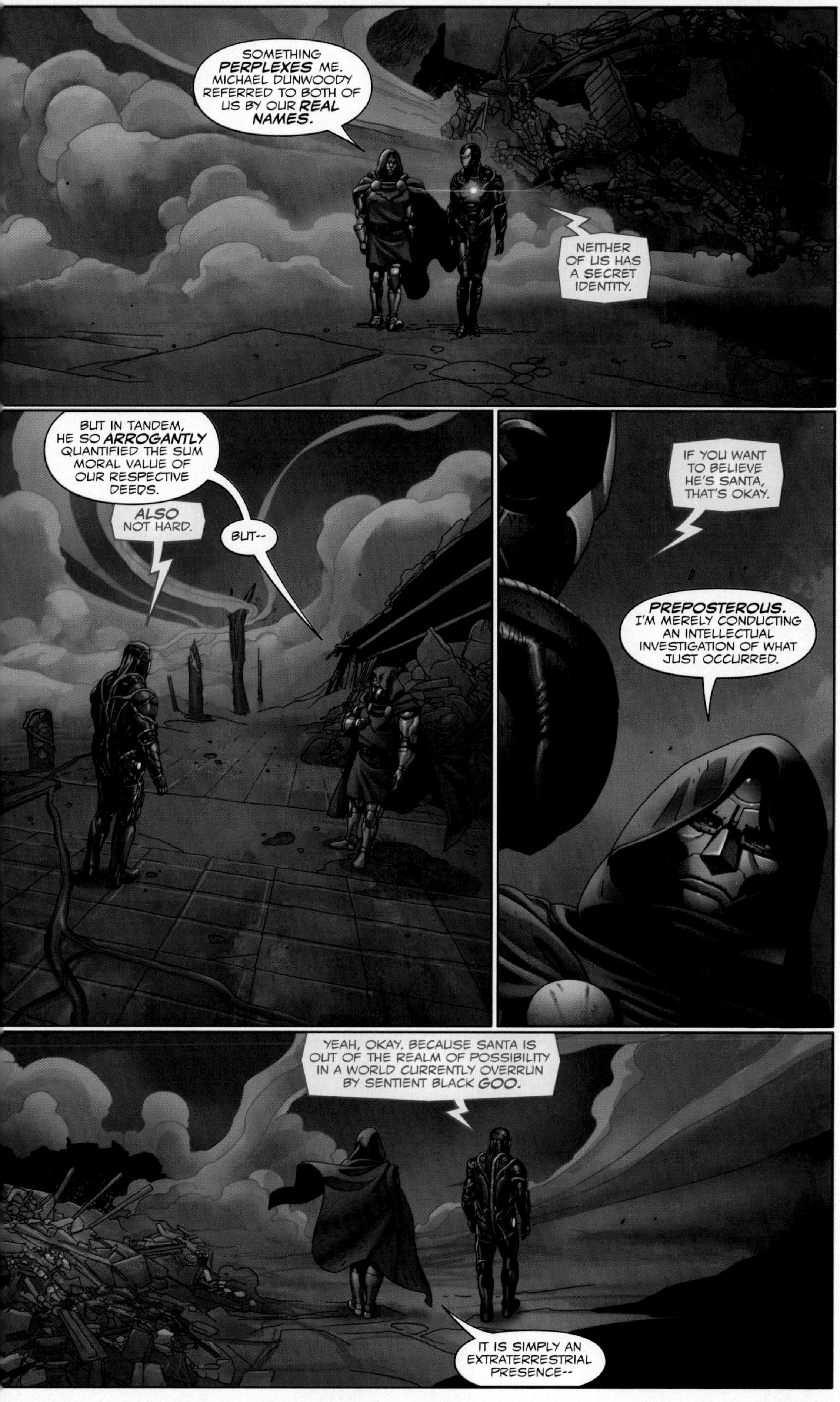
SOMETHING PERPLEXES ME. MICHAEL DUNWOODY REFERRED TO BOTH OF US BY OUR REAL NAMES.
NEITHER OF US HAS A SECRET IDENTITY.
BUT IN TANDEM, HE SO ARROGANTLY QUANTIFIED THE SUM MORAL VALUE OF OUR RESPECTIVE DEEDS.
ALSO NOT HARD.
BUT--
IF YOU WANT TO BELIEVE HE'S SANTA, THAT'S OKAY.
PREPOSTEROUS. I'M MERELY CONDUCTING AN INTELLECTUAL INVESTIGATION OF WHAT JUST OCCURRED.
YEAH, OKAY. BECAUSE SANTA IS OUT OF THE REALM OF POSSIBILITY IN A WORLD CURRENTLY OVERRUN BY SENTIENT BLACK GOO.
IT IS SIMPLY AN EXTRATERRESTRIAL PRESENCE--

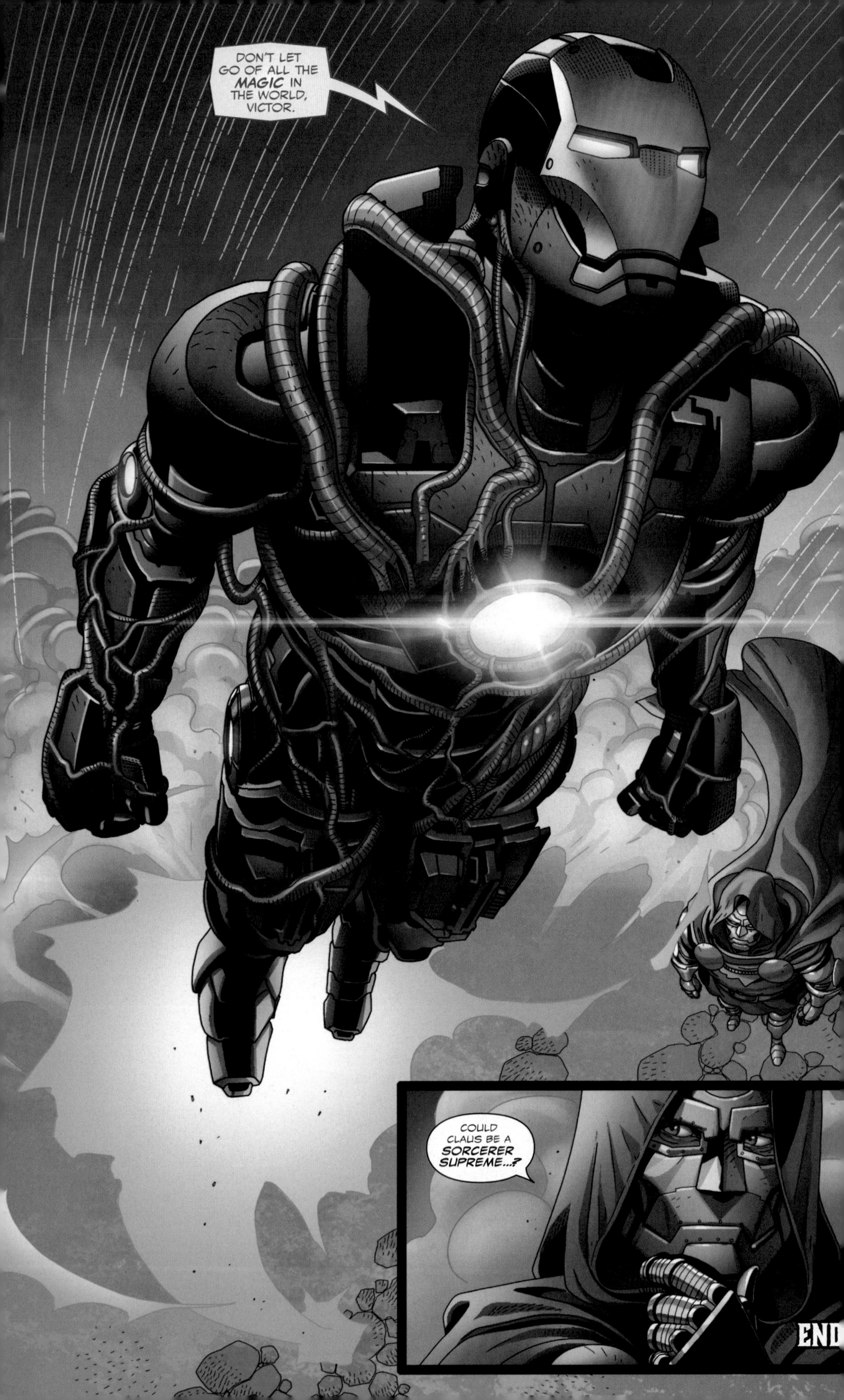
DON'T LET GO OF ALL THE MAGIC IN THE WORLD, VICTOR.
COULD CLAUS BE A SORCERER SUPREME...?
END

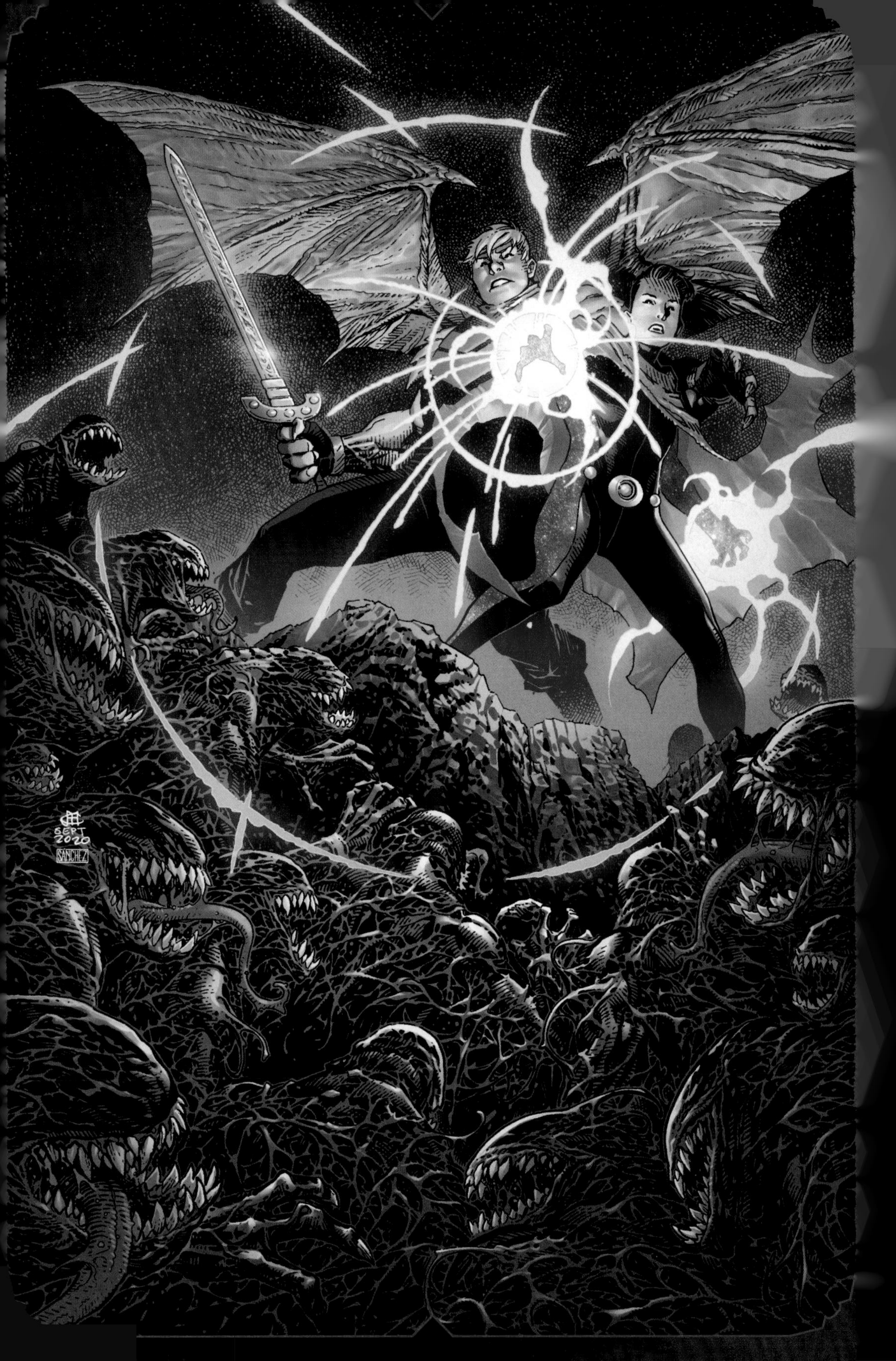
SEPT
2020
SANCHEZ

WICCAN AND HULKLING

IN THE NAME OF THE HONEYMOON

Young Avenger **HULKLING** recently fulfilled his
destiny to become the emperor of the newly united
KREE-SKRULL ALLIANCE. Before leaving Earth, he quietly
married the love of his life, fellow Young Avenger **WICCAN**,
but in the chaos of intergalactic war, they've
had no time to celebrate.

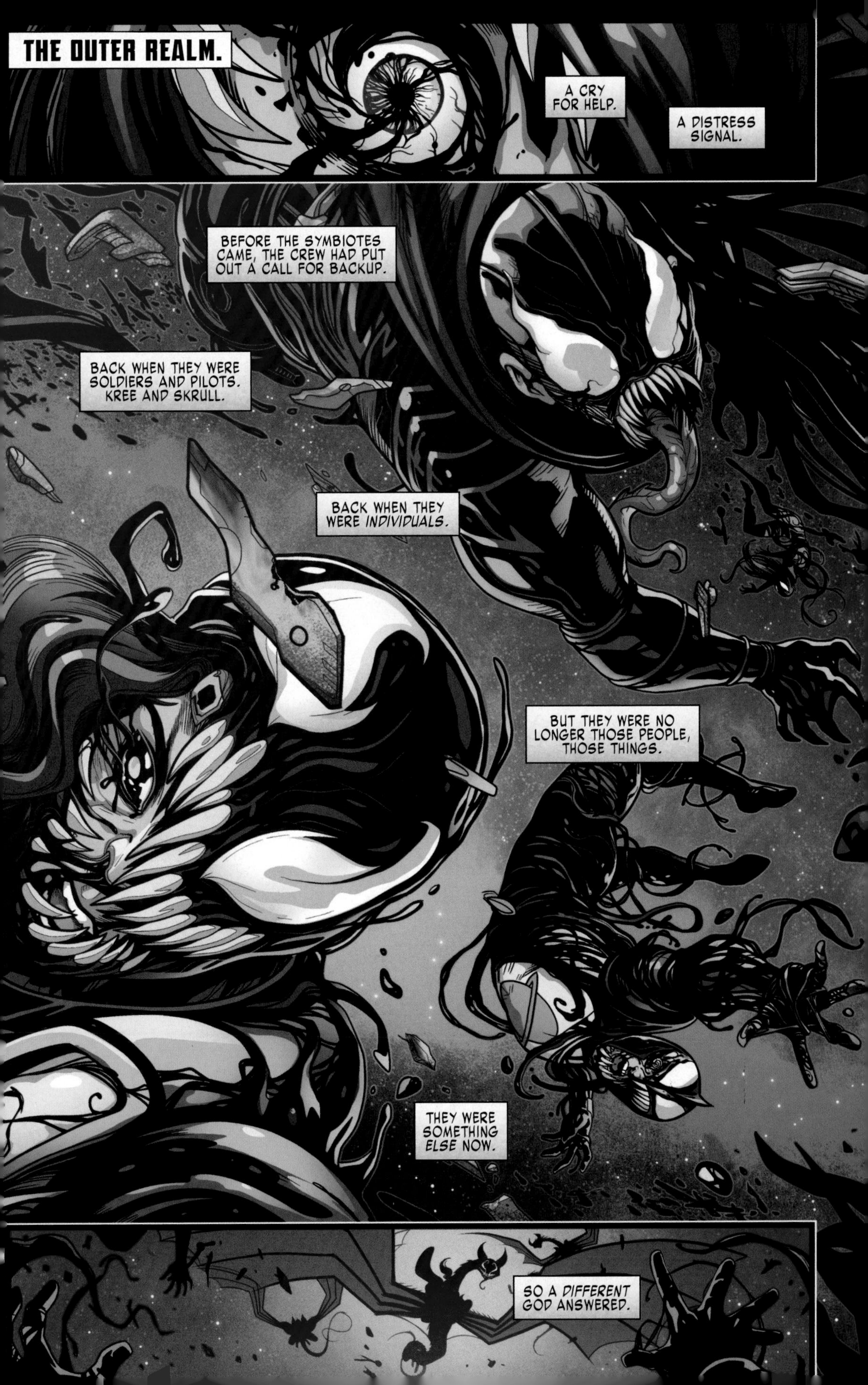
THE OUTER REALM.
A CRY FOR HELP.
A DISTRESS SIGNAL.
BEFORE THE SYMBIOTES CAME, THE CREW HAD PUT OUT A CALL FOR BACKUP.
BACK WHEN THEY WERE SOLDIERS AND PILOTS. KREE AND SKRULL.
BACK WHEN THEY WERE INDIVIDUALS.
BUT THEY WERE NO LONGER THOSE PEOPLE, THOSE THINGS.
THEY WERE SOMETHING ELSE NOW.
SO A DIFFERENT GOD ANSWERED.

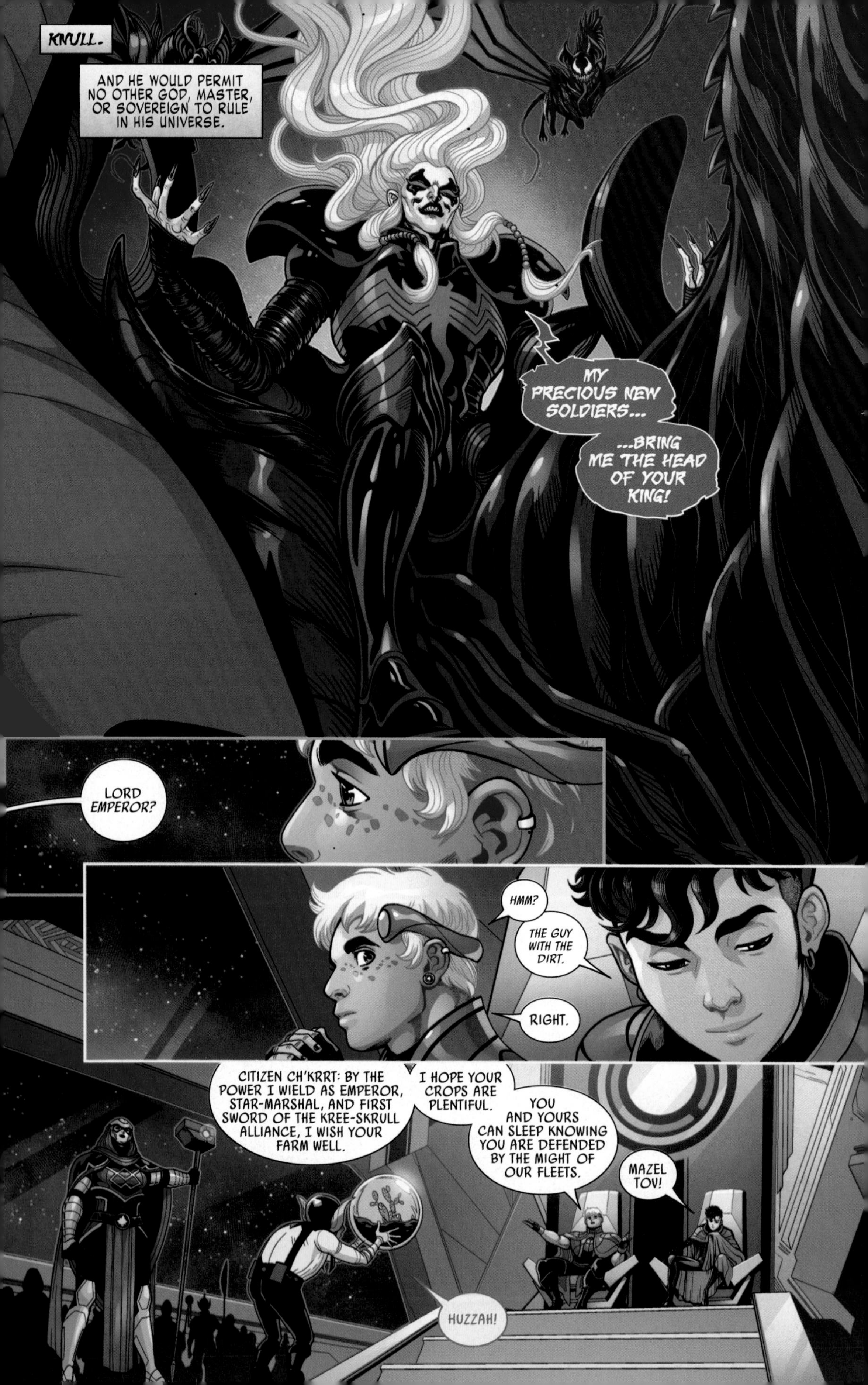
KNULL.
AND HE WOULD PERMIT NO OTHER GOD, MASTER, OR SOVEREIGN TO RULE IN HIS UNIVERSE.
MY PRECIOUS NEW SOLDIERS...
...BRING ME THE HEAD OF YOUR KING!
LORD EMPEROR?
HMM?
THE GUY WITH THE DIRT.
RIGHT.
CITIZEN CH'KRRT: BY THE POWER I WIELD AS EMPEROR, STAR-MARSHAL, AND FIRST SWORD OF THE KREE-SKRULL ALLIANCE, I WISH YOUR FARM WELL.
I HOPE YOUR CROPS ARE PLENTIFUL.
YOU AND YOURS CAN SLEEP KNOWING YOU ARE DEFENDED BY THE MIGHT OF OUR FLEETS.
MAZEL TOV!
HUZZAH!

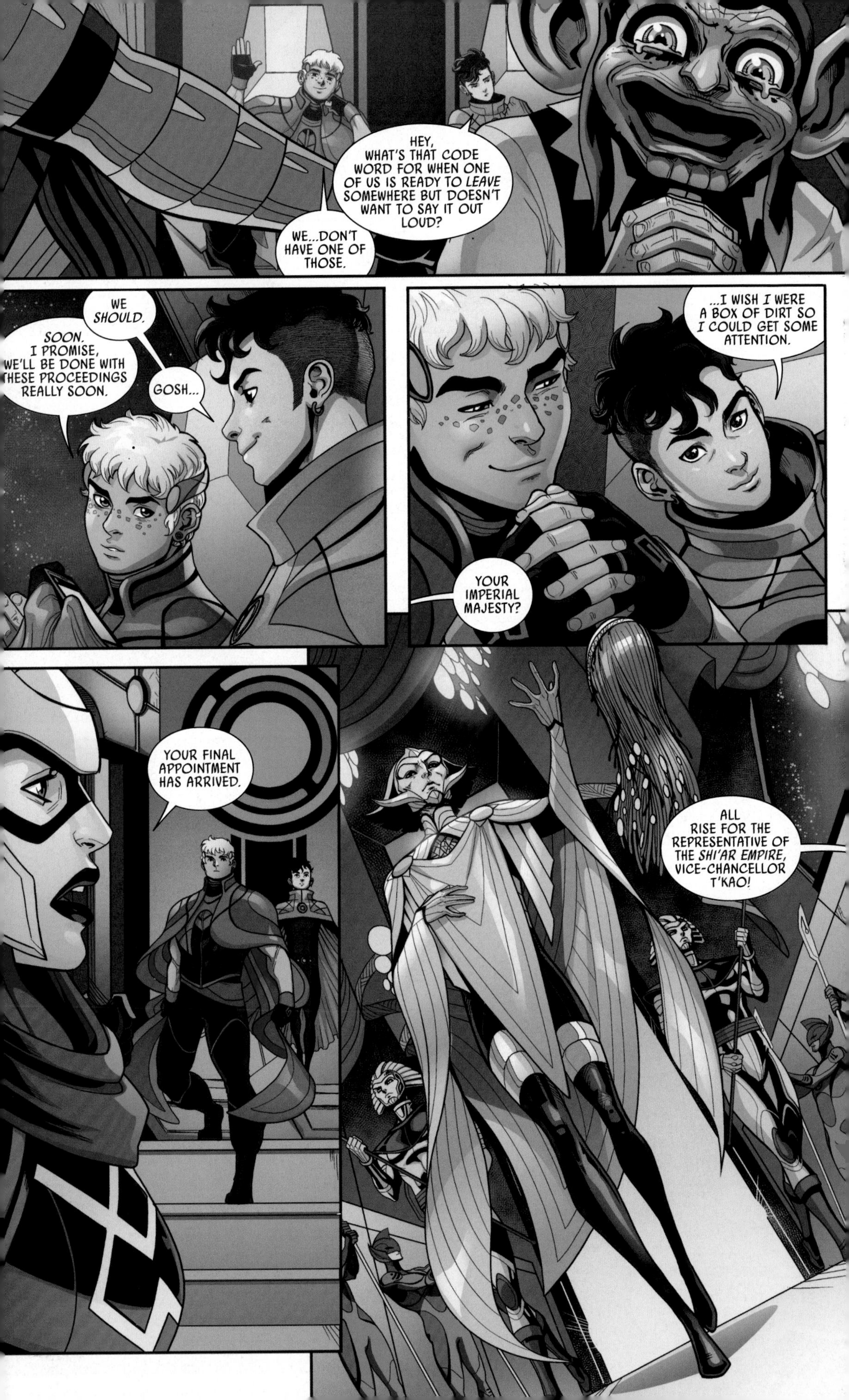
HEY, WHAT'S THAT CODE WORD FOR WHEN ONE OF US IS READY TO LEAVE SOMEWHERE BUT DOESN'T WANT TO SAY IT OUT LOUD?
WE...DON'T HAVE ONE OF THOSE.
WE SHOULD.
SOON. I PROMISE, WE'LL BE DONE WITH THESE PROCEEDINGS REALLY SOON.
GOSH...
...I WISH I WERE A BOX OF DIRT SO I COULD GET SOME ATTENTION.
YOUR IMPERIAL MAJESTY?
YOUR FINAL APPOINTMENT HAS ARRIVED.
ALL RISE FOR THE REPRESENTATIVE OF THE SHI'AR EMPIRE, VICE-CHANCELLOR T'KAO!

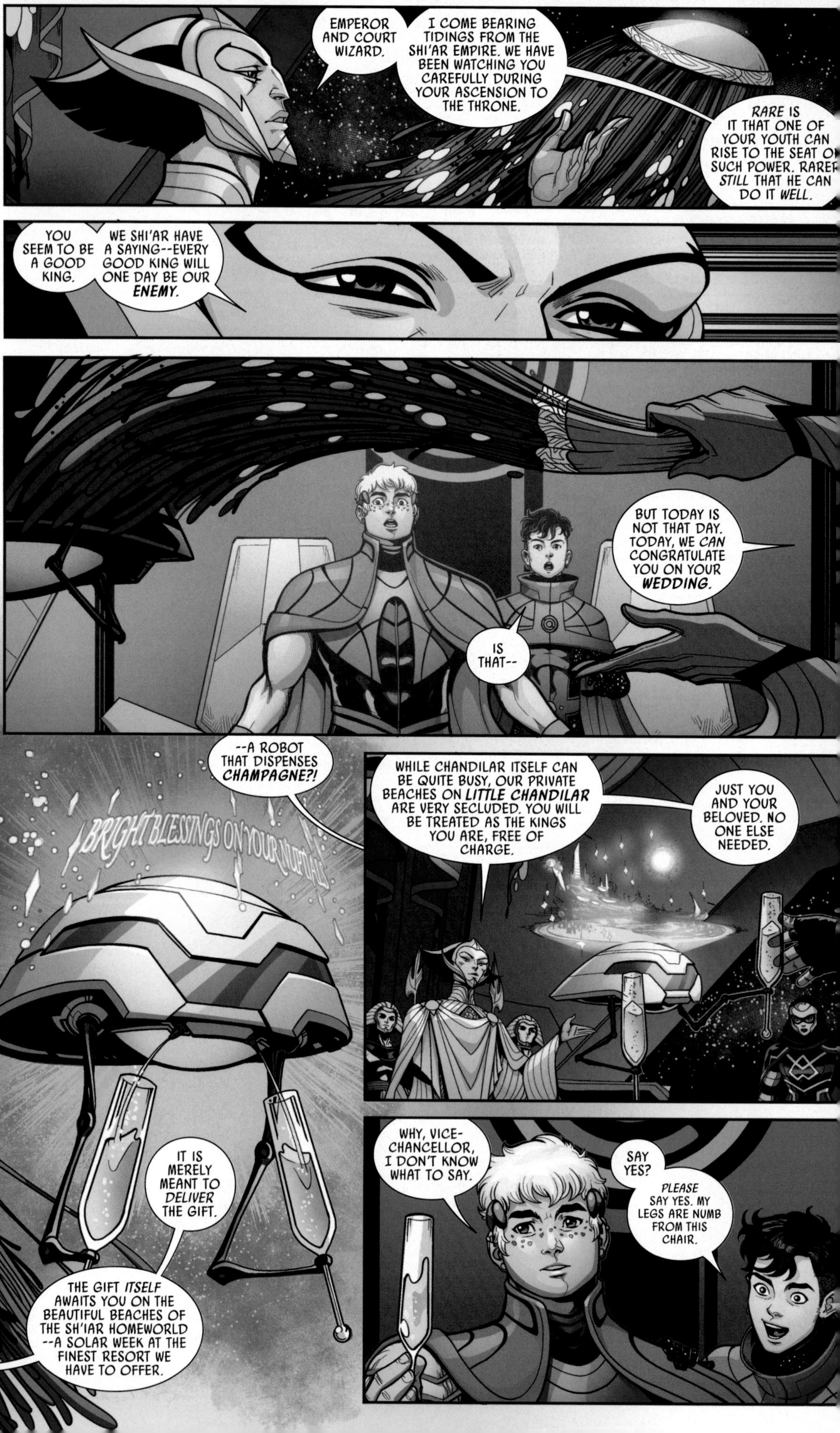
EMPEROR AND COURT WIZARD.
I COME BEARING TIDINGS FROM THE SHI'AR EMPIRE. WE HAVE BEEN WATCHING YOU CAREFULLY DURING YOUR ASCENSION TO THE THRONE.
RARE IS IT THAT ONE OF YOUR YOUTH CAN RISE TO THE SEAT OF SUCH POWER. RARER STILL THAT HE CAN DO IT WELL.
YOU SEEM TO BE A GOOD KING.
WE SHI'AR HAVE A SAYING--EVERY GOOD KING WILL ONE DAY BE OUR ENEMY.
BUT TODAY IS NOT THAT DAY. TODAY, WE CAN CONGRATULATE YOU ON YOUR WEDDING.
IS THAT--
--A ROBOT THAT DISPENSES CHAMPAGNE?!
BRIGHT BLESSINGS ON YOUR NUPTIALS
IT IS MERELY MEANT TO DELIVER THE GIFT.
THE GIFT ITSELF AWAITS YOU ON THE BEAUTIFUL BEACHES OF THE SH'IAR HOMEWORLD --A SOLAR WEEK AT THE FINEST RESORT WE HAVE TO OFFER.
WHILE CHANDILAR ITSELF CAN BE QUITE BUSY, OUR PRIVATE BEACHES ON LITTLE CHANDILAR ARE VERY SECLUDED. YOU WILL BE TREATED AS THE KINGS YOU ARE, FREE OF CHARGE.
JUST YOU AND YOUR BELOVED. NO ONE ELSE NEEDED.
WHY, VICE-CHANCELLOR, I DON'T KNOW WHAT TO SAY.
SAY YES?
PLEASE SAY YES. MY LEGS ARE NUMB FROM THIS CHAIR.

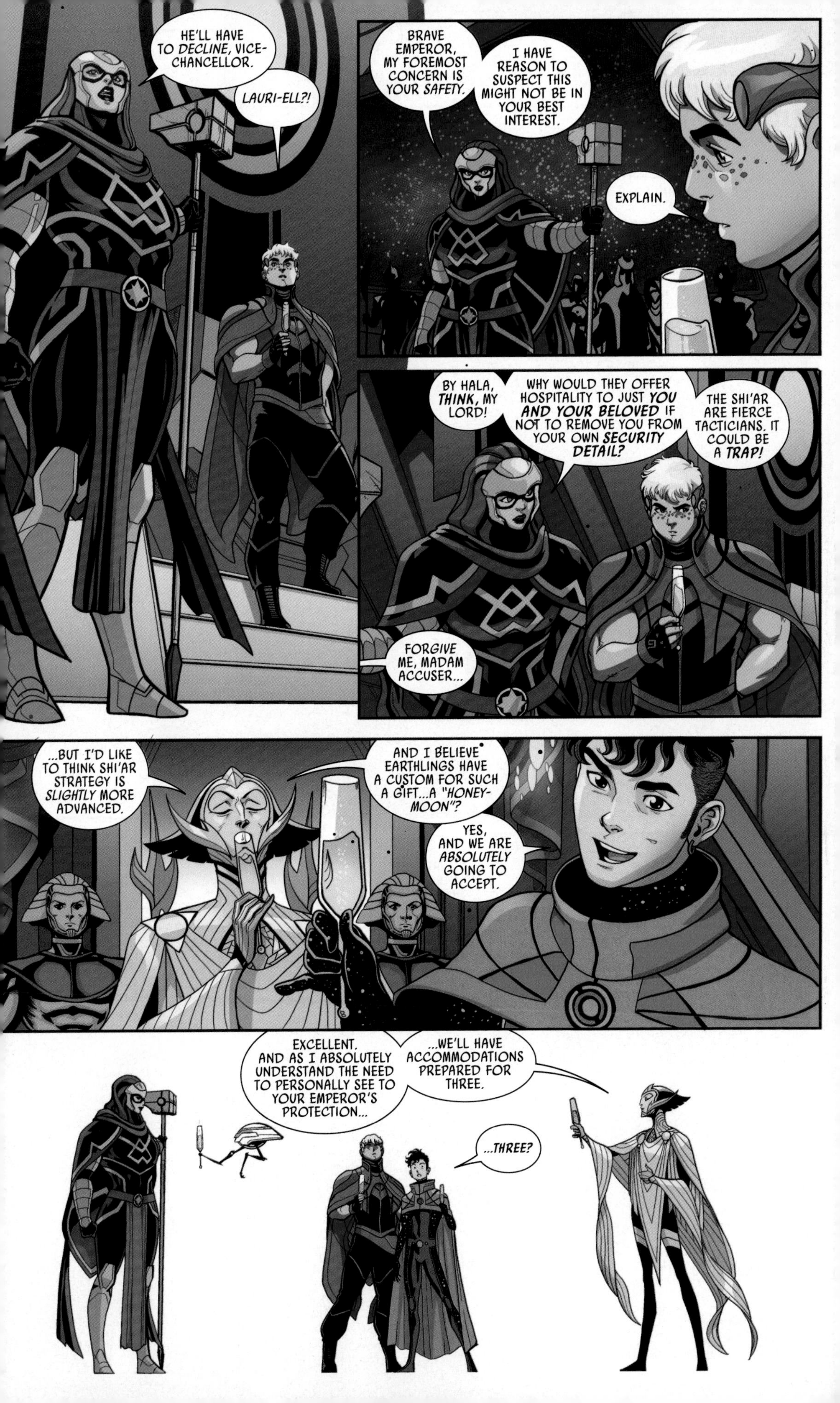
HE'LL HAVE TO DECLINE, VICE-CHANCELLOR.
LAURI-ELL?!
BRAVE EMPEROR, MY FOREMOST CONCERN IS YOUR SAFETY.
I HAVE REASON TO SUSPECT THIS MIGHT NOT BE IN YOUR BEST INTEREST.
EXPLAIN.
BY HALA, THINK, MY LORD!
WHY WOULD THEY OFFER HOSPITALITY TO JUST YOU AND YOUR BELOVED IF NOT TO REMOVE YOU FROM YOUR OWN SECURITY DETAIL?
THE SHI'AR ARE FIERCE TACTICIANS. IT COULD BE A TRAP!
FORGIVE ME, MADAM ACCUSER...
...BUT I'D LIKE TO THINK SHI'AR STRATEGY IS SLIGHTLY MORE ADVANCED.
AND I BELIEVE EARTHLINGS HAVE A CUSTOM FOR SUCH A GIFT...A "HONEY-MOON"?
YES, AND WE ARE ABSOLUTELY GOING TO ACCEPT.
EXCELLENT. AND AS I ABSOLUTELY UNDERSTAND THE NEED TO PERSONALLY SEE TO YOUR EMPEROR'S PROTECTION...
...WE'LL HAVE ACCOMMODATIONS PREPARED FOR THREE.
...THREE?

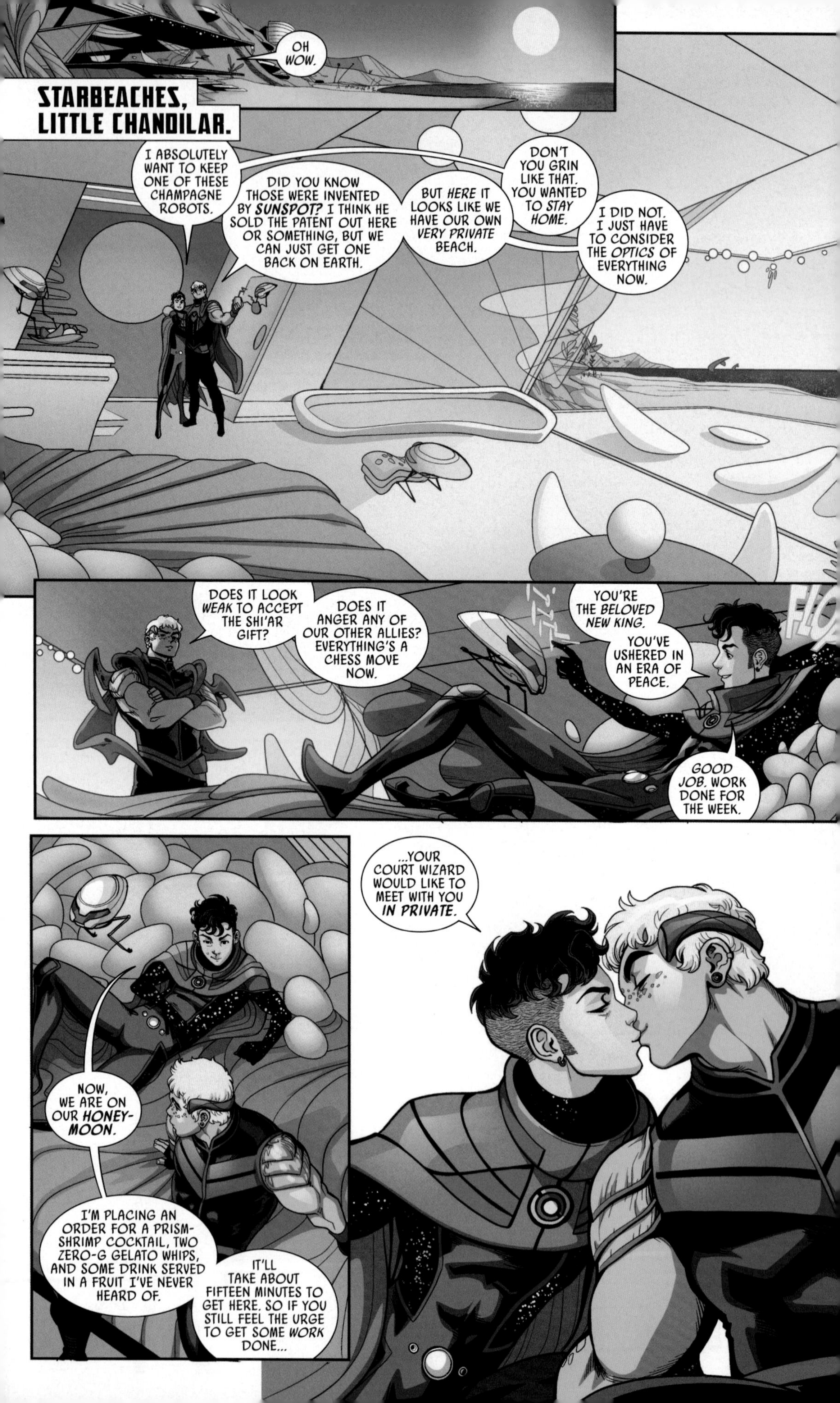

OH WOW.
STARBEACHES, LITTLE CHANDILAR.
I ABSOLUTELY WANT TO KEEP ONE OF THESE CHAMPAGNE ROBOTS.
DID YOU KNOW THOSE WERE INVENTED BY SUNSPOT? I THINK HE SOLD THE PATENT OUT HERE OR SOMETHING, BUT WE CAN JUST GET ONE BACK ON EARTH.
BUT HERE IT LOOKS LIKE WE HAVE OUR OWN VERY PRIVATE BEACH.
DON'T YOU GRIN LIKE THAT. YOU WANTED TO STAY HOME.
I DID NOT. I JUST HAVE TO CONSIDER THE OPTICS OF EVERYTHING NOW.
DOES IT LOOK WEAK TO ACCEPT THE SHI'AR GIFT?
DOES IT ANGER ANY OF OUR OTHER ALLIES? EVERYTHING'S A CHESS MOVE NOW.
YOU'RE THE BELOVED NEW KING.
YOU'VE USHERED IN AN ERA OF PEACE.
GOOD JOB. WORK DONE FOR THE WEEK.
NOW, WE ARE ON OUR HONEY-MOON.
I'M PLACING AN ORDER FOR A PRISM-SHRIMP COCKTAIL, TWO ZERO-G GELATO WHIPS, AND SOME DRINK SERVED IN A FRUIT I'VE NEVER HEARD OF.
IT'LL TAKE ABOUT FIFTEEN MINUTES TO GET HERE. SO IF YOU STILL FEEL THE URGE TO GET SOME WORK DONE...
...YOUR COURT WIZARD WOULD LIKE TO MEET WITH YOU IN PRIVATE.

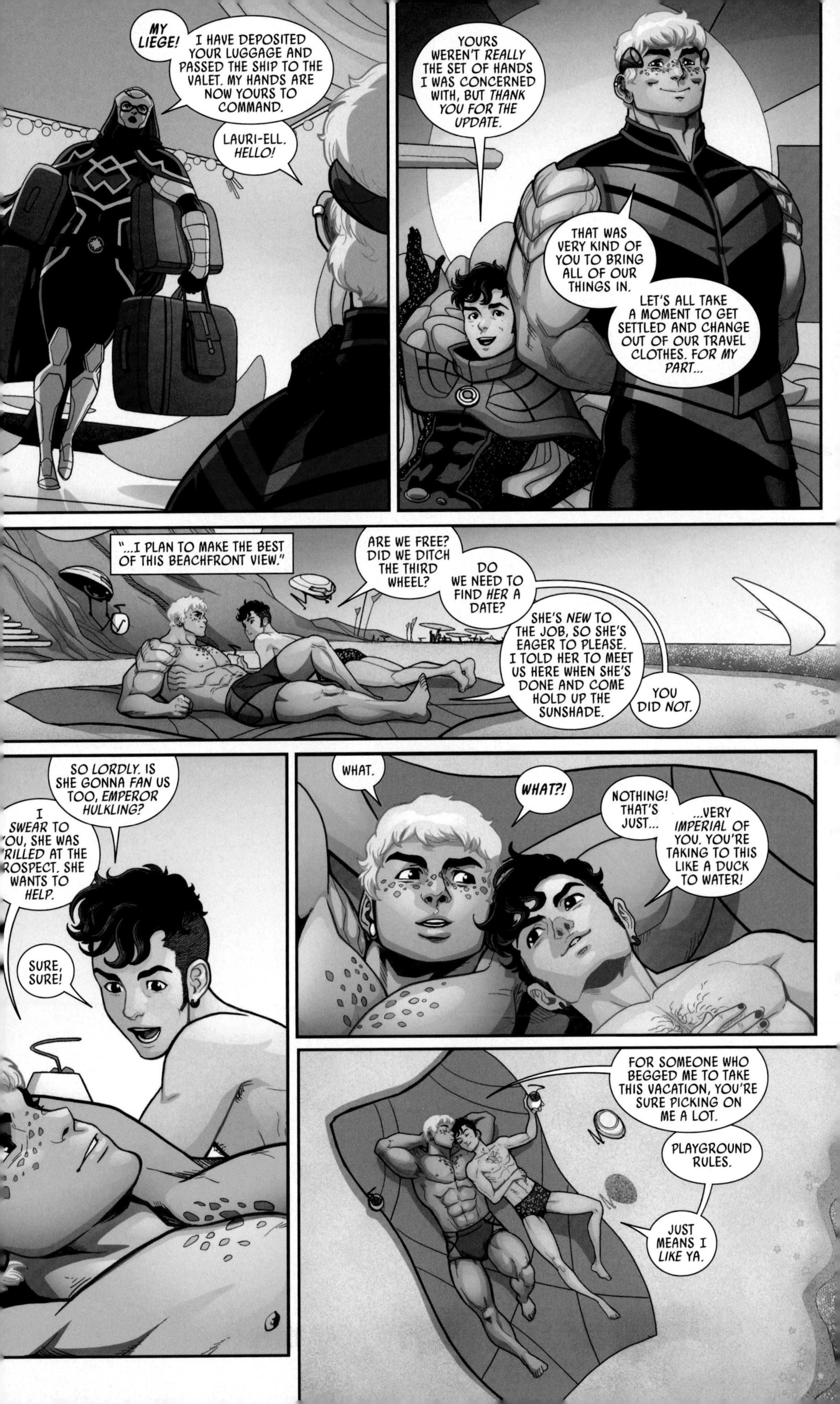
MY LIEGE!
I HAVE DEPOSITED YOUR LUGGAGE AND PASSED THE SHIP TO THE VALET. MY HANDS ARE NOW YOURS TO COMMAND.
LAURI-ELL. HELLO!
YOURS WEREN'T REALLY THE SET OF HANDS I WAS CONCERNED WITH, BUT THANK YOU FOR THE UPDATE.
THAT WAS VERY KIND OF YOU TO BRING ALL OF OUR THINGS IN.
LET'S ALL TAKE A MOMENT TO GET SETTLED AND CHANGE OUT OF OUR TRAVEL CLOTHES. FOR MY PART...
"...I PLAN TO MAKE THE BEST OF THIS BEACHFRONT VIEW."
ARE WE FREE? DID WE DITCH THE THIRD WHEEL?
DO WE NEED TO FIND HER A DATE?
SHE'S NEW TO THE JOB, SO SHE'S EAGER TO PLEASE. I TOLD HER TO MEET US HERE WHEN SHE'S DONE AND COME HOLD UP THE SUNSHADE.
YOU DID NOT.
SO LORDLY. IS SHE GONNA FAN US TOO, EMPEROR HULKLING?
I SWEAR TO YOU, SHE WAS RILLED AT THE ROSPECT. SHE WANTS TO HELP.
SURE, SURE!
WHAT.
WHAT?!
NOTHING! THAT'S JUST...
...VERY IMPERIAL OF YOU. YOU'RE TAKING TO THIS LIKE A DUCK TO WATER!
FOR SOMEONE WHO BEGGED ME TO TAKE THIS VACATION, YOU'RE SURE PICKING ON ME A LOT.
PLAYGROUND RULES.
JUST MEANS I LIKE YA.

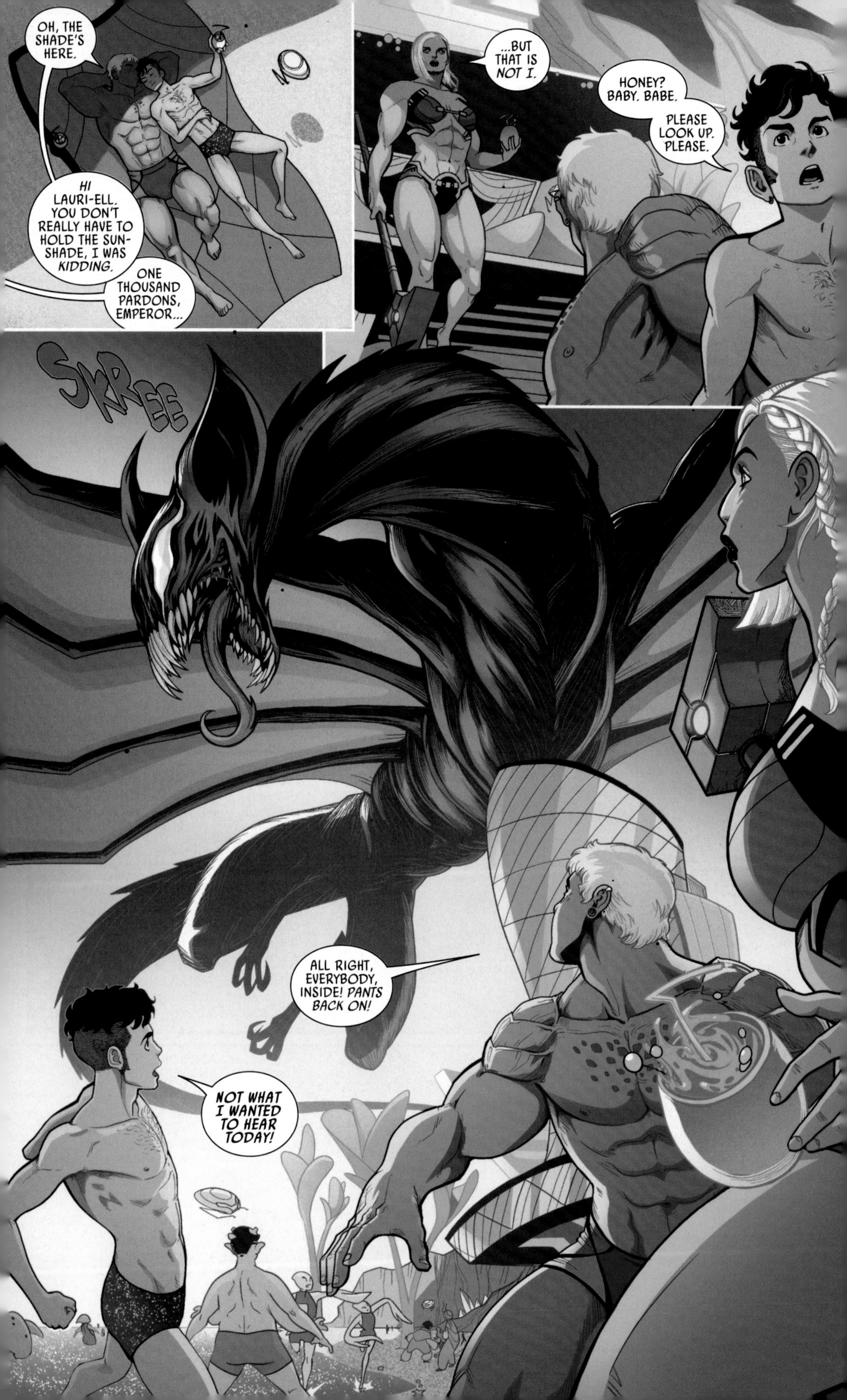
OH, THE SHADE'S HERE.
HI LAURI-ELL. YOU DON'T REALLY HAVE TO HOLD THE SUN-SHADE, I WAS *KIDDING.*
ONE THOUSAND PARDONS, EMPEROR...
...BUT THAT IS *NOT* I.
HONEY? BABY. BABE.
PLEASE LOOK UP. PLEASE.
SKREE
ALL RIGHT, EVERYBODY, INSIDE! *PANTS BACK ON!*
NOT WHAT I WANTED TO HEAR TODAY!

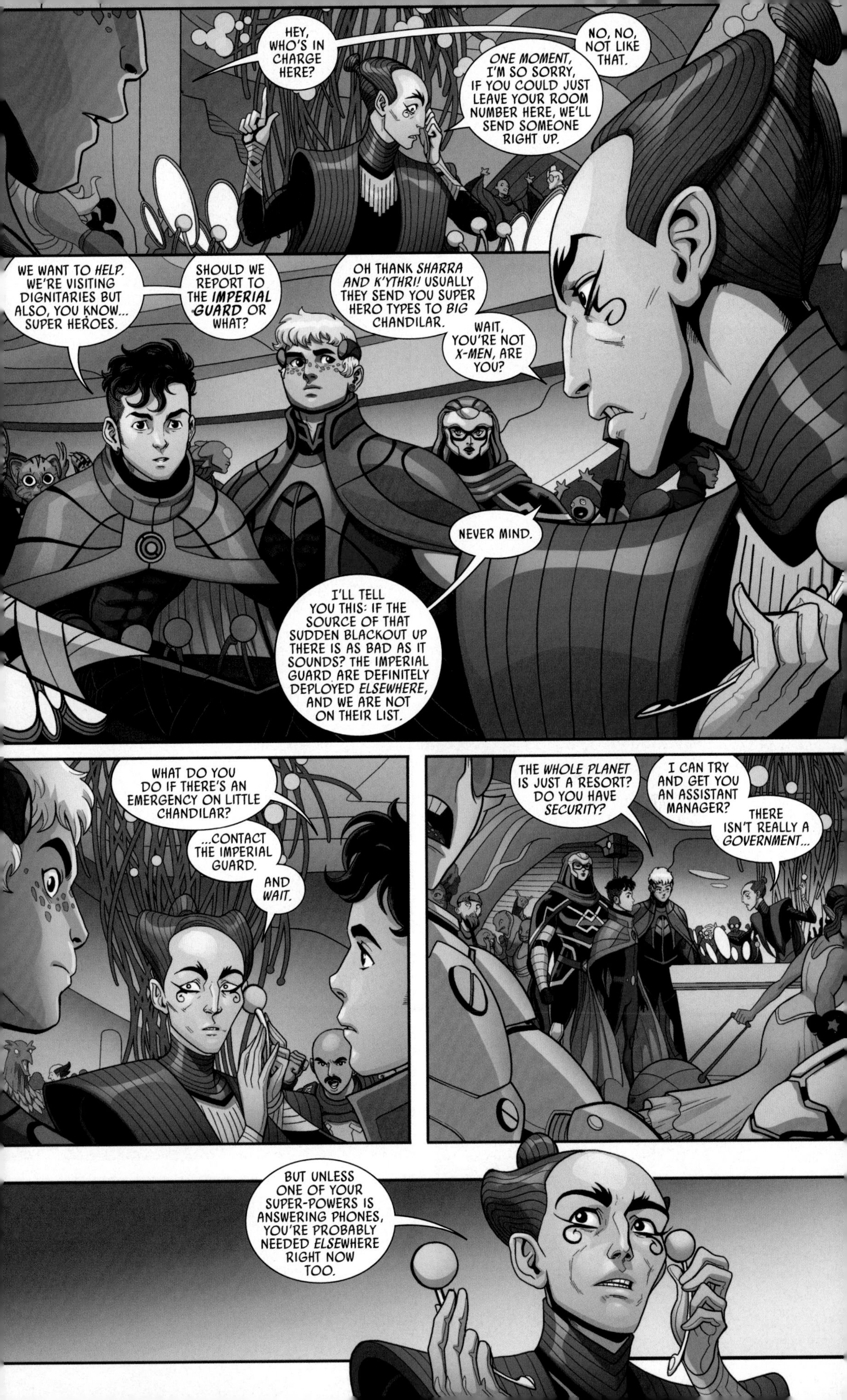
HEY, WHO'S IN CHARGE HERE?
NO, NO, NOT LIKE THAT.
ONE MOMENT, I'M SO SORRY, IF YOU COULD JUST LEAVE YOUR ROOM NUMBER HERE, WE'LL SEND SOMEONE RIGHT UP.
WE WANT TO HELP. WE'RE VISITING DIGNITARIES BUT ALSO, YOU KNOW... SUPER HEROES.
SHOULD WE REPORT TO THE IMPERIAL GUARD OR WHAT?
OH THANK SHARRA AND K'YTHRI! USUALLY THEY SEND YOU SUPER HERO TYPES TO BIG CHANDILAR.
WAIT, YOU'RE NOT X-MEN, ARE YOU?
NEVER MIND.
I'LL TELL YOU THIS: IF THE SOURCE OF THAT SUDDEN BLACKOUT UP THERE IS AS BAD AS IT SOUNDS? THE IMPERIAL GUARD ARE DEFINITELY DEPLOYED ELSEWHERE, AND WE ARE NOT ON THEIR LIST.
WHAT DO YOU DO IF THERE'S AN EMERGENCY ON LITTLE CHANDILAR?
...CONTACT THE IMPERIAL GUARD.
AND WAIT.
THE WHOLE PLANET IS JUST A RESORT? DO YOU HAVE SECURITY?
I CAN TRY AND GET YOU AN ASSISTANT MANAGER?
THERE ISN'T REALLY A GOVERNMENT...
BUT UNLESS ONE OF YOUR SUPER-POWERS IS ANSWERING PHONES, YOU'RE PROBABLY NEEDED ELSEWHERE RIGHT NOW TOO.

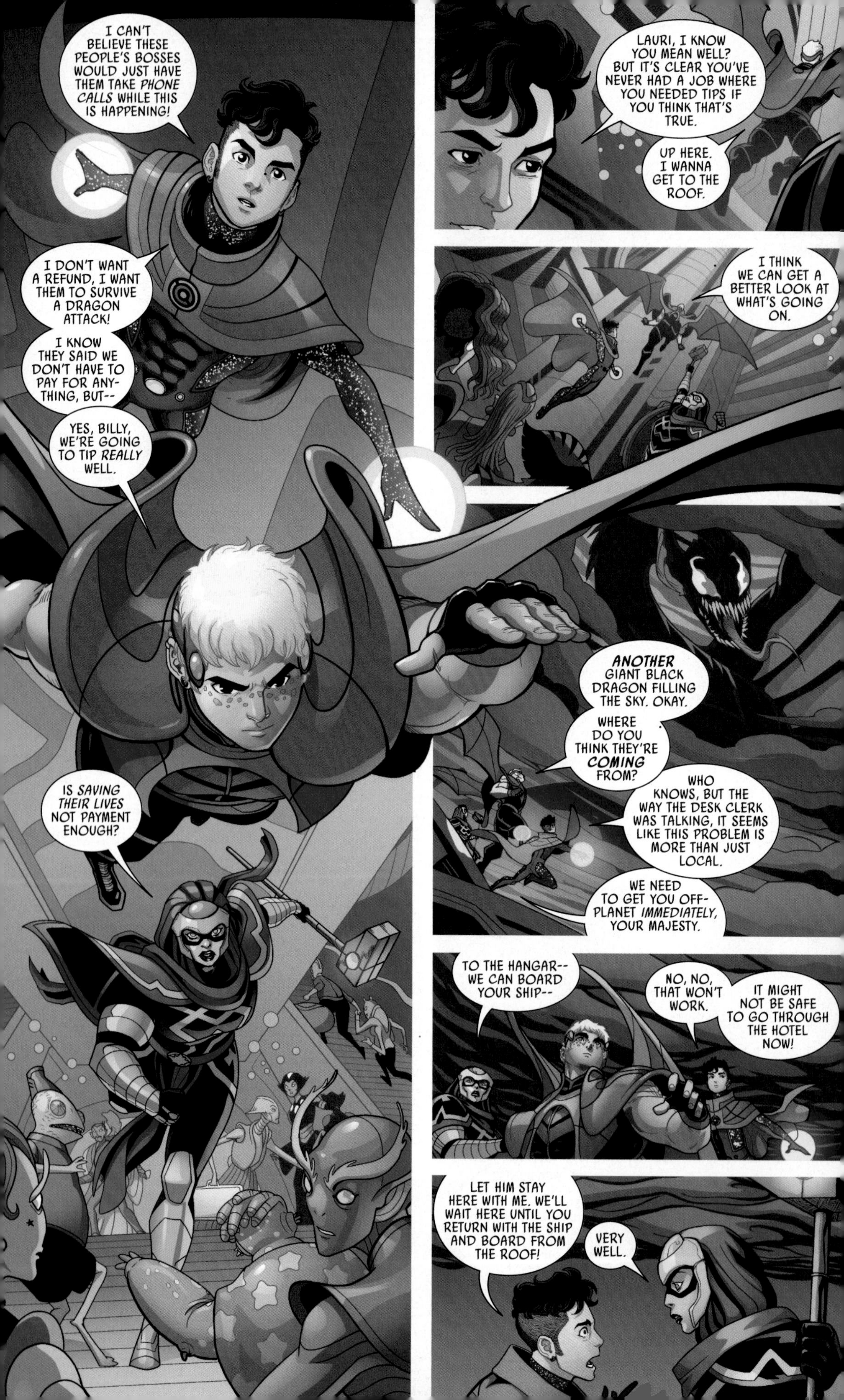
I CAN'T BELIEVE THESE PEOPLE'S BOSSES WOULD JUST HAVE THEM TAKE *PHONE CALLS* WHILE THIS IS HAPPENING!
I DON'T WANT A REFUND, I WANT THEM TO SURVIVE A DRAGON ATTACK!
I KNOW THEY SAID WE DON'T HAVE TO PAY FOR ANYTHING, BUT--
YES, BILLY, WE'RE GOING TO TIP *REALLY* WELL.
IS *SAVING THEIR LIVES* NOT PAYMENT ENOUGH?
LAURI, I KNOW YOU MEAN WELL? BUT IT'S CLEAR YOU'VE NEVER HAD A JOB WHERE YOU NEEDED TIPS IF YOU THINK THAT'S TRUE.
UP HERE. I WANNA GET TO THE ROOF.
I THINK WE CAN GET A BETTER LOOK AT WHAT'S GOING ON.
ANOTHER GIANT BLACK DRAGON FILLING THE SKY. OKAY.
WHERE DO YOU THINK THEY'RE **COMING** FROM?
WHO KNOWS, BUT THE WAY THE DESK CLERK WAS TALKING, IT SEEMS LIKE THIS PROBLEM IS MORE THAN JUST LOCAL.
WE NEED TO GET YOU OFF-PLANET *IMMEDIATELY*, YOUR MAJESTY.
TO THE HANGAR-- WE CAN BOARD YOUR SHIP--
NO, NO, THAT WON'T WORK.
IT MIGHT NOT BE SAFE TO GO THROUGH THE HOTEL NOW!
LET HIM STAY HERE WITH ME. WE'LL WAIT HERE UNTIL YOU RETURN WITH THE SHIP AND BOARD FROM THE ROOF!
VERY WELL.

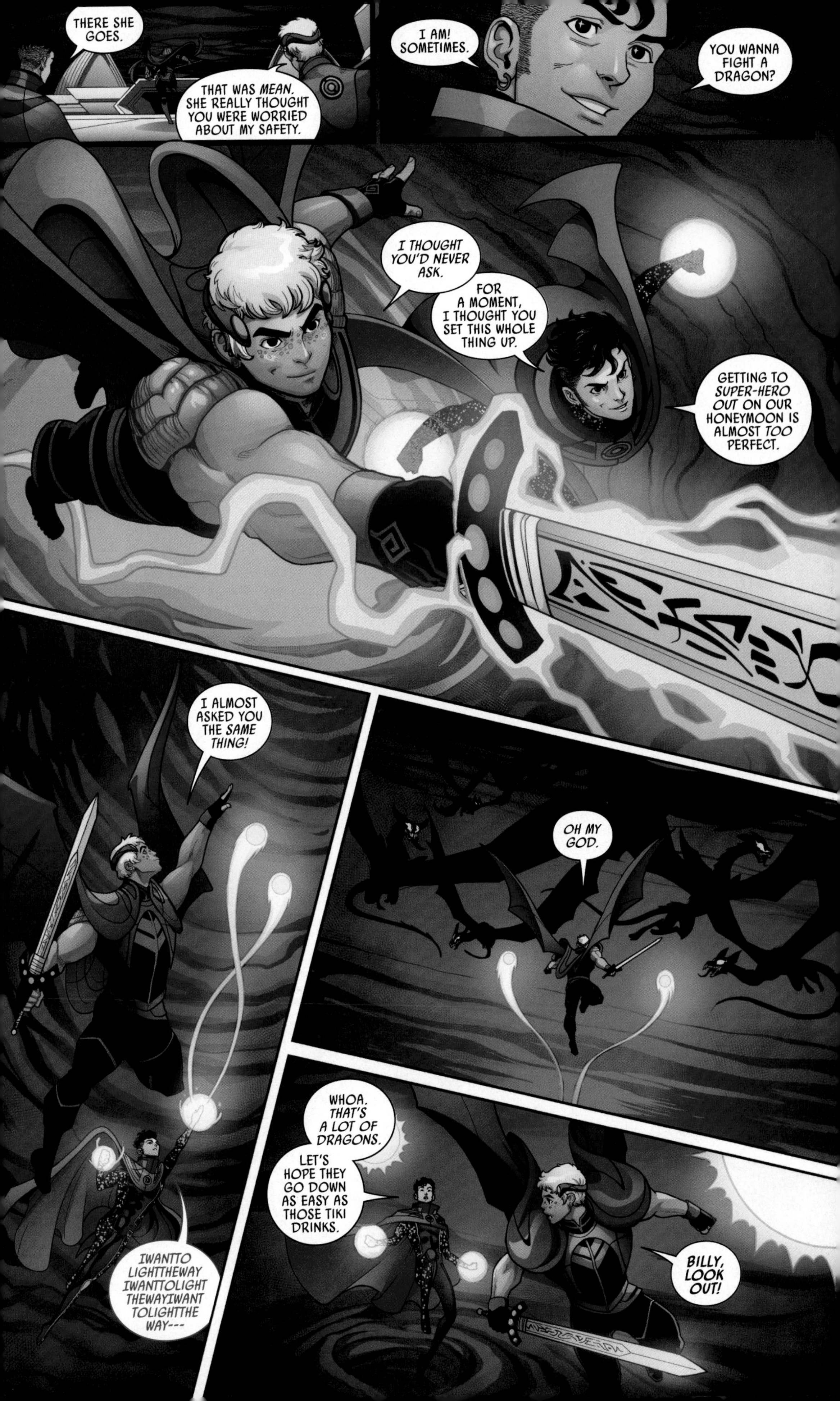
THERE SHE GOES.
THAT WAS MEAN. SHE REALLY THOUGHT YOU WERE WORRIED ABOUT MY SAFETY.
I AM! SOMETIMES.
YOU WANNA FIGHT A DRAGON?
I THOUGHT YOU'D NEVER ASK.
FOR A MOMENT, I THOUGHT YOU SET THIS WHOLE THING UP.
GETTING TO SUPER-HERO OUT ON OUR HONEYMOON IS ALMOST TOO PERFECT.
I ALMOST ASKED YOU THE SAME THING!
IWANTTO LIGHTTHEWAY IWANTTOLIGHT THEWAYIWANT TOLIGHTTHE WAY---
OH MY GOD.
WHOA. THAT'S A LOT OF DRAGONS.
LET'S HOPE THEY GO DOWN AS EASY AS THOSE TIKI DRINKS.
BILLY, LOOK OUT!

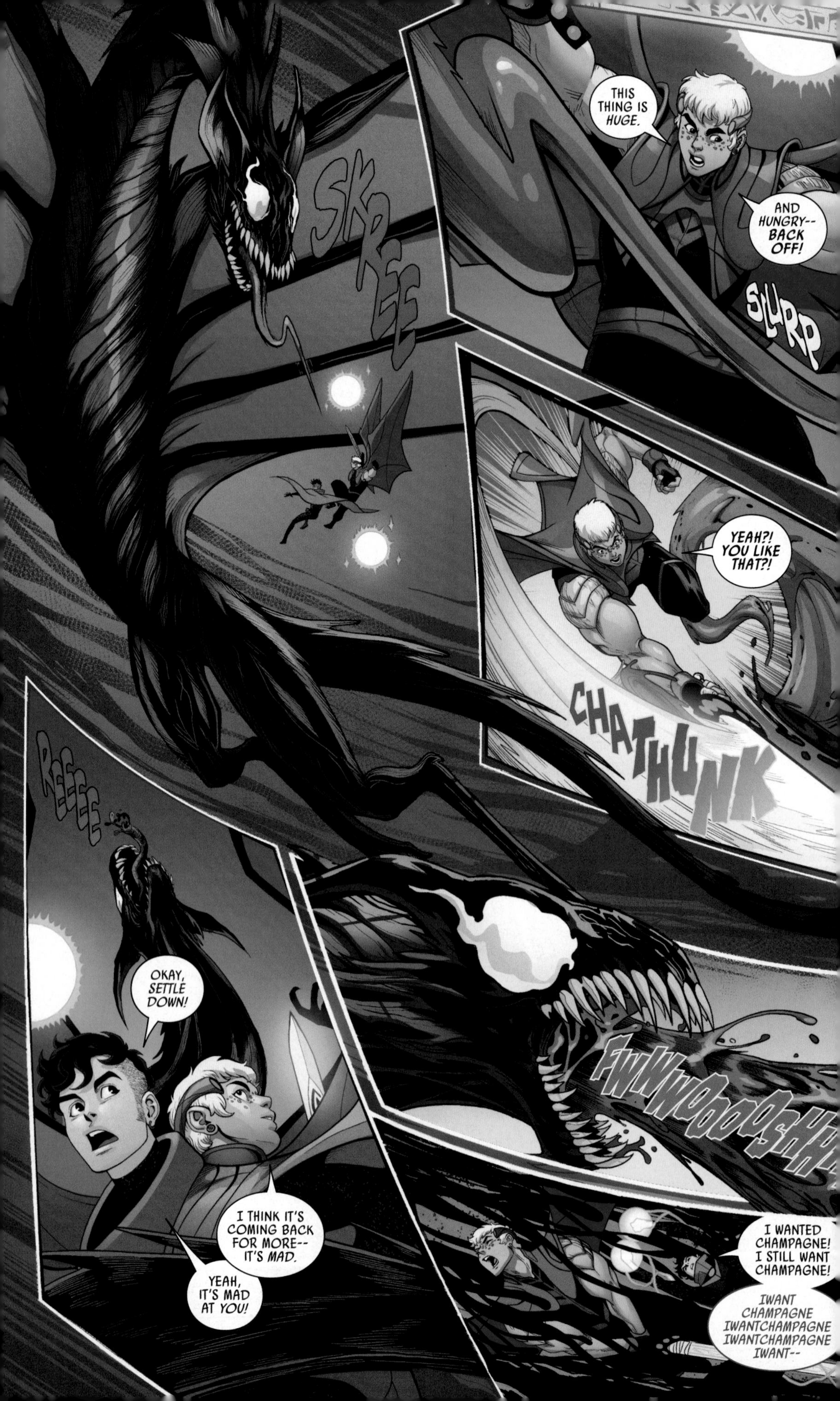
SKREE
THIS THING IS HUGE.
AND HUNGRY-- BACK OFF!
SLURP
YEAH?! YOU LIKE THAT?!
CHATHUNK
REEEE
OKAY, SETTLE DOWN!
I THINK IT'S COMING BACK FOR MORE-- IT'S MAD.
YEAH, IT'S MAD AT YOU!
FWWWOOOSHH
I WANTED CHAMPAGNE! I STILL WANT CHAMPAGNE!
IWANT CHAMPAGNE IWANTCHAMPAGNE IWANTCHAMPAGNE IWANT--

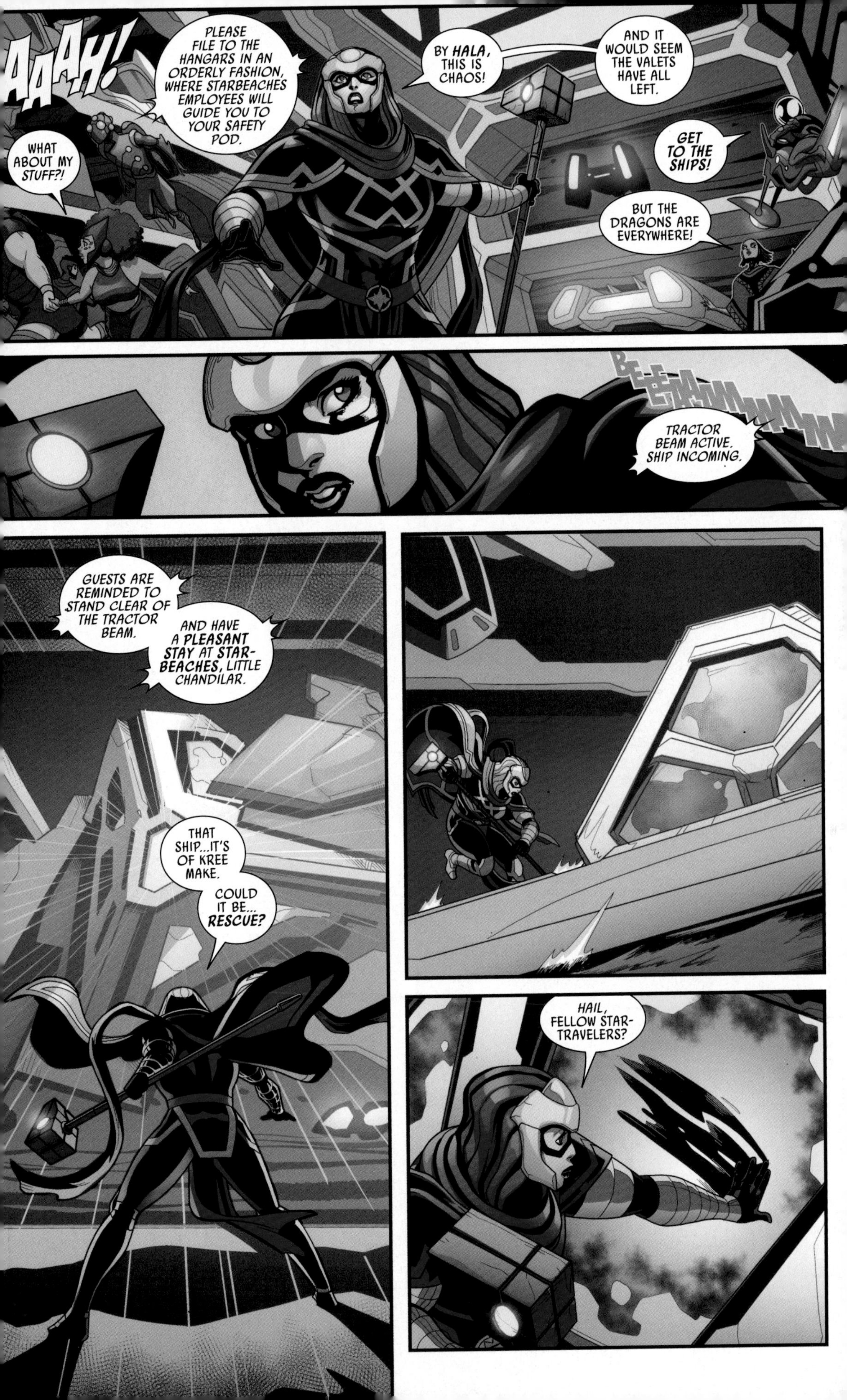
AAAH!
PLEASE FILE TO THE HANGARS IN AN ORDERLY FASHION, WHERE STARBEACHES EMPLOYEES WILL GUIDE YOU TO YOUR SAFETY POD.
WHAT ABOUT MY STUFF?!
BY HALA, THIS IS CHAOS!
AND IT WOULD SEEM THE VALETS HAVE ALL LEFT.
GET TO THE SHIPS!
BUT THE DRAGONS ARE EVERYWHERE!
TRACTOR BEAM ACTIVE. SHIP INCOMING.
GUESTS ARE REMINDED TO STAND CLEAR OF THE TRACTOR BEAM.
AND HAVE A PLEASANT STAY AT STAR-BEACHES, LITTLE CHANDILAR.
THAT SHIP...IT'S OF KREE MAKE.
COULD IT BE... RESCUE?
HAIL, FELLOW STAR-TRAVELERS?

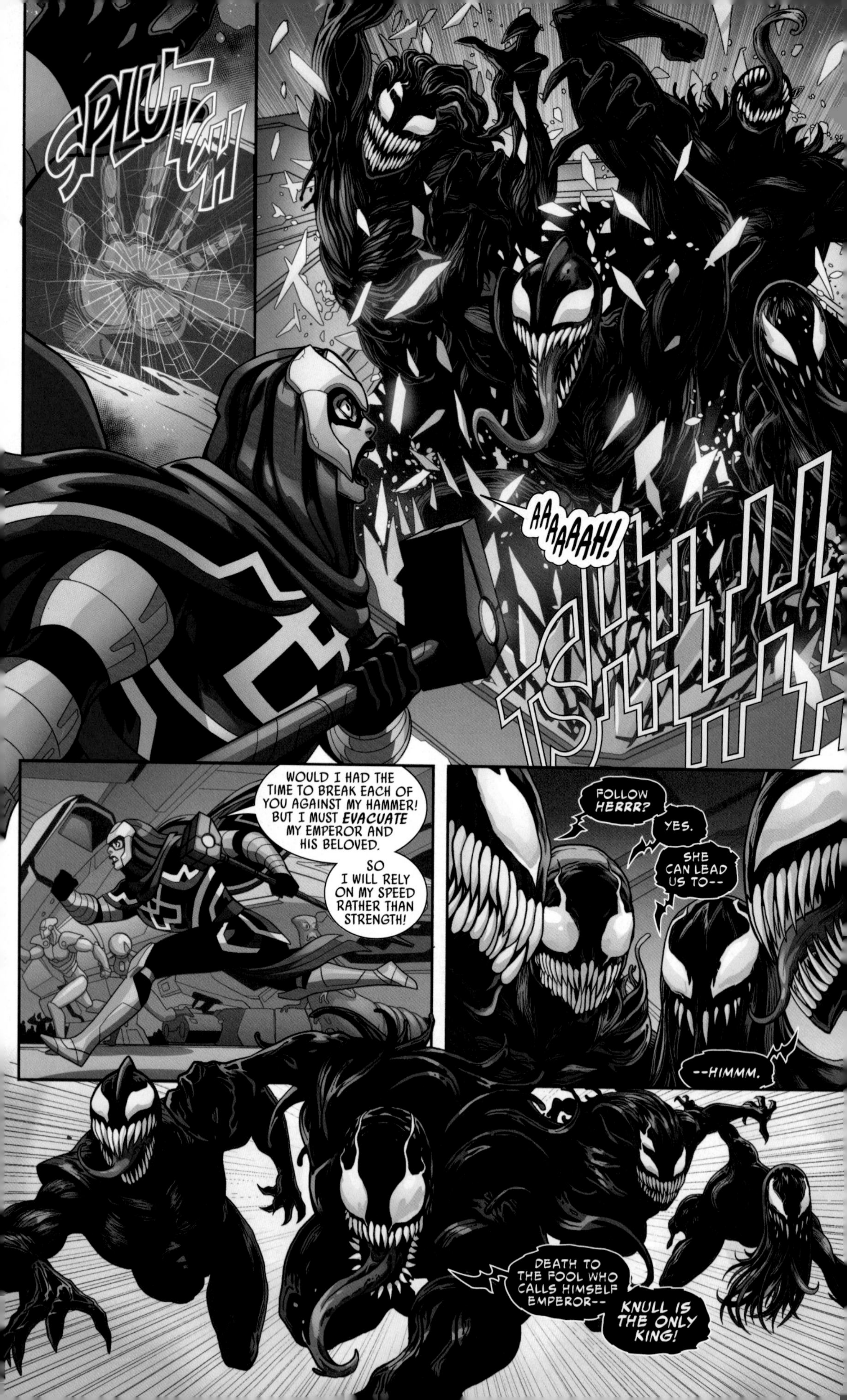
SPLUTCH
AAAAAAH!
TSHHH
WOULD I HAD THE TIME TO BREAK EACH OF YOU AGAINST MY HAMMER! BUT I MUST EVACUATE MY EMPEROR AND HIS BELOVED.
SO I WILL RELY ON MY SPEED RATHER THAN STRENGTH!
FOLLOW HERRR?
YES.
SHE CAN LEAD US TO--
--HIMMM.
DEATH TO THE FOOL WHO CALLS HIMSELF EMPEROR--
KNULL IS THE ONLY KING!

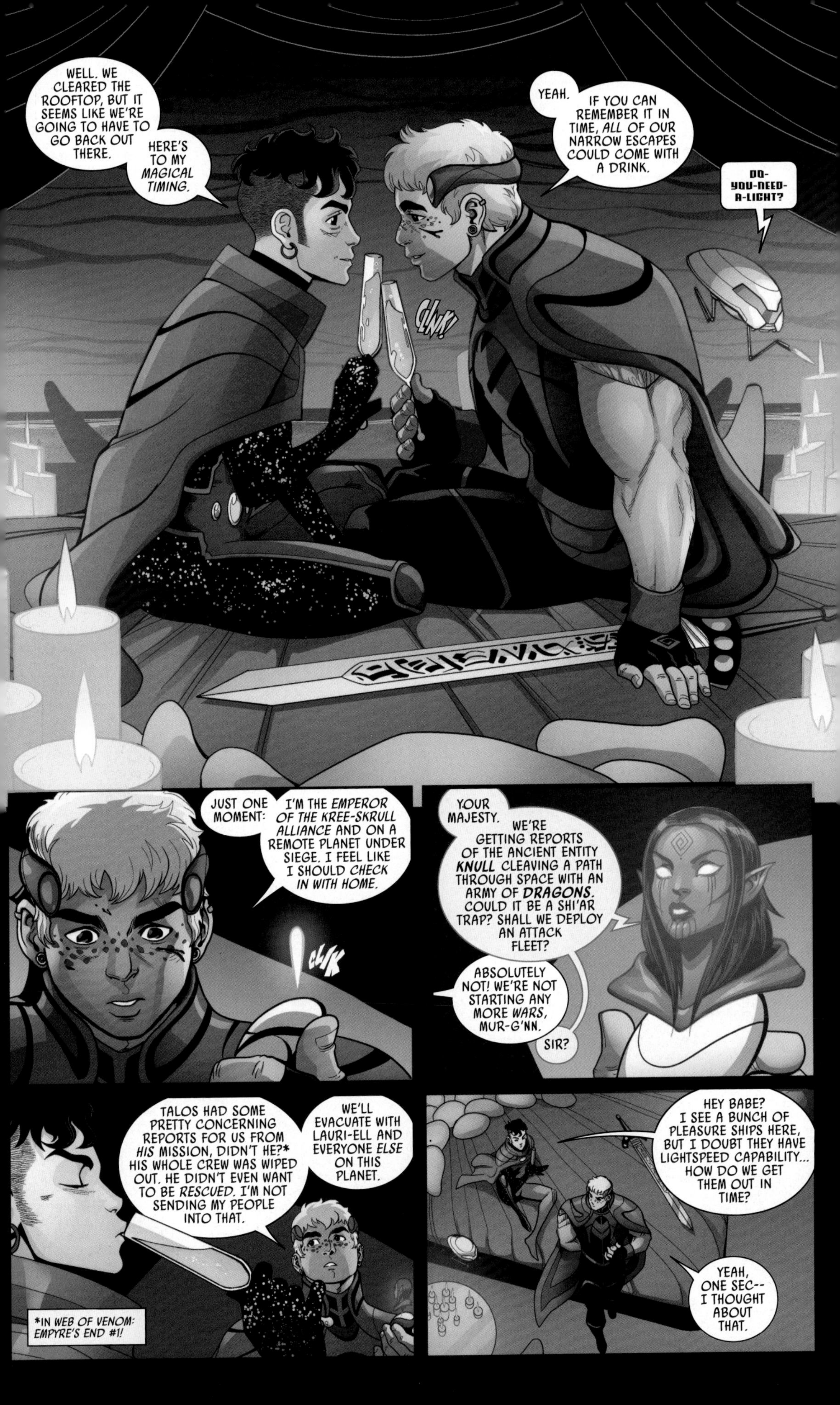
WELL. WE CLEARED THE ROOFTOP, BUT IT SEEMS LIKE WE'RE GOING TO HAVE TO GO BACK OUT THERE.
HERE'S TO MY MAGICAL TIMING.
YEAH.
IF YOU CAN REMEMBER IT IN TIME, ALL OF OUR NARROW ESCAPES COULD COME WITH A DRINK.
DO-YOU-NEED-A-LIGHT?
CLINK!
JUST ONE MOMENT:
I'M THE EMPEROR OF THE KREE-SKRULL ALLIANCE AND ON A REMOTE PLANET UNDER SIEGE. I FEEL LIKE I SHOULD CHECK IN WITH HOME.
CLIK
YOUR MAJESTY.
WE'RE GETTING REPORTS OF THE ANCIENT ENTITY KNULL CLEAVING A PATH THROUGH SPACE WITH AN ARMY OF DRAGONS. COULD IT BE A SHI'AR TRAP? SHALL WE DEPLOY AN ATTACK FLEET?
ABSOLUTELY NOT! WE'RE NOT STARTING ANY MORE WARS, MUR-G'NN.
SIR?
TALOS HAD SOME PRETTY CONCERNING REPORTS FOR US FROM HIS MISSION, DIDN'T HE?* HIS WHOLE CREW WAS WIPED OUT. HE DIDN'T EVEN WANT TO BE RESCUED. I'M NOT SENDING MY PEOPLE INTO THAT.
WE'LL EVACUATE WITH LAURI-ELL AND EVERYONE ELSE ON THIS PLANET.
*IN WEB OF VENOM: EMPYRE'S END #1!
HEY BABE? I SEE A BUNCH OF PLEASURE SHIPS HERE, BUT I DOUBT THEY HAVE LIGHTSPEED CAPABILITY... HOW DO WE GET THEM OUT IN TIME?
YEAH, ONE SEC-- I THOUGHT ABOUT THAT.

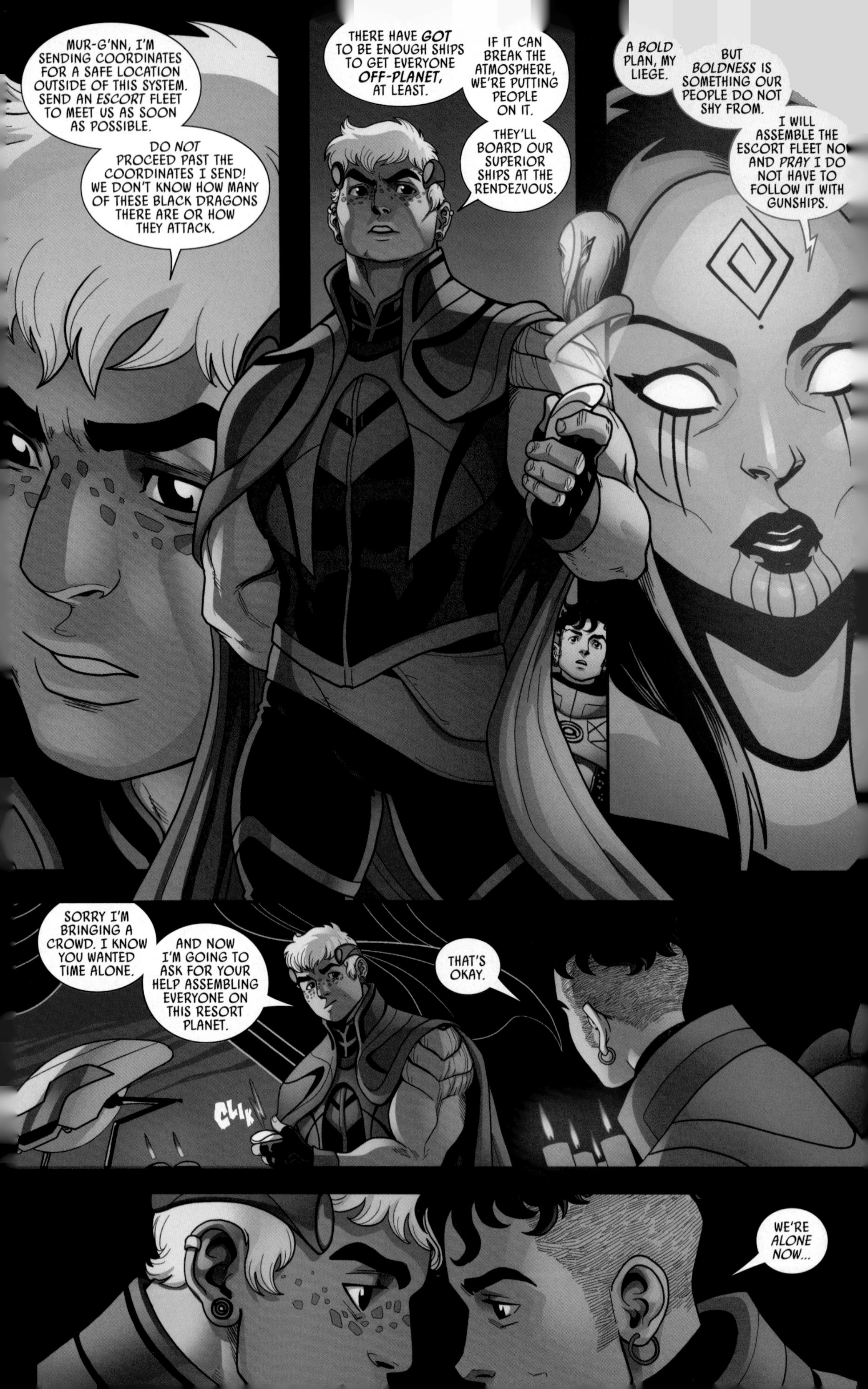
MUR-G'NN, I'M SENDING COORDINATES FOR A SAFE LOCATION OUTSIDE OF THIS SYSTEM. SEND AN *ESCORT* FLEET TO MEET US AS SOON AS POSSIBLE.
DO *NOT* PROCEED PAST THE COORDINATES I SEND! WE DON'T KNOW HOW MANY OF THESE BLACK DRAGONS THERE ARE OR HOW THEY ATTACK.
THERE HAVE ***GOT*** TO BE ENOUGH SHIPS TO GET EVERYONE ***OFF-PLANET,*** AT LEAST.
IF IT CAN BREAK THE ATMOSPHERE, WE'RE PUTTING PEOPLE ON IT.
THEY'LL BOARD OUR SUPERIOR SHIPS AT THE RENDEZVOUS.
A *BOLD* PLAN, MY LIEGE.
BUT *BOLDNESS* IS SOMETHING OUR PEOPLE DO NOT SHY FROM.
I WILL ASSEMBLE THE ESCORT FLEET NOW AND *PRAY* I DO NOT HAVE TO FOLLOW IT WITH GUNSHIPS.
SORRY I'M BRINGING A CROWD. I KNOW YOU WANTED TIME ALONE.
AND NOW I'M GOING TO ASK FOR YOUR HELP ASSEMBLING EVERYONE ON THIS RESORT PLANET.
CLIK
THAT'S OKAY.
WE'RE *ALONE* NOW...

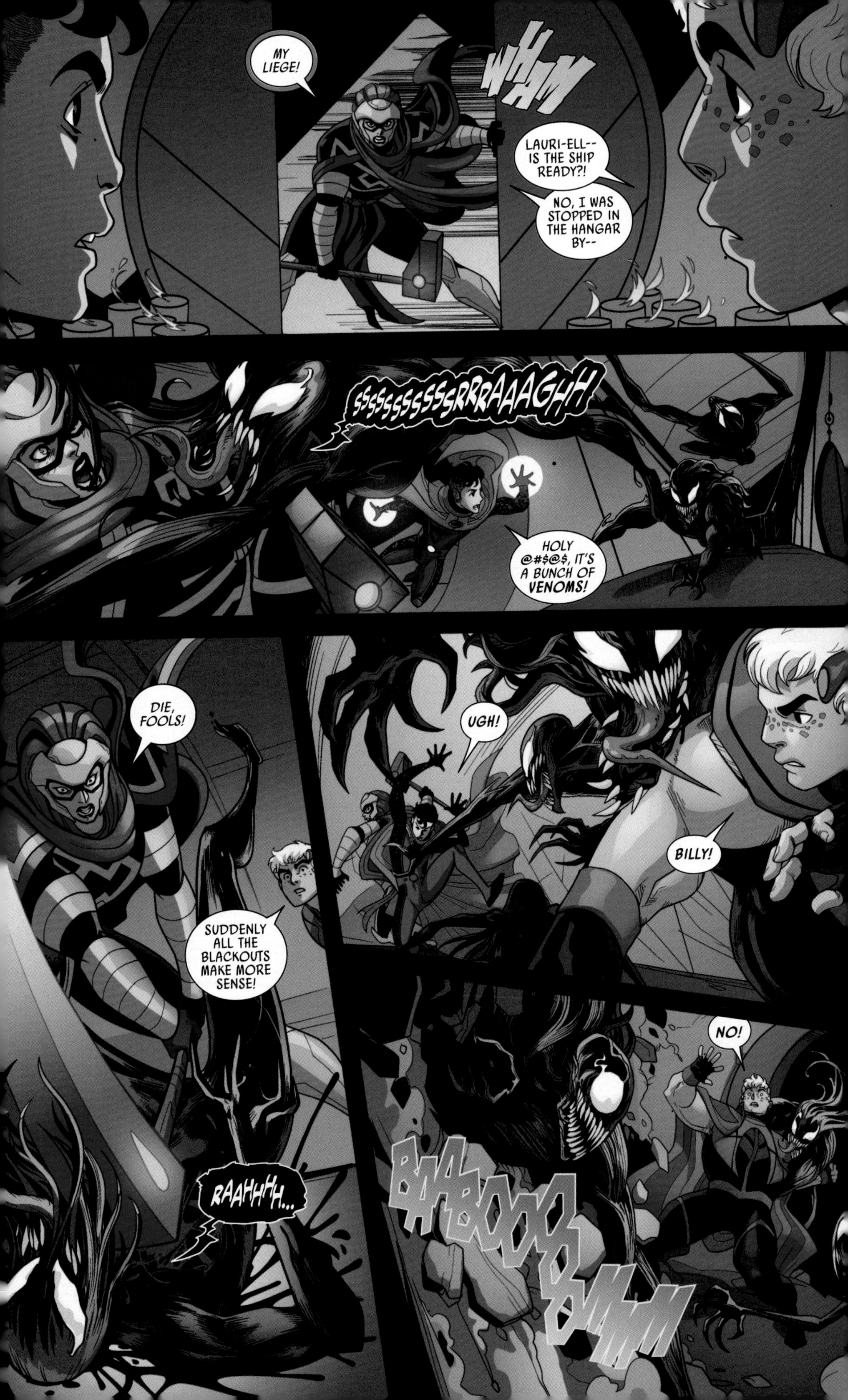
MY LIEGE!
WHAM
LAURI-ELL-- IS THE SHIP READY?!
NO, I WAS STOPPED IN THE HANGAR BY--
SSSSSSSSSSSRRRAAAGHH
HOLY @#$@$, IT'S A BUNCH OF VENOMS!
DIE, FOOLS!
SUDDENLY ALL THE BLACKOUTS MAKE MORE SENSE!
UGH!
BILLY!
RAAHHHH...
NO!
BABOOOBMMM

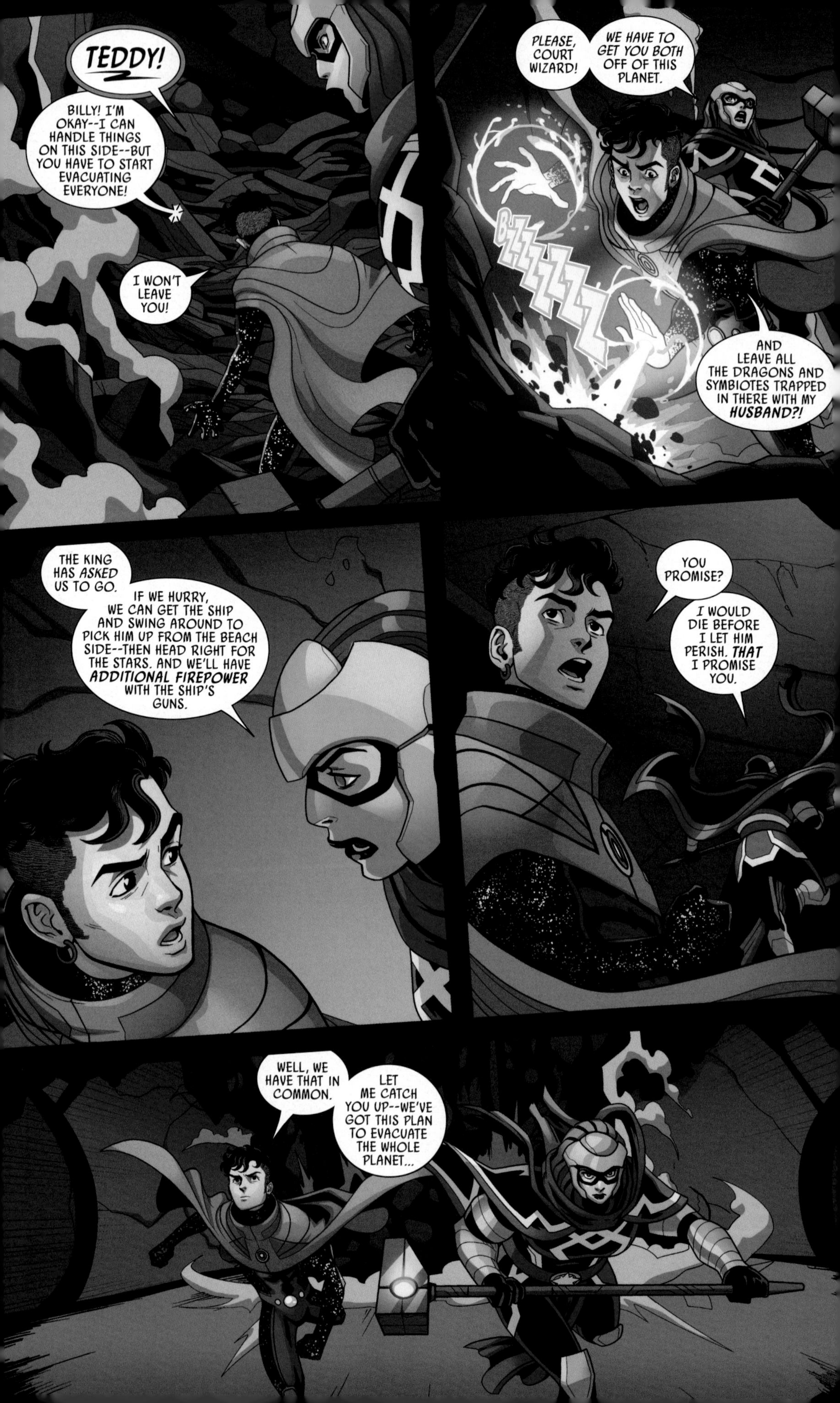
TEDDY!
BILLY! I'M OKAY--I CAN HANDLE THINGS ON THIS SIDE--BUT YOU HAVE TO START EVACUATING EVERYONE!
I WON'T LEAVE YOU!
PLEASE, COURT WIZARD!
WE HAVE TO GET YOU BOTH OFF OF THIS PLANET.
BZZZZZZZ
AND LEAVE ALL THE DRAGONS AND SYMBIOTES TRAPPED IN THERE WITH MY HUSBAND?!
THE KING HAS ASKED US TO GO.
IF WE HURRY, WE CAN GET THE SHIP AND SWING AROUND TO PICK HIM UP FROM THE BEACH SIDE--THEN HEAD RIGHT FOR THE STARS. AND WE'LL HAVE ADDITIONAL FIREPOWER WITH THE SHIP'S GUNS.
YOU PROMISE?
I WOULD DIE BEFORE I LET HIM PERISH. THAT I PROMISE YOU.
WELL, WE HAVE THAT IN COMMON.
LET ME CATCH YOU UP--WE'VE GOT THIS PLAN TO EVACUATE THE WHOLE PLANET...

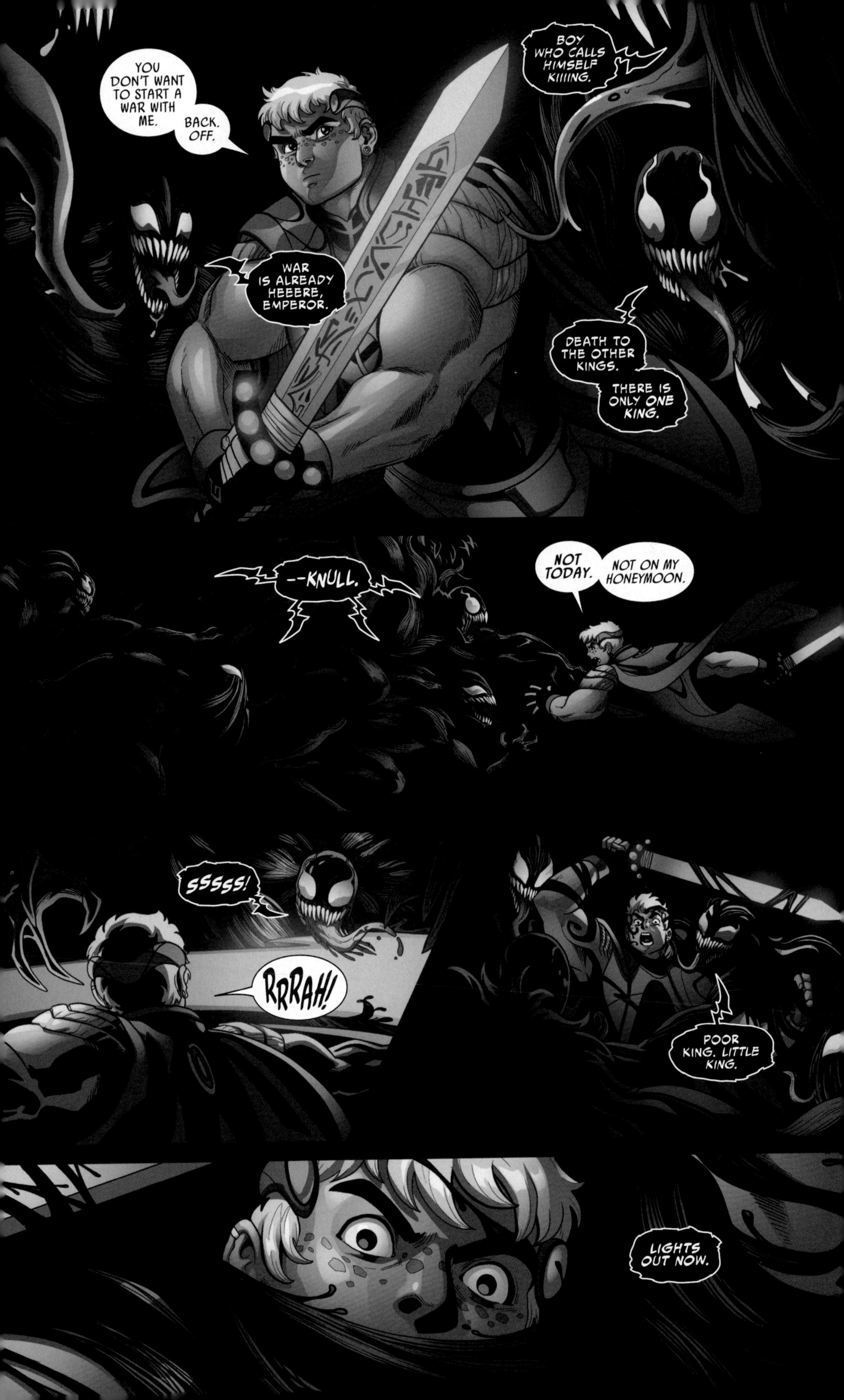

YOU DON'T WANT TO START A WAR WITH ME.
BACK. OFF.
BOY WHO CALLS HIMSELF KIIIING.
WAR IS ALREADY HEEERE, EMPEROR.
DEATH TO THE OTHER KINGS.
THERE IS ONLY ONE KING.
--KNULL.
NOT TODAY.
NOT ON MY HONEYMOON.
SSSSS!
RRRAH!
POOR KING. LITTLE KING.
LIGHTS OUT NOW.

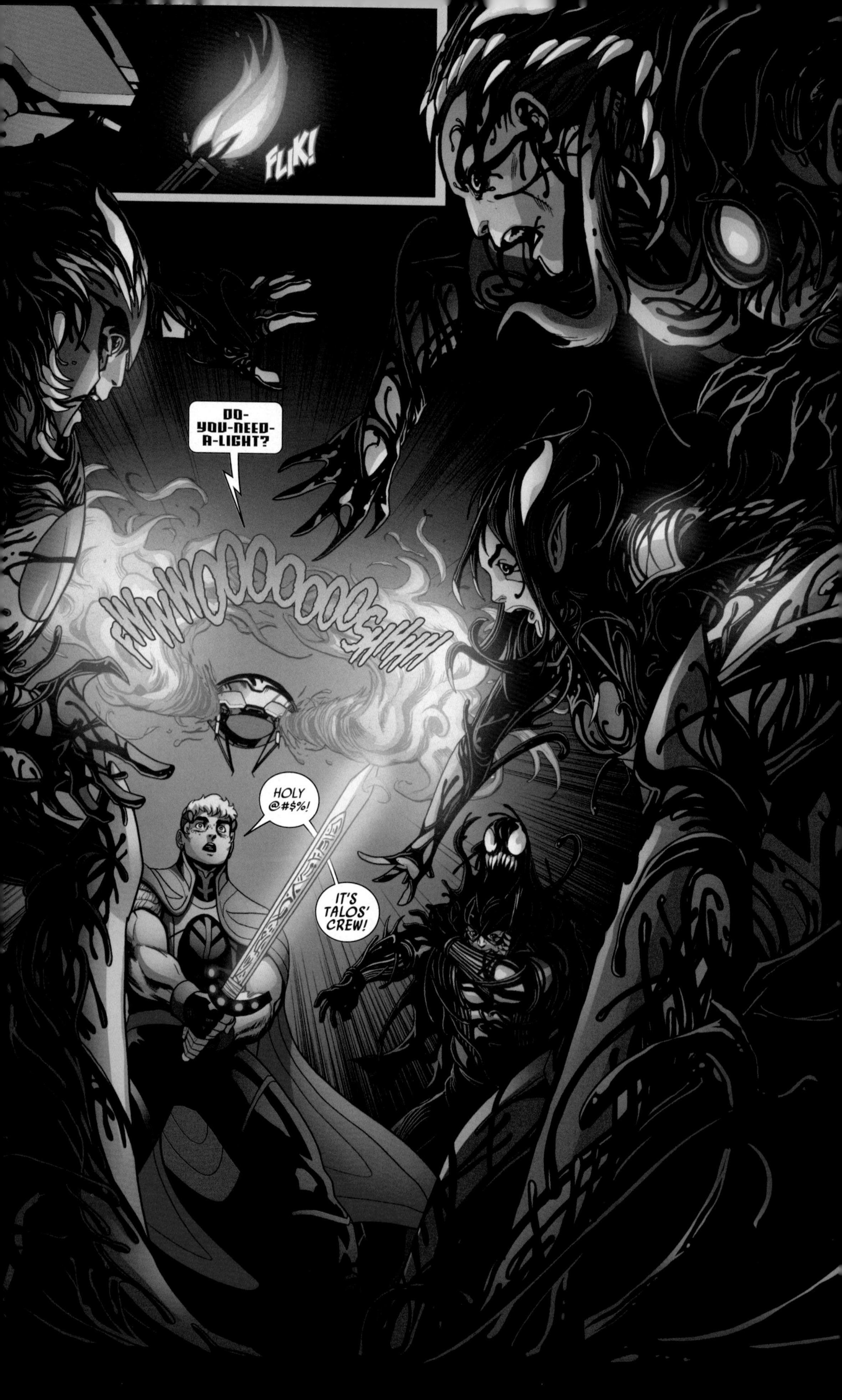
FLIK!
DO-
YOU-NEED-
A-LIGHT?
FWWWOOOOOOOSHHH
HOLY
@#$%!
IT'S
TALOS'
CREW!

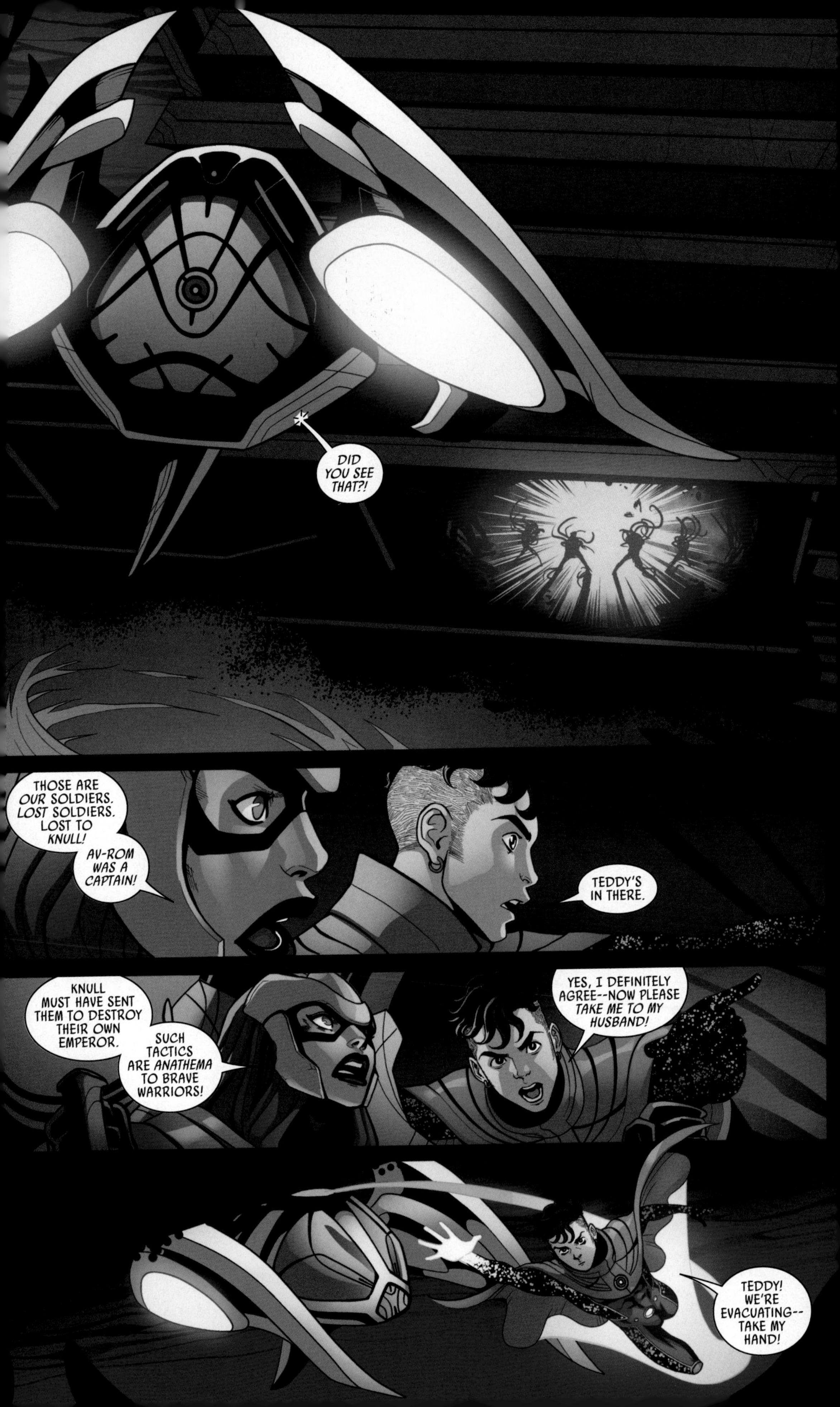
DID YOU SEE THAT?!
THOSE ARE OUR SOLDIERS. LOST SOLDIERS. LOST TO KNULL!
AV-ROM WAS A CAPTAIN!
TEDDY'S IN THERE.
KNULL MUST HAVE SENT THEM TO DESTROY THEIR OWN EMPEROR.
SUCH TACTICS ARE ANATHEMA TO BRAVE WARRIORS!
YES, I DEFINITELY AGREE--NOW PLEASE TAKE ME TO MY HUSBAND!
TEDDY! WE'RE EVACUATING--TAKE MY HAND!

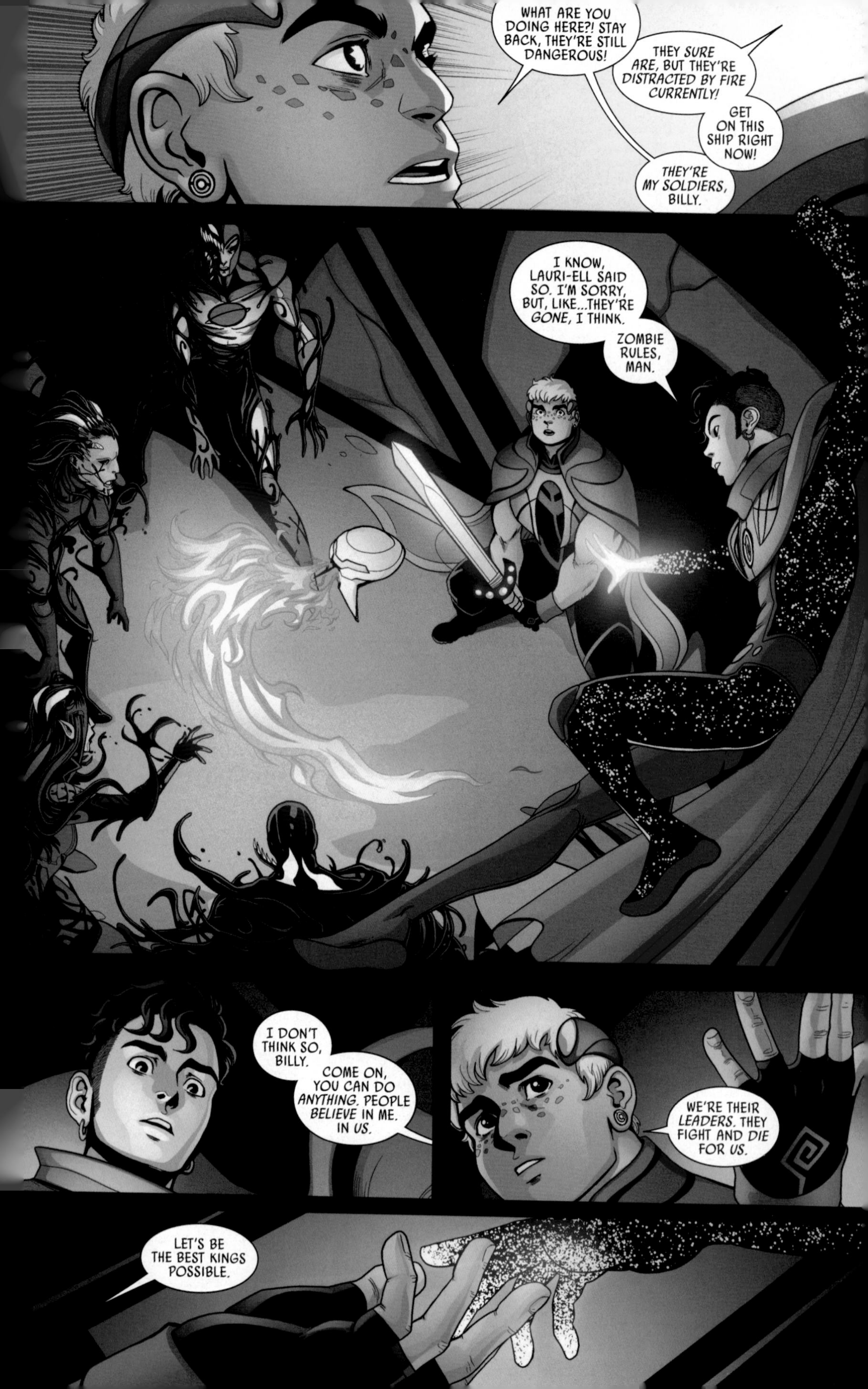
WHAT ARE YOU DOING HERE?! STAY BACK, THEY'RE STILL DANGEROUS!
THEY *SURE* ARE, BUT THEY'RE DISTRACTED BY FIRE CURRENTLY!
GET ON THIS SHIP RIGHT NOW!
THEY'RE MY SOLDIERS, BILLY.
I KNOW, LAURI-ELL SAID SO. I'M SORRY, BUT, LIKE...THEY'RE *GONE*, I THINK.
ZOMBIE RULES, MAN.
I DON'T THINK SO, BILLY.
COME ON, YOU CAN DO *ANYTHING*. PEOPLE *BELIEVE* IN ME. IN *US*.
WE'RE THEIR *LEADERS*. THEY FIGHT AND *DIE* FOR US.
LET'S BE THE BEST KINGS POSSIBLE.

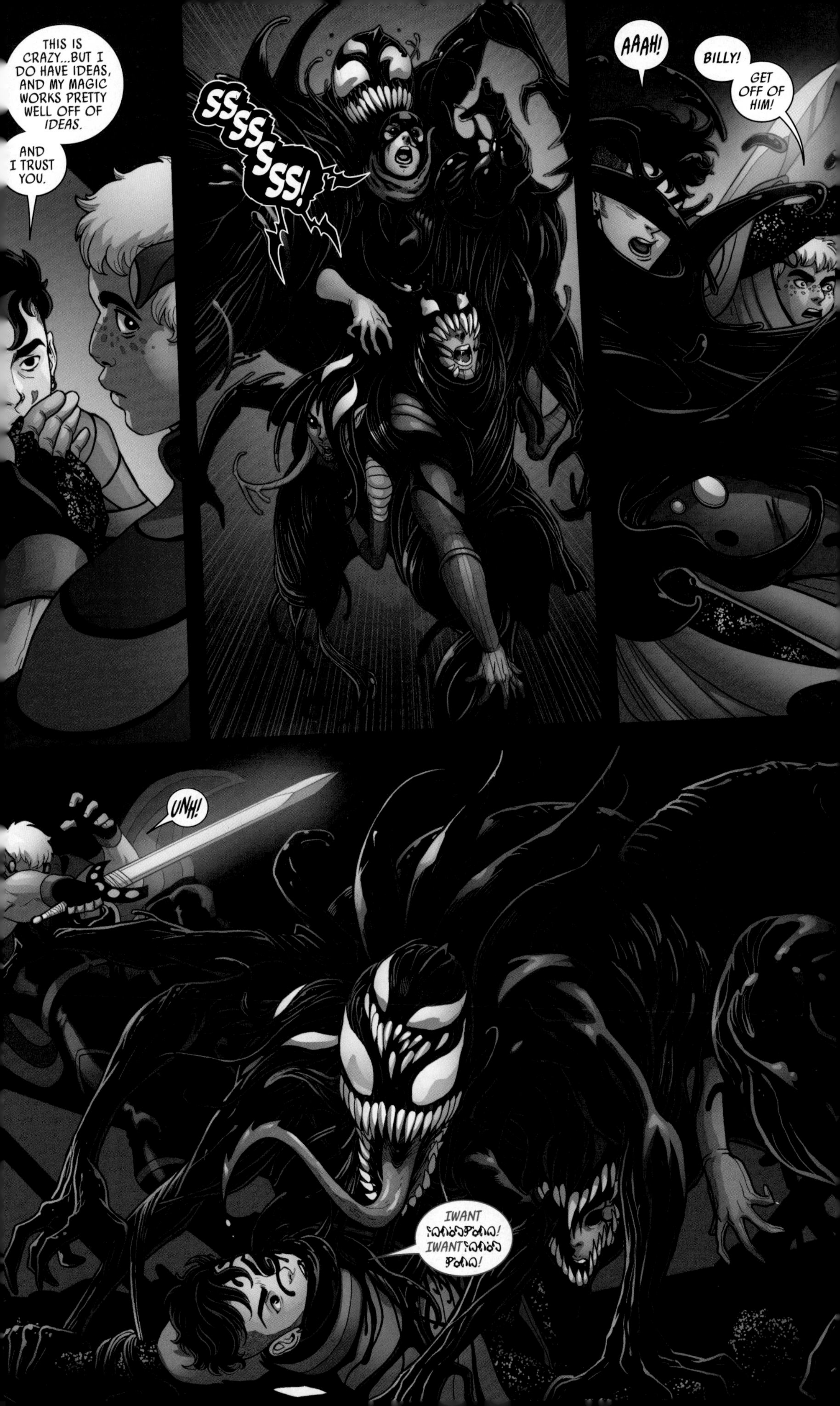
THIS IS CRAZY...BUT I DO HAVE IDEAS, AND MY MAGIC WORKS PRETTY WELL OFF OF IDEAS.
AND I TRUST YOU.
SSSSSSS!
AAAH!
BILLY!
GET OFF OF HIM!
UNH!
IWANT
IWANT

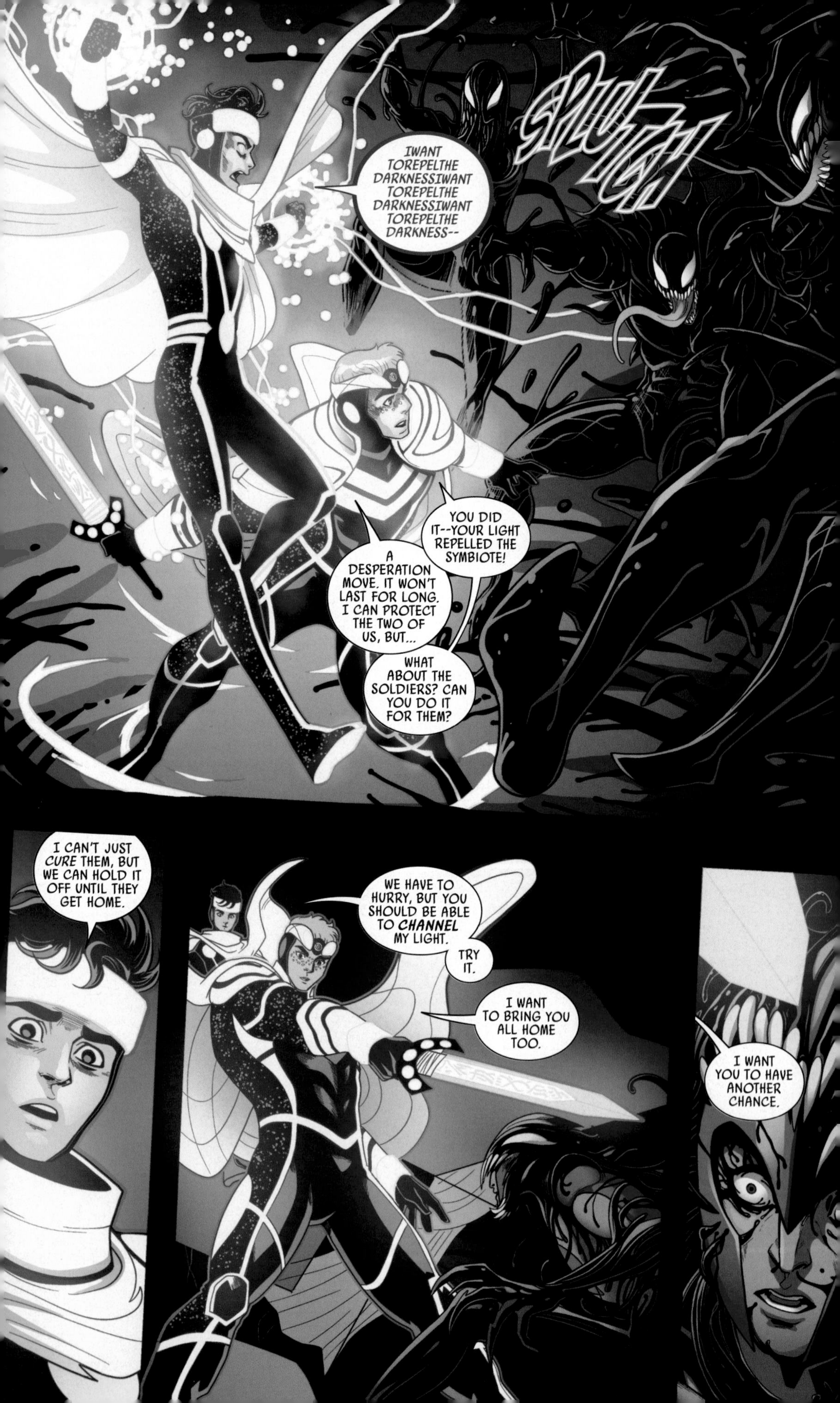
IWANT TOREPELTHE DARKNESSIWANT TOREPELTHE DARKNESSIWANT TOREPELTHE DARKNESS--
SPLUTCH
YOU DID IT--YOUR LIGHT REPELLED THE SYMBIOTE!
A DESPERATION MOVE. IT WON'T LAST FOR LONG. I CAN PROTECT THE TWO OF US, BUT...
WHAT ABOUT THE SOLDIERS? CAN YOU DO IT FOR THEM?
I CAN'T JUST CURE THEM, BUT WE CAN HOLD IT OFF UNTIL THEY GET HOME.
WE HAVE TO HURRY, BUT YOU SHOULD BE ABLE TO CHANNEL MY LIGHT.
TRY IT.
I WANT TO BRING YOU ALL HOME TOO.
I WANT YOU TO HAVE ANOTHER CHANCE.

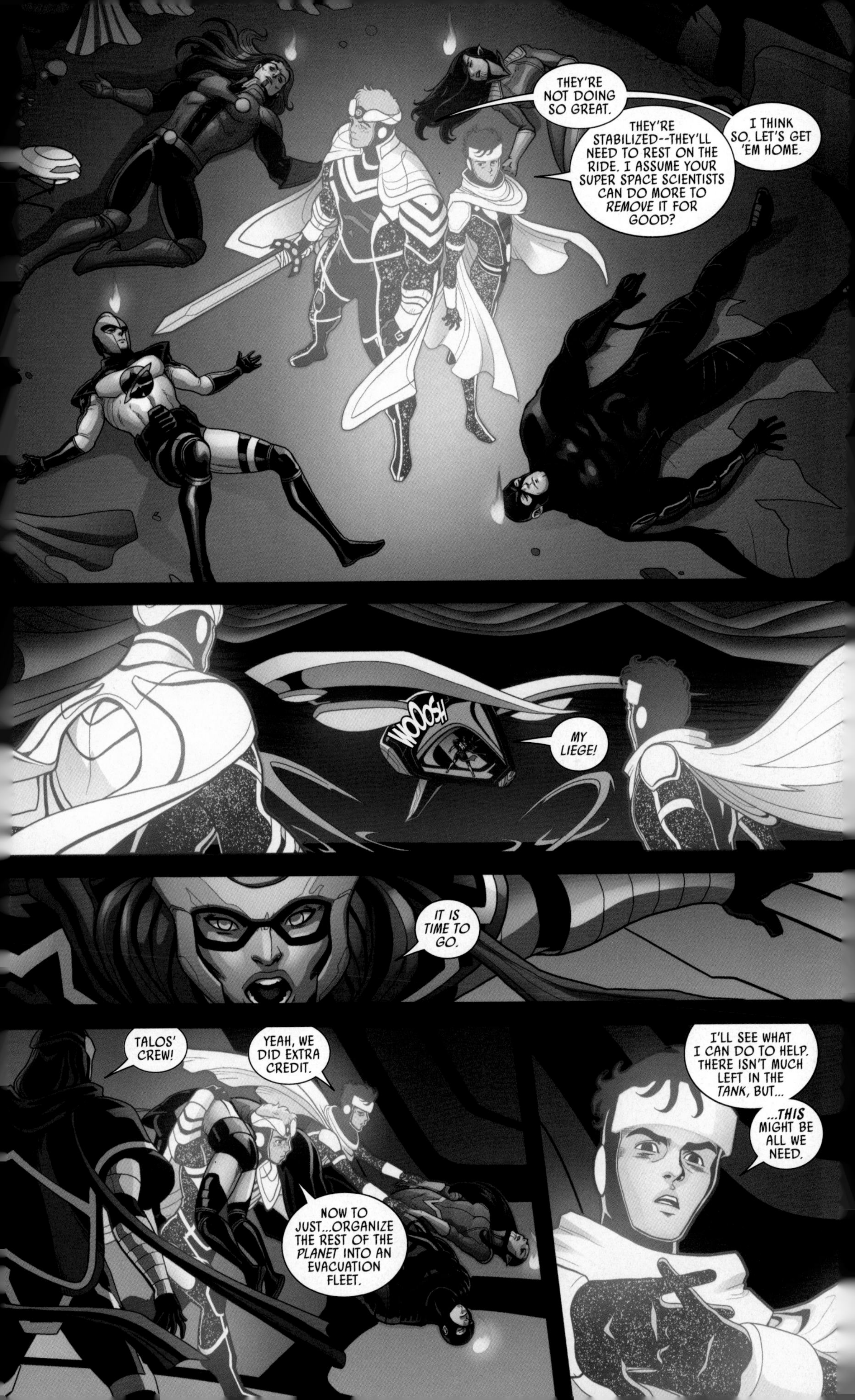
THEY'RE NOT DOING SO GREAT.
THEY'RE STABILIZED--THEY'LL NEED TO REST ON THE RIDE. I ASSUME YOUR SUPER SPACE SCIENTISTS CAN DO MORE TO *REMOVE* IT FOR GOOD?
I THINK SO. LET'S GET 'EM HOME.
WOOOSH
MY LIEGE!
IT IS TIME TO GO.
TALOS' CREW!
YEAH, WE DID EXTRA CREDIT.
NOW TO JUST...ORGANIZE THE REST OF THE *PLANET* INTO AN EVACUATION FLEET.
I'LL SEE WHAT I CAN DO TO HELP. THERE ISN'T MUCH LEFT IN THE *TANK*, BUT...
...*THIS* MIGHT BE ALL WE NEED.

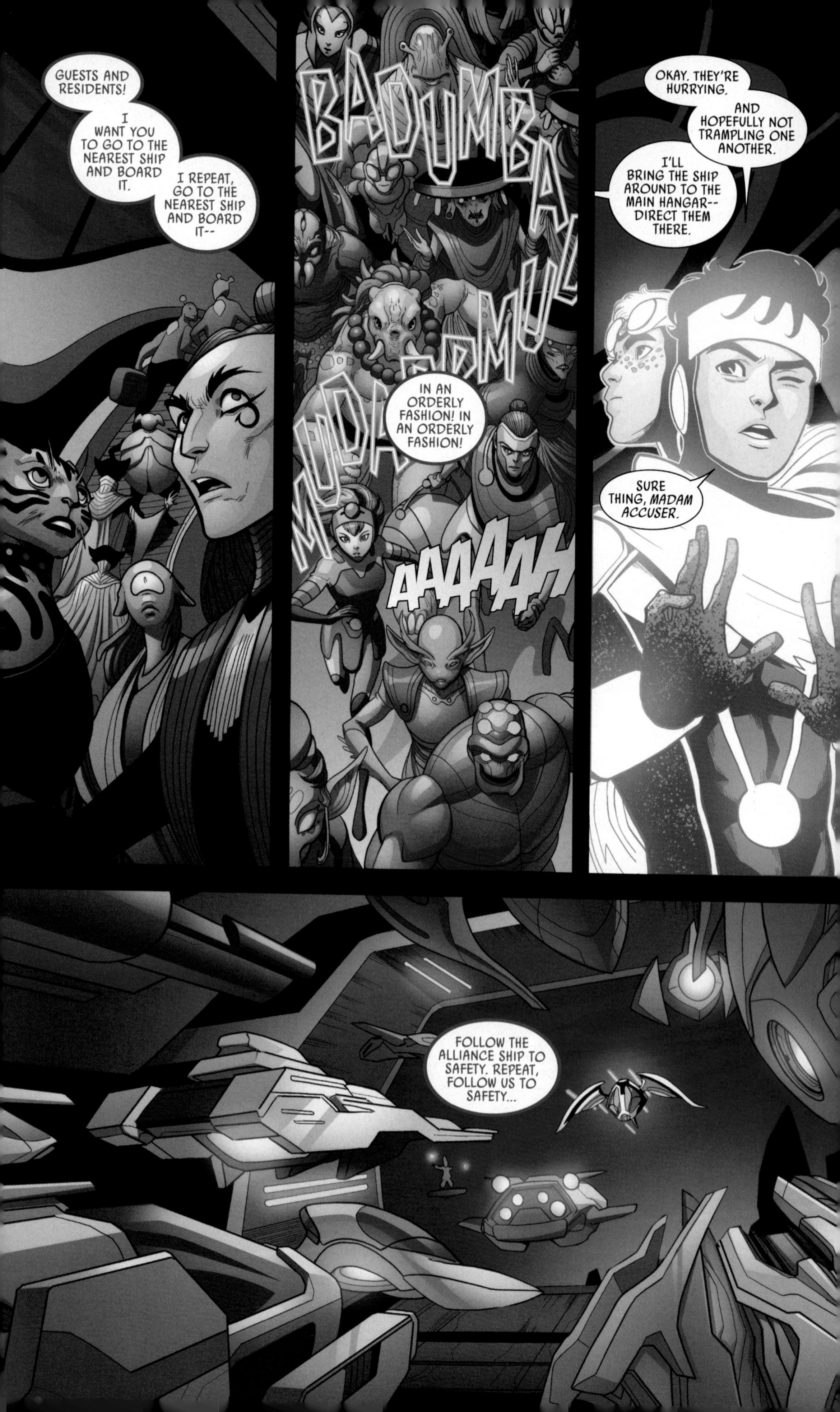
GUESTS AND RESIDENTS!
I WANT YOU TO GO TO THE NEAREST SHIP AND BOARD IT.
I REPEAT, GO TO THE NEAREST SHIP AND BOARD IT--
BADUMBA
MUDADUMDUM
IN AN ORDERLY FASHION! IN AN ORDERLY FASHION!
AAAAAH
OKAY. THEY'RE HURRYING.
AND HOPEFULLY NOT TRAMPLING ONE ANOTHER.
I'LL BRING THE SHIP AROUND TO THE MAIN HANGAR-- DIRECT THEM THERE.
SURE THING, *MADAM ACCUSER.*
FOLLOW THE ALLIANCE SHIP TO SAFETY. REPEAT, FOLLOW US TO SAFETY...

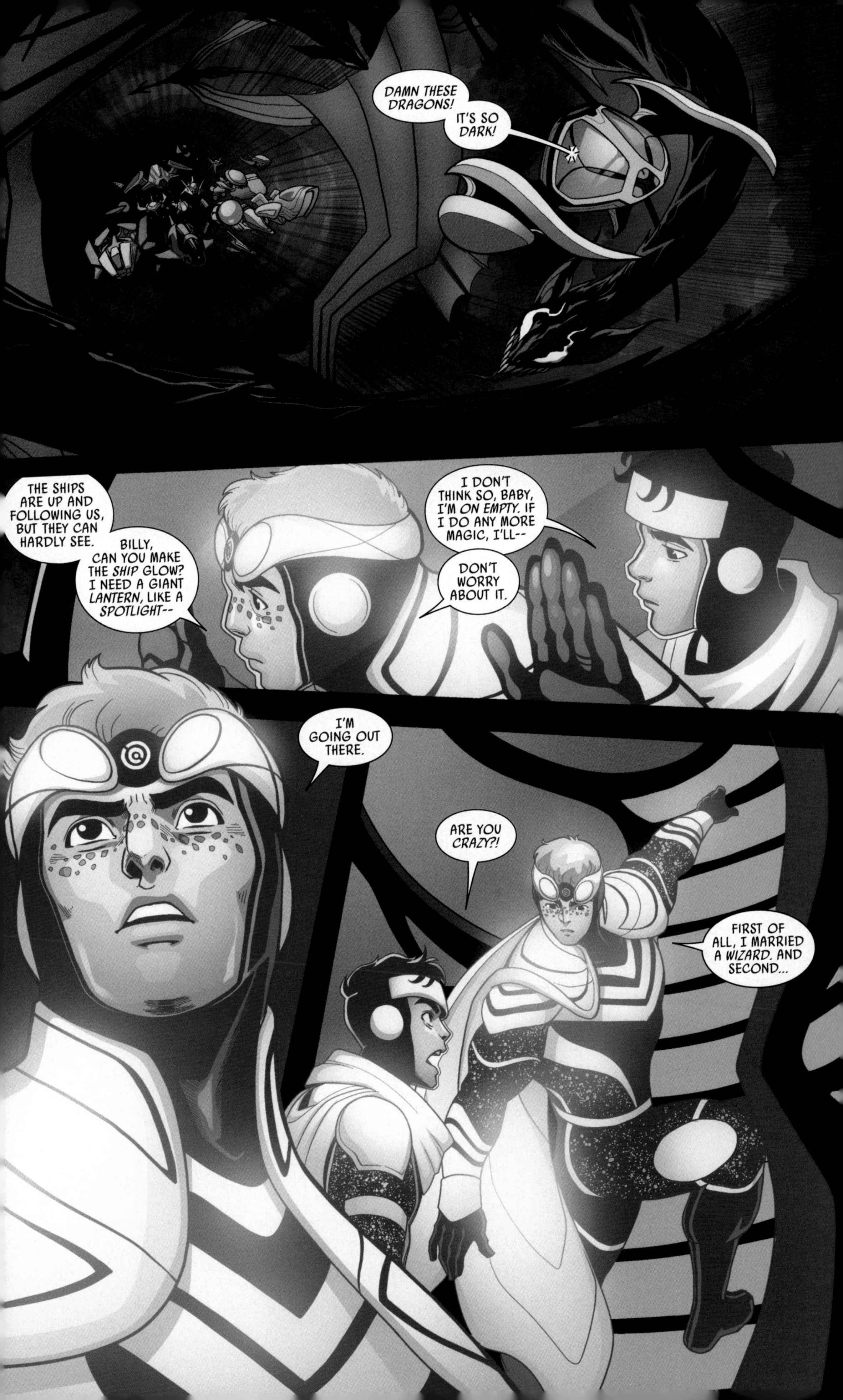
DAMN THESE DRAGONS!
IT'S SO DARK!
THE SHIPS ARE UP AND FOLLOWING US, BUT THEY CAN HARDLY SEE.
BILLY, CAN YOU MAKE THE *SHIP* GLOW? I NEED A GIANT *LANTERN*, LIKE A *SPOTLIGHT*--
I DON'T THINK SO, BABY, I'M *ON EMPTY*. IF I DO ANY MORE MAGIC, I'LL--
DON'T WORRY ABOUT IT.
I'M GOING OUT THERE.
ARE YOU *CRAZY*?!
FIRST OF ALL, I MARRIED A *WIZARD*. AND SECOND...

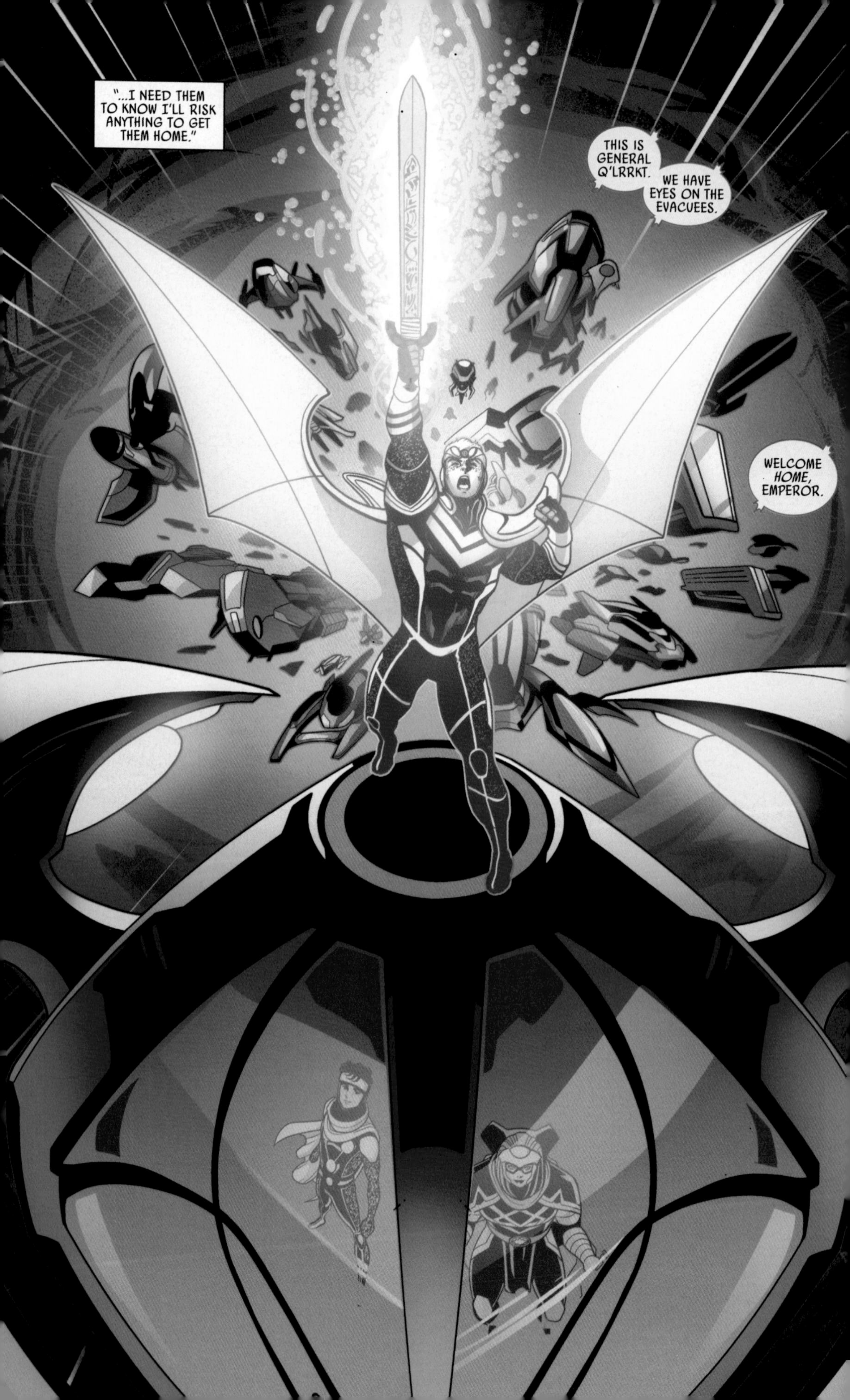
"...I NEED THEM TO KNOW I'LL RISK ANYTHING TO GET THEM HOME."
THIS IS GENERAL Q'LRRKT.
WE HAVE EYES ON THE EVACUEES.
WELCOME *HOME*, EMPEROR.

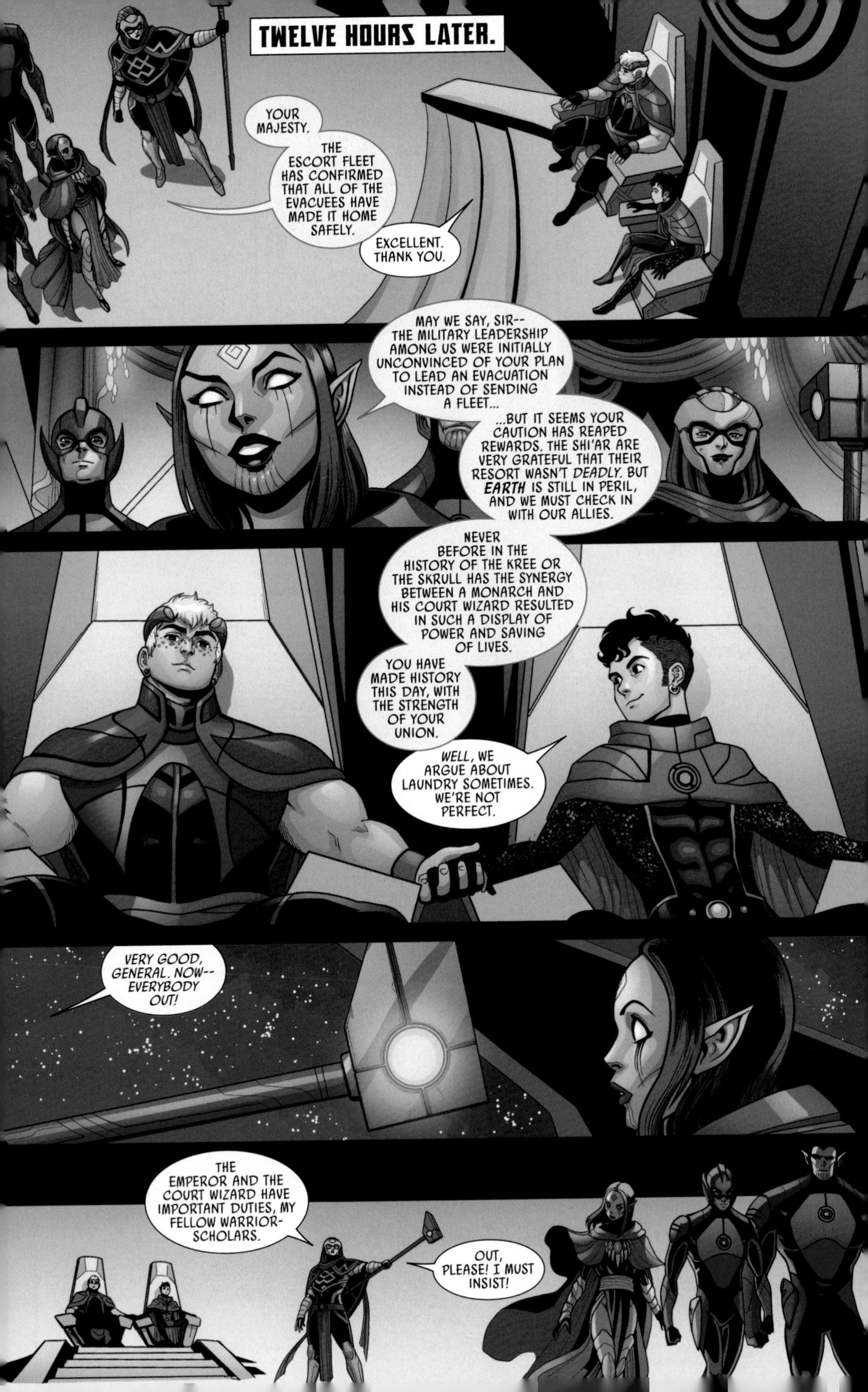
TWELVE HOURS LATER.
YOUR MAJESTY.
THE ESCORT FLEET HAS CONFIRMED THAT ALL OF THE EVACUEES HAVE MADE IT HOME SAFELY.
EXCELLENT. THANK YOU.
MAY WE SAY, SIR-- THE MILITARY LEADERSHIP AMONG US WERE INITIALLY UNCONVINCED OF YOUR PLAN TO LEAD AN EVACUATION INSTEAD OF SENDING A FLEET...
...BUT IT SEEMS YOUR CAUTION HAS REAPED REWARDS. THE SHI'AR ARE VERY GRATEFUL THAT THEIR RESORT WASN'T *DEADLY*. BUT ***EARTH*** IS STILL IN PERIL, AND WE MUST CHECK IN WITH OUR ALLIES.
NEVER BEFORE IN THE HISTORY OF THE KREE OR THE SKRULL HAS THE SYNERGY BETWEEN A MONARCH AND HIS COURT WIZARD RESULTED IN SUCH A DISPLAY OF POWER AND SAVING OF LIVES.
YOU HAVE MADE HISTORY THIS DAY, WITH THE STRENGTH OF YOUR UNION.
WELL, WE ARGUE ABOUT LAUNDRY SOMETIMES. WE'RE NOT PERFECT.
VERY GOOD, GENERAL. NOW-- EVERYBODY OUT!
THE EMPEROR AND THE COURT WIZARD HAVE IMPORTANT DUTIES, MY FELLOW WARRIOR-SCHOLARS.
OUT, PLEASE! I MUST INSIST!

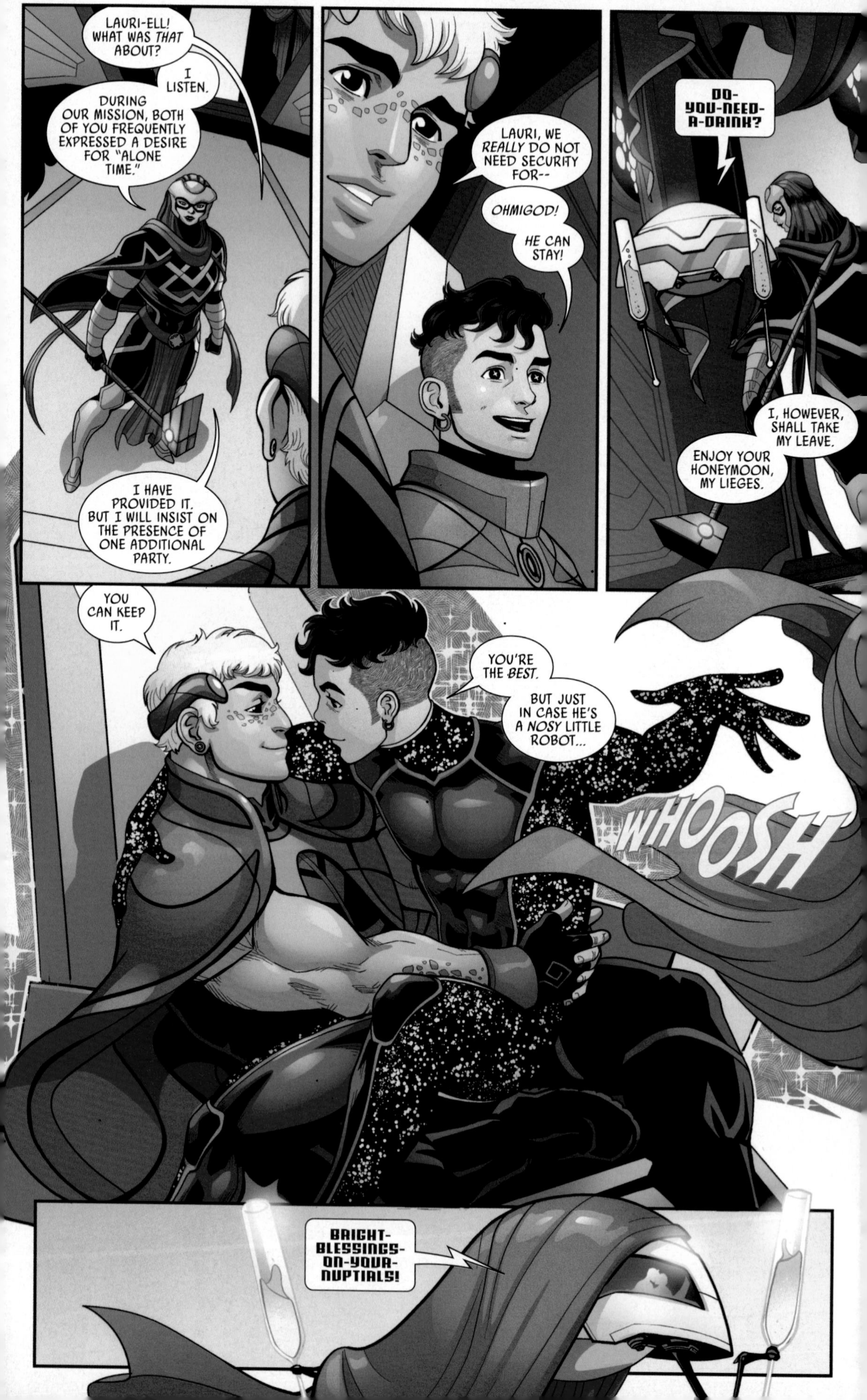
LAURI-ELL! WHAT WAS THAT ABOUT?
I LISTEN.
DURING OUR MISSION, BOTH OF YOU FREQUENTLY EXPRESSED A DESIRE FOR "ALONE TIME."
I HAVE PROVIDED IT. BUT I WILL INSIST ON THE PRESENCE OF ONE ADDITIONAL PARTY.
LAURI, WE REALLY DO NOT NEED SECURITY FOR--
OHMIGOD!
HE CAN STAY!
DO-YOU-NEED-A-DRINK?
I, HOWEVER, SHALL TAKE MY LEAVE.
ENJOY YOUR HONEYMOON, MY LIEGES.
YOU CAN KEEP IT.
YOU'RE THE BEST.
BUT JUST IN CASE HE'S A NOSY LITTLE ROBOT...
WHOOSH
BRIGHT-BLESSINGS-ON-YOUR-NUPTIALS!

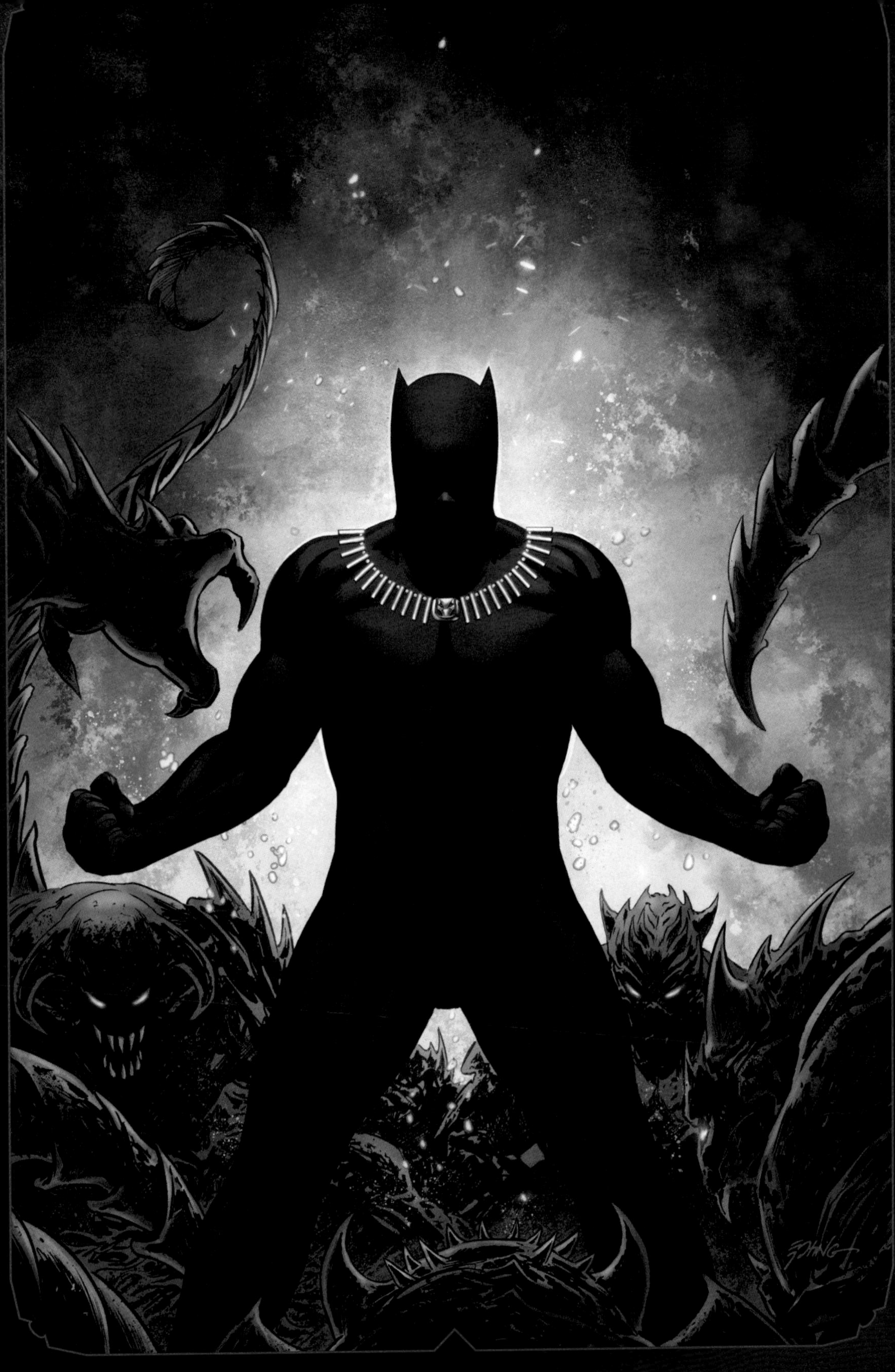

BLACK PANTHER VARIANT BY **STEVE EPTING**

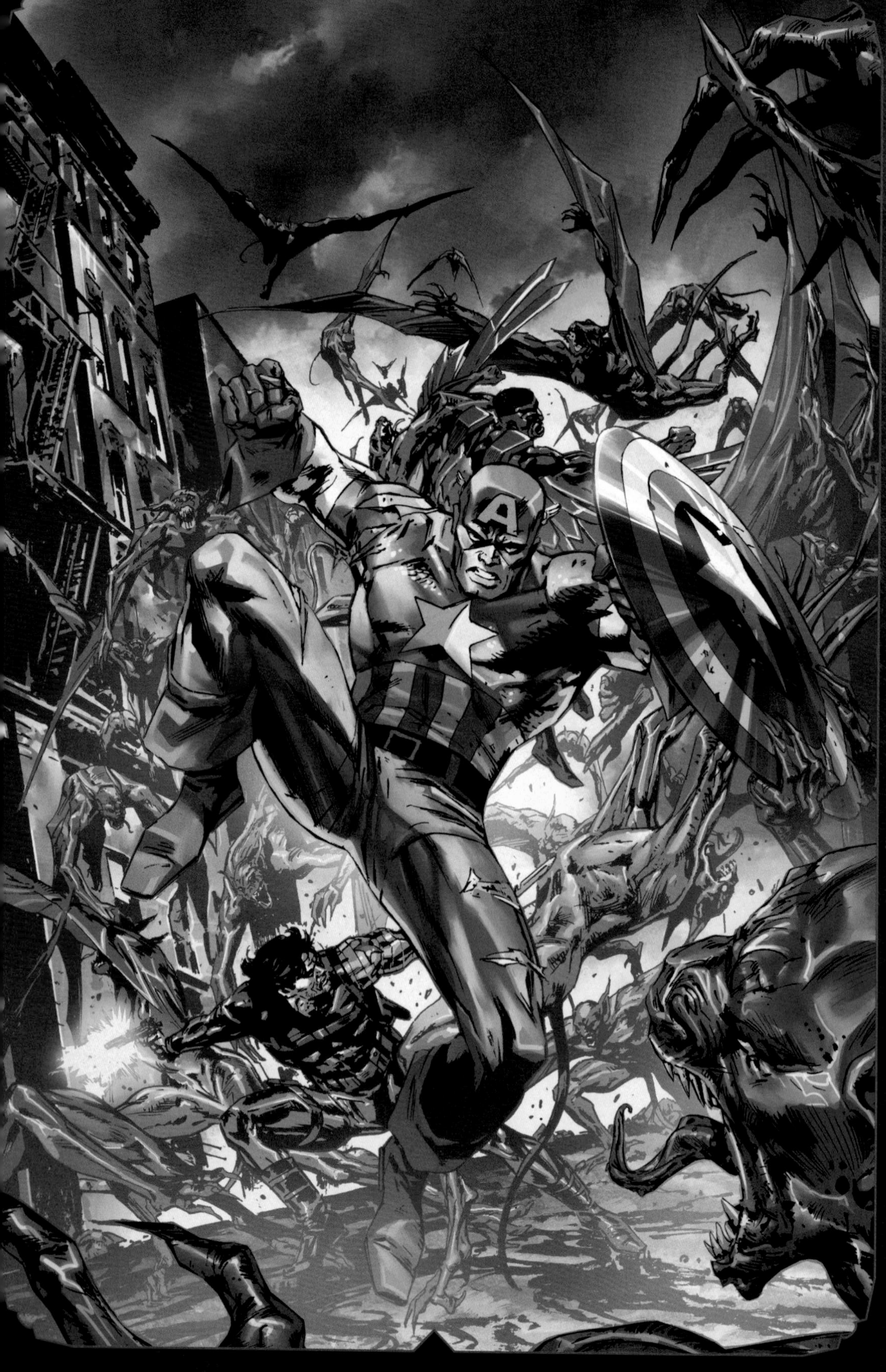

CAPTAIN AMERICA VARIANT BY

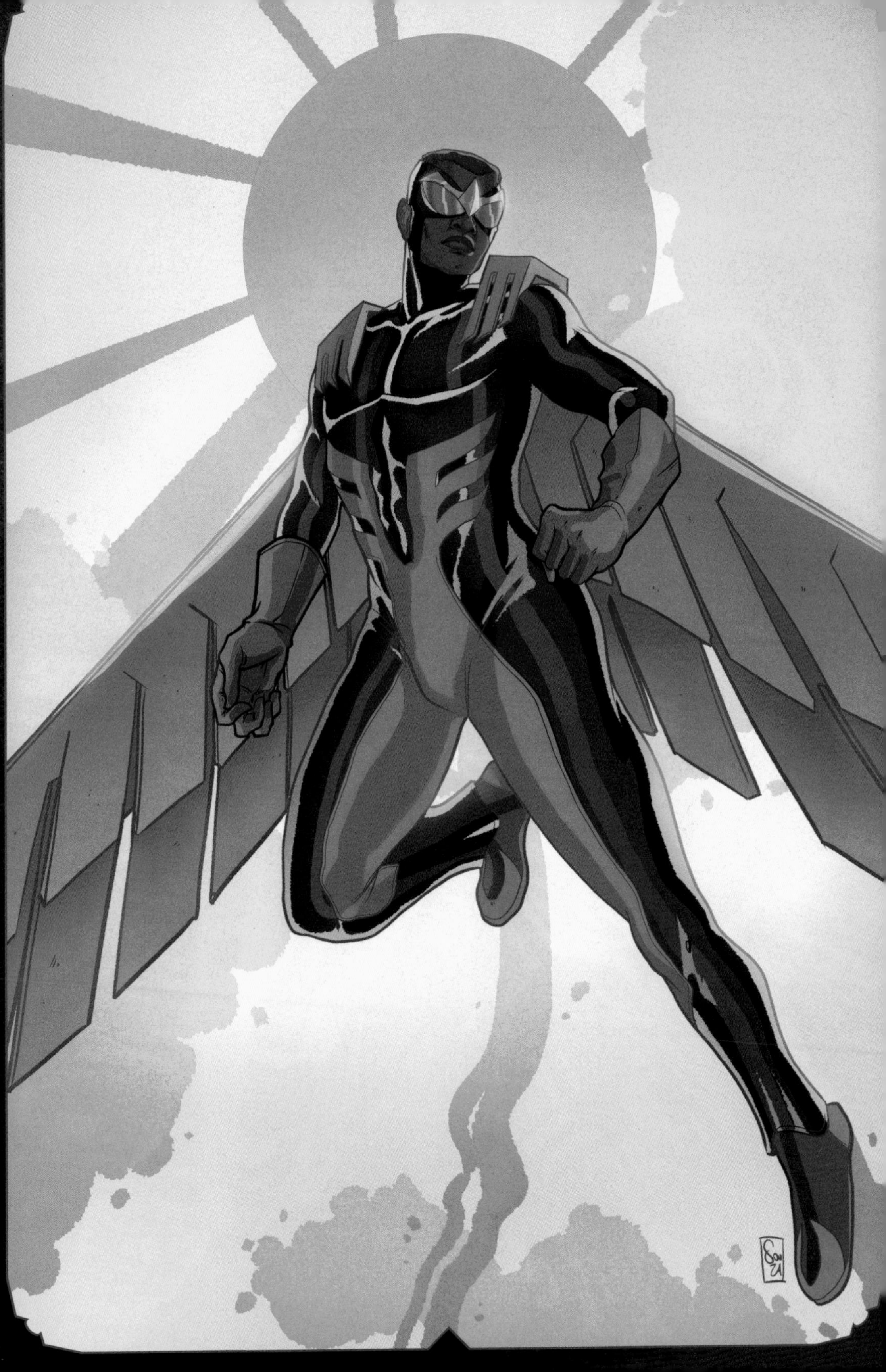

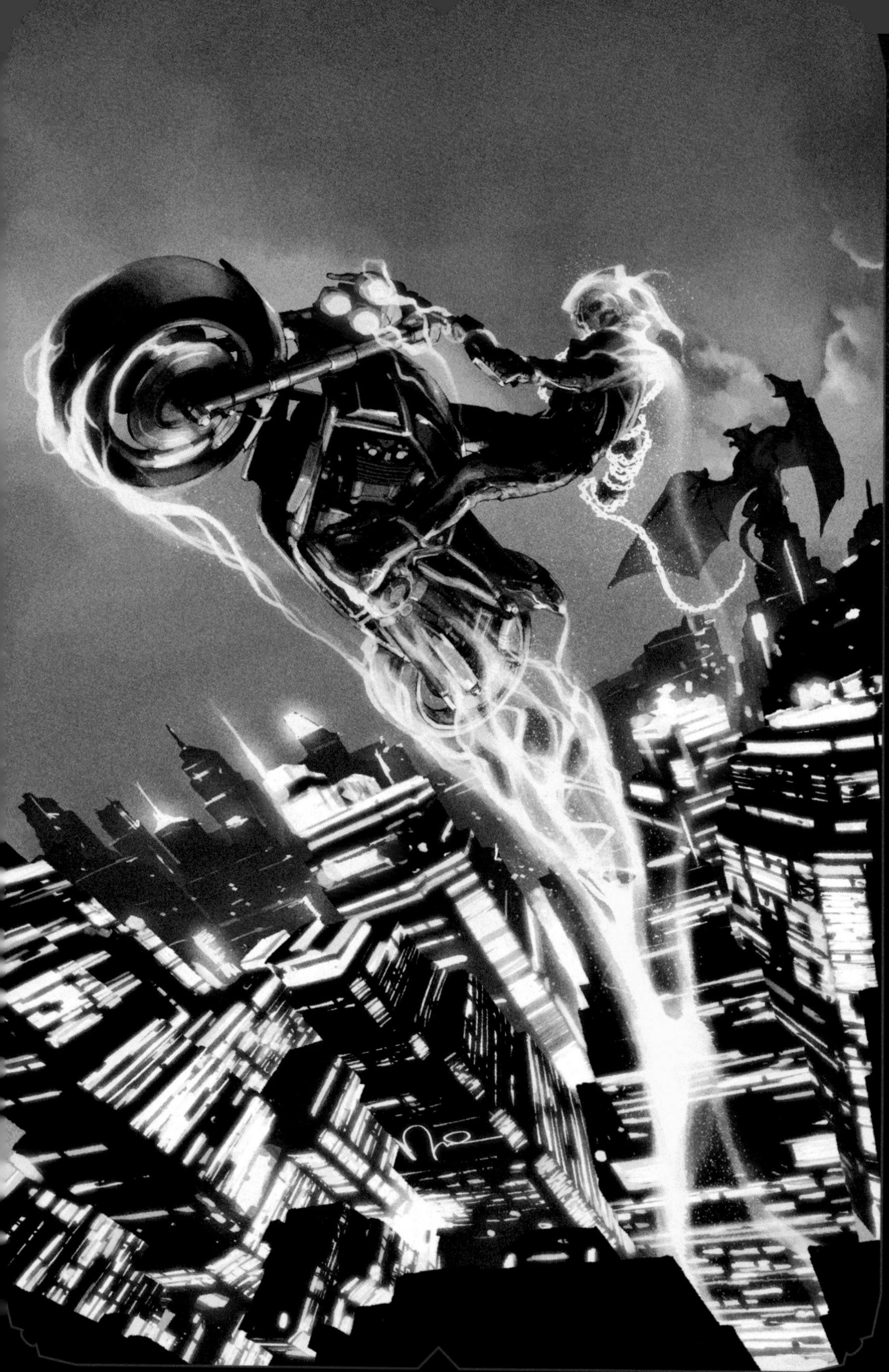

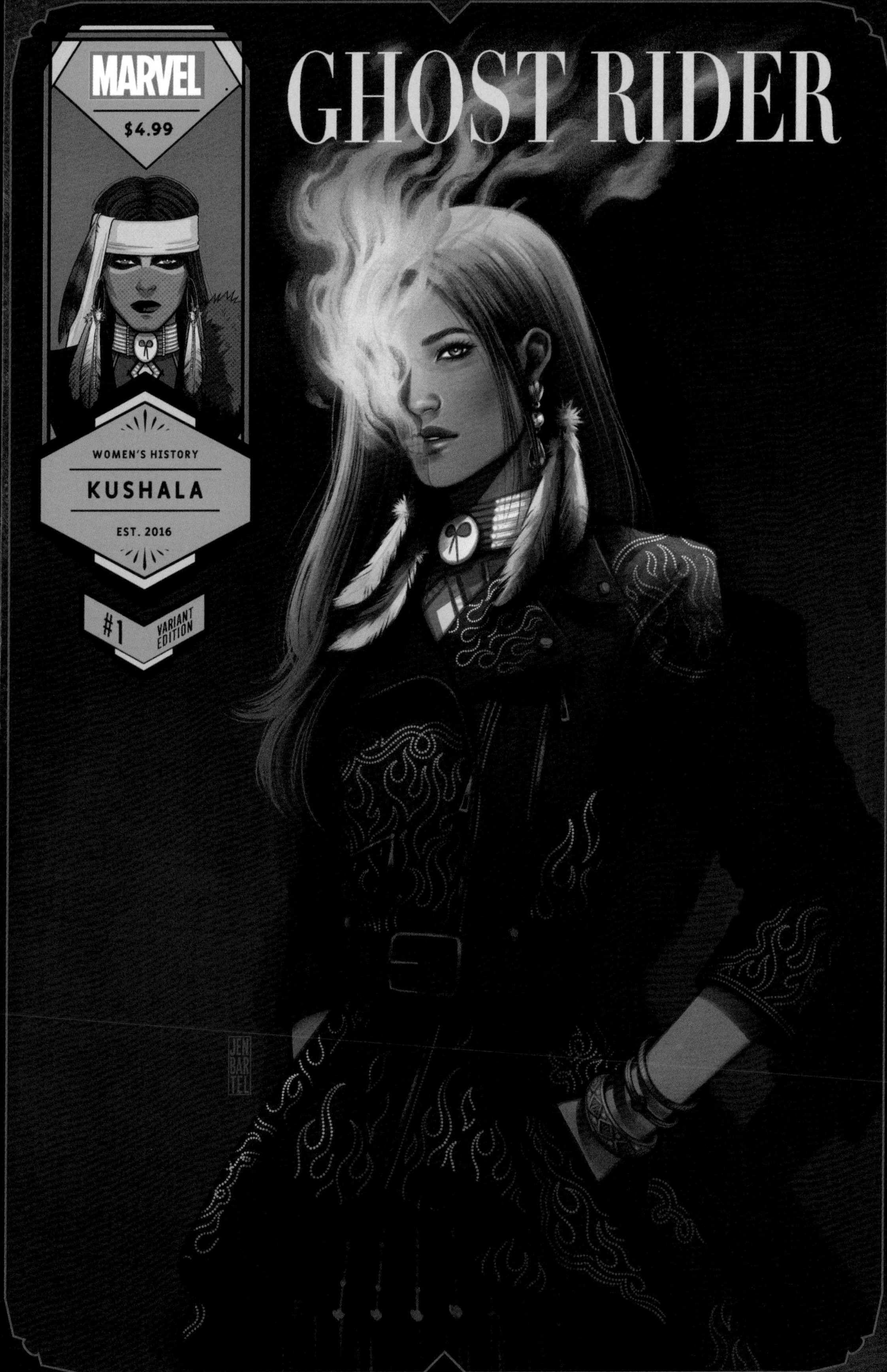
MARVEL
$4.99
GHOST RIDER
WOMEN'S HISTORY
KUSHALA
EST. 2016
#1 VARIANT EDITION
JEN BARTEL

GHOST RIDER WOMEN'S HISTORY MONTH VARIANT BY **JEN BARTEL**

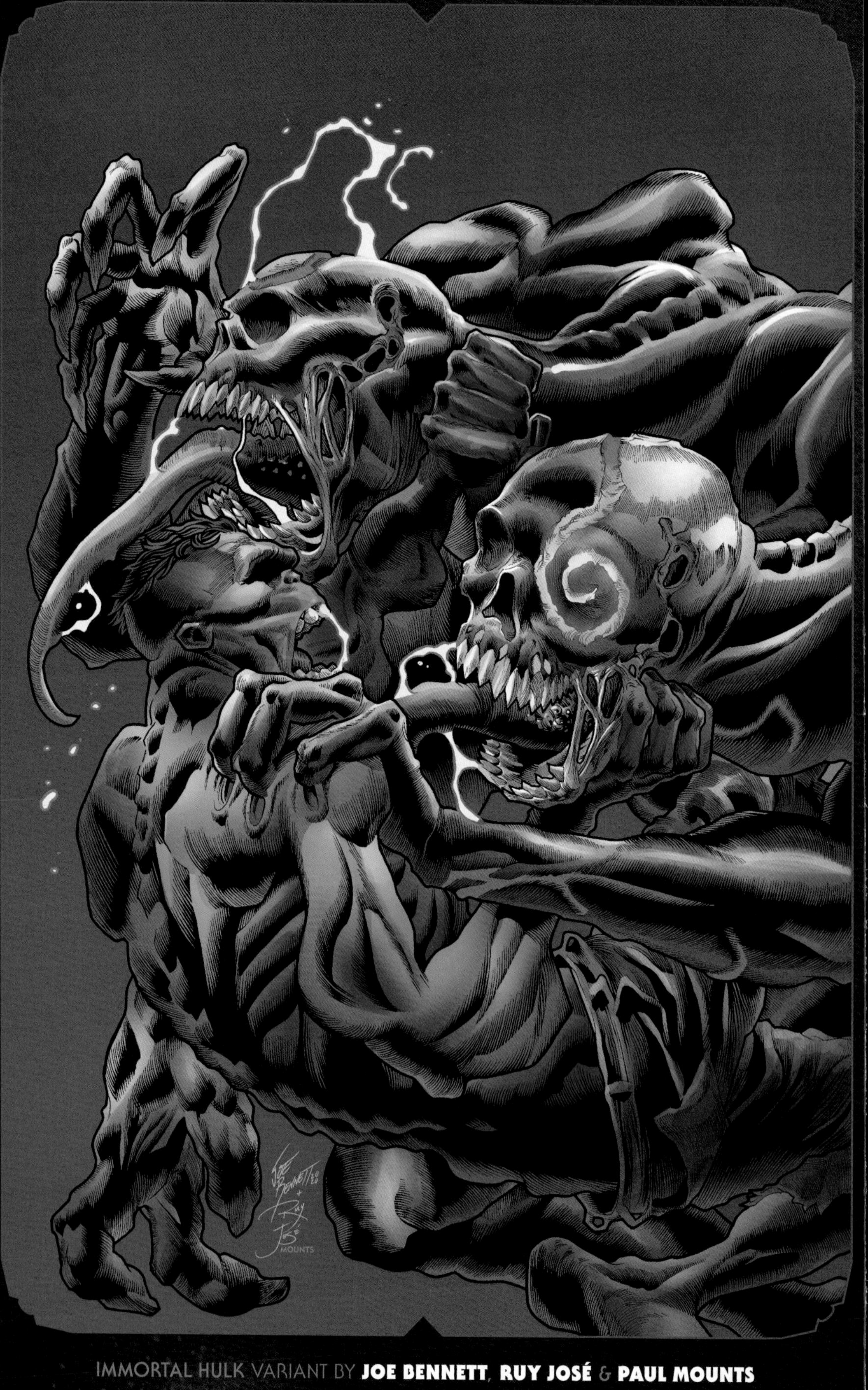

JOE BENNETT '20
+
Ruy José
MOUNTS

IMMORTAL HULK VARIANT BY **JOE BENNETT, RUY JOSÉ & PAUL MOUNTS**

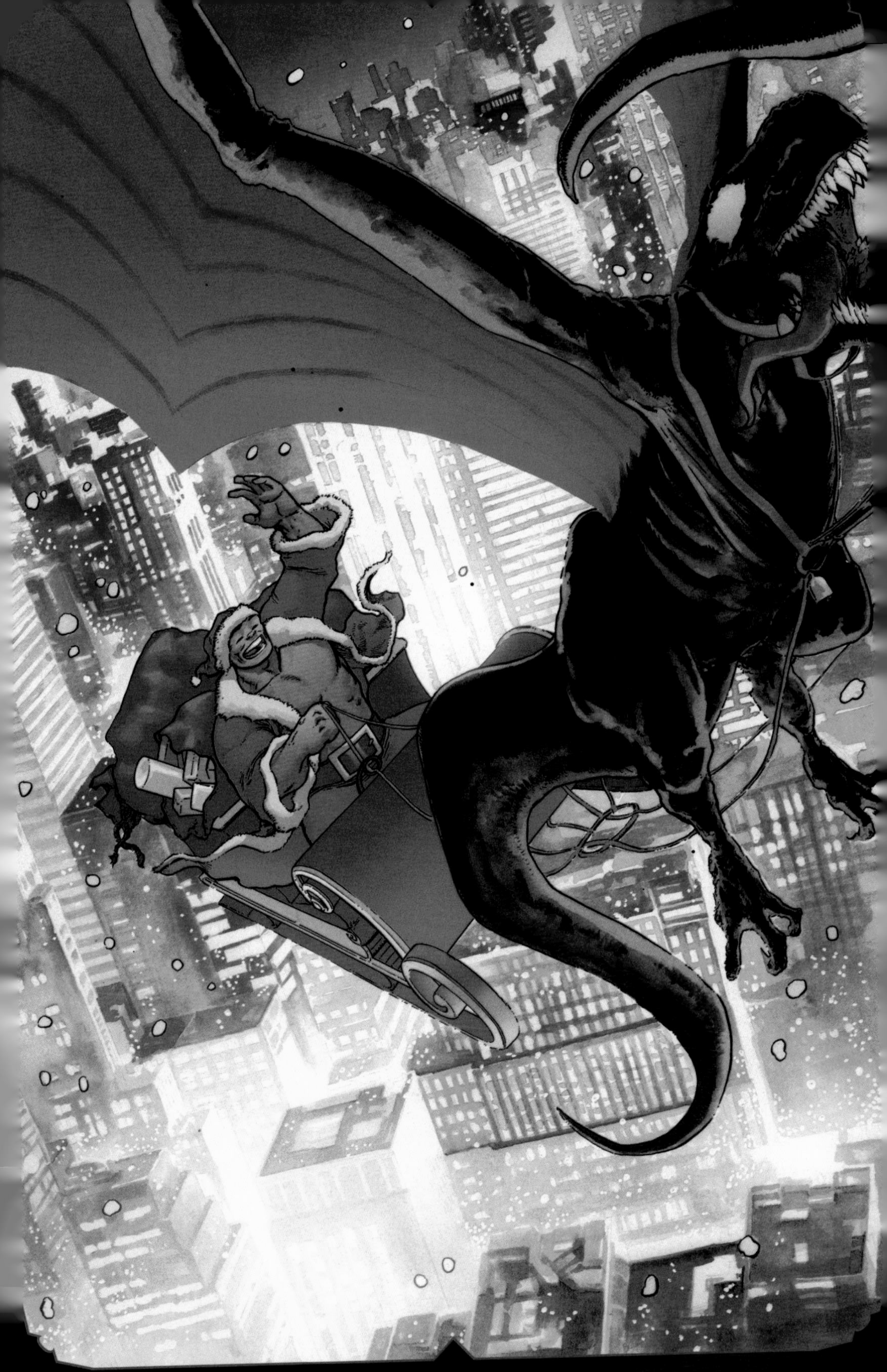

VARIANT BY AARON KUDER & MATTHEW WILSON

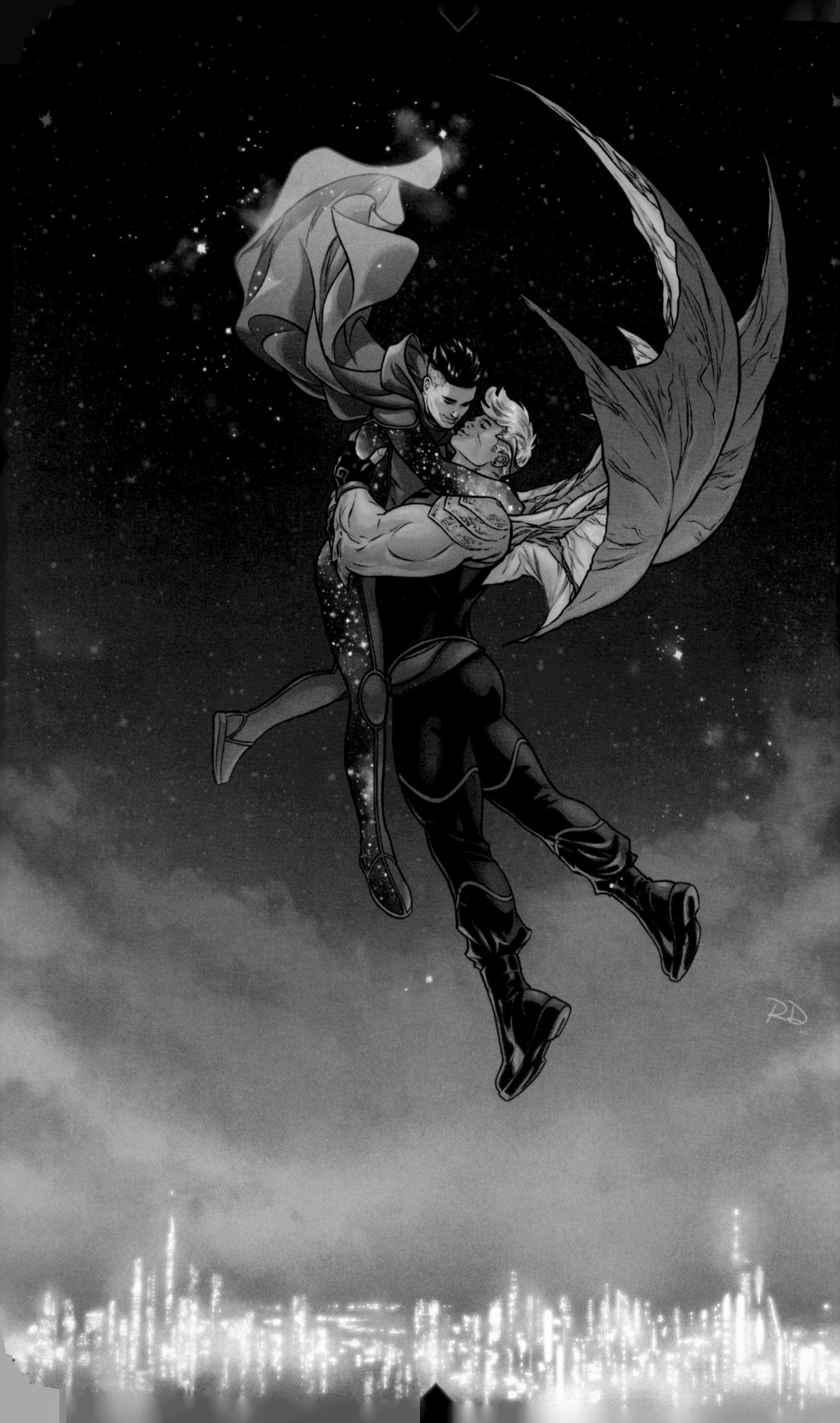
RD

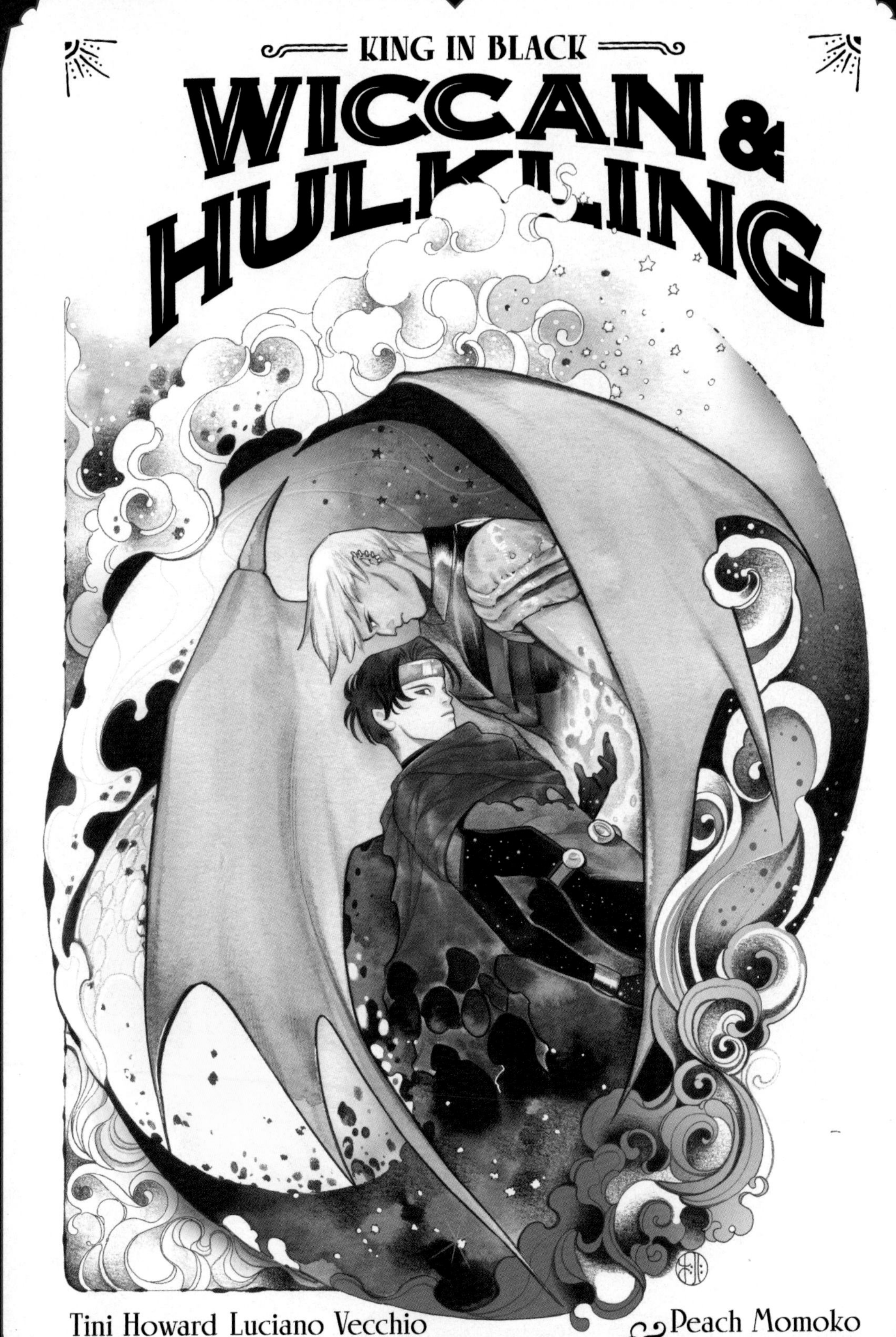
KING IN BLACK
WICCAN & HULKLING
Tini Howard WRITER
Luciano Vecchio ARTIST
& Peach Momoko STORMBREAKERS VARIANT

WICCAN AND HULKLING STORMBREAKERS VARIANT BY **PEACH MOMOKO**

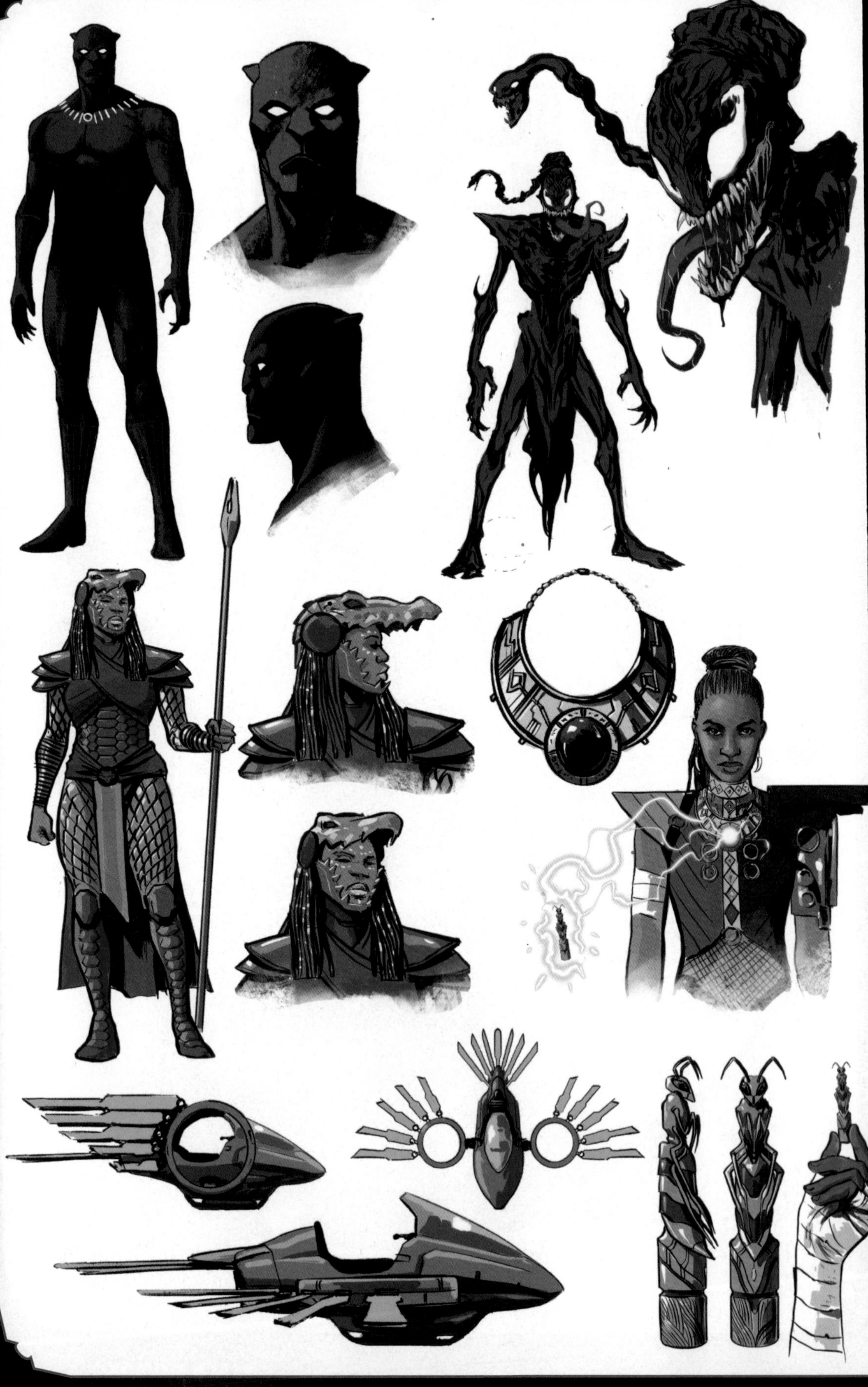

BLACK PANTHER CHARATER DESIGNS BY **GERMÁN PERALTA**

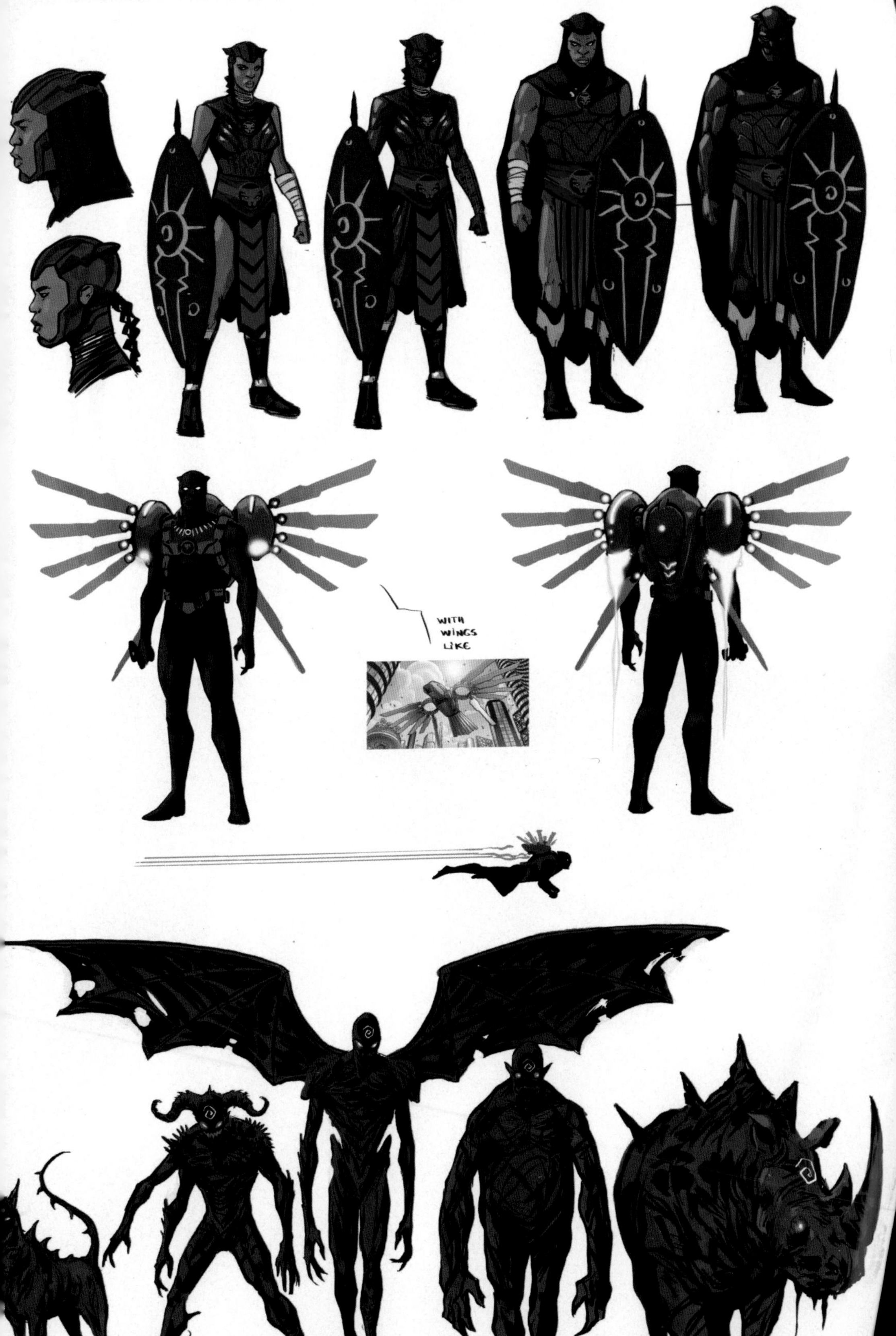
WITH WINGS LIKE

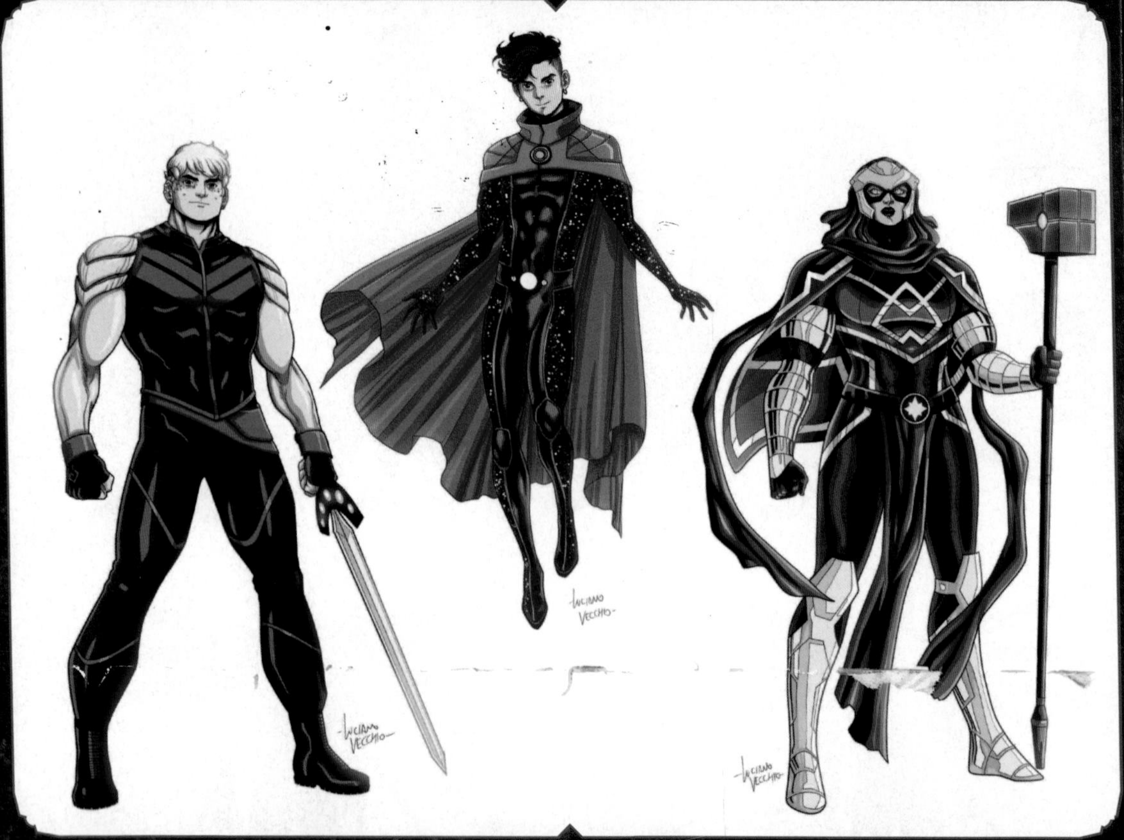

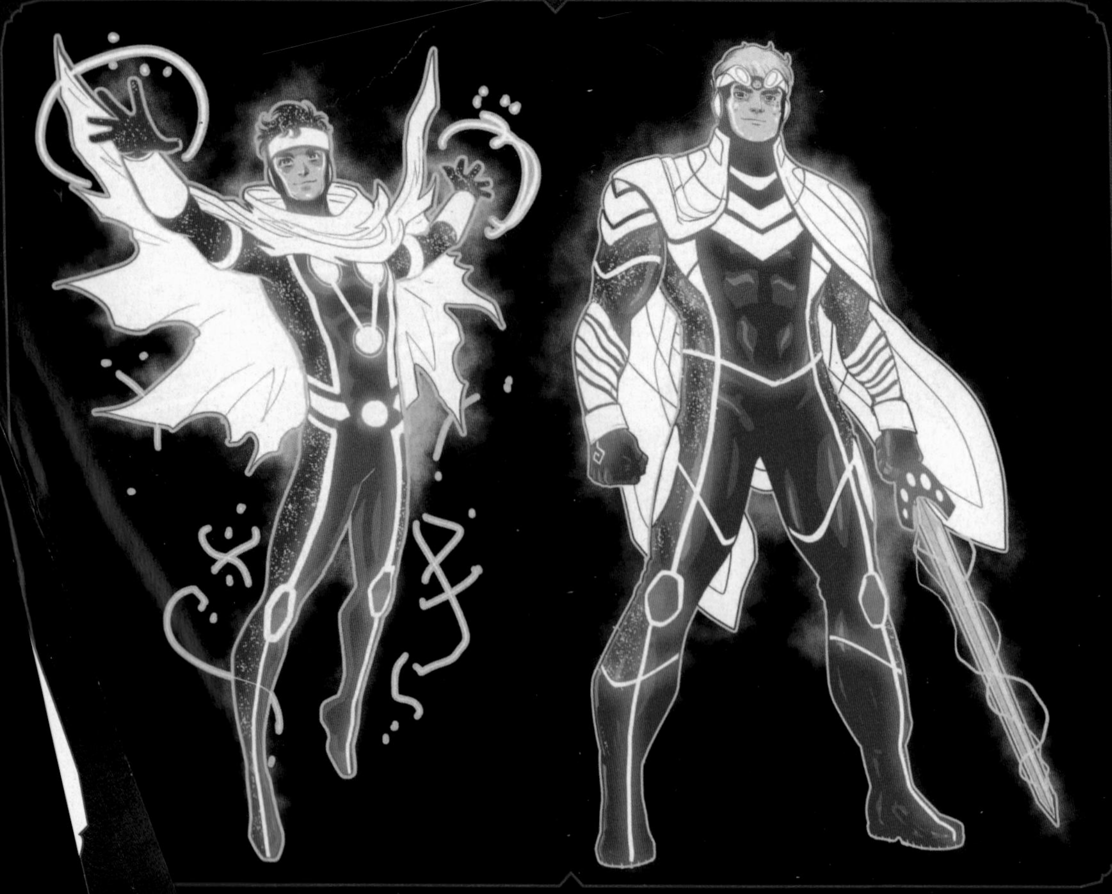

WICCAN AND HULKLING CHARATER DESIGNS BY **LUCIANO VECCHIO**